THE MESSIANIC HOPE

A DIVINE SOLUTION FOR THE HUMAN PROBLEM

by

Arthur W. Kac, M.D.

A CANON PRESS BOOK

BAKER BOOK HOUSE
Grand Rapids, Michigan

Books by the same author:

THE REBIRTH OF THE STATE OF ISRAEL:
IS IT OF GOD OR OF MEN?

THE SPIRITUAL DILEMMA OF THE JEWISH PEOPLE

THE DEATH AND RESURRECTION OF ISRAEL

Biblical references used in this book are from a number of Biblical versions including the following: the Hebrew text of the Old Testament; *The Holy Scriptures,* copyright 1936 by Hebrew Publishing Company, and used by permission; *The Amplified New Testament,* copyright 1958 by the Lockman Foundation, La Habra, California, and used by permission; *New American Standard Bible* (New Testament), copyright 1960, 1962, 1963 by the Lockman Foundation, and used by permission; *American Standard Version,* copyright 1901 by Thomas Nelson & Sons; *Revised Standard Version,* copyright 1946 (New Testament Section) and 1952 (Old Testament Section) by the Division of Christian Education of the National Council of the Churches of Christ in the United States of America, and used by permission; *The New Testament in Modern English* by J.B. Phillips, copyright 1958 by J.B. Phillips, and used by permission of the Macmillan Company.

Library of Congress Catalog Number 75-4483
ISBN: 0-8010-5362-5 (PAPER)
        0-8010-5363-3 (CLOTH)

PRINTED BY REESE PRESS, INC., BALTIMORE, MARYLAND

CONTENTS

ACKNOWLEDGMENTS

The author wishes to thank all publishers and copyright owners for permission to use in this book excerpts from their copyright works. If any acknowledgment has inadvertently been omitted apologies are offered. The author also desires to make grateful mention of the following individuals for their helpfulness in the preparation of this book: Harold Lindsell, Ph.D., Editor-Publisher of CHRISTIANITY TODAY, who wrote the Foreword; the staff of Canon Press; Roger D. Derby, Ph.D.; John D. Elder, Sc.D.; last, but certainly not least, Mrs. Charlotte T. Hatcher who typed the manuscript.

FOREWORD

This book was written by one who believes that Jesus is the Messiah and who wants Jews and Gentiles, Christians and non-Christians, to understand the full scope of the Biblical teaching concerning this.

The work itself is divided into three segments: the first has to do with the unveiling of the Messianic hope in the Old Testament; the second has to do with the Messianic mission of Jesus of Nazareth; and the third deals with the resurrection hope.

The author has given us a rather complete statement of all aspects of the Messianic hope and covers not only the Old and New Testaments but also the inter-testamental period. He adverts to non-canonical Jewish writings to support his thesis too. He traces the Messianic hope in the Old Testament from the Pentateuch, the Nathan prophecy, and the writings of Micah and Isaiah. He treats the subject of the Suffering Servant and shows that Jesus of Nazareth is the Suffering Servant of the Old Testament Scriptures.

The second part of the work deals with the incarnation, the birth of Jesus by the virgin, followed by Messiah's teaching and His death, as well as the universal and permanent validity of that death.

In the third section the major emphasis is on the resurrection, based, of course, upon the New Testament teaching, that without it there could be no abiding Christian faith. He traces the resurrection hope in the Old Testament, in the apocryphal books, on into the New Testament, ending with reasons why the resurrection assures men of a new life and of their own resurrection at the last day.

This is an important work, a Biblical work, and a solid contribution to the thinking of any person who sincerely seeks to know what Messianism is and how Jesus is related to it. The author has done his research well and his conclusions are based upon solid foundations. It is a work one can recommend with the hope that it will be read carefully and prayerfully.

Harold Lindsell
Editor-Publisher
CHRISTIANITY TODAY

This book is dedicated to the memory of the many loved ones of the author and his wife who perished in the Nazi holocaust

And the LORD said, "What have you done? The voice of your brother's blood is crying to me from the ground".

Genesis 4:10

INTRODUCTION

There is an acute awareness at the present juncture of history of the reality and enormity of evil in the world, and of man's utter incapacity to cope with it. It is becoming increasingly evident that man is man's greatest problem. Western civilization, some of the main ingredients of which have become part and parcel of the civilization of the remainder of the world, is sick at heart. It is reaping the bitter harvest of secularism which began in Europe in the seventeenth century. Secularism is a world view and a way of life which conceives of man as the be-all and end-all. God is ignored, if not expelled altogether from human life. Secularism is thus not only non-religious, it is actually anti-religious.

While modern secularism was born in Europe of the seventeenth century, it was not a new phenomenon. Greco-Roman civilization — the Western civilization of the ancient world — in its final stage, at least, was also pervaded by the principle of secularism, namely, that man can live by human reason and human resources alone. It was this philosophy of secularism which was one of the main factors which in the end brought about the downfall of Greco-Roman civilization.

The events of the twentieth century have revealed the emptiness and moral bankruptcy of the philosophy of secularism. It is secularism which is at the heart of the profound and intractable world crisis of today. The human spirit cries out against the meaninglessness and purposelessness of life which are the hallmark of secularism. It was this lack of meaning and purpose which was the mainspring of many of the student riots in the United States in the 1960's and which dragged thousands of young people into the drug culture with its disastrous consequences. Two destructive world wars, an unrelentless population explosion, famines in large parts of the world, depletion of the earth's mineral resources, pollution of man's earthly environment, mounting piles of nuclear weapons consuming a large part of the nations' hard-earned income, with their constant threat of world destruction — all these developments have brought mankind face to face with a crisis the like of which the world had never known before. The twentieth century has rightly been called the age of anxiety, an age in which mankind is adrift, not knowing what tomorrow will bring. The most concerned men are those engaged in intellectual fields, the men of science, and knowledgeable people in other areas. There is a fear that before our century draws to a close the whole world system will collapse. The happiest generation, it was stated, will be the one that will have left this earthly sphere before the twentieth century comes to an end.

And yet, secularism which is at the basis of the present world calamity, dates much further back than Greco-Roman civilization. Its roots extend all the way to the beginning of human existence. The words of the Evil one, addressed to the woman as recorded in Genesis chapter three, that God had imposed certain limitations on man in order to prevent him from becoming Divine, these words were in reality a reflection of man's unholy pride and man's ambition to usurp God's place. Man's determination to cross the bounds within which he was necessarily placed was the beginning of his downfall.

The tragedy of all this is that God had from the very beginning intended man to occupy a most exalted position in creation. "When I look at thy heavens, the work of thy fingers," the psalmist declares, "the moon and the stars which thou hast established. What is man that thou art mindful of him, and the son of man that thou dost care for him? Yet thou hast made him little less than God, and dost crown him with glory and honor. Thou hast given him dominion over the works of thy hands; thou hast put all things under his feet" (Psalm 8:3-6; 8:4-7 Heb.)

Of all created beings on earth man alone was made in God's image, i.e., God implanted into man something of His own personality, in order to enable man to communicate with God and to live in fellowship with Him. The story of God's redemptive purpose, unfolded in the Bible, is the account of God's mighty acts designed to make man fit for the exalted position which God had intended for man from the very beginning. This is the story of the Messianic Hope as presented in the pages of this work.

PART ONE

THE UNVEILING OF THE MESSIANIC HOPE

*"And beginning with Moses and all the prophets,
he interpreted to them in all the scriptures the things
concerning himself."*

Luke 24:27

CHAPTER 1
THE MESSIANIC HOPE IN THE PENTATEUCH

I. The Biblical Concept of History

II. The Centrality Of The Biblical Messianic Hope

III. The Genesis Of The Messianic Hope
   1. The Beginning Of Man's Alienation From God
   2. The First Promise Of Redemption

IV. The Prophetic Utterance Of Noah
   1. The Exalted Spiritual Position Of Shem
   2. The Supremacy Of Japheth
   3. The Association Between Shem And Japheth

V. The Messianic Hope In The Patriarchal Period
   1. The Call Of Abraham
   2. The Shiloh Prophecy

CHAPTER I
THE MESSIANIC HOPE IN THE PENTATEUCH
I. THE BIBLICAL CONCEPT OF HISTORY

With the nations of antiquity human history was just another series of cycles which rotate perennially with the change of the seasons of the year. From their observations of the recurrent periodicity of the movements of the sun and other heavenly bodies, and of the regularity which characterizes the coming and going of the seasons of the year, the ancients came to think of human events in similar cyclical terms. "The cosmic law of growth and decay was also the pattern for their understanding of history."[1] The Greek Herodotus is considered as the first historian. But to the Greeks history writing was no more than the recording of facts. They were unable to see the meaning of these facts.

"In Greek authors of classical times," Butcher observes, "there is no trace of the thought that the human race as a whole, or any single people, is advancing towards a Divinely appointed goal . . . Greek thought turned mainly to the past. The Greek orators and political writers drew their inspiration either from mythical heroes or from the achievements of their ancestors . . . In the absence of Hope and of an ideal of progress, we strike upon one great difference between the classical Greeks and the Hebrews . . . In the darkest hour of adversity the prophets did not despair of Israel. When Jerusalem was desolate, when the people were in captivity, and national existence had been crushed, the voice of prophecy speaks out the more confidently. It points back to the Divine guidance that had watched over the race, and tells of the mighty destiny that was in store for Israel. Through the prophets an ideal and glorified national sentiment was created, transcending local limits, and intertwined with the highest hopes that could be conceived for humanity. They looked to a spiritual restoration and triumph, what should be for the world at large the beginning of a glorious future. This ideal, ardently desired, possessed the mind of the pious Jew; it fed in him a

---

1. Karl Lowith, MEANING IN HISTORY (The University of Chicago Press: Chicago, 1955), p. 4. Copyright 1949 by The University of Chicago. Used by permission.

secret fund of joy, and kept alive a spark of hope in a world of spiritual despair against the day when He who was 'the Desire of the nations' should come."[2]

The Bible was the first body of writings to present to the world what may be called a philosophy of history. The Bible does not merely record facts, it interprets them. According to the Bible history displays a purpose and is moving towards a goal. The goal of history is the redemption of the human race and the establishment of God's rule on earth. This redemptive purpose is the sum and substance of the Biblical Messianic hope.

II. THE CENTRALITY OF THE BIBLICAL MESSIANIC HOPE

There is a great deal of truth in the statement that history is made by individuals. In some instances these individuals embody contemporary trends and movements, in others they shape events, whether knowingly or not, in accordance with their own ideas. In support of this statement one needs but list the names of a few of those who dominated events in the first half of the twentieth century, such as, Kaiser Wilhelm, Hindenburg, Foch, Clemenceau, Lloyd George, Balfour, Woodrow Wilson, Kerensky, Lenin, Trotzky, Stalin, Mussolini, Hitler, Chamberlain, Roosevelt, Churchill, Truman. Apart from these men the first half of the twentieth century is unthinkable. What is true of the first half of the twentieth century is equally true of history in general.

The same phenomenon may be discerned in Biblical history, except that the Bible represents God as not only being involved in human history, but as exercising the decisive role in the final outcome of world events. From the beginning to the end of Holy Writ we see God making use of individual men and women to accomplish His purpose in the world. He selected one man — Abraham — to lay the foundation of the Kingdom of God.

> Look to Abraham your father and to Sarah who bore you; for when he was but one I called him, and I blessed him and made him many.
>
> *Isaiah 51: 2*

---

2. S. H. Butcher, SOME ASPECTS OF GREEK GENIUS (Macmillan Co.: London, 1891). pp. 155-158.

When the hour struck for the deliverance of the Hebrews from Egyptian bondage, God summoned one man — Moses — to accomplish this mission. It was through this one man Moses that the foundation of the nationhood and faith of Israel was laid in the Wilderness.

It was one man — Joshua — whom God appointed after the death of Moses to lead the Israelites into the Promised Land.

It was one man after another that God raised to rule the newly settled tribes of Israel during the period of Judges.

It was one man — Samuel — whom God chose to inaugurate the kingly form of government in Israel.

It was one prophet after another whom God inspired to interpret His will to each particular generation. And so from the beginning to the end of Biblical history, it is God who speaks and acts through individuals of His choice.

To give expression to the fact that all those who were pressed into God's service were acting by God's enabling power, the rite of anointing with oil was performed on these servants of God. This rite signified that the anointed person was acting under the guidance of the Spirit of God and doing God's will, not his own will. The patriarchs Abraham, Isaac and Jacob are referred to as anointed persons. Speaking of the patriarchs the Psalmist says:

> He suffered no man to do them wrong; yea, he rebuked kings on their account. Saying, "Touch not my anointed ones, do my prophets no harm."
>
> *Psalm 105: 14-15*

The Judges and Kings, i.e. those who were to dispense justice and maintain law and order, were inaugurated into their office by the rite of anointment.[3] Priests, whose function was to mediate between God and man, were inducted into their office by the rite of anointment.[4] Prophets were either anointed, or counted as having been anointed.[5]

The English word "anointed" is a translation of the Hebrew

---

3   Judges 9:8, 15; I Samuel 2: 35; 10: 1; 24:6.
4.   Exodus 29:7; 30:30; Leviticus 4:3.
5.   I Kings 19:16.

word 'Messiah.' Thus all those who were initated into their offices by the rite of anointment were called anointed ones or Messiahs.[6] This was true whether or not the rite of anointing was actually carried out, for the rite of anointing was merely a symbolic act, an external sign that a given individual was acting under the leadership of the Spirit of God. Thus, the holder of each of the three offices — king, priest, and prophets through whom God was seeking to work out His redemptive purpose — was an anointed, or a Messianic, person.

In the beginning of every new phase in the Biblical period of Israel's history all three Messianic offices were held by a single person. This was true of Abraham. When the Cities of the Plain were invaded by a hostile confederacy Abraham assembled a military force of 318 trained men all of whom were born in his domain, attacked a detachment of the invaders, rescued some of the prisoners of war and recovered some of the spoil carried off by the invaders.[7] In his capacity as chief of a clan Abraham made treaties with neighboring rulers.[8] Abraham was a ruler in his realm. Abraham also acted in the capacity of a priest,[9] and he is referred to as a prophet.[10] Thus Abraham, the founder of the Hebrew nation, was ruler, priest and prophet.

The Exodus from Egypt was the second great turning-point in Israels history. The man who left an indelible mark on that formative period was Moses. For all practical purposes Moses was Israel's first king. In fact, he exercised more power than any of the crowned kings of Israel. Moses was also a priest. At the conclusion of the all-important Sinai Covenant the twelve young men, acting on behalf of the twelve tribes of Israel, killed the sacrificial oxen, since normally the sacrificial animals had to be killed by the persons who brought the sacrifice. But it was Moses as the officiating priest who manipulated the blood of the offerings which was the function of the priest.[11] When Moses consecrated Aaron to the priesthood he

6.   Leviticus 4:3, 5, 16; 6:22(6:15 Heb.); I Samuel 2:10, 35; 12:3, 5; 16:6; 24:6 (24:7 Heb), 10(24:11 Heb.); 26:9, 11, 16, 23; 2 Samuel 1: 14, 16, 21; 19:21 (19:22 Heb.); 22:51; 23:1; I Chronicles 16:22; 2 Chronicles 6:42; Psalm 2:2; 18:50 (18:51 Heb.); 20:6 (20:7 Heb.); 28:8; 84:9 (84:10 Heb.); 89:38 (89:39 Heb.), 51 (89:52 Heb.); 105:15; 132:10, 17; Isaiah 45:1; Lamentations 4:20.
7.   Genesis 14:13-16.
8.   Genesis 12:7-8; 13:3-4; 22:9-10.
9.   Genesis 21:22-32.
10. Genesis 20:7.
11. Exodus 24:4-6.

merely delegated to him his priestly functions. This is why it was Moses, rather than Aaron, who inducted Eleazar into the priesthood just before Aaron's death.[12] Moses was also a prophet.[13] Indeed, as a prophet he holds a most unique place in the Old Testament.

Samuel was the last representative of the group of uncrowned rulers designated in the Old Testament by the name of Judges. Samuel was the one who inaugurated the kingly form of government in Israel. He stood therefore in the transition period between two epochs. Not only was Samuel a ruler,[14] he was also a priest.[15] And he exercised the function of a prophet.

Thus, Abraham, Moses and Samuel, who initiated new periods in Biblical history, combined in their person the office of ruler, priest and prophet, the three offices the holders of which were anointed or Messianic agents, through whom God was striving to accomplish His redemptive purpose in the world.

The Mosaic Law kept these three offices separate. I believe this was done for two reasons. First, in order to avoid the concentration of excessive powers in the hands of one person which concentration had so often been the means by which political oppression and economic injustice were practiced in the ancient world. Second, to demonstrate to Israel and to the world at large, from centuries of Jewish experience, that mere separation of authority and powers is no safeguard of liberty, nor guarantee of justice. By and large, Israel's kings turned out to be wicked men; Israel's priests, since, at least, Solomon's days, were state officials who served their own interest rather than the interests of the people. Even many of the prophets were motivated by financial gain and were denounced as false prophets by that small group of Divinely inspired men of God, the genuine prophets of Israel.

Thus the sheer weight of historical experience led Israel to look for the coming of God's anointed Servant, the true Messiah, who in the fullness of time would inaugurate a new era in mankind's history. Like Abraham, Moses and Samuel, He would combine in His own Person the three offices of king, priest and prophet, and estab-

---

12. Numbers 20:23-28.
13. Numbers 12:6-8; Deuteronomy 18:15; 34:10.
14. I Samuel 7:15.
15. I Samuel 7:9.

lish on earth the kingdom of God. He would be the true embodiment of the highest Israelite ideal, and through Him Israel's mission
in the world should be fully accomplished.

III. THE GENESIS OF THE MESSIANIC HOPE

1. THE BEGINNING OF MAN'S ALIENATION FROM GOD

And Jehovah God took the man and put him in the garden
of Eden to till it and keep it. And Jehovah God commanded the
man, saying, "Of every tree in the garden you may freely eat.
But of the tree of the knowledge of good and evil you shall not
eat, for in the day that you eat of it you shall die."

Now the serpent was more subtle than any other wild
creature that Jehovah God had made; and he said to the
woman, "Did God say, 'You shall not eat of any tree of the
garden'?" And the woman said to the serpent, "We may eat of
the fruit of the trees of the garden. But God said, 'You shall not
eat of the fruit of the tree which is in the midst of the garden,
neither shall you touch it, lest you die.'" But the serpent said to
the woman, "You will not die. For God knows that when you eat
of it your eyes will be opened, and you will be like God, knowing
good and evil." And when the woman saw that the tree was good
for food, and that it was pleasant to the eyes, and that the tree
was to be desired to make one wise, she took of its fruit and ate;
and she gave also to her husband, and he ate. Then the eyes of
both were opened, and they knew that they were naked; and
they sewed fig leaves together and made themselves aprons.

And they heard the sound of Jehovah God walking in the
garden in the cool of the day, and the man and his wife hid
themselves from the presence of Jehovah God among the trees
of the garden. But Jehovah God called to the man, and said to
him, "Where are you?" And he said, "I heard the sound of thee
in the garden, and I was afraid, because I was naked; and I hid
myself." He said, "Who told you that you were naked? Have you
eaten of the tree of which I commanded you not to eat?" The
man said, "The woman whom thou gavest to be with me, she
gave me fruit of the tree, and I ate." Then Jehovah God said to
the woman, "What is this that you have done?" The woman said,
"The serpent beguiled me, and I ate."

Genesis 2:15-17, 3:1-13

"The chapter describes how man was seduced into disobedience. . .The sinful desire, though it has its real seat in the soul is

excited by an outward object, appealing to the senses; and here it is stimulated into activity, and directed towards its object (the forbidden fruit) by the serpent. The serpent is introduced in the first instance simply as one of the animals which had passed before man: it appears soon, however, that it is more, at any rate, than an ordinary animal: it possesses the faculty of speech, which it exercises with supreme intelligence and skill."[16]

"Profound as the teaching of this narrative is, its meaning does not lie on the surface. Literal interpretation will reach a measure of its significance, but plainly there is more here than appears in the letter. When we read that the serpent was more subtle than any beast of the field which Jehovah God had made, and that he tempted the woman, we at once perceive that it is not with the outer husk of the story we are to concern ourselves, but with the kernel.[17]

The serpent was worshipped in Egypt, Babylon, Palestine, China, India, America, England, France, Italy, Ireland, Scandinavia (Sweden and Norway), Greece, Africa in its most savage parts — in a word, all over the heathen world. "Deified as the serpent has been all over the world, it has always been the emblem of the evil principle in nature, and its worship was inspired rather to avert evil than to express reverence or gratitude. A god it might become in the perverted judgment of fallen men, but the feeling of antipathy and aversion with which it was regarded has never abated. It might be feared, but loved it never was nor could be. Thus, we are told that while many Hindus pay religious homage to the serpent at the present day, they regard it, notwithstanding, 'as a hideous reptile, whose approach inspires them with a secret awe, and insurmountable horror.' Worshipped universally, the serpent was still 'cursed above all and above every beast of the field'."[18]

"The reader of this perennially fresh story is first of all struck with the account given of man's primitive condition . . . Certainly he is described as innocent and at peace with God, and in this respect no

16. S. R. Driver, THE BOOK OF GENESIS (Methuen and Co: London, 1904), p.44.
17. Marcus Dods, "The Book of Genesis.", THE EXPOSITOR'S BIBLE (S.S. Scranton Co: Hartford, Conn., 1914), p.8.
18. Prof. W. G. Moorhead, "Universality of Serpent-Worship," essay in THE OLD TESTAMENT STUDENT (Wm. R. Harper, Editor: Chicago, September 1884-June 1885), vol. 4, p. 206.

terms can exaggerate his happiness. But in other respects the language of the Bible is surprisingly moderate. Man is represented as living on fruit, and as going about unclothed, and, so far as appears, without any artificial shelter either from the heat of the sun or the cold of night. None of the arts were as yet known. All working of metals had yet to be discovered, so that his tools must have been of the rudest possible description; and the arts, such as music, which adorn life and make leisure enjoyable,were also still in the future. But the most significant elements in man's primitive condition are represented by the two trees of the garden; by trees, because with plants alone man had to do. In the center of the garden stood the tree of life, the fruit of which bestowed immortality. Man was therefore naturally mortal, though apparently with a capacity for immortality . . . In Eden man's immortality was suspended on the condition of obedience. And the trial of man's obedience is imaged in the other tree, the tree of the knowledge of good and evil. From the child-like innocence in which man originally was, he was to pass forward into the condition of moral manhood, which consists not in mere innocence, but in innocence maintained in the presence of temptation. The savage is innocent of many of the crimes of civilized men because he has no opportunity to commit them; the child is innocent of some of the vices of manhood because he has no temptation to them. But this innocence is the result of circumstance, not of character; and if savage or child is to become a mature moral being he must be tried by altered circumstances, by temptation and opportunity. To carry man forward to this higher stage trial is necessary, and this trial is indicated by the tree of knowledge. The fruit of this tree is prohibited, to indicate that it is only in the presence of what is forbidden that man can be morally tested, and that it is only by self-command and obedience to law, and not by mere following of instincts, that man can attain to moral maturity. The prohibition is that which makes him recognize a distinction between good and evil. He is put in a position in which good is not the only thing he can do; an alternative is present to his mind, and the choice of good in preference to evil is made possible to him. In the presence of this tree childlike innocence was no longer possible. The self-determination of manhood was constantly required. Conscience, hitherto latent, was now evoked and took its place as man's supreme faculty."[19]

---

19. Marcus Dods, Op. Cit., p.9.

2. THE FIRST PROMISE OF REDEMPTION

> Jehovah God said to the serpent, "Because you have done this, cursed are you above all cattle, and above every beast of the fields; upon your belly you shall go, and dust you shall eat all the days of your life. I will put enmity between you and the woman, and between your seed and her seed; he shall bruise your head, and you shall bruise his heel." To the woman he said, "I will greatly multiply your pain in childbearing; in pain you shall bring forth children, yet your desire shall be for your husband, and he shall rule over you." And to Adam he said, "Because you have listened to the voice of your wife, and have eaten of the tree of which I commanded you, 'You shall not eat of it,' cursed is the ground because of you; in toil you shall eat of it all the days of your life; thorns and thistles it shall bring forth to you; and you shall eat the plants of the field. In the sweat of your face you shall eat bread till you return to the ground, for out of it you were taken; you are dust, and to dust you shall return" . . and Jehovah God made for Adam and for his wife garments of skins, and clothed them.
>
> *Genesis 3: 14-19, 21*

"The first result of sin is shame. The form in which the knowledge of good and evil comes to us is the realization that we are naked, the consciousness that we are stripped of all that made us walk unabashed before God and men. The promise of the serpent while broken in substance is fulfilled in the sense that the eyes of Adam and Eve were indeed opened and they knew that they were naked. Self-reflection began, and the first movement of conscience produced shame. Had they resisted temptation, conscience would have been born, but not in self-condemnation. Like children they had hitherto been conscious only of what was external to themselves, but now their consciousness of a power to choose good and evil is awakened and its first exercise is accompanied with shame. They feel that in themselves they are faulty, that they are not in themselves complete; that though created by God, they are not fit for His eye . . .

But when Adam found that he was no longer fit for God's eye, God provided a covering which might enable him again to live in His presence without dismay. Man had exhausted his own ingenuity and resources, and exhausted them without finding relief to his shame. If his shame was to be effectually removed, God must do it. And the clothing in coats of skins indicates the restoration of man, not indeed to pristine innocence, but to peace with God . . . It is also to be remarked that the clothing which God provided was in itself differ-

ent from what man had thought of. Adam took leaves from an
inanimate, unfeeling tree; God deprived an animal of life, that the
shame of its creature might be relieved. This was the last thing Adam
would have thought of doing. To us life is cheap and death familiar,
but Adam recognized death as the punishment of sin. Death was to
early man a sign of God's anger. And he had to learn that sin could
be covered not by a bunch of leaves snatched from a bush as he
passed by and that would grow again next year, but only by pain and
blood. Sin cannot be atoned for by any mechanical action nor without expenditure of feeling. Suffering must ever follow wrongdoing.
From the first sin to the last, the track of the sinner is marked with
blood. Once we have sinned we cannot regain permanent peace of
conscience except through pain, and this not only pain of our own.
The first hint of this was given as soon as conscience was aroused in
man. It was made apparent that sin was a real and deep evil, and that
by no easy and cheap process could the sinner be restored. The same
lesson has been written on millions of consciences since. Men have
found that their sin reaches beyond their own life and person, that it
inflicts injury and involves disturbance and distress, that it changes
utterly our relation to life and to God, and that we cannot rise above
its consequences except by the intervention of God Himself, by an
intervention which tells us of the sorrow He suffers on our
account."[20]

The far reaching and long-range consequences which were to
follow man's alienation from God are indicated in the words addressed by God to Eve and Adam. The woman who was created man's
equal and his helpmate was to sink to an inferior position—a development which was literally fulfilled in the history of mankind.
Moreover, this earth which was intended to be a vast garden of Eden
created for man's sake was to suffer the effects of man's wilfullness,
the dire results of which are only now beginning to be fully ap-
preciated.

As to the serpent which in our text represents the Evil one, God
Himself established a perpetual hostility between the seed of the
woman and the seed of the serpent. The seed of the serpent are the
forces of evil in this world. But the seed of the woman cannot
possibly refer to all the natural seed of the woman, the whole human
race, since the forces of evil, i.e. the seed of the serpent, are made up
of that portion of the seed of the woman which follows the guidance

---

20.   Marcus Dods, Op. Cit., pp. 10-11.

of the Evil one. The conflict ordained by God is therefore between the portion of the seed of the woman to whom Jehovah is God, and that other portion of the seed of the woman to whom Satan is god.

It is to that part of the seed of the woman who follow Jehovah that the promise of eventual victory over the forces of evil is given in our text. Thus the words addressed to the serpent contain at the very beginning of redemptive history the assurance of the eventual defeat of evil in the world; it "strikes at the very outset of redemptive history the note of promise and hope."[21] At its very inception Biblical revelation sets forth the three great principles of redemptive history, "on which rests the whole Biblical teaching concerning the Messiah and His Kingdom: that man is capable of salvation; that all evil springs from sin, with which mortal combat must be waged; and that there will be a final victory over sin through the Representative of humanity"[22]—the seed of the woman.

IV. THE PROPHETIC UTTERANCE OF NOAH

The sons of Noah who went forth from the ark were Shem, Ham and Japheth; Ham was the father of Canaan. These three were the sons of Noah; and from these the whole earth was peopled.

Noah was the first tiller of the soil; he planted a vineyard. And he drank of the wine, and became drunk, and lay uncovered in his tent. And Ham, the father of Canaan, saw the nakedness of his father, and told his two brothers outside. Then Shem and Japheth took a garment, laid it upon both their shoulders, and walked backward and covered the nakedness of their father; their faces were turned away, and they did not see their father's nakedness. When Noah awoke from his wine and knew what his younger[23] son had done to him, He said, "Cursed be Canaan; a slave of slaves shall he be to his brothers." He also said, "Blessed be Jehovah the God of Shem; and let Canaan be his slave. God enlarge Japheth, and let him dwell in the tents of Shem; and let Canaan be his slave . . ."

---

21. Ottley, HISTORY OF THE HEBREWS, p.11; quoted by S. R. Driver, Op. Cit., note on p. 48.
22. Alfred Edershei , PROPHECY AND HISTORY IN RELATION TO THE MESSIAH (Longmans, Green and Co.: London, 1885), p. 34.
23. This is the more correct reading for Ham was not the youngest, but the younger, son in relation to Shem.

> After the flood Noah lived three hundred and fifty years.
> All the days of Noah were nine hundred and fifty years; and he
> died.
>
> *Genesis 9:18-29*

This writer accepts the Biblical statement which attributes this prophetic declaration to Noah. But its wonder is not diminished one particle even if we should take the position that the prophecy of Noah is in reality an observation made centuries after Noah. If we examine the contents of this prophecy we shall see that certain of its features did not even begin to fulfill themselves until some time after the writing of the Old Testament had been completed. Not only so, but certain elements of this prophecy have continued to work themselves out to this very day. Noah's personal knowledge of the moral corruption of the generation which perished in the Great Flood, his many years of observation of the moral and intellectual characteristics of his numerous progeny after the Flood, and the illumination of the Spirit of God enabled him to pass on to posterity a general foreview of history. The future of each of the three main branches of mankind is foretold, but not assigned. Though it is undoubtedly true that certain racial traits are transmitted from one generation to another, the destiny of each generation is determined by its own conduct, not by that of its ancestors. For the purpose of our study we will limit our discussion to what Noah had said with reference to the future destinies of Shem and Japheth.

1. THE EXALTED SPIRITUAL POSITION OF SHEM

"Blessed be Jehovah, the God of Shem"

Noah's prophecy foresaw no permanent material advantages for Shem. Spiritual supremacy was to be his unique treasure. "God has been the Lord God of Shem in an altogether peculiar and distinctive sense. The savior of the world descended from this son of Noah. Revealed religion has flowed through Semitic channels . . . Every psalm of David, and every Christian hymn and sacred song of later days, every authentic narrative of the earliest ages of humanity, the sublime law of Sinai, and the beatitudes and parables of Christ, the visions of prophecy, the teachings of apostles, the testimony of the martyrs, the missions of modern Christianity — all that has lifted our world from ruin and misery and darkness and death, all that has purified and ennobled it and opened to it a·door of hope for the future — all has come to it through Shem",[24] or rather through this God who was pleased to become the God of Shem, in order that through Shem He may become the God of all nations.

2. *THE SUPREMACY OF JAPHETH*

"God enlarge Japheth"

According to the Table of the Nations in Genesis 10 the Japhethites are the peoples of the isles or the coastland, a term used in the Old Testament to designate the European continent. In secular history the Japhethites bear the name of Caucasian, Indo-European or Aryan peoples. The Japhethites were the last of the three divisions of mankind after the Great Flood to assume world leadership. The conquest of Semitic Babylon by Cyrus the Persian in 538 B.C. was the beginning of Japhethic world power since Persia is a Japhethic nation. A few years later, in 525 B.C., Hamitic Egypt was conquered by Cambyses, a successor of Cyrus. From the Japhethic Persians world leadership passed on to Alexander the Great, also a Japhethite. After Alexander's untimely death his empire was split up among four of his generals, and for a brief period there was no single world-dominating power. But soon Japhethic Rome began to reach out for world mastery. Rome's ambitions in this direction were challenged by Carthage, a rich and powerful city-state situated in North Africa. The gifted and brave Carthaginian general Hannibal invaded Italy and defeated the Roman armies in several battles. But at the last moment the army of Hannibal was hurled back, and in a decisive battle at Sama, south of Carthage, in 202 B.C., it was crushed, and Carthage was destroyed. With the elimination of Carthage the last serious obstacle in the path of Japhethic world power was swept away.

In later centuries, when the European Japhethites were emerging into distinctive nation-states, Japhethic supremacy was again challenged: by the Huns in the fourth and fifth centuries, the Arabs in the eighth century, the Mongols in the thirteenth century, and the Turks from the middle of the sixteenth to the second half of the seventeenth century. One by one, all these assaults were repelled, and beginning with the sixteenth century the European Japhethites

---

24.   H. Grattan Guinness, THE DIVINE PROGRAMME OF THE WORLD'S HIS-
        TORY (Hodder and Stoughton: London, 1889), p. 109.

initiated a period of world-wide expansion. In the course of time they spread out over the whole face of the earth. At the present juncture of history the Japhethites are in full possession of three continents: Europe, America, Australia and New Zealand. They hold a dominant place in South Africa, and even in present-day Asia the Japhethites as represented by America and Russia exert a decisive influence. In world politics, in the various branches of art and science, in agriculture and industry, in medicine, in the field of education, child care, the status of women, social welfare, the rights of the individual, freedom of speech and religion — in all these areas the Western branch of Japhethic civilization has been the leader and teacher of the rest of the world. In the last 25 centuries world leadership has remained in the hands of the Japhetic peoples. "God enlarge Japheth," said Noah, and God certainly did.

3. THE ASSOCIATION BETWEEN SHEM AND JAPHETH

"God enlarge Japheth and let him dwell in the tents of Shem"

There are two views about the meaning of the second part of this statement, "and let him dwell in the tent of Shem." According to one view we have here a prediction of the extension of Japhethic political control over Semitic territories. Another (shared by the Palestinian Targum) maintains that the passage foretells participation by the Japhethites in the spiritual heritage of the Semites. In actual history both views found remarkable verification. Beginning with the ascendancy of the Japhetic Persian empire Semitic lands came under Japhethic rule on several occaisions. But the prediction that Japeth will dwell in the tents of Shem found its most glorious fulfillment in the spiritual sphere. For since the beginning of the Christian era the spiritual heritage of Israel, a descendant of Shem, has been one of the main ingredients in the religious, moral and cultural life of Japhethic peoples.

The first translation of the Hebrew Sacred Scriptures into a non-Semitic tongue took place on the island of Pharos with the encouragement of King Ptolemy Philadelphus, the son and successor of the founder of the Japhethic dynasty of the Ptolemies who ruled Egypt for 300 years. This Greek translation, begun in the third century B.C., and known as the Septuagint, is the oldest version of the Old Testament. When Christianity came on the scene, before the apostolic age drew to a close, the torch of the new evangelical faith was passed on into the hands of Japhethic believers. It was the

Japhethites who translated the Bible into hundreds of other languages and took the Biblical message to the far corners of the earth. And it is not without deep significance that in the last 19 centuries the bulk of the Jewish people have lived among Japhethic peoples.

When in the fullness of time God sent forth into the world the promised Redeemer, the world of that day had been prepared for His coming by Greco-Roman civilization. In our days, when we see so many signs everywhere of history, as we know it, coming to an end, when so many people speak of the imminent return of Jesus the Messiah, the world is becoming unified once again by the technology, industrial know-how, and certain other features of Japhethic civilization. "God enlarge Japheth and let him dwell in the tents of Shem."

V. THE MESSIANIC HOPE IN THE PATRIARCHAL PERIOD

1. THE CALL OF ABRAHAM

In the centuries following the flood the descendants of Noah multiplied and spread out all over the then known world. In the course of time they grew into nations differing in language, manners and customs. The knowledge and worship of the true God which they inherited from the Noah family gradually became corupt until idolatrous polytheism became the religion of mankind.

The emergence of nations created the necessity of dealing with mankind on a national level. To communicate His redemptive purpose to the nations of the world God needed the services of one particular nation as His messenger to all nations of the earth. To accomplish His purpose God did not choose one of the then existing nations. Had He selected this course of action, He might have been accused of partiality by the other nations of the earth, and the nation so chosen would have attributed God's choice to its own superiority.

Consequently, God determined to create a new nation. To this end He summoned one man, Abram, and called on him to leave his native Mesopotamia and settle in Canaan which was to become the country of the nation to descend from him. That mankind's redemption was the reason for the call of Abraham may be seen from the first recorded Divine communication to Abraham.

Now Jehovah said to Abram,

Go from your country and your kindred and your father's house to the land that I will show you. And I will make of you a great nation, and I will bless you, and make your name great, so that you will be a blessing. I will bless those who bless you, and him who curses you I will curse; and by you all the families of the earth will be blessed.

Genesis 12:1-3

The same message was restated in God's last communication to Abraham.

And the angel of Jehovah called to Abraham a second time from heaven. And said, "By myself I have sworn, says Jehovah, because you have done this, and have not withheld your son, your only son. I will indeed bless you and I will multiply your descendants as the stars of heaven and as the sand which is on the seashore; and your descendants shall possess the gate of their enemies. And by your descendants shall all the nations of the earth be blessed, because you have obeyed my voice."

Genesis 22: 15-18

The promise that the nation to descend from Abraham shall become a channel through which God's blessings would reach all nations was renewed to Isaac[25] and reiterated to Jacob.[26]

2. THE SHILOH PROPHECY

Then Jacob called his sons, and said "Gather yourselves together, that I may tell you what shall befall you in the latter days . . . The scepter shall not depart from Judah, nor the ruler's staff from between his feet, until Shiloh comes, and to him shall be the obedience of the peoples."

Genesis 49:1, 10

The Shiloh prophecy is the most complete Messianic revelation in the book of Genesis. It was uttered by Jacob just before his death and on the eve of the Egyptian phase of Hebrew history. "Gather yourselves together that I may tell you what shall befall you in the latter days." This is the first time we encounter the phrase "the latter days." It is found in the following additional passages: Numbers 24:14; Deuteronomy 31:29; Isaiah 2:2; Jeremiah 23:20; 30:24;

---

25. Genesis 26:4.
26. Genesis 28:14.

48:47; 49:39; Ezekiel 38:16; Hosea 3:5; Micah 4:1; Daniel 2:28; 10:14. In all these references the phrase "latter days" points to the period of, or events associated with, the establishment of God's Kingdom on earth under the leadership of the Messianic King.

It is said that the earliest extant interpretation of the word "Shiloh" is found in Ezekiel 21 where we read the following:

> And you profane wicked prince of Israel, whose day has come, the time of your final punishment. Thus says the Lord God: Remove the mitre, and take off the crown; exalt him that is low, and abase him that is high. I will overturn, overturn, overturn it; and it shall be no more until he comes whose right it is; and to him I will give it.
>
> *Ezekiel 21:25-27 (21:30-32Heb.)*

The "wicked prince" addressed in this passage was Zedekiah, the last king of the Davidic dynasty. The message which Ezekiel was instructed to deliver had reference to the approaching destruction of Judea, which event took place in 587 B.C. In his comment on this passage in the Soncino Hebrew-English edition of Ezekiel, Rabbi Fisch interprets this passage to mean that the ultimate restoration of the Judean state will take place with the coming of the Messiah, and "the phrase, 'until he comes whose right it is,' recalls the Messianic prophecy in Genesis 49:10."[27]

Traditional Jewish interpreters follow Ezekiel's lead, except that in place of the word "right" as found in Ezekiel, they used the word "kingdom," as seen from the following expositions of the Shiloh prophecy.

"He who exercises dominion shall not pass away from the house of Judah, nor the scribe from his children's children for ever, until Messiah shall come, whose is the kingdom, and whom the peoples shall obey."[28]

"Kings shall not cease from the house of Judah, nor scribes teaching the law from his children's children, until the time that the King Messiah shall come, whose is the kingdom, and to whom all the

---

27. S Fisch, EZEKIEL (The Soncino Press: London, 1950), p. 141.
28. Targum Onkelos. The Aramaic Version of the Pentateuch known as Targum Onkelos and the Aramaic version of the prophetic writings known as Targum Jonathan were composed not later than the second century A.D., and probably much earlier.

kingdoms of the earth shall be obedient."[29]

"The scepter shall not depart from Judah, nor a declarer [of the law] from between his feet, until he shall come whose it is."[30]

The Midrash takes "Shiloh" to refer to "King Messiah."[31]

In the Babylonian Talmud "Shiloh" is listed as one of the names of the Messiah.[32]

The great medieval Jewish Biblical expositor Rashi makes the following comment on the word "Shiloh:" "Shiloh — i.e., King Messiah whose is the kingdom."

The words "scepter" and "ruler's staff" which occur in the Shiloh prophetic utterance by Jacob symbolize royal power or sovereignty. The idea which these two words intend to convey is that the Jewish people will retain national sovereignty until Messiaih's advent. When Messiah comes, He will take over the reigns of the Judean government, and He will at the same time receive the obedience or homage of the nations of the earth. The Hebrew word in our text translated "obedience" is an uncommon word. It occurs only once again in Proverbs 30:17, in connection with obedience to a mother. It also expresses the notion of piety, fear or reverence of God. It is thought that the word as used in the Shiloh prophecy suggest not mere blind obedience, but willing and loving obedience, such as obedience to parents, or veneration of God.

In conclusion, the Shiloh prophecy declares that the Jewish people will exercise national sovereignty in their own land until Messiah comes. This was true in the days of the first advent of Jesus of Nazareth — when the Jews lived on their own soil under a Jewish King, though this king was only partly Jewish and not of the Davidic line. It is also deeply significant that as the signs of Messiah's return are multiplying round about us, the Jewish people have resumed their national life in the Land of Israel, after an interruption of some 18 centuries.

---

29. Palestinian Targum.
30. Peshitta - The Syriac version of the Old Testament, considered to be a Jewish production, thought by some to have been composed before the end of the apostolic age, by ohers - in the second century A.D.
31. Genesis R. 98:13.
32. Sanhedrin 98b.

CHAPTER 2
THE NATHAN PROPHECY

I. The Historical Background

II. The Meaning And Purpose Of The Nathan Prophecy

CHAPTER 2
THE NATHAN PROPHECY
I. THE HISTORICAL BACKGROUND

Saul was the first king of the newly-established kingdom of Israel. His death put an end to his dynasty. David, a member of the tribe of Judah, became now Israel's king. Having witnessed the downfall of the Saul dynasty David was determined that a similar fate should not happen to his family. David was fully aware of the existence of many who had remained faithful to the surviving members of Saul's family, and of the strong separatist tendencies which seemed always to prevail among the northern tribes. To unify the whole nation under his leadership and to put his dynasty on a firm foundation, David set out to execute a cleverly-devised plan. To this end he directed his troops to conquer the fort of Zion. The city of Jerusalem with the fort of Zion were located between the territories belonging to the tribes of Benjamin and Judah. While the town of Jerusalem had been captured by the Israelites in the days of Joshua, the fort of Zion which dominated the whole area remained in the hands of the Jebusites who managed to beat off every attempt to take the stronghold. Acting on David's orders a detachment of his warriors stormed the stronghold and captured it. The fort of Zion now became the city of David. David then erected here the royal palace and by this move the city of Jerusalem with the fort of Zion became the political capital of the Israelitish kingdom. Centrally placed, located in mountainous territory, easily defensible, Jerusalem was marked out by destiny, as it were, to become Israel's capital.

But David also knew that what kept the tribes of Israel together was their loyalty to a common religious inheritance as represented by the Ark of the Covenant, that central religious shrine which originated under Moses in the Wilderness and which to the Israelites symbolized God's presence among them. Consequently, David toyed with the idea of constructing alongside the royal palace an imposing sanctuary to become the fixed residence of the national shrine. This would make the city of David the center of Israel's religious as well as political life, and thus inseparable from the Davidic dynasty.

The importance of this association was fully realized by Jeroboam who in the days of Rehoboam, David's grandson, influenced the so-called ten tribes to secede from the Davidic dynasty and form the Northern Kingdom of Israel, as seen from this statement:

> And Jeroboam said in his heart, "Now shall the kingdom[1] return to the house of David: If this people go up to do sacrifice in the house of Jehovah at Jerusalem, then shall the heart of this people turn again unto their lord, even unto Rehoboam king of Judah, and they will kill me, and go back to Rehoboam king of Judah."
>
> *1 Kings 12: 27*

To prevent this from happening Jeroboam set up two national shrines in the northern kingdom, one in its southern and one in its northern region, which were to take the place of the Temple in Jerusalem.

David confided his desire to build a Temple to the prophet Nathan, his court chaplain and counsellor. Nathan saw nothing objectionable in this and gave to the king his wholehearted approval. But that same night Nathan received the following Divine message for David.

> Go and tell my servant David, "Thus says Jehovah, Shall you build me a house for me to dwell in? For I have not dwelt in a house since the time that I brought up the children of Israel out of Egypt, even to this day, but I have walked in a tent and in a tabernacle. In all the places wherein I have walked with all the children of Israel spoke I a word with any of the tribes of Israel, whom I commanded to feed my people Israel, saying, Why build you not me a house of cedar?" Now therefore so shall you say unto my servant David, "Thus says Jehovah of hosts, I took you from the sheepcote, from following the sheep, to be ruler over my people, over Israel. And I was with you withersoever you went, and have cut off all your enemies out of your sight, and have made you a great name, like unto the name of the great men that are in the earth. Moreover, I will appoint a place for my people Israel, and I will plant them, that they may dwell in a place of their own, and move no more; neither shall the children of wickedness afflict them any more, as formerly. From the time that I commanded judges to be over my people Israel; and I have caused you to rest from all your enemies; moreover, Jehovah declares to you that he will make you a house. When your days are fulfilled; and you lie down with your

---

1. Of the ten tribes.

fathers, I will set up your seed after you, who shall proceed out of your body, and I will establish his kingdom. He shall build a house for my name, and I will establish the throne of his kingdom for ever. I will be his father, and he shall be my son; if he commits iniquity, I will chasten him with the rod of men, and with the stripes of the children of men. But my mercy I will not take away from him, as I took it from Saul, whom I put away from before you. And your house and your kingdom shall be established for ever before me; your throne shall be established for ever.

2 Samuel 7: 5-16

The above declaration is another instance of how human circumstances and historical events became the occasion for great Divine revelations. David was assured that his dynasty will not suffer the fate of the dynasty of Saul. But the preservation of his dynasty will be accomplished not by what David, but by what God, will do. In accordance with God's will, the Temple shall be built by David's son. If any of David's successors will become unfaithful to God, he will be chastised, but this will never nullify God's promise to David through the prophet Nathan. No matter what happens, the Davidic dynasty shall endure forever.

The Nathan prophecy caused David to think that the Messianic substance of God's revelation to Nathan will probably be fulfilled in the reign of Solomon, his son and appointed successor, as may be seen from the following statement by David made near the end of his earthly life.

Yet Jehovah the God of Israel chose me before all the house of my father to be king over Israel for ever; for he has chosen Judah to be the ruler;[2] and of the house of Judah, the house of my father; and among the sons of my father he took pleasure in me to make me king over Israel. And of all my sons (for Jehovah has given me many sons) he has chosen Solomon my son to sit upon the throne of the kingdom of Jehovah over Israel. And he said unto me, "Solomon thy son, he shall build my house and my courts; for I have chosen him to be my son and I will be his father. Moreover, I will establish his kingdom for ever, if he be constant to my commandments and my judgments, as he is at this day.

1 Chronicles 28: 4-7

---

2.   An allusion to the Shiloh declaration in Genesis 49.

II. THE MEANING AND PURPOSE OF THE NATHAN PROPHECY

Many things happened in David's life since he became the recipient of the Divine message contained in the Nathan prophecy. A most unsettling incident was his affair with Bathsheba, the wife of Uriah, captain in the Israel army. To conceal his sin and to gain permanent possession of Bathsheba he decided to dispose of Uriah. He accomplished this by issuing instructions to the commander-in-chief to place Uriah in the front lines of a battle raging outside of Rabbah, the besieged capital of the Ammonites. In the battle Uriah was killed and David was then left free to add Bathsheba to the royal harem.

The Biblical writer's comment on this tragic incident is contained in the following brief but ominous sentence: "But the thing that David had done was evil in the eyes of Jehovah."[3] Commissioned by God, Nathan presented himself before the king and in a parable taken from every-day life he uncovered before David the dastardly nature of his sin. A heap of evils rolled down on David's head in consequence of his fall. The child that was born of his adulterous act with Bathsheba died. Amnon, one of David's sons, raped his half-sister Tamar. For this he was murdered by Absalom, another of David's sons and Tamar's brother. Later on this Absalom incited a rebellion against David hoping thereby to unseat his father and place himself on the throne. The rebellion was crushed and Absalom was killed.

Thus when David was approaching the end of his earthly pilgrimage, "after the splendor of his personality had almost entirely faded away in his own eyes and in the eyes of those about him," he may have been wondering as to the true meaning and purpose of the Nathan prophecy communicated to him many years ago. How could any human dynasty be made to last forever? Why did God single him out for the reception of this promise?

The answer to these questions came to him, probably towards the end of his life, in a prophetic message direct from God and recorded in the following passage.

> Now these are the last words of David: The oracle of David,
> the son of Jesse, the oracle of the man who was raised on high,

---

3.   2 Samuel 11: 27.

the anointed of the God of Jacob, the sweet psalmist of Israel.
The Spirit of Jehovah spoke by me, and his word was upon my
tongue. The God of Israel has spoken, the Rock of Israel said to
me: "A ruler over men, [he shall] be just, a ruler in the fear of
God. [And he shall be]⁴ as the light of the morning when the sun
rises, a morning without clouds; as the tender grass springing
out of the earth by clear shining after a rain.

2 Samuel 23: 1-4

In these few words we have a Divine interpretation of the
meaning of the Nathan prophecy. It points to a universal ruler ("a
ruler over men") who in relation to those he will rule will be the
personfication of justice, and in relation to God — the embodiment
of godly fear. Many years later, when speaking of this future universal ruler, Isaiah will say in his Messianic chapter: "And the Spirit of
Jehovah shall rest upon him . . . and the fear of Jehovah . . . Righteousness shall be the girdle of his waist, and faithfulness — the girdle
of his loins."⁵ The effect upon the world of the coming of this
universal ruler is likened to the brightness of a cloudless morning
and the tender grass springing forth after a rain.

As to the question why David was singled out to be the progenitor of this universal, godly and righteous ruler, by this time David
was fully aware of the fact that he was chosen for this dignity not
because of his moral excellence or the moral excellence of his human
descendants. What then is the assurance that the house of David will
bring forth this universal ruler? The assurance rests on God's promise made in the Nathan prophecy, a promise by virtue of which God
entered into a special covenant relationship with David, a covenant
which no moral lapses of David or his descendants can render
invalid.⁶

Inasmuch as this revelation was communicated to David in his
last days, Solomon must have become acquainted with its contents.
Consequently, we have a further delineation of the person and
mission of this universal ruler in Psalm 72, attributed to Solomon,
and representing in many respects an expansion of the ideas contained in the last Divine message to David cited above.

---

4. The words in the brackets are not in the text, but they express the sense of the
    sentence.
5. Isaiah 11: 2, 5.
6. 2 Samuel 7: 14-16; 23: 5.

Give the king thy judgments, O God, and thy righteousness unto the king's son. He shall judge thy people with righteousness, and thy poor judgment. The mountains shall bring peace to the people, and the hills, in righteousness. He shall judge the poor of the people, he shall save the children of the needy, and shall break in pieces the oppressor. They shall fear thee as long as the sun and moon endure, throughout all generations. He shall come down like the rain on mown grass, as showers that water the earth. In his days shall the righteous flourish, and abundance of peace so long as the moon endures. He shall have dominion also from sea to sea, and from the river unto the ends of the earth. They that dwell in the wilderness shall bow before him, and his enemies shall lick the dust. The kings of Tarshish and of the isles[7] shall bring presents; the kings of Sheba and Seba shall offer gifts. Yea, all kings shall fall down before him: all nations shall serve him. For he shall deliver the needy when he cries; the poor also, and him that has no helper. He shall spare the poor and needy, and shall save the souls of the needy. He shall redeem their soul from deceit and violence, and precious shall their blood be in his sight. And he shall live, and to him shall be given of the gold of Sheba; prayer also shall be made for him continually, and daily shall he be praised. There shall be an abundance of corn in the earth upon the top of the mountains; the fruit thereof shall shake like Lebanon, and they of the city shall flourish like the grass of the earth. His name shall endure forever; his name shall be continued as long as the sun; and men shall be blessed in him, all nations shall call him blessed. Blessed be Jehovah, the God of Israel, who alone does wondrous things. Blessed be his glorious name for ever; and let the whole earth be filled with his glory! Amen and Amen!

Psalm 72: 1-19

We know from history that Solomon was not the person depicted in the above psalm. He neither attained to world-wide rule, nor was he the kind of godly and righteous ruler described in the psalm. In his old age Solomon adopted idolatrous practices from the surrounding nations. "And Solomon," we are told, "did evil in the sight of Jehovah, and did not wholly follow Jehovah, as David his father had done."[8]

Jewish tradition attached a Messianic interpretation to Psalm 72. The ancient and authoritative Jewish Biblical commentator, the

_____

7.   "Tarshish and the isles," i.e., Spain and the countries of Europe.
8.   1 Kings 11:6.

Targum, thus translates the first sentence: "O God, give thy judgments to King Messiah . . . "; while the first half of verse 17 is thus rendered in the Talmud: "May his [Messiah's] name be Yinnon as long as the sun."[9]

We have in this Psalm a description of an era of justice, peace, and prosperity which shall attend Messiah's universal rule in the world. The second half of verse 17: "and men shall be blessed in him, all nations shall call him blessed," takes us back to God's promise to Abraham: "and in you shall all the families of the earth be blessed."[10] In other words, Israel's mission in this world will be accomplished by her Messianic King.

What exactly was Israel's mission supposed to be? This was spelled out in the third month after the departure from Egypt when the Israelites arrived in the vicinity of Mount Sinai.

> You have seen what I did to the Egyptians, and how I bore you on eagles' wings and brought you unto myself. Now therefore, if you will obey my voice indeed, and keep my covenant, then you shall be a peculiar treasure unto me from among all people: for all the earth is mine. And you shall be unto me a kingdom of priests, and a holy nation.
>
> *Exodus 19: 4-6*

Israel's function was to be that of a priestly nation. "The whole earth is mine," i.e., all nations are God's since He created them, and Israel's mission is to see that the nations of the earth be not only God's by virtue of having been created by God, but by becoming the children of God. Since according to Psalm 72 Israel's mission will be accomplished by her Messianic King, it follows that Messiah's highest mission will be of a priestly character, i.e. to bring the nations to God.

But how can Messiah discharge a priestly function, if he is a descendant of David, i.e. of the tribe of Judah, while the priesthood was vested by Moses in the house of Aaron, i.e. in the tribe of Levi? David himself, who in accordance with Nathan's prophecy was chosen as Messiah's progenitor, must have felt his separation from the priesthood to be a contradiction. He was king, he was also prophet in the sense that God made certain revelations to him, but he was

---

9. Sanh. 98 b.
10. Genesis 12: 3.

deprived of priestly function. This difficulty was cleared up for him by another Divine revelation as recorded in the following psalm.

> Jehovah says to my lord: "Sit at my right hand until I make your enemies your footstool. Jehovah sends forth from Zion your mighty scepter; rule in the midst of your enemies . . . Jehovah has sworn and will not change his mind: You are a priest for ever after the manner of Melchizedek.
>
> *Psalm 110: 1-2, 4*

In Jewish traditional writings Psalm 110 is interpreted as speaking of the Messiah. Notice, that though David is his human ancestor, he addresses this Messianic person as "my lord." The reference in this psalm to Melchizedek takes us back to the story of Abraham. When Abraham returned from his victorious engagement with the invaders of the Cities of the Plain, a certain Melchizedek, king of Salem, came out to greet him and brought with him bread and wine for the refreshment of Abraham's weary warriors. We are told that Melchizedek worshipped the same God as Abraham did, and Melchizedek was also a priest. Salem is the ancient name of Jerusalem. "Melchizedek" means king of righteousness. "Salem" or "Jerusalem" means peace or the possession or inheritance of peace. There is an implied connection between the name of Salem and the name of Melchizedek. Jerusalem is a city of peace when, or because, she is ruled by a king of righteousness. Throughout its long recorded history Jerusalem experienced wars, bloodshed, sieges and famine — anything but peace. But she will become a city of peace, not only for Israel, but for the whole world, when at the end of the age, i.e., the end of history as we know it, Messiah ascends the throne of David. This, because as the second Melchizedek He will be a King of righteousness and a priest for ever, who will bring all nations to a saving knowledge of God.

CHAPTER 3
THE MESSIANIC HOPE IN MICAH

I. Micah's Prediction Of The Babylonian Exile

II. Messiah's Coming Announced
  1. Messiah's Humble Human And Exalted Divine Position
  2. The Two Stages Of Messiah's Mission

CHAPTER 3
THE MESSIANIC HOPE IN MICAH

Prior to the eighth century B.C. Israel was frequently forced to defend her borders against hostile neighbors. In some of these local wars Israel suffered defeat, in others she was victorious. Under David, Solomon and Uzziah Israel attained a commanding position in the immediate area. With the beginning of the eighth century B.C. this situation changed radically. With the emergence of Assyria as a world power Israel was brought face to face with Mesopotamian world power. The outcome of this confrontation was the destruction of northern Israel in 722 B.C. and the downfall of the southern kingdom in 587 B.C. During the period of this confrontation — roughly about 150 years — Old Testament Messianism had reached its high watermark. The channels by which this Divine truth came to Israel were Israel's prophets, chiefly Micah and Isaiah in the eighth century, and Jeremiah and Ezekiel in the sixth century. The prophets were enabled to see that God was using the world power of their day to execute His corrective judgment on Israel and the other nations of the ancient world of that day. They gained the conviction that from then on Israel will remain in a subordinate position until the consummation of history, i.e., until all Gentile world power will have come to an end, and God's rule will become established on earth. They stressed the fact that the ushering in of this new world order will coincide with the coming of the Messiah, and that only then, and not until then, will Israel and the world at large experience peace and security.

> "Behold, the days are coming, says Jehovah, when I will raise up for David a righteous Branch, and he shall reign as king and deal wisely, and shall execute justice and righteousness in the earth. In his days Judah will be saved, and Israel will dwell securely; and this is the name by which he will be called: 'Jehovah is our righteousness.' "[1]
>
> *Jeremiah 23: 5-6*

Thus says the Lord God: Behold, I will take the people of Israel from the nations among which they have gone, and will

---

1.   Or 'Jehovah our righteousness'. See, also, Isaiah 11.

gather them from all sides, and bring them to their own land.
And I will make them one nation in the land, upon the mountains of Israel; and one king shall be king over them all; and they
shall be no longer two nations, and no longer divided into two
kingdoms . . . My servant David shall be king over them; and
they shall all have one shepherd; they shall follow my ordinances and be careful to observe my statutes. They shall dwell in
the land where your fathers dwelt that I gave to my servant
Jacob; they and their children and their children's children
shall dwell there for ever; and David my servant shall be their
prince for ever.

Ezekiel 37: 21-22, 24-25

That "my servant David" mentioned in the above passage is a Messianic person may be inferred from the fact that in a statement
addressed to Zedekiah on another occasion Ezekiel intimated that
Zedekiah is the last earthly member of the Davidic dynasty.[2]

I. MICAH'S PREDICTION OF THE BABYLONIAN EXILE

The destruction of northern Israel by Assyria as predicted by
Hosea had no enduring salutary effect on the southern kingdom of
Judah. Social injustice and violence were the prevailing evils. The
whole body politic of Judean society was sick. The three Divinely
appointed agents of the nation — the princes, priests and prophets
— were debasing their high calling. Micah's indictment of the rulers
of the nation is contained in the following passage.

And I said: Hear, you heads of Jacob and rulers of the
house of Israel: Is it not for you to know justice? — You who
hate the good and love the evil, who tear the skin from off my
people, and their flesh from off their bones. Who eat the flesh
of my people, and flay their skin from off them, and break their
bones in pieces, and chop them up like meat in a kettle, like flesh
in a caldron.

Micah 3: 1-3

The false prophets are similarly denounced.

Thus says Jehovah concerning the prophets who lead my
people astray, who cry "Peace" when they have something to

---

2.   Ezekiel 21: 25-27 (21: 30-32 Heb.).

eat, but declare war against him who puts nothing into their
mouths.

Micah 3: 5

All three leading classes are upbraided in the following passage.

> Hear this, you heads of the house of Jacob and rulers of the
> house of Israel who abhor justice and pervert all equity. Who
> build Zion with blood and Jerusalem with iniquity. Its heads
> judge for reward, its priests teach for hire, and its prophets
> divine for money.

Micah 3: 9-11a

Thus the very agents by which God was seeking to prepare
Israel for its mission had by their abysmal failures brought defeat
and disaster upon the people and its land.

> Therefore shall Zion for your sake be plowed as a field, and
> Jerusalem shall become heaps, and the mountain of the house[3]
> as the high places of the forest . . . Now why do you cry out
> aloud? Is there no king in you? Has your counsellor perished
> that pangs have seized you like a woman in travail? Be in pain
> and groan, O daughter of Zion, like a woman in travail; for now
> you shall go forth out of the city, and you shall dwell in the open
> country; and you shall go even to Babylon.

Micah 3: 12; 4: 9-10a

The Babylonian captivity predicted by Micah took place a little
over a century later. But the cause of world redemption would not
have been advanced had God permitted the permanent extinction
of the Judean kingdom. Therefore God had determined that after
His work of correction had been accomplished on the Judean kingdom, a remnant should return and resume Israel's national existence.

> There[4] you shall be delivered; there Jehovah shall redeem
> you from the hand of your enemies. Now many nations are
> assembled against you, that say, Let her be defiled, and let our
> eyes gaze upon Zion. But they know not the thoughts of
> Jehovah, neither do they understand his counsel: for he shall
> gather them as sheaves to the threshing-floor. Arise and thresh,
> O daughter of Zion, for I will make your horn iron and your
> hoofs brass; and you shall beat in pieces many peoples, and I will

---

3. Temple.
4. In Babylon.

consecrate their gain unto Jehovah and their substance unto the
Lord of the whole earth.

Micah 4: 10 b - 13

II. MESSIAH'S COMING ANNOUNCED

The Babylonian exile did take place in fulfillment of Micah's
prediction. But the end of the exile was not the result of a victory
over Babylon by the Jewish exiles. The exile was terminated as a
gesture of goodwill by Cyrus after he had destroyed the Babylonian
empire. Evidently, the above passage has in view another delivery,
one associated with the coming of the Messiah.

Therefore he[5] shall give them[6] up until she who is in travail
has brought forth . . .

Micah 5: 3a (5: 2a Heb.)

Who this person is whom a certain woman should bring forth is the
subject described in the next section.

1. MESSIAH'S HUMBLE HUMAN AND EXALTED DIVINE POSITION

But you, Bethlehem Ephratha, though you are little among
the thousands of Judah, yet out of you shall one come forth
unto me that is to be ruler in Israel, whose goings forth are from
of old, from everlasting.

Micah 5: 2 (5: 1 Heb.)[7]

Bethlehem was not large enough to have a thousand families or
family clans, a truly insignificant town. The mention of Bethlehem
was not merely to indicate Messiah's birthplace, but his lowly human
background as contrasted with His exalted Divine origin, "whose
goings forth are from of old, from everlasting." The future Ruler of
Israel, whose goings forth reach back into eternity is to spring from
insignificant Bethlehem, like His ancestor king David. The reference to Bethlehem shows by implication that Messiah is to be of

---

5. God.
6. Israel.
7. With the exception of substituting "you" for "thou" and "thee", the passage is
    exactly as rendered in THE HOLY SCRIPTURES, published by the Hebrew
    Publishing Company, 1951.

Davidic origin, but it also pre-supposes that Messiah will be born after the Davidic dynasty had gone out of existence, otherwise He would have been born in Jerusalem, the royal city of David's royal house.

It so happened — humanly speaking — that when Jesus of Nazareth was about to be born a census of the population was being conducted in the Roman empire including Palestine which was then a Roman province. Since both Joseph and Miriam were descendants of David they had to go, by government order, to Bethlehem, the city of their ancestors, to register. While in Bethlehem Miriam went into labor. Unable to secure a tourist or hotel room — and the census may have occasioned the shortage of tourist accommodations — a place was hastily prepared in a stable and there Miriam brought forth her firstborn son Jesus. And so it came about that Messiah Jesus was born not only in the insignificant town of Bethlehem but in a stable with a manger for His temporary crib. What a combination of circumstances to give fulfillment to Micah's prophecy uttered eight centuries in advance, and how inscrutable and wonderful are the ways of God!

2. THE TWO STAGES OF MESSIAH'S MISSION

"Therefore he shall give them up until she who is in travail has brought forth." God will give up Israel to her enemies until Messiah comes. Micah had already foretold the destruction of the Judean state by Babylonian world power. Had this not taken place, Messiah would have been born in the royal city of Jerusalem, not in Bethlehem. Messiah's birth in Bethlehem is the direct effect of the surrender of Israel by God to the power of Babylon. Israel, Micah tells us, will remain in this position of inferiority and subordination until Messiah comes. The Old Testament prophets were not given to distinguish clearly between the two phases of Messiah's mission; the lowly aspect of the first phase, and the triumphant aspect of the second phase. The birth in Bethlehem represents the first phase, during which He is a mere twig from the remaining stump of Jesse,[8] a root out of dry ground,[9] when He comes to suffer for and with His people. His second appearance will be, not in Bethlehem, but . . .

---

8. Isaiah 11: 1.
9. Isaiah 53: 2.

> On that day his feet shall stand on the Mount of Olives
> which lies before Jerusalem on the east.
>
> *Zechariah 14: 4*

The effect of the second phase of Messiah's mission is described by Micah in the following words:

> And he shall stand and feed his flock in the strength of Jehovah, in the majesty of the name of Jehovah his God. And they shall dwell secure, for now he shall be great to the ends of the earth. And this shall be peace,[10] when the Assyrian comes into our land and treads upon our soil, that we will raise against him seven shepherds and eight princes of men. They shall rule the land of Assyria with the sword, and the land of Nimrod with the drawn sword; and they shall deliver us from the Assyrian when he comes into our land and treads within our border.
>
> *Micah 5: 4-6 (5: 3-5 Heb.)*

The name "Assyria" is not always restricted to the Mesopotamian Assyria. It is also used to designate Babylon, the last representative of Mesopotamian world power.[11] Nimrod was the founder of the ungodly world power in the Mesopotamian valley. "Nimrod" and "Assyria" in the Micah passage are used to indicate the last Gentile world empire whose origin goes back all the way to the beginning of ungodly world power in the Mesopotamian valley and which shall be destroyed once and for all in the triumphant phase of Messiah's mission; "for now", i.e., in the triumphant phase of His mission, he, i.e., Messiah, "will be great to the ends of the earth."

The second effect which will attend the victorious phase of Messiah's coming has to do with the new spiritual life which He will initiate in the world and which will be channeled through Israel to the nations of the earth.

> Then the remnant of Jacob shall be in the midst of many
> peoples like dew from Jehovah, like showers upon the grass,
> which tarry not for men nor wait for the sons of men.
>
> *Micah 5: 7 (5: 6 Heb.)*

"Israel will come upon many nations, like a refreshing dew from

---

10. "And He shall be peace", is another rendering of this sentence, "He" referring to the Messiah.
11. Isaiah 7: 17; Lamentations 5:6.

Jehovah, which falls plentifully in drops upon the grass, and will produce and promote new and vigorous life among them . . . The spiritual dew, which Jacob will bring to the nations, comes from Jehovah, and falls in rich abundance without the cooperation of men."[12] It will be then, and not until then, that God's promise to Abraham will be fulfilled.

> And in you shall all the families of the earth be blessed.
> *Genesis 12: 3*

The destruction of the evil forces in the world and the spiritual rebirth of the nations will, for the first time in the history of the world, bring universal peace and prosperity, an ideal the world has been seeking to achieve from time immemorial but never succeeded.

> And it comes to pass at the end of the days, that the mountain of Jehovah's house[13] will be established on the head of the mountains, and it will be exalted above the hills, and nations stream to it. And many nations go and say, Up, let us go up to the mountain of Jehovah, and to the house of the God of Jacob, that he may teach us of his ways, and we may walk in his paths: for from Zion will instruction go forth, and the word of Jehovah from Jerusalem. And he will judge between many nations, and pronounce sentence on strong nations afar off; and they shall forge their swords into plowshares, and their spears into pruning hooks; nation will not lift up sword against nation, nor will they learn war any more. And they will sit, every one under his vine, and under his fig-tree, and no one will make them afraid; for the mouth of Jehovah of hosts has spoken.
> *Micah 4: 1-4*

When will this blessed event take place? - "And it shall come to pass at the end of the days." In Biblical prophecy the phrase "at the end of the days" always denotes the Messianic era, and, to be more specific, the triumphant phase of Messiah's mission.

---

12. C. F. Keil and F. Delitzsch, THE TWELVE MINOR PROPHETS (T. and T. Clark: Edinburgh, 1868), Vol. 1, p.488.
13. The Temple in Jerusalem.

CHAPTER 4
THE MESSIANIC HOPE IN ISAIAH

CHAPTER 4
THE MESSIANIC HOPE IN ISAIAH
I. THE ASSYRIAN CRISIS

Chronologically, Isaiah's ministry began when Uzziah was still alive. Uzziah ruled over the Judean Kingdom 52 years. His reign was an era of power, progress and prosperity. After Solomon the reign of Uzziah was the most glorious period in the history of the Judean Kingdom. Uzziah's death coincided with the emergence or re-emergence of Assyria as the representative of the Mesopotamian world power. Pursuing a policy of world conquest Assyria was determined to subjugate all nations which lay in her path towards world dominion. In those days the ability of a nation to defend itself depended largely on the power and prestige of kings. When Uzziah died the nation was deprived of a strong leader at a most dangerous time in her history.

Isaiah was a young man when Uzziah died, probably not more than 25 years old. When Uzziah died young Isaiah must have felt as if his whole world was slipping away from under his feet. Gone was the glory of an entire era and all those things which make life worthwhile, stable and secure. It was in this mood of despondency that the young man made his way one day to the sanctuary. While there he passed through an experience which catapulted him into the forefront of Old Testament prophecy. His experience was a prophetic vision which contained God's answer to what had been perplexing Isaiah's heart and mind, namely, the Assyrian threat to Israel's national survival. He came away with the profound conviction that the real threat to Israel's survival was not Assyria, but Israel's hardness of heart, her spiritual callousness, her failure to identify herself wholeheartedly with the Divine purpose of world redemption for which reason she was brought into existence. Isaiah was now certain that it was Israel's spiritual condition, rather than Assyrian aggression, which will eventually bring about the destruction of Israel, both people and land.

But the destruction of Israel would not mean that God's purpose can be frustrated. A remnant, which Isaiah calls the holy seed, will be saved. Out of this holy seed a new holy people will emerge

39

which under the leadership of King Messiah will accomplish Israel's mission.[1]

II. THE BIRTH OF THE MESSIANIC KING

Behold, the almah[2] shall conceive, and bear a son, and shall call his name Immanuel

Isaiah 7:14

For unto us a child is born, unto us a son is given; and the government rests on his shoulders: and his name shall be called,[3] Wonderful, Counsellor,[4] Mighty God, Eternal Father, Prince of Peace.

Isaiah 9:6

And there comes forth a twig out of the stump of Jesse;[5] and a shoot from its roots brings forth fruit.

Isaiah 11:1[6]

The above excerpts are from three prophetic messages in which Isaiah unfolds the Personality and mission of the Messianic King. The emphasis in the first message is on his human side; the second passage stresses His Divine-Human origin; while the third message reveals His descent from the royal house of David and implies that He will come after the downfall of the Davidic dynasty. Referring to the person depicted in these three messages, Dr. Horodetzky, writing in the Hebrew periodical "Moznaim" ("Balances" or "Scales") over forty years ago, makes the following statement: "He[7] is singled out and more marvelous than any of the holy children in the Bible. When the Judean Kingdom was in danger of being destroyed Isaiah prophesied in God's name, saying: 'Behold, the almah conceives and gives birth to a son and calls his name Immanuel.' About the quality and character of this child the prophet says laconically: 'Butter and

---

1. See, f.e., Isaiah 4:2-6; 6:1-13; 10:21-22.
2. A discussion of the meaning of the word "almah" will be found in Part Two.
3. "One calls his name," "they call his name," are other renderings of this phrase.
4. Or "Wonderful Counsellor".
5. "Jesse", David's father, stands here in place of David.
6. With minor variations the translation of the above three passages are according to the work of the Semitic scholar, Dr. Franz Delitzsch, entitled THE PROPHECIES OF ISAIAH.
7. i.e. Immanuel.

honey shall he eat, despising the evil and choosing the good.' Isaiah prophesies again about the same child, but calls him by a different name, namely, 'A child is born unto us, a son is given unto us; and the government rests on his shoulders: and his name shall be called, Wonderful, Counsellor, Mighty God, Eternal Father, Prince of Peace,' etc., etc. In another place, the prophet relates in more clear and more detailed words the descent, character and mission of this child (Isaiah 11). All these descriptions, namely, Immanuel, Wonderful, Counsellor, Root of Jesse's stock," are linked together by one, namely, Immanuel. This last name is the principal name of the child, so much so that in Isaiah 8:8 the whole land of Judah is called the land of Immanuel."[8]

III. IMMANUEL

HISTORICAL BACKGROUND

It came to pass, in the days of Ahaz the son of Jotham, the son of Uzziah, king of Judah, that Rezin, the king of Syria, and Pekah the son of Remaliah, king of Israel, went up toward Jerusalem to make war against it, but could not conquer it. When the house of David[9] was told, "Syria has settled down upon Ephraim"[10]: Then his[11] heart and the heart of his people shook as trees of the forest shake before the wind. Then said Jehovah to Isaiah, "Go forth now to meet Ahaz, you and Shear-Yashub your son, to the end of the aqueduct of the upper pool, on the highway to the Fuller's Field. And say unto him, take heed, and keep quiet; and let not your heart be faint because of these two smoking fire-brand stumps, at the fierce anger of Rezin and Syria, and the son of Remaliah. Because Syria with Ephraim and the son of Remaliah have devised evil against you, saying, We will march against Judah, and terrify it, and conquer it for ourselves, and make the son of Tabeal king in the midst of it, thus says the Lord Jehovah, It will not be brought about, and will not take place. For the head of Syria is Damascus, and the head of Damascus is Rezin, (and within sixty-five

---

8. S.A. Horodetsky, in MOZNAIM, first year, Vol. 1, No. 10; quoted by J. I. Landsman in DER WEG (Warsaw), Nov.-Dec., 1929.
9. i.e. Ahaz, the Davidic king of the Judean Kingdom.
10. i.e. the armies of the two allies, the Northern Kingdom of Israel and Syria, have linked up in preparation for a joint expedition against Jerusalem.
11. King Ahaz.

years Ephraim as a people will be broken in pieces). And the head of Ephraim is Samaria, and the head of Samaria the son of Remaliah; if you do not believe, surely you will not remain. And Jehovah continued to speak to Ahaz as follows: Ask a sign of Jehovah your God, whether it be as deep as Hades or as high as heaven. But Ahaz replied, I dare not ask, and dare not put Jehovah to the test.

Isaiah 7: 1-12

To get all the details connected with the historical event which forms the background of the three Messianic messages which we are discussing now, the reader is referred to the Second Book of Kings, chapters 15, 16, 17; and Second Chronicles, chapter 28. Syria and Northern Israel had formed an alliance aiming to shake off the yoke of Assyria. For this plan to succeed they had to make themselves secure against the Judean Kingdom in the south, especially in view of the fact that there are indications of the existence at that time of friendly relations between Assyria and the Judean Kingdom. The two northern allies conceived of a plan to eliminate the Davidic dynasty by placing on its throne a certain person identified in the text as the son of Tabeal who is believed to have been a Syrian army captain. Rezin, the Syrian ruler, marched into the south of Judah through trans-Jordanian territory, captured Elath and handed it over to the Edomites, as Syria could hardly be expected to hold this isolated outpost so far south; furthermore, through this clever act of generosity he gained the Edomites as allies against the Judean Kingdom. Pekah, Northern Israel's king, proceeded into Judea and defeated its armies in a great battle and laid siege to Jerusalem but failed to conquer it. When Rezin returned from his expedition in the south, the Syrian and Northern Israel armies joined their forces for another march against Jerusalem with the avowed purpose to take the capital, depose Ahaz, and set up another dynasty in the Judean Kingdom.

Two events then took place, fraught with great political and theocratic significance. The first was the decision by Ahaz to appeal to Assyria for help. The second was the prophet Isaiah's intervention. In our own days, eastern Germany, Poland, Hungary and Czechoslovakia, with Russian soldiers stationed in their countries, have learned the meaning of being "protected" by a great power. Some twenty-six centuries ago Isaiah was fully aware of the disastrous consequences which would follow an appeal to Assyria. Commissioned by God, Isaiah appeared before Ahaz with a two-fold message. First, Ahaz was told not to fear, and to stand firm. Second, he was assured that the whole plan to depose him will fail.[12] This, not because Ahaz was worth saving, he was a weak, and idolatrous character, but on account of the Divine promise made to David concerning the permanence of his dynasty. To permit the destruction of the Davidic dynasty at that particular juncture of history would have interfered with God's redemptive purpose for the world.

To persuade the King to change his mind in the matter of his decision to appeal for Assyrian intervention, Isaiah challanged him to ask for any sign from God which would give him instant proof of the certitude of Isaiah's message. But Ahaz would not be swayed. Mighty Assyria was so much more real and tangible than all this talk about help from a God whom he could not see and of whose real character he was totally ignorant.

The die was cast. Isaiah was now convinced that the King's decision will have far-reaching disastrous consequences for the Judean Kingdom. Isaiah then gave to the King another sign, one which the King did not ask for, and which would be verified by events taking place in the course of history. The sign was of a two-fold character. In the first place, it announced God's coming judgment upon all Israel, north and south. In the second place, it contained a message of consolation and reassurance for the faithful remnant.

> Therefore the Lord himself will give you a sign: Behold, the almah shall conceive and bear a son and shall call his name Immanuel. He shall eat curds and honey when he knows how to refuse the evil and choose the good. For before the boy shall understand to refuse the evil and choose the good, the land will be desolate of whose two kings you are afraid.
> *Isaiah 7: 14-16*

God's judgment will first fall upon northern Israel and Syria for their attempt to overthrow the Davidic dynasty.

> Then Jehovah said to me, "Take a large slab, and write upon it with common characters, 'The spoil speeds, the prey hastens.' And I took to me trustworthy witnesses, Uriah the priest, and Zechariah the son of Jeberechiah. And I drew near to the prophetess, and she conceived and bore a son; and

---

12.   Isaiah 7: 4-5, 8.

> Jehovah said to me, Call his name the spoil speeds, the prey
> hastens. For before the boy shall know how to cry, My father
> and my mother, they will carry away the riches of Damascus,
> and the spoil of Samaria,[13] before the king of Assyria.
>
> Isaiah 8: 1-4

The words engraved on the slab which were adopted as the name of
the prophet's child born nine months later carried an announcement of the approaching doom. Within three years Damascus, the
capital of Syria, was taken by the Assyrian army, the northern
provinces of Northern Israel were annexed by Assyria, and Pekah,
the king of Northern Israel, was assassinated. For Northern Israel
this was the beginning of her national extinction.

But there was a judgment reserved also for the Judean Kingdom as seen from the following words addressed to Ahaz.

> Jehovah will bring upon you, and upon your people, and
> upon your father's house, days such as have not come since the
> day when Ephraim broke away from Judah—the king of As-
> syria.
>
> Isaiah 7:17

IV. THE MEANING OF THE IMMANUEL PROPHECY

George Adam Smith, one of the great Old Testament scholars
of another generation, was certainly right when he said that we
cannot dissociate the announcement of the birth of Immanuel from
the expectation of the coming of a glorious Prince which was current
in the royal Davidic family since the days of the founder of the
dynasty. "Mysterious and abrupt as the intimation of Immanuel's
birth may seem to us at this juncture, we cannot forget that it fell
from Isaiah's lips on hearts which cherished as their dearest hope
the appearance of a glorious descendant of David, and which were
just now the more sensitive to this hope that both David's city and
David's dynasty were in peril."[14]

---

13. Reference to the coming destruction of Syria and Northern Israel by Assyria.
14. George Adam Smith, THE BOOK OF ISAIAH (Harper and Brothers: New
    York, 1927), Vol. 1, p.114 Used by permission of Harper & Row, Publishers,
    Inc.

Before we can grasp the full meaning of the Immanuel Prophecy we must first inquire into the time of Immanuel's coming. Isaiah does not give a fixed date of his coming. But he does intimate that he was to be born after the destruction of the Davidic Kingdom, and that this destruction of the Judean Kingdom will be accomplished by the Mesopotamian world power on whose help Ahaz staked his survival.

> And in that day Jehovah will whistle for the fly which is at the end of the Nile-arms of Egypt, and the bees that are in the land of Assyria; and they will settle all of them in the valleys of the slopes, and in the clefts of the rocks, and in all the thorn-hedges, and on all the pastures.
>
> *Isaiah 7: 18-19*

Historically this collision between the armies of Egypt and Mesopotamia implied in the above passage took place in the days of Josiah, king of Judah, when Pharaoh-Necho attempted to defeat the emerging Babylonian empire. In a battle at Carchemish the Egyptian army was routed by the military might of Nebuchadnezzar, and Babylon entered into the heritage of Assyria and assumed power over the territories of the Assyrian empire, at least in western Asia, including the Judean Kingdom. It was the Babylonian representative of the Mesopotamian world power that ultimately destroyed the Davidic Kingdom as indicated by Isaiah in the next line of chapter seven . . .

> In That day will the Lord shave with a razor which is hired beyond the River[15]—with the king of Assyria—the head and the hair of the feet; and even the beard it will take away.
>
> *Isaiah 7:20*

"Assyria" used in the above passages actually stands for Babylon. Jeremiah also designates Babylon by the name of Assyria.[16] Even the Persian empire is so identified.[17] This, because both Babylon and Persia were in fact a continuation of the Mesopotamian world empire. This is especially true of Babylon which is geographically part of Mesopotamia and was the center of the first world empire in the days of Nimrod. As a matter of fact, Isaiah at a later period distinctly predicted the collapse of the Davidic Kingdom in the days of Baby-

---

15.   Euphrates - another designation of the Mesopotamian Valley.
16.   Jeremiah 2:18; Lamentations 5:6.
17.   Ezra 6:22.

lon, as seen from the following words addressed by him to King Hezekiah.

> Behold, the days are coming, that all that is in your house, and all that your fathers have laid up unto this day, will be carried away to Babylon; nothing will be left behind, says Jehovah. And your children, who are born to you, shall be taken away; and they will be eunuchs in the palace of the king of Babylon.
>
> *Isaiah 39: 6-7*

Ahaz himself became a tributary to the Assyrian king, and held his crown at the mercy of the world power whose intervention he invited in defiance of Isaiah's pleadings. From then on Assyria held a tight grip on the Judean Kingdom. The destruction of the Judean Kingdom by Babylon was merely the completion of the work begun by Assyria in the days of Ahaz.

In the Immanuel Prophecy Isaiah sought to impress on King Ahaz that by his reckless policy dictated by his shortrightedness and his unfaithfulness to God he will disestablish the Davidic dynasty, mortgage away the Messianic hope of Israel, and disinherit the promised Messianic King.

> If you will not believe, surely you will not be established . . . For before the boy[18] shall understand to refuse the evil, and choose the good,[19] the land will be desolate, of whose two kings you are afraid. Jehovah will bring upon you, and upon your people, and upon your father's house[20] days such as have not come since the day when Ephraim broke away from Judah — the king of Assyria.
>
> *Isaiah 7:9b, 16-17*

In conclusion, in consequence of the growing spiritual callousness of Israel — of the Davidic dynasty and of the people — the promised Messianic King will come after the Land of Israel, north and south, will have been devastated,[21] and the Davidic dynasty will have ceased to exist. Instead of in the royal city of Jerusalem, His

---

18. i.e. Immanuel, the promised Messianic King.
19. i.e.before he will reach discerning age, or maturity.
20. Davidic dynasty.
21. This devastation and depopulation of the Land had already been predicted in Isaiah 6.

birth will therefore take place, as Micah tells us, in the insignificant town of Bethlehem. The lowliness of His birth is further stressed by Isaiah in his prediction that she of whom He is to be born will not be the queen of the royal palace, but merely "the almah," some un-named woman.

But though human folly and unfaithfulness can bring about a delay or detour in the execution of God's purpose, they can never nullify it. By God's overruling power, He who because of human willfulness will be so lowly at his appearing, will nevertheless be the Immanuel, God-with-us.

V. DIVINE JUDGMENT

The judgment of God which with one voice the prophets had foretold had finally overtaken the northern kingdom. Its capital was taken in 722 B.C. and its territory became an Assyrian province. For the first time in her history the Judean Kingdom was now directly confronted by the Assyrian world power. It was soon to realize the utter worthlessness of the alliance concluded by Ahaz with Assyria and the folly of trusting an unscrupulous world power.

Isaiah was convinced that, treaty or no treaty, Assyria will in-vade the Judean Kingdom. He even described the route which the Assyrian army was likely to take from the northern border of Judea until it had reached the heights over against Jerusalem.[22] Histori-cally this took place when Sennacherib sent a detachment of his expeditionary force into Judea as recorded in 2 Kings, chapters 18 and 19.

Isaiah's interpretation of the meaning of the Assyrian victories over Israel and the other nations is given in the following passage.

> Woe to Assyria the rod of my anger, in whose hand is the staff of my fury. Against a hypocritical nation will I send him, and against the people of my wrath will I give him charge, to take spoil and to seize plunder, and to tread them down like the mire of the streets. Nevertheless he does not so intend, neither

---

22.   Isaiah 10:28-32.

does his mind think so; for it is in his heart to destroy and cut off nations not a few. For he says, "Are not my generals all kings? Is not Calno as Carchemish, or Hamath as Arpad, or Samaria as Damascus?[23] As my hand has found the kingdoms of the idols whose graven images did excel those of Jerusalem and Samaria. Shall I not, as I have done unto Samaria and her idols, so do to Jerusalem and her idols?"[24]

Wherefore when the Lord has finished his work[25] on Mount Zion and on Jerusalem I will punish the arrogant boasting of the king of Assyria and his haughty pride. For he has said, "By the strength of my hand I have done it, and by my own wisdom, for I am prudent; and I have removed the boundaries of peoples, and have robbed their treasures and threw down rulers like a bull. My hand extracted the wealth of the nations like a nest; and as men sweep up forsaken eggs, have I swept the whole earth; there was none that moved a wing, or opened the mouth, or chirped."

Dare the ax boast itself against him that hews with it, or the saw magnify itself against him that wields it? As if a rod were to swing those that lift it up, and as if a stick should lift him who is not wood! Therefore will the Lord, Jehovah of hosts, send wasting sickness against his fat men; and under his glory he shall kindle a burning like the burning of a fire. The light of Israel will become a fire, and his Holy One a flame; and it shall set on fire and devour its thistles and thorns in one day. And he shall consume the glory of his forest, and of his fruitful field, both soul and body; and it will be as when a sick man wastes away. And the remnant of the trees of his forest will be so few that a child can write them down.

Isaiah 10: 5-19

"Belief in God had hitherto been local and circumscribed. Each nation had walked in the name of its god, and limited his power and prevision to its own life and territory. We do not blame the peoples for this. Their conception of God was narrow, and they confined the power of their deity to their own borders because, in fact, their

---

23.   A reference to the various foreign kingdoms which Assyria had conquered.
24.   It should be noted that this statement about the Judean Kingdom's God was made by Sennacherib in the days of Hezekiah who purged Judea of idolatry. To Assyria Judea's God stood on the same level as the gods of the other nations that she conquered.
25.   Of corrective judgment.

thoughts seldom strayed beyond. But the barriers, that had so long enclosed mankind in narrow circles, were being broken down,[26] and men learned that outside their fatherland there lay the world. Their lives thereupon widened immensely, but their theologies stood still. They felt the great forces which shook the world, but their gods remained the same petty, provincial deities.

"Then came this great Assyrian power, hurtling through the nations, laughing at their gods and idols, boasting that it was by his own strength that he overcame them . . . No wonder that men's hearts were drawn from unseen spiritualities to this very visible brutality. No wonder all real faith in the gods seemed to be dying out, and that men made it the business of their lives to seek peace with this world force, which was carrying everything, including the god's themselves, before it! Mankind was in danger of practical atheism: of placing, as Isaiah tells us, the ultimate faith which belongs to a righteous God in this brute force, of substituting embassies for prayers, tribute for sacrifice, and the tricks and compromises of diplomacy for the endeavor to live a holy and righteous life.

"Behold, what questions were at issue, questions that have come up again and again in the history of human thought, and that are tugging at us today harder than ever! — whether the visible [and brutal] forces of the universe . . . are what we men have to make our peace with, or whether there is behind them a Being, who wields them for purposes, far transcending them, of justice and love; whether, in short, we are to be materialists, or believers in God. It is the same old and ever-new debate. The factors of it have only changed a little as we have become more learned . . . Everything that has come forcibly and gloriously to the front of things, every drift that appears to dominate history, all that asserts its claim on our wonder, and offers its own simple and strong solution to our life — is our Assyria.

"Our Assyria may be . . . that flood of successful, heartless, unscrupulous, scornful forces which burst on our innocence, with their challenge to make terms and pay tribute, or go down straightway in struggle for existence. Beside their frank and forceful demands, how commonplace and irrelevant do the simple precepts of religion often seem; and how the great brazen face of the world seems to bleach the beauty out of purity and honor! According to our temper,

---

26. Indeed, Assyria was used of God to break them down.

we either cower before its insolence, whining that character and energy of struggle and religious peace are impossible against it; and that is the Atheism of Fear, with which Isaiah charged the men of Jerusalem, when they were paralyzed before Assyria. Or we seek to insure ourselves against disaster by alliance with the world. We make ourselves one with it, its subjects and its imitations. We absorb the world's temper, get to believe in nothing but success, regard men only as they can be useful to us, and think so exclusively of ourselves as to lose the faculty of imagining about us any other right or need or pity. And all that is the Atheism of Force, with which Isaiah charged the Assyrian . . .

"Our Assyria may be the forces of nature, which have swept upon the knowledge of this generation with the novelty and impetus, with which the northern hosts burst across the horizon of Israel. Men today, in the course of their education, become acquainted with laws and forces which dwarf the simpler theologies of their boyhood, pretty much as the primitive beliefs of Israel dwindled before the arrogant face of Assyria. The alternative confronts them either to retain, with a narrowed and fearful heart, their old conceptions of God, or to find their enthusiasm in studying, and their duty in relating themselves to, the forces of nature alone. If this be the only alternative, there can be no doubt but that most men will take the latter course . . . But is this the only alternative? . . .

"Isaiah's greatness lay in this, that it was given to him to attack the problem the first time it presented itself to humanity with any serious force, and that he applied to it the only sure solution — a more lofty and spiritual view of God than the one which it had found wanting . . . Beneath his idea of God, exalted and spiritual, even the imperial Assyrian, in all his arrogance, fell subordinate and serviceable. The prophet's faith never wavered, and in the end was vindicated by history."[27] As was with Assyria in Isaiah's day, with Babylon in Jeremiah's day, so it has been with the other world powers in history: they are preparing the way for Messiah's coming. God has used them as instruments with which to accomplish His purpose. When this phase of God's redemptive program has been brought to completion, the world powers will be discarded as tools for which He has no more use, and Messiah will come to set up God's rule on earth.

---

27.   George Adam Smith, Op.Cit., Vol. 1, pp. 176-181.

VI. MESSIAH'S DUAL NATURE

Like the Immanuel Prophecy in chapter 7, the prophetic message in chapter 9 was also occasioned by historical circumstances. The northern area of the Land of Israel comprising the lands of Zebulun and Naphtali was also known as Galilee or Galilee of the nations, because it was inhabited by both Israelites and heathen peoples. The Israelites dwelling there were involved in incessant warfare with the surrounding peoples and in a never-ending struggle with heathenism. Around 732 B.C. the Assyrian army under Tiglath-Pileser burst, like a mighty flood, over the Northern Kingdom of Israel which was the beginning of the fulfillment of Isaiah's prediction. The first province to be submerged by the Assyrian flood was Galilee. It was annexed by Assyria and its Jewish inhabitants transported into exile. It was the night of Israel's first captivity. The opening lines of the prophetic message in chapter nine was a message of consolation addressed especially to the northern, i.e. Galilean, provinces, then under Assyrian rule.

> For there will be no darkness where there is distress now: in the former time he brought into disgrace the land of Zebulun and the land of Naphtali, but in the latter time he will bring to honor the road by the sea,[28] the land beyond the Jordan, Galilee of the Gentiles. The people who walked in darkness have seen a great light; they who dwelt in the land of the shadow of death, upon them a light shines. Thou hast multiplied the nation, thou hast increased its joy; they rejoice before thee like the joy in harvest, as men rejoice when they share the spoil.
>
> *Isaiah 9:1-3 (8:23; 9:1-2 Heb.)*

The light of future deliverance, the prophet declares, will shine forth first in those areas which suffered first.[29] The nation or area which because of wars and deportations was depopulated will become repopulated: "Thou has multiplied the nation, thou hast increased its joy."

The deliverance which is the cause of the change in Israel's position is described in the next passage.

---

28. The Sea or Lake of Galilee.
29. "King Messiah will reveal Himself in the Land of Galilee"-ZOHAR, p. 1, fol. 119, ed. Amstelod; fol. 74 ed. Solisbac quoted by E.W. Hengstenberg, CHRISTOLOGY OF THE OLD TESTAMENT (Kregel Publications: Grand Rapids, Michigan, 1956), Vol. 2, p. 75.

> For thou hast broken the yoke of his burden, and the staff
> of his shoulder, the rod of his oppressor, as in the day of Midian.
> For every boot of the tramping warrior in the tumult of battle
> and cloak rolled in blood will be burned as fuel for the fire.
>
> *Isaiah 9:4-5 (9:3-4 Heb.)*

The words "burden" and "oppresssor" are terms familiar to us from
the oppression during the period of the Egyptian bondage. The
future deliverance will be like a second redemption from Egypt,
with this difference however, that the defeat of Israel's enemy will
take place on Israel's soil as it happened in the war with Midian
under the leadership of Gideon. The reference to the victories over
the hosts of Egypt and Midian aims to emphasize an important
phenomenon in Israel's history, namely, that at every critical period
when Israel's survival is at stake, God steps in and saves the day for
Israel. So will it be in the last attack upon Israel by the Gentile world
power of the last days. Its power will be broken on Israel's soil by
Divine intervention. Victory over Israel's enemies in the last days of
the Times of the Gentiles will be the work of God. It is God who will
break the burden of Israel's oppressors, it is God who will multiply
the nation.[30]

In the sphere of human history God works through leaders of
His choice. Israel's final deliverance described above will be accomplished through her Messianic King, as seen from the next passage
in chapter 9.

> For unto us a child is born, unto us a son is given; and the
> government will be upon his shoulder, and his name will be
> called Wonderful, Counsellor,[31] Mighty God, Everlasting
> Father, Prince of Peace. Of the increase of his government and
> of peace there will be no end, upon the throne of David, and
> over his kingdom, to strengthen it, and to support it through
> judgment and righteousness from henceforth even for ever.
> The zeal of Jehovah of host will do this.
>
> *Isaiah 9:6-7 (9:5-7 Heb.)*

It would not be too far-fetched to say that the above prophetic
message saw a partial fulfillment in the days of Jesus of Nazareth
who not only grew up in Galilee, but concentrated the first part of
His ministry in that part of the Land of Israel.

---

30. See also Ezekiel 38 and 39; Zechariah 12.
31. Or Wonderful Counsellor.

VII. MESSIAH'S DAVIDIC DESCENT

There shall come forth a twig out of the stump of Jesse, and a shoot shall grow out from its roots.

Isaiah 11:1

The Davidic dynasty is here likened to a stump which has been cut down. Then, in the fullness of time, a twig springs forth from the stump of the felled tree, and from its roots covered with earth a shoot comes forth. It should be noted that the Hebrew word used for "shoot" is "netzer." Netzer or Nitzereth is the Hebrew name for Nazareth — the town in Galilee where Jesus grew up. "Notzri" is the Hebrew word identifying a follower of Jesus the Messiah. In this first sentence of chapter 11 Isaiah reiterates what he has been trying to say in chapters 7 and 8 that the promised Messianic King will come some time after the downfall of the Davidic dynasty.

VIII. MESSIAH'S SPIRITUAL EQUIPMENT

And the Spirit of Jehovah shall rest upon him, the spirit of wisdom and understanding, the spirit of counsel and might, the spirit of knowledge and of the fear of Jehovah.

Isaiah 11:2

We have in this statement seven spirits — the Spirit of Jehovah and six other spirits. They correspond to the seven-lighted candlesticks in the Tabernacle and Temple. The Spirit of Jehovah is the central shaft of this candlestick and the six other spirits emerge in three pairs from both sides of the central shaft. Together they symbolize Messiah's anointment for His Messianic mission. As was mentioned before, the act of anointing with oil in Biblical times suggested that the anointed individual was equipped with God's purpose. In the Old Testament period the descent of God's Spirit upon the anointed individual was of a transient duration. It often lasted only long enough for that particular individual to accomplish his mission. In the case of the Messianic King the Spirit of God is his permanent possession: "The Spirit of Jehovah shall rest upon him."

And his delight shall be in the fear of Jehovah.

Isaiah 11: 3a

George Adam Smith renders this sentence thus: "He shall draw his breath in the fear of Jehovah." "It is a most expressive definition of sinlessness — sinlessness which was the attribute of Jesus Christ alone. We, however well intentioned we be, are compassed about by an atmosphere of sin. We cannot help breathing what now inflames our passions, now chills our warmest feelings, and makes our throats incapable of honest testimony or glorious praise. As oxygen to a dying fire, so the worldliness we breathe is the sin within us. We cannot help it; it is the atmosphere into which we are born. But from this Christ alone was free. He was His own atmosphere, drawing breath in the fear of Jehovah. Of Him alone it is recorded, that, though living in the world, He was never infected with the world's sin. The blast of no man's cruelty ever kindled unholy wrath within his breast; nor did men's unbelief carry to His soul its deadly chill. Not even when He was led of the devil into the atmosphere of temptation, did His heart throb with one rebellious ambition. Christ drew breath in the fear of Jehovah."[32]

All of those to whom Messiah Jesus became the Savior and Lord of their lives can truly say with the apostle Paul that in Him "we live and move and have our being."[33] "And what else is heaven to be, if not this? God, we are told, shall be its Sun; but its atmosphere shall be His fear, which is clean and endures for ever. Heaven seems most real as a moral open-air, where every breath is an inspiration, and every pulse a healthy joy, where no thoughts from within us find breath but those of obedience and praise, and all our passions and aspirations are of the will of God. He that lives near to Christ, and by Christ often seeks God in prayer, may create for himself even on earth such a heaven."[34] "If any one belongs to Messiah Jesus," Paul testifies from personal experience, "he is a new creation; the old has passed away, behold, the new has come."[35]

IX. MESSIAH'S MISSION

1. THE ESTABLISHMENT OF RIGHTEOUSNESS

He shall not judge by what his eyes see, or decide by what

---

32. George Adam Smith, Op. Cit., Vol. 1, pp. 187-8.
33. Acts 17:28.
34. George Adam Smith, Op. Cit., Vol. 1, p. 188.
35. 2 Corinthians 5:17.

his ears hear. But with righteousness shall he judge the poor,
and decide with equity for the poor of the earth; and he shall
smite the earth with the rod of his mouth, and with the breath of
his lips shall he slay the wicked. Righteousness shall be the girdle
of his loins, and faithfulness the girdle of his waist.

Isaiah 11: 3b-5

The meek, the poor and oppressed will be the special objects of His
concern. The forces of evil will be subdued everywhere on earth,
and universal righteousness will be established. In chapter 32, also a
Messianic chapter, we are told that righteousness and peace will
reign in the world when society will experience a spiritual rebirth.

Until the Spirit is poured upon us from on high, and the
wilderness becomes a fruitful field, and the fruitful field be
deemed a forest. Then justice will dwell in the wilderness, and
righteousness will abide in the fruitful field. And the effect of
righteousness will be peace, and the result of righteousness,
quietness and trust for ever.

Isaiah 32: 15-17

2. THE REUNIFICATION OF THE WORLD

According to the Biblical interpretation of the Tower of Babel
event, the nations of the earth were born in rebellion against God
and in hostility to one another. The unity of mankind was broken.
The various world powers have tried to reunite the world but have
failed dismally. The world will not be reunited until King Messiah
comes. The Jewish people have tasted more of international enmity
than any other nation in the world. Some one said that as long as the
Jews are away from their ancestral land, the Jews are out of place
and the world is out of place. The reunification of the world in
Messianic times will therefore begin with Israel's restoration to the
Land of Israel.

And it shall come to pass in that day that the Lord will
stretch out his hand again a second time to recover the remnant
of his people which shall be left, from Assyria, and from Egypt,
and from Pathros, and from Ethiopia, from Elam, from Shinar,
from Hamath, and from the coastlands of the sea. He will raise
an ensign for the nations, and will assemble the outcasts of
Israel, and gather the dispersed of Judah from the four corners
of the earth.

Isaiah 11: 11-12

The restoration of Israel will be the first act of Messiah's work in the sphere of international relations. The second act of his work in this sphere will be the reunification of the world. Messiah will become the focus of world union.

> In that day the root of Jesse shall stand as an ensign of the peoples; him shall the nations seek, and his dwellings shall be glorious.
>
> *Isaiah 11:10*

3. WORLD PEACE AND ECONOMIC SECURITY

> It shall come to pass in the latter days[36] that the mountain of the house of Jehovah[37] shall be established as the highest of mountains, and shall be exalted above the hills; and peoples shall stream to it. And many nations shall come, and say: "Come, let us go up to the mountain of Jehovah, to the house of the God of Jacob; and he will instruct us in his ways, that we may walk in his paths"; for out of Zion shall go forth instruction, and the word of God from Jerusalem.[38] He shall arbitrate between many peoples, and settle disputes among strong and distant nations; and they shall beat their swords into plowshares, and their spears into pruning hooks; nation shall not lift up sword against nation, nor shall they train for war any more. And they shall sit every one under his vine and under his fig tree, and none shall make them afraid; for the mouth of Jehovah of hosts has spoken.
>
> *Micah 4:1-4*

---

36. The Messianic significance of the phrase "the latter days" has been described in chapter 1.
37. The Jerusalem Temple.
38. Unlike the revelation made in the Sinai desert, containing elements suitable for one people and for a particular period of history, the new revelation addressing itself to all nations will come out of Jerusalem.

CHAPTER 5
THE SUFFERING SERVANT IN THE OLD TESTAMENT

I. The End Of The Babylonian Exile

II. The Three Servants
   1. The Powers Of The World
   2. The People Of Israel
   3. The Messianic Person

III. The Vicarious And Atoning Death Of The Suffering Servant
   1. The Untenableness Of Modern Jewish Interpretations
      a. The Suffering Servant of Isaiah is a perfectly innocent Person
      b. The Suffering Servant of Isaiah suffers on account of the sins of others
      c. The Suffering Servant of Isaiah is a willing Sufferer
      d. The sufferings of the Suffering Servant of Isaiah culminated in His death
   2. Medieval Jewish Interpretations
   3. The Suffering Servant In The Talmud
   4. The Suffering Servant In The Midrashim
   5. The Suffering Servant In The Zohar
   6. The Suffering Servant In The Prayer Book

IV. The Mission Of The Suffering Servant
   1. Humiliation And Apparent Failure
   2. His Mission To Israel
      a. The spiritual aspect of Messiah's mission to Israel
      b. The physical aspect of Messiah's mission to Israel
   3. His Mission To The World

V. Is The Atoning Aspect Of Isaiah's Suffering Servant An Isolated Concept?
   1. The Sacrifice Of Isaac
   2. Moses
   3. Hosea
   4. Isaiah
   5. Jeremiah
   6. Ezekiel
   7. The Generation Of The Babylonian Exile

THE SUFFERING SERVANT IN THE OLD TESTAMENT

We now come to the heart of the Biblical Messianic hope — the Suffering Servant of Jehovah depicted in the second part of Isaiah. The second part of Isaiah consists of 27 chapters — 40 to 66 — which fall into three divisions, each consisting of nine chapters. The first division is brought to a close at the end of chapter 48 where the blessed state of the righteous is contrasted with the state of the wicked and is concluded with the words: "There is no peace, says Jehovah, for the wicked".[1] The righteous are those Israelites who remained faithful to Jehovah; the wicked are those who denied Jehovah and thus placed themselves on a level with the heathen. The second division, chapters 49-57, closes with a similar refrain: "There is no peace, says my God, for the wicked".[2] The last division, chapters 58-66, omits the familiar refrain "There is no peace", and, instead, concludes with a description of the miserable end of the wicked: "Their worm shall not die, neither shall their fire be quenched, and they shall be an abhorring to all flesh".[3] "One great line of thought unfolded in the whole prophesy [of the second half of Isaiah] is the development of evil and the final overthrow of the wicked, who are excluded from the blessings of Messiah's Kingdom; the sufferings but final glory of the righteous remnant, who are the citizens of that Kingdom, and whose King is described as leading the way along the same path of suffering and glory".[4]

The main theme of the first division is the restoration from Babylonian captivity through Cyrus, God's appointed instrument. The subject of the second or central division is Israel's final and full restoration accomplished by One far greater than Cyrus, the Servant of Jehovah, whose mission is not only to raise up "the tribes of Jacob" and to restore "the preserved of Israel", but to be also "a light to the Gentiles" and God's salvation "to the end of the earth". The

---

1. Isaiah 48:22.
2. Isaiah 57:21.
3. Isaiah 66:24.
4. David Baron, THE SERVANT OF JEHOVAH (Morgan & Scott: London, 1922), p.6.Used by permission of Marshall, Morgan & Scott.

substance of the last division is the blessed condition of a restored and redeemed Israel who becomes the channel through which Messiah's message of salvation reaches all nations.

I. THE END OF THE BABYLONIAN EXILE

The point of departure of the first division, as indicated above, is the end of the Babylonian captivity. The catastrophe which befell the Judean Kingdom at the beginning of the sixth century B.C., and the termination of the exile in 538 B.C., were used by the prophet to prove the trustworthiness of God's promises; while the partial restoration following the end of the Babylonian exile was cited by him as forshadowing a future and full restoration.

In the opening statement of the first division of the second half of Isaiah the prophet declares, among other things, that the Babylonian disaster was the consequence of Israel's sinfulness:

> Comfort you, comfort you my people, says your God. Speak you to the heart of Jerusalem, and cry to her that her affliction is ended, that her iniquity is pardoned, that she received from Jehovah's hand double for all her sins.
> *Isaiah 40: 1-2*

When King Ahaz in the eighth century B.C. refused to change his mind about appealing to Assyria for help, Isaiah declared to him that he was laying the foundation for the destruction of the Judean Kingdom.[5] In his vision in the Temple as recorded in the sixth chapter, Isaiah was told that it was not Assyria that was Israel's problem, but rather the nation's growing alienation from God and its increasing spiritual callousness.[6]

Again and again, in the Biblical period of her history, Israel was taught that her national welfare will be determined by her faithfulness to Jehovah and by the quality of her moral life. This truth is implicit in the law concerning the Jubilee Year, one of the most remarkable social institutions in the Old Testament. While still in the Wilderness, Israel was told that, when she had taken possession of

---

5.   Isaiah 7:17.
6.   Isaiah 6: 9-13.

the Promised Land, every fiftieth year should be proclaimed the
Jubilee Year.

> And you shall number seven sabbaths of years, seven times
> seven years, and the space of the seven sabbaths of years shall be
> unto you forty and nine years. Then shall you send abroad the
> loud trumpet on the tenth day of the seventh month; on the day
> of atonement you shall send abroad the trumpet throughout all
> your land. And you shall hallow the fiftieth year, and proclaim
> liberty throughout the land to all its inhabitants; it shall be a
> jubilee for you, when each of you shall return to his property
> and each of you shall return to his family. A jubilee shall that
> fiftieth year be to you; in it you shall neither sow, nor reap what
> grows of itself, nor gather the grapes from the undressed vines.
> For it is a jubilee; it shall be holy to you; you shall eat what it
> yields out of the field.
>
> *Leviticus 25: 8-13*

During the Jubilee Year the land shall lie fallow, in order that it may
recover its fertility. Sold land and, under certain circumstances, sold
houses must revert to the original owners. The servitude of Israelites, irrespective of when it had begun, was to terminate in the
Jubilee Year. The Jubilee Year institution aimed to prevent the
permanent excessive accumulation of property in the hands of the
few. It sought to check the development in Israel of the two evils:
excessive wealth of the few and abject poverty of the many. It tended
to hinder the rise of a landless peasantry, and to block the growth of
slavery. It was designed to assure the existence of a sound, stable and
just social and economic order. It was for this reason that the Jubilee
Year was called a year of liberty.

We should note, however, that the Jubilee Year was to be
ushered in on the Day of Atonement, undoubtedly after the solemn
services and sacrifices prescribed for that day had already been
completed. The sacrifices offered up on the Day of Atonement were
intended to cleanse the nation of its sins and thus to restore its
covenant-relation with God which during the year had become
disrupted through sin. Thus, the renewal which the Jubilee Year
was to initiate in Israel's social and economic relations had to be
preceded by Israel's moral renewal. The Jubilee Year provisions pertaining to the restoration of property and emancipation of slaves did
not apply to heathen persons living in Israel. But once these heathen
individuals accepted Israel's faith and joined the spiritual household
of Israel, they were granted the same rights and privileges as the
native Israelites. These considerations serve to emphasize a Biblical

truth of permanent and universal validity, namely, that only a morally cleansed people can be a truly free people, while a morally unregenerated people is capable of corrupting the most just social and economic system.

Sacrifices were practiced in the ancient world long before Israel came into existence. The rationale underlying its introduction into the Mosaic Law is given in the following passage.

> For the life of the flesh is in the blood; and I have appointed it for you upon the altar to make an atonement for your souls; for it is the blood that makes atonement for the soul.
>
> *Leviticus 17:11*

To this writer the above passage means that atonement, i.e. at-one-ment between God and man, cannot take place until man receives a new kind of life, and this new kind of life can only come at the cost of another life.

There is no doubt that the Mosaic sacrificial system had deepened the Israelite sense of sin to a degree unknown among any other people in antiquity. However, since the animal is neither a moral creature, nor a willing substitute for man, the animal sacrifice may have freed the Israelite from his sense of guilt, but it did not weaken the power of sin. Hence King David, when confronted with the heinous character of his sin with Bathsheba, became conscience-stricken, and in the agony of his soul he cried out, not for mere forgiveness, but for a renewal of his human nature, which the animal sacrifice symbolized but could not bestow.

> Wash me thoroughly from my iniquity, and cleanse me from my sin. For I am conscious of my transgressions, and my sin is ever before me . . . Behold, in iniquity was I born, and in sin did my mother conceive me . . . O purge me with hyssop,[7] and I shall be clean; wash me, and I shall be whiter than snow . . . Create in me a clean heart, O God, and renew a right spirit within me.
>
> *Psalm 51: 2-3, 5, 7, 10 (51: 4-5, 7, 9, 12 Heb.)*

The prophet Isaiah, when he saw a vision of God's holy character, exclaims:

---

7. Hyssop was used by the priest in ritual cleansings (see Leviticus 14, Numbers 19).

> Woe is me, for I am lost; for I am a man of unclean lips, and I dwell in the midst of a people of unclean lips; for my eyes have seen the King, Jehovah of hosts.
>
> *Isaiah 6:5*

These words were uttered by the prophet even as he stood in the Temple, with all the visible means provided for the purpose of atoning for sin available to him.

The prophet Micah reflects the same state of mind when he says:

> With what shall I come before Jehovah, and bow myself before God on high? Shall I come before him with burnt offerings, with calves a year old? Will Jehovah be pleased with thousands of rams, or with ten thousands of rivers of oil? Shall I give my first-born for my transgression, the fruit of my body for the sin of my soul? He has showed you, O man, what is good; and what does Jehovah require of you but to do justice, and to love kindness, and to walk humbly with your God?
>
> *Micah 6: 6-8*

One needs only to read the Old Testament, from Exodus to Malachi, to see that Israel did not walk humbly before God. From the beginning to the end Israel had been designated a stiff-necked people, a people in rebellion against God. Here are the words of Moses who spent forty years in the Wilderness with his people.

> Know therefore that Jehovah your God is not giving you this good land to possess it because of your righteousness; for you are a stubborn people. Remember and do not forget how you provoked Jehovah your God to wrath in the wilderness; from the day when you departed from the land of Egypt, until you came to this place, you have been rebellious against Jehovah . . . You have been rebellious against Jehovah from the day that I knew you.
>
> *Deuteronomy 9: 6-7, 24*

The opening words of Isaiah give a similar description of Israel as a rebellious people.

> Hear, O heavens, and give ear, O earth; for Jehovah has spoken: "Sons have I reared and brought up, but they have rebelled against me".
>
> *Isaiah 1: 2*

Because Israel did not walk humbly with God, it did not practice justice and righteousness.

> When you spread forth your hands,[8] I will hide my eyes from you; even though you make many prayers, I will not listen; your hands are full of blood. Wash yourselves; make yourselves clean; remove the evil from your doings from before my eyes; cease to do evil. Learn to do good; seek justice, relieve the oppressed; defend the fatherless, plead for the widow.
>
> *Isaiah 1: 15-17*

And so the cry, "Create in me a clean heart", "Woe is me, for I am lost!", "With what shall I come before God on high and what will enable me to walk humbly with Him" — by a David, Isaiah, Micah, and many others of the most spiritual representatives of ancient Israel, continued right on, until it found the answer in the Suffering Servant.

> Surely ours were the sicknesses that he bore and ours the sorrows that he carried . . . but he was wounded for our sins, bruised for our iniquities, the chastisement that secured our well-being was upon him, and with his wounds we are healed . . . By his knowledge shall the righteous one, my servant, make many to be accounted righteous, and he shall bear their iniquities.
>
> *Isaiah 53: 4-5, 11b.*

II. THE THREE SERVANTS[9]

In the Old Testament any agent appointed by God to perform a service for Him is designated God's servant. In the Bible we encounter three kinds of such agents: the powers of the world, the people of Israel, and the Person of the Messiah. How God's redemptive purpose for the world is being accomplished through these three servants forms the contents of the second half of Isaiah.

---

8. In prayer.
9. I am indebted to the Rev. H.L. Ellison for calling my attention to this fact in his booklet, THE SERVANT OF JEHOVAH, published by the International Hebrew Christian Alliance, London, England.

1. THE POWERS OF THE WORLD

When the nations of Asia Minor including the Judean Kingdom were in need of discipline and correction in the beginning of the sixth century B.C., God used Nebuchadnezzar, the world power of that day, to execute corrective punishment upon these nations.

> Therefore thus says Jehovah of hosts: "Because you have not obeyed my words, Behold, I will send and take all the tribes of the north, says Jehovah. and for Nebuchadnezzar the king of Babylon, my servant, against this land,[10] and against all these nations round about . . .
>
> *Jeremiah 25: 8-9*

The earthly powers are God's servants insofar as they advance God's purpose in the world. But these powers of the world are not aware of the fact that they are carrying out God's will. In the eighth century B.C., God made use of Assyria to discipline Israel, especially the Northern Kingdom which became corrupt religiously and morally:

> O Assyria, the rod of my anger, the staff of my wrath is in their hand. Against a hypocritical nation I will send him, and against the people of my fury I will command him, to take spoil, and to seize plunder, and to tread them down like the mire of the streets.
>
> *Isaiah 10: 5-6*

But when Assyria invaded Israel or the other small nations, she had no knowledge or intention of accomplishing God's purpose.

> But he[11] does not so intend, neither does his mind think so; but it is in his mind to destroy, and to cut off many nations.
>
> *Isaiah 10:7*

Ignorant of, or not caring to know, God's purpose in the world, the arrogant earthly powers attribute their success to their own resources.

> For he says: 'By the strength of my hand I have done it, and by my wisdom, for I have understanding'.
>
> *Isaiah 10:13*

---

10. The Judean Kingdom.
11. The Assyrian king.

But what does God say about this?

> Shall the ax boast itself against him who hews with it, or
> shall the saw magnify itself against him who wields it?
>
> *Isaiah 10:15*

Once a particular earthly power has accomplished God's purpose, it is discarded by Him like a tool for which there is no further use.

> When Jehovah has performed all his work[12] upon Mount
> Zion and on Jerusalem, he will punish the arrogant boasting of
> the king of Assyria and his haughty pride.
>
> *Isaiah 10:12*

Babylon in the sixth century B.C. is treated the same way.

> And all nations shall serve him,[13] and his son, and his son's
> son, until the time of his own land comes; and then many
> nations and great kings shall make him serve.
>
> *Jeremiah 27:7*

As the Babylonian exile drew to a close, God made use of another world power. In fact, Scripture represents the rise of Persia as the work of God for the purpose of terminating the Babylonian captivity.

> Who raised up the man from the east, whom victory meets
> at every step? . . . I, Jehovah, the first, and with the last; I am
> He.
>
> *Isaiah 41: 2a, 4b*

2. THE PEOPLE OF ISRAEL

One of the first references to Israel as God's servant is found in Leviticus.

> For unto me are the people of Israel servants; they are my
> servants whom I brought forth out of the land of Egypt: I am
> Jehovah your God.
>
> *Leviticus 25:55*

---

12. Of correction.
13. The king of Babylon.

In the second half of the book of Isaiah Israel is addressed as God's servant on a number of occasions.

> But you, Israel, my servant, Jacob, whom I have chosen, the offspring of Abraham, my friend.
>
> *Isaiah 41:8*[14]

But Israel has often refused to let God accomplish the purpose for which she was brought into existence. The sacred historian's interpretation of why the ancient State of Israel was destroyed by the Babylonians is found in the following passage.

> Jehovah, the God of their fathers, sent persistently to them by his messengers, because he had compassion on his people and on his dwelling-place.[15] But they continued to mock the messengers of God, and despised his words, and scoffed at his prophets, until the wrath of Jehovah rose against his people, till there was no remedy.
>
> *2 Chronicles 36: 15-16*

The portrayal of Israel as the kind of servant who resisted God's will, a fact which is recorded on many pages of the Old Testament, is reiterated in the second half of Isaiah.

> Hear, you deaf; and look, you blind, that you may see. Who is blind but my servant, or deaf, as my messenger that I sent? Who is blind as my confidant,[16] and blind as the servant of Jehovah? You have seen much, but you do not observe; his ears are open, but he does not hear.
>
> *Isaiah 42: 18-19*

Throughout the Biblical period Israel has been the kind of God's servant who had known God's will but refused to identify herself with it.

3. THE MESSIANIC PERSON

The third agent designated in the Bible the servant of Jehovah is the Messianic Person. In the second half of Isaiah He is introduced

---

14. See, also, Isaiah 43:10; 44:1,21.
15. The Jerusalem Temple.
16. He whom I trusted.

to us in the 42nd chapter, i.e. in the first of its three divisions. This arrangement may seem out of place, because the Messianic Servant of Jehovah forms the subject of the second of the three divisions, beginning with chapter 49. But this was done intentionally, in order to underscore the relation which the Messiah bears to the new historic era which was initiated by the defeat of the Babylonian empire by Cyrus the Great. The introduction of the Messianic Servant of Jehovah was part of the prophetic message to the world of that day. The burden of that message was that, however important the consequences of the victory of Cyrus the Great were, the salvation of the world, of both Jews and Gentiles, is bound up not with a change in the political structure of the world, or with the exploits of a military conqueror, but with Him who is the Servant of Jehovah's choice, Israel's Messiah and the Saviour of the world.

> Behold my servant, whom I uphold, my chosen, in whom my soul delights; I have put my Spirit upon him; he will bring forth justice to the nations. He will not cry nor lift up his voice nor cause it to be heard in the street. A bruised reed he will not break and a glimmering wick he will not put out; he shall bring forth justice according to truth. He will not fail or be discouraged until he has established justice upon the earth; and the islands wait for his law.
>
> Thus says God, Jehovah, who created the heavens, and stretched them out; who spread forth the earth and that which comes out of it; who gives the spirit of life to the people upon it, and the breath of life to them that walk upon it: I, Jehovah, have called you in righteousness, and will hold your hand, and keep you; and I give you as a covenant to the people, a light to the nations. To open blind eyes, to bring out the prisoners from the prison, them that sit in darkness out of the prison-house. I am Jehovah, that is my name, and my glory I give not to another, nor my renown to graven images.
>
> *Isaiah 42: 1-8*

"Behold my servant". The ancient Jewish Targum thus paraphrases these words: "Behold my servant the Messiah". The Messianic Servant of Jehovah is introduced here by way of contrast with the two other servants of Jehovah: that of Cyrus, the world ruler of that day, who was performing a service for Jehovah whom he did not even know;[17] and with Israel, whom the prophet, in the same 42nd chapter, describes as having ears but refusing to hear, eyes — but

---

17. Isaiah 45:4.

failing to see, who, though delivered to the enemy on account of her sin against Jehovah, has remained unrepentant at heart.[18]

"Behold my servant, whom I uphold." "God has been faithful to His covenanted word and has upholden Israel at all times. Though the waters may have gone over his head, they have never overwhelmed him. But Israel, like so many Christians, has only wanted God's upholding hand when he has been too battered and bruised to stand by himself. But the Messianic Servant of Jehovah is one who so welcomes Jehovah's upholding hand that God's soul is delighted in him.

"When we turn to the New Testament we find in the life of Messiah Jesus supremely the story of one who voluntarily abandoned everything that man, even regenerate man, instinctively turns to for help. The manger at Bethlehem was truly typical of all that was to follow. His reputed father was too poor to melt the heart of a churlish innkeeper in the hour of greatest need — for where there is money enough there is always room enough. He was brought up in a province out of which no prophet was thought to have come and in a small town of which it could be said that no good could come out of it. He was given the minimun of schooling, and His supporters were, with few exceptions, poor and despised, so here too we look in vain for any human advantage. We do not find Him using oratory, that most powerful of means for stirring the human heart; there was no effort to meet the scholar on his own ground and to defeat him with his own weapons; His miracles were the fruit of sheer compassion, and in many cases He tried to hide them from the multitude. He made no effort to conciliate either the leaders of the people or the mob. Here then was the One of whom it could be supremely said, "My servant, whom I uphold!"[19]

"He will bring forth justice to the nations". The word "justice" or "judgment" is used to render into English the word "mishpat" in the Hebrew original. Two great scholars of the Old Testament maintain that the word "mishpat" is used here in the sense of religion or faith, "religion as the law of life".[20] The Messianic Ser-

---

18.   Isaiah 42: 18-25.
19.   H. L. Ellison, Op. Cit. pp. 16-17.
20.   Franz Delitzsch, THE PROPHECIES OF ISAIAH (Wm. B. Eerdmans Publishing Company, Grand Rapids, Michigan, 1949), vol. 2, p.175; George Adam Smith, THE BOOK OF ISAIAH (Harper and Brothers: New York, 1927), vol. 2, p. 307. Used by permission of Harper & Row, Publishers, Inc.

vant of Jehovah will carry to the nations the true knowledge of Jehovah.

"A bruised reed he will not break and a glimmering wick he will not put out." A bruised reed and a glimmering wick, or dimly burning wick — this is a description of the moral and spiritual state of Israel and the Gentile world at the end of the Babylonian exile. This was the condition of Israel and of the world at the first advent of Messiah Jesus. This will be the condition of Israel and the world at the time of the return of Messiah Jesus. He comes not to destroy the life that is hanging on a slender thread, but to save it.

In the second part of the introduction God addresses His Messianic Servant directly. "I, Jehovah, have called you in righteousness," i.e., the Messianic Servant comes into the world in accordance with God's faithfulness to His redemptive purpose.

"I give you", i.e., I have appointed you, "as a covenant to the people, a light to the nations." That "covenant to the people" refers to Israel may be seen from a perusal of a similar passage in Isaiah 49 where both phrases "covenant to the people" and "light to the nations" are used separately, and where there is no doubt whatsoever that a "covenant to the people" refers to Israel. We recall that on the eve of the destruction of the Judean Kingdom by the Babylonians Jeremiah predicted the conclusion of a New Covenant. The Sinai Covenant was given through Moses, the New Covenant was to be mediated through the Messiah.

The spiritual character of Messiah's mission is depicted in the following statement: "To open up eyes, to bring out the prisoners from the prison, them that sit in darkness out of the prison-houses. I am Jehovah, that is my name, and my glory I give not to another, nor my renown to graven images." Cyrus through his military victories, and the Greeks through their philosophy, prepared the way for the destruction of idolatry. But neither the Persians nor the Greeks had anything positive to offer which would take the place of idolatry. This will be done by the Messianic Servant of Jehovah. It is He who by His gentle and unselfish love will open spiritually-blind eyes, and illumine the dark heathen world.

III. THE VICARIOUS AND ATONING DEATH
OF THE SUFFERING SERVANT

Lest we assume that the sufferings of the Servant of Jehovah are merely an incidental episode in His Messianic career, this idea is dispelled in the description of the Suffering Servant as recorded in Isaiah 52: 13-15, 53: 1-12.

> Behold, my servant shall prosper, he shall be exalted and be lifted up and shall be very high. Just as many were appalled at him[21] (so disfigured, his appearance was not human and his form unlike that of the sons of men). So shall he sprinkle many nations; kings shall shut their mouths[22] because of him, for they see what has not been told them, and of that which they had not heard shall they discern the meaning.

> Who has believed what we have heard, and over whom has the arm of Jehovah been revealed? For he sprang up before him as a sapling, and like a root-sprout out of dry ground; he had no form nor stateliness that we should look at him, and no beauty that we should desire him. He was despised and forsaken by men; a man of sorrows and acquainted with sickness; and as one from whom men hide their face; he was despised and we esteemed him not.

> Surely ours were the sicknesses that he bore and ours the sorrows that he carried; we, however, regarded him stricken, smitten of God, and afflicted. But he was wounded for our sins, bruised for our iniquities; the chastisement that secured our well-being was upon him, and with his wounds we are healed. All we like sheep have gone astray; we have turned every one to his own way; and Jehovah has caused the iniquity of us all to fall on him.

> He was oppressed and he was afflicted, yet he opened not his mouth, like a lamb that is led to the slaughter and like a sheep that before its shearers is dumb, so he opened not his mouth. He was taken away from prison and judgment; and of his generation, who considered that he was snatched away out of the land of the living, stricken for the transgression of my people? And they assigned him his grave with sinners, and with a rich man in his death, because he had done no wrong and there was no deceit in his mouth.

---

21. This, more correct, reading is adopted by the Targum.
22. "They will become dumbfounded", is another rendering.

Yet it was the will of Jehovah to bruise him, to put him to grief; when he makes himself an offering for sin, he should see posterity, he should prolong his days, and the purpose of Jehovah should prosper through him. He shall see the fruit of the travail of his soul and be satisfied: by his knowledge shall the righteous one, my servant, make many to be accounted righteous, and he shall bear their iniquities. Therefore I will give him a portion among the great, and he shall divide the spoil with the strong;[23] because he has poured out his soul to death, and was numbered with transgressors; yet he bore the sin of many and makes intercession for the transgressors.

Isaiah 52: 13-15; 53:1-12

1. THE UNTENABLENESS OF MODERN JEWISH INTERPRETATIONS

Among many modern Jews, and in certain Gentile circles, the Suffering Servant of Jehovah as depicted in Isaiah 52: 13-15, 53: 1-12 is taken to represent the Jewish people. That such an interpretation lacks any factual basis may be seen from the following considerations.

a. The Suffering Servant of Isaiah is a perfectly innocent Person.

He had done no wrong and there was no deceit in his mouth . . .

Isaiah 53: 9b

The Isaiah prophecy also tells us that God's purpose in the death of the Servant of Jehovah will be accomplished only when He will offer up His life as an offering for sin. The word in the Hebrew text meaning an offering for sin is "asham." According to the Mosaic Law an offering for sin had to be physically perfect, as seen, for example, from the following passage in which the word "asham" is used.

And Jehovah spoke to Moses, saying, "If any one commits a trespass, and sins through ignorance in any of the holy things of

---

23. The sense of this statement is better conveyed by the following rendering: "Therefore I will assign him the many for his portion, and numberless shall be his spoil," given by Christopher R. North, THE SUFFERING SERVANT IN DEUTERO-ISAIAH (Oxford University Press: London, 1956), p. 122. Used by permission.

Jehovah, he shall bring as his trespass offering to Jehovah a ram without blemish out of the flocks . . .

Leviticus 5:14

As the sacrificial animal brought as an offering for sin had to be physically perfect, even so must the Servant of Jehovah be morally perfect, if he were to offer up his life as an offering for sin. If two criminals are condemned to die, one of them could not possibly offer to die in the place of the other. It is because the Servant of Jehovah in Isaiah is morally perfect that His death has the effect of transforming sinners into holy people.

By his knowledge shall the righteous one, my servant, make many to be accounted righteous, and he shall bear their iniquities.

Isaiah 53:11

No other human being is regarded in the Bible as morally spotless, or perfectly righteous.

Jehovah looked down from heaven upon the children of men, to see if there were any that did understand, that seek after God. They are all gone aside; they are all together become filthy, there is none that does good, no, not one.

Psalm 14: 2-3

If thou, O Jehovah, shouldst mark iniquities, Lord, who could stand?

Psalm 130: 3

For there is no man who does not sin.

I Kings 8:46

Surely there is not a righteous many on earth, who does good and never sins.

Ecclesiastes 7:20

As far as Israel is concerned, she is neither sinless nor righteous.

Ah, sinful nation, a people, laden with iniquity, offspring of evildoers, sons that deal corruptly; they have forsaken Jehovah, they have despised the Holy one of Israel, they have turned away backwards.

Isaiah 1:4

Even the godly portion of Israel do not consider themselves righteous.

> We all became like the unclean thing, and all our virutes
> like a garment soiled with blood; and we all faded away together
> like the leaves; and our iniquities, like the storm, they carried us
> away.
>
> *Isaiah 64: 6 (64: 5 Heb.)*

b. The Suffering Servant of Isaiah suffers on account of the sins of
others.

> Surely ours were the sickness that he bore and ours the
> sorrows that he carried . . . He was wounded for our sins,
> bruised for our iniquities . . . Jehovah has caused the iniquity of
> us all to fall on him.
>
> *Isaiah 53: 4, 5, 6*

Israel, however, is everywhere in the Bible represented as suffering
for her own misconduct.

> But if you will not hearken to me, and will not do all these
> commandments. If you shall despise my statutues, and if your
> soul abhors my ordinances, so that you will not do all my
> commandments . . . I will set my face against you, and you shall
> be smitten before your enemies; they that hate you shall reign
> over you; and you shall flee when none pursues you . . . And if
> you will not for all this hearken to me, but walk contrary to
> me . . . I will lay your cities waste, and will make your sanc-
> tuaries desolate . . . And I will devastate the land, so that your
> enemies that settle in it shall be astonished at it. And I will scatter
> you among the nations, and I will draw out a sword after you;
> and your land shall be a desolation, and your cities a waste.
>
> *Leviticus 26: 14-15, 17, 27, 31-33*

The evils predicted by Moses in the Wilderness were all fulfilled in
the history of the Jewish people centuries after the words cited above
were spoken.

As to the generation of Jews who belonged to the Babylonian
exile period, to whom especially the message of the Suffering Servant of Jehovah was addressed, Isaiah has this to say:

> Who delivered Jacob to the spoiler, and Israel to the rob- ·

bers? Was it not Jehovah, against whom we have sinned, in whose ways they would not walk and whose law they would not obey? Therefore he poured upon him[24] the fury of his anger, and the might of battle; it set him on fire round about, yet he did not understand; it burned him, yet he did not take it to heart.

Isaiah 42: 24-25

c. The Suffering Servant of Isaiah is a willing Sufferer

He was oppressed and he was afflicted, yet he opened not his mouth, like a lamb that is led to the slaughter and like a sheep that before its shearers is dumb, so he opened not his mouth.

Isaiah 53:7

Never in Jewish history have the Jewish people been willing sufferers. They have resisted whenever and wherever they could. One aspect of the Nazi holocaust which makes it so grievous and so deeply tragic in Jewish eyes is the fact that Jewish victims perished without being able to resist or defend themselves. Isaiah's Suffering Servant goes to His death knowingly, willingly and offering no resistance.

d. The sufferings of the Suffering Servant of Isaiah culminated in His death.

He has poured out his soul to death.

Isaiah 53:12

Israel has suffered much, but she never died. All this, of course, is due to the faithfulness of God to His promise.

Jehovah has chastened me sorely, but he has not given me over to death.

Psalm 118:18

Many a time have they afflicted me from my youth,[25] may Israel now say. Many a time have they afflicted me from my youth; yet they have not prevailed against me.

Psalm 129:1-2

---

24. Israel.
25. From the beginning of my national existence.

2. MEDIEVAL JEWISH INTERPRETATIONS

Rashi, the Jewish Biblical and Talmudic commentator of the eleventh century, was the first one to suggest that the Suffering Servant of Isaiah 53 represents Israel. It is thought that the sufferings inflicted on the Jews by the crusaders was a determining factor in Rashi's interpretation. Until then the Suffering Servant of Isaiah 53 was almost universally understood by the Jews as referring to the Messiah. A number of other Jewish Biblical expositors of note accepted Rashi's position, as, for example Aben Ezra and Kimchi. Aben Ezra[26] betrays some uncertainty since he states in the beginning of his exposition that this chapter, referring to Isaiah 52: 13-15, 53: 1-12, "is an extremely difficult one. Our Opponents[27] say that it refers to their God." Kimchi is said to have admitted that he wrote controversially, "in answer to the heretics"[28], meaning those who interpret the Suffering Servant of Isaiah 53 as having been fulfilled in the life of Jesus of Nazareth. Rashi himself is not entirely consistent, for while in his Biblical exposition of Isaiah 53 he maintains that the Suffering Servant refers to Israel, he applies it to the Messiah in his Talmudic commentary.[29] He uses a similar double standard in his exposition of the Messianic passage in Zechariah 12:10 ("They shall look upon me whom they have pierced"): in his Biblical commentary he applies this prophecy to Israel, but in his Talmudic exposition he interprets it of the Messiah.[30] In his opening statement on the Messianic Psalm 21 he says: "Our Rabbis have expounded it of King Messiah, but it is better to expound it of David himself in order to answer heretics."

Rabbi Moshe Cohen Iben Crispin (fourteenth century) states that those who for controversial reasons apply the prophecy of the Suffering Servant to Israel find it impossible to understand the true meaning of this prophecy, "having forsaken the knowledge of our teachers, and inclined after the stubborness of their own opinions." Their misinterpretation, he declares, "distorts the passage from its

---

26. Aben Ezra or Iben Ezra (1092-1167).
27. Referring to Christians.
28. David, Baron, RAYS OF MESSIAH'S GLORY (Zondervan Publishing House: Grand Rapids, Michigan, n.d.), p. 227.
29. Sanhedrin fol. 93, col. 1.
30. Succah, fol. 52, col. 1.

natural meaning," for "it was given of God as a description of the Messiah, whereby, when any should claim to be the Messiah, to judge by the resemblance or non-resemblance to it whether he were the Messiah or no."[31]

Rabbi Elijah de Vidas, Cabbalist scholar at Safed, upper Galilee, in the sixteenth century, affirms that "the meaning of 'He was wounded for our transgressions, . . . bruised for our iniquities,' is, that since the Messiah bears our iniquities, which produce the effect of his being bruised, it follows that whoso will not admit that the Messiah thus suffers for our iniquities must endure and suffer for them himself."[32]

Alshech (Rabbi Moshe el Sheikh, second half of the sixteenth century), who was chief Rabbi of Safed, makes this statement in his *Commentaries On The Earlier Prophets:* "Our Rabbis with one voice accept and affirm the opinion that the prophet is speaking of the King Messiah, and we shall ourselves also adhere to the same view."[33]

Isaac Abrabanel (1437-1508), a bitter opponent of Christianity, in his exposition of Isaiah 53, makes the following statement: "The first question is to ascertain to whom this prophecy refers, for the learned among the Nazarenes expound it of the man who was crucified in Jerusalem at the end of the second Temple, and who according to them was the Son of God and took flesh in the virgin's womb, as is stated in their writings. Jonathan ben Uzziel interprets it in the Targum of the future Messiah; and this is also the opinion of our learned men in the majority of their Midrashim."[34]

3. THE SUFFERING SERVANT IN THE TALMUD

Commenting on a passage in the Messianic chapter eleven of Isaiah, Rabbi Alexandri said: "This teaches us that God will burden the Messiah with commandments and sufferings as with millstones."[35]

---

31. David Baron, Op. Cit., p. 228.
32. Ibid, p. 229.
33. Ibid, p. 271.
34. Quoted by David Baron, THE SERVANT OF JEHOVAH (Morgan and Scott, Ltd: London, 1922), p.12.
35. Sanhedrin 93 b.

There is a whole discussion in the Talmud about Messiah's name. The several discussants suggested various names and cited Scriptural references in support of these names. The disciples of the school of Rabbi[36] said "The sick one is his name," for it is written, 'Surely he has borne our sicknesses and carried our sorrows and pains, yet we considered him stricken, smitten, and afflicted of God.'[37]

4. THE SUFFERING SERVANT IN THE MIDRASHIM[38]

a. Midrash Ruth R.

The following Midrashic discussion revolves around the story of Ruth who through her marriage to Boaz became the ancestress of the royal family of David, who in turn became the progenitor of the Messiah. The Scriptural passage which is the subject of this Midrashic exposition reads as follows:

> And at mealtime Boaz said to her, "Come this way, eat from the bread and dip your morsel in the sour wine."
>
> *Ruth 2:14*

Rabbi Yochanan made several suggestions as to the meaning of this passage, one of which reads like this: "Come this way', refers to the King Messiah, 'eat from the bread', means the bread of royalty, and 'dip your morsel in the sour wine', refers to the sufferings of the Messiah, as it is written, 'But he was wounded for our transgressions, bruised for our iniquities' (Isaiah 53:5)."

Having accepted Boaz' invitation, Ruth

> Sat beside the reapers; and he [Boaz] served her roasted grain; and she ate until she was satisfied, and she had some left over.
>
> *Ruth 2:15*

---

36.   Rabbi Yehudah Ha'Nasi, compiler of the Mishnah, third century A.D.
37.   Sanhedrin 98b.
38.   Jewish commentaries on the Old Testament, some of which are of quite ancient origin.

"She sat beside the reapers", "this", Rabbi Yochanan states, "means that for a short while the kingship will be snatched away from the Messiah, as it is written, 'For I will gather all nations to Jerusalem to wage war' . . . (Zechariah 14:2), while the passage, 'and he served her roasted grain', means that the kingship will be restored to Him, as it is written, 'He shall strike the earth with the rod of his mouth' . . . (Isaiah 11:4)'."

Rabbi Berachya, speaking in the name of Rabbi Levi, made the following comment on the above Scriptural passage in the Book of Ruth: "It will be with the last deliverer,[39] as with the first;[40] as the first deliverer revealed himself first to the Israelites and then withdrew (Exodus 5:20), so also will the last deliverer reveal Himself to the Israelites and then withdraw [for a while].[41] "The Messiah of the Midrash Ruth Rabba is a king robbed for a time of his kingship, who, however, will then win ascendancy over his adversaries again."[42]

b. Midrash on Psalm 2

Psalm 2 is a prophetic forecast of a revolt of the nations against the God and the Messiah of Biblical revelation. We shall confine ourselves to the Midrashic exposition of that passage in Psalm 2 which contains a Divine declaration addressed to the Messiah.

> I will tell of the decree: Jehovah said to me, "You are my son, today I have begotten you. Ask of me, and I will make the nations your heritage, and the ends of the earth your possession."
>
> *Psalm 2: 7-8*

Rabbi Huna in the name of Rabbi Acha says: "The sufferings are divided into three parts: one for David and the fathers, one for our own generation, and one for the King Messiah, and this is what is written,'He was wounded for our transgressions,' etc. And when the hour comes, says the Holy One, blessed be He, to them: 'I must

---

39. The Messiah.
40. Moses.
41. Midrash Ruth R. 5:6. This Midrash which was compiled in the ninth century A.D. is said to contain material of a much older date.
42. Kurt Hruby, "The Suffering of the Messiah," art. in JUDAICA (Zwingli Verlag, Zurich, Switzerland, Dec. 1964). Used by permission.

create Him[43] a new creation, as even it is said, 'This day have I begotten you.' "[44]

The revolt of the nations against Israel's God and His Messiah is mentioned in the following passage in Psalm 2.

> The kings of the earth set themselves, and the rulers take counsel together, against Jehovah and his anointed.
>
> *Psalm 2:2*

The following is an interesting Midrashic comment on the above statement. The Gentile nations are likened to a robber who stands defiantly behind the palace of the king and says, "If I shall find the son of the king, I shall lay hold on him, and crucify him, and kill him with a cruel death. But the Holy Spirit mocks at him, 'He that sits in the heavens laughs, Jehovah has them in derision' (Psalm 2:4).[45]

c. The Pesiqta Rabbati

The Pesiqta de-Rab Cahana and the Pesiqta Rabbati are a group of sermonic Midrashim centered around the portion of Scripture read in the Synagogue on the Sabbath and festival days. They originated in the fifth century of our era, but were arranged in their present form toward the middle of the ninth century.[46]

Messiah's willingness to suffer for His people is described in chapter 36 of this Pesiqta. "And the Holy One made an agreement with (the Messiah) and said to Him, 'The sins of those which are forgiven for your sake will cause you to be put under an iron yoke, and they will make you like this calf whose eyes are dim, and they will choke your spirit under the yoke, and on account of their sins your tongue shall cleave to your mouth. Are you willing to do this?' Said Messiah before the Holy One: 'Perhaps this agony will last many years?' And the Holy One said to Him: 'By your life and by the life of

---

43. The Messiah.
44. Midrash Tehillim on Psalm 2, and Midrash Samuel, chapter 19.
45. Yalkut, vol. 2, par. 620, p. 90a, quoted by Alfred Edersheim in THE LIFE AND TIMES OF JESUS THE MESSIAH (Longmans, Green, and Co.: London, 1899), Vol. 2, p. 716.
46. Kurt Hruby, Idem.

my head, one week[47] only have I decreed for you; but if your soul is grieved I shall destroy them even now.' But (the Messiah) said to Him: 'Sovereign of the world, with the gladness of my soul and the joy of my heart I take it upon me, on condition that not one of Israel shall perish, and not only those alone should be saved who are in my days, but also those who are hid in the dust; and not only should the dead of my own time be saved, but all the dead from the first man until now; also the unborn and those whom thou hast intended to create. Thus I agree, and on this condition I will take it upon myself.'

"In the week when the Son of David comes, they will bring beams of iron and put them like a yoke on his neck until His stature is bent down. He cries and weeps, and his voice ascends to heaven, and in God's presence He will say: 'Sovereign of the world, how long will my strength last, how long my breath, my soul, and my limbs? Am I not flesh and blood?' With a view to this hour David groaned aloud, saying, 'My strength is dried up like a potsherd' (Psalm 22: 15 (22:16 Heb.). Then the Holy One — blessed be He! — says to Him: 'Ephraim,[48] my righteous Messiah, you took all this upon yourself from the six days of creation;[49] now your suffering shall be like my suffering; for from the time that Nebuchadnezzar,[50] the wicked one destroyed my house, burned my sanctuary, and scattered my children among the peoples of the world, I have not sat down on my throne.'[51]

"The Patriarchs will one day rise again in the month of Nisan and will say to the Messiah: 'Ephraim, our righteous Messiah, although we are your ancestors, you are nevertheless greater than we, for you have borne the sins of our children, as it is written: 'Surely he has borne our diseases and carried our sorrows; yet we regarded him stricken, smitten of God, and afflicted. But he was wounded for our sins, bruised for our iniquities, upon him was the chastisement-that makes us well, and through his wounds we are healed' (Isaiah 53: 4-5). Heavy oppressions have been imposed upon you, as it is written: 'As a result of oppression and judgment he was taken away;

---

47. The word translated "week" may also mean seven years instead of seven days.
48. The Messiah in these chapters is called Ephraim.
49. One of the many references reflecting the belief in the pre-existence of the Messiah.
50. The mention of Nebuchadnezzar who destroyed the Solomonic Temple may be a disguised reference to Rome which destroyed the Second Temple.
51. Pesiqta Rabbati, chap. 36, of Friedmann's edition.

but in his day, who considered that he was torn from the land of the living because of the transgressions of my people?' (Isaiah 53:8). You have been a laughing-stock and a derision among the peoples of the world, and because of you they jeered at Israel, as it is written (Psalm 22:6). You have dwelt in darkness and in gloominess, and your eyes have not seen light, your skin was cleaving to your bones, and your body withered like wood. Your eyes became hollow from fasting, and your strength was dried up like a potsherd, as it is written (Psalm 22:15; 22:16 Heb.).[52] All this happened because of the sins of our children, as it is written: 'And Jehovah laid on him the iniquity of us all' (Isaiah 53:6).[53]

We will conclude the discussion of the sufferings of the Messiah as presented in the Pesiqta Rabbati with the following remarks by Hruby: "If we now attempt an analysis of the ideas in the quoted texts, we see that one of the main tasks of Messiah's work of deliverance, perfected by the sufferings He took upon Himself, consists in hurling into the infernal regions 'Satan and the princes of the peoples of the world,'[54] that is the demons, under whose malign influence they stand. The Messiah appears loaded with chains; he suffers thirst in a dark dungeon, which surely constitutes a reference to Psalm 22.

"An important element is the fact that the Messiah voluntarily takes his sufferings on himself, on the condition that all of Israel who died since Adam should be saved! The Messiah whom the Pesiqta Rabbati brings before our eyes exists 'since the six days of creation', and already at that time he had assumed His future sufferings. The Patriarchs render honor to the Messiah and acknowledge that he is 'greater than they because he bears the sins of their children.' This passage contains a clear reference to Isaiah 53. The Patriarchs remind the Messiah of all the sufferings that he was obliged to endure on behalf of Israel when he was in prison. The peoples of the world, too, are against him (compare Psalm 22), and when he emerges from prison, they want to destroy him. But God rescues him from their hands . . .

"The sufferings of the Messiah are genuine physical and moral

---

52.   As may be seen from the above, Psalm 22 is treated as a Messianic psalm.
53.   Chapter 37 of the Pesiqta Rabbati, Friedmann's edition.
54.   This passage of the Pesiqta Rabbati, chapter 36, is not included in our discussion.

sufferings even if they do not lead to his death. He takes them on himself voluntarily and thus becomes Israel's deliverer. Deliverance will also redound to the dead since, in virtue of the atoning sufferings of the Messiah, they will rise to eternal life. Spiritual deliverance is assumed, since it is taught in the text that the impulse to do evil will be rendered harmless in the Messianic period. There also ensues a general forgiveness of sins, death will cease, and the Israelites will be released from the infernal regions . . .

"The twenty-second Psalm of suffering, where we have the well-known passage, 'They pierced my hands and feet'[55] is applied in its entirety to the suffering Messiah.

"Naturally, the comparison with the Gospels forces itself upon us, where Jesus applies the twenty-second Psalm to His own Person, and on the cross He quotes the first verse of this Psalm. 'My God, my God, why hast thou forsaken me?' Like the Messiah of the Pesiqta, Jesus, too, is cast into prison. He too asks the Father, if possible, to keep this suffering away from Him.[56] while at the same time submitting Himself willingly, totally and unhesitantly to the death of the cross."[57]

5. THE SUFFERING SERVANT IN THE ZOHAR

The Zohar is a commentary on the Pentateuch written partly in Hebrew and partly in Aramaic. It appeared for the first time in Spain in the thirteenth century. Its authorship was ascribed to the famous Talmudist of the second century, Simeon ben Yohai. But its real authorship and date are uncertain. It became the holy book of the Jewish mystics. In its commentary on Exodus we find the following passage. "The souls which are in the Garden of Eden below go to and fro every new moon in order to ascend to the place called the Walls of Jerusalem . . . Then they journey on and consider all those that are martyrs for the unity of their Lord, and then return and announce it to the Messiah. As they tell Him of the misery of Israel in their captivity, and of those wicked ones among them who are not mindful of knowing their Lord, He lifts up His voice and weeps on account of their wickedness, — as it is written, 'He was wounded for

---

55. Psalm 22: 16 (22: 17 Heb.).
56. This has reference to His prayer in the Garden of Gethsemane just before His arrest.
57. Kurt Hruby, Idem.

our transgressions, etc.' Then those souls return and abide in their own place.

"There is in the Garden of Eden a palace named the Palace of the Sons of Sickness. This palace the Messiah enters, and He summons every pain and every chastisement of Israel. All of these come and rest upon Him. And had He not thus lightened them off Israel and taken them upon Himself, there had been no man able to bear Israel's chastisements for the transgressions of the law; as it is written, 'Surely our sicknesses he has carried.' "[58]

6. THE SUFFERING SERVANT IN THE PRAYER BOOK

The many references to the Suffering Servant of Isaiah 53 interpreted of the Person of the Messiah, some of which we cited thus far from the Talmud, the Midrashim and the Zohar, are too numerous to constitute isolated statements. They are often attributed to authors who hold an eminent place in Jewish religious history. But even if one should for a moment concede that these pronouncements are not necessarily representative of the teachings of Judaism, the following two passages contained in the Prayer-Book bear the stamp of approval of the Synagogue which for many centuries was representative of all Israel and religious Judaism. The first of these is recited among the prayers on the Feast of the Passover.

> Flee my beloved, until the end of the vision shall speak; hasten and the shadows shall take their flight hence: high and exalted and lofty shall be the despised one: he shall be prudent in judgment and shall sprinkle many! Cry out, and say: "The voice of my beloved; behold he comes."

Two sentences in this prayer contain portions from the Suffering Servant taken from Isaiah 52 and 53. David Levi, the English translator of the liturgy for the festival services, declares that this prayer refers to "the true Messiah."

In the Service for the Day of Atonement there is a hymn composed by the Jewish hymn-writer Eleazar ben Qualir. According to the Jewish historian Zunz he lived in the ninth century of our era. This remarkable hymn or prayer reads as follows.

---

58. The Zohar, vol. II, 212a.

Before the world was created,
His dwelling place[59] and Yinnon[60] God prepared.
The Mount of His house, lofty from the beginning,
He established, ere people and language existed.
It was His pleasure that there His Shekhina[61] should dwell,
To guide those gone astray into the path of rectitude.
Though their sins were red like scarlet,
They were preceded by "Wash you, make you clean,"[62]
If His anger was kindled against His people,
Yet the Holy One poured not out all His wrath.
We are ever threatened by destruction because of our evil deeds,
And God does not draw nigh us — He, our only refuge.
Our righteous Messiah has departed from us,
We are horror-stricken, and have none to justify us.
Our iniquities and the yoke of our transgressions
He carries, and He is wounded because of our transgressions.
He bears on His shoulder the burden of our sins,
To find pardon for all our iniquities.
By his stripes we shall be healed —
O, Eternal One, it is time that thou shouldst create Him anew!
O, bring Him up from the land of Seir[63]
To announce salvation to us from Mount Lebanon,[64]
Once again through the hand of Yinnon.

IV. THE MISSION OF THE SUFFERING SERVANT

1. HUMILIATION AND APPARENT FAILURE

But I said, "I have toiled in vain, I have spent my strength for nothing and to no purpose . . . Thus says Jehovah, the Redeemer of Israel, his holy one, to one deeply despised to an abhorred of the people, to the servant of tyrants . . .

Isaiah 49:4, 7a

---

59. Probably referring to the Jerusalem Sanctuary, or rather the Mount on which the Temple was later erected.
60. Yinnon - one of the names of the Messiah.
61. Shekhina - Divine presence.
62. The last sentence is from Isaiah 1:16.
63. Rome - where, as legend has it, the Messiah lives in humiliation and suffering.
64. Lebanon stands here for the mount of the Temple from where the Messiah is supposed to proclaim to Israel the hour of redemption.

a. "An abhorred of the people"

The Hebrew word "goi" means here people in general, the mass of men. In the first phase of His mission the Servant of Jehovah will be "deeply despised," "aborred by the mass of men." "If instead of a prophecy uttered centuries before the advent of Jesus Nazareth, it had been a history, written subsequent to the events, no more terse or graphic account could have been given of the attitude and feeling of men generally, and of the nation of Israel in particular, to our Lord Jesus Christ. No person in the history of the Jews has provoked such deep-seated abhorrence as He who came only to bless them, and who even on the cross prayed, 'Father forgive them, for they know not what they do.' When on earth, at the end of three and a half years of a blessed ministry among them, they finally rejected Him, their hatred was intense and mysterious. 'Away with this man; release unto us Barabas . . . crucify him, crucify him!' was their cry.

"All through the centuries no name has called forth such intense abhorrence among the Jewish people as the name of Jesus . . . In the filthy legends about Him in the Talmud, and later productions, the very names by which He is called are blasphemies. The precious name Yeshua ('Jesus' — Savior) — has been changed into "Yeshu" made up of initial letters, which mean 'Let His name and His memory be blotted out.' This Holy One who knew no sin, nor was guile found in His mouth, was often styled 'The Transgressor': There are other filthy designations, such as 'Ben Stada', or 'Ben Pandera' which imply blasphemies not only against Him, but against her who is 'blessed among women.'

"Israel's blind hatred to the Messiah did not stop short of His Person or His virgin mother, but extended also to those of their nation who took upon themselves His reproach and followed Him . . . Not satisfied with classifying them as 'apostates' and 'worse than heathen,' the Rabbis at the end of the first century of our era instituted a daily public prayer in the most solemn part of their liturgy that 'the Nazarenes' may, together with all apostates, 'be suddenly destroyed,' and 'be blotted out of the book of life' . . .

"Let it be remembered also that Jewish hatred to Christ and His followers is partly to be traced to the sufferings which they have endured at the hands of so-called Christians, and also that it is not our Lord Jesus as we know Him that Israel in ignorance did so blaspheme, but the carricature of Him as presented to them by the apostate Christendom in the Dark Ages."[65] It nevertheless is true that Jewish hatred of Jesus Christ dates back to the first century when His Messianic movement was predominantly Jewish. The apostle John was so impressed with this hostility that he saw in it a fulfillment of a certain statement in the Psalms, "They hated me without a cause."[66]

Thanks be to God that in recent years the Jewish attitude to Jesus had undergone a profound change. The fact, however, remains, that for many centuries no person had been despised by the Jewish people so persistently and so intensely as Jesus of Nazareth.

b. "A servant of tyrants"

The Servant of Jehovah who was to be initially despised by the mass of men was to be a servant of tyrants. Soon after His birth the parents of the newly-born Jesus took Him to Egypt to escape the murderous designs by the tyrant Herod the Great. At the other end of His earthly life we hear Pilate, the representative of the tyrannical heathen world power of Rome, say to Him: "I have power to crucify you, and I have power to release you."[67] Tyrannical Roman rulers waded deep in the blood of the early followers of Messiah Jesus. Persecution of genuine Christians has never ceased. The real issue at the present juncture of world history is not between communism and capitalism, but between secular humanism of which communism is the logical end-product, and Jesus Christ. Many thousands of genuine Christians have suffered severely in countries under communist rule, and the New Testament anticipates a resurgence of bitter anti-Christian hostility in the days preceding the return of Messiah Jesus.

The first phase of Messiah's mission was to be marked by deep humiliation and seeming failure. He was to be abhorred by the mass of men, so much so that He was led to say:

---

65. David Baron, TYPES, PSALMS AND PROPHECIES (Morgan & Scott, Ltd.: London, 1924), pp. 331-333. Used by permission of Marshall, Morgan and Scott, Ltd.
66. John 15:25.
67. The Gospel of John 19:10.

> I have toiled in vain, I have spent my strength for nothing and to no purpose.
>
> *Isaiah 49:4*

Did He therefore give up, or decide to change the method or direction of His ministry? By no means! Here are His words:

> I was not rebellious, neither turned back. I offered my back to the smiters, and my cheeks to them that pluck off the hair; I hid not my face from shame and spitting. But the Lord Jehovah will help me; therefore have I not suffered myself to be overcome by mockery; therefore did I make my face like the flint, and knew that I should not be put to shame.
>
> *Isaiah 50: 5-7*

His confidence had its source in the Divine assurance that ultimately His mission will be crowned with success.

> Thus says Jehovah, the Redeemer of Israel and his Holy One . . .: "Kings shall see and arise; princes, and they shall prostrate themselves; because of Jehovah, who is faithful, the Holy One of Israel, who has chosen you."
>
> *Isaiah 49:7*

2. HIS MISSION TO ISRAEL

The mission of the Servant of Jehovah is of a two-fold character: It is a mission to Israel, and a mission to the nations of the world. The mission to Israel has a spiritual and national aspect.

a. The spiritual aspect of Messiah's mission to Israel

> Thus says Jehovah: "In a time of favor have I heard you, and in a day of salvation have I helped you; I have preserved you, and I have appointed you for a covenant of the people, to raise up the land, to apportion the desolate inheritances. That you may say to the prisoners, 'Come forth,' to those who are in darkness, 'Show yourselves.' "
>
> *Isaiah 49: 8-9a*

The first phase of Messiah's work was to be a time of trouble for Him and His cause. The second phase of His mission is to be a time of favor, a time of grace and goodwill, a time of success and victory. It is for this great day of salvation that He was preserved. The spiritual aspect of His mission to Israel is described in the words, "I have appointed you for a covenant of the people." The Sinai Covenant which was made in the Wilderness established a covenant relationship between Jehovah and ancient Israel. On the eve of the destruction of ancient Israel Jeremiah declared that the Sinai Covenant was broken, and that Jehovah will some day make a New Covenant with His people. This New Covenant, Jeremiah asserts, will not be a renewal of the Sinai Covenant. Unlike the Sinai Covenant, this New Covenant will be written, not on stone or parchment, but on human hearts. The outstanding effect of this New Covenant will be that every one belonging to it will experientially know God, for this New Covenant will remove man's alienation from God through the forgiveness of sin.[68]

In the book of the New Covenant the birth of Jesus was announced as the coming of a Savior.[69] He was to be given the name of Yeshua, a word which in the Hebrew means "he will save." The reason He was to have this name, we are told, is because "he will save his people from their sins."[70] On the night when He celebrated the last Passover with His disciples, only a few hours before He was arrested and then crucified, He took a cup of the Passover wine, distributed it among the disciples sitting at the Passover table, and said:

> Drink all of you out of it. For this is my blood of the covenant, that which is poured out for many for forgiveness of sins.
>
> *Matthew 26:27-28*

b. The physical aspect of Messiah's mission to Israel

> Thus says Jehovah: "In a time of favor have I heard you, in a day of salvation have I helped you: I have preserved you and I have appointed you for a covenant of the people, to raise up the land, to apportion the desolate inheritances. That you may say to the prisoners, 'Come forth,' to those who are in darkness, 'Show yourselves.' They shall feed by the ways, and in all high places shall be their pasture. They shall not hunger nor thirst, neither shall the heat nor sun smite them; for he who has mercy

---

68. Jeremiah 31:31-34 (31:30-33 Heb.).
69. Luke 2:11.
70. Matthew 1:21.

on them shall lead them, and by the springs of water shall he guide them. And I will make all my mountains a way, and my highways shall be exalted. Behold, these shall come from afar, and, lo, these from the north and from the west, and these from the land of the Sinese.[71] Sing, O heavens; and be joyful, O earth; and break forth into singing, O mountains! For Jehovah has comforted his people, and will have compassion upon his afflicted . . .

Thus says the Lord Jehovah, "Behold, I will lift up my hand to the nations, and raise my signal to the peoples: and they shall bring your sons in their bosom, and your daughters shall be carried on their shoulders. And kings shall be your foster-fathers, and their queens your nursing mothers; with their faces to the ground they shall bow down to you, and lick the dust of your feet and you shall know that I am Jehovah: for they who wait for me shall not be ashamed."

Can the prey be taken from the mighty, or will the captive host of the righteous escape? Surely, thus says Jehovah: "Even the captives of the mighty shall be taken, and the prey of the tyrant be rescued; for I will contend with those who contend with you, and I will save your children. And I will make your oppressors eat their own flesh, and they shall be drunk with their own blood as with wine; then all flesh shall know that I Jehovah am your Savior, and your Redeemer is the Mighty One of Jacob.

Isaiah 49:8-13, 22-26

The national restoration of Israel depicted above was not fulfilled with the return of the exiles from Babylon. The small group of Jews who went back to the Land of Israel at the end of their Babylonian exile was much in need of this message. They were only permitted to rebuild their religious center in Judea. Even so, they encountered fierce opposition on the part of those aliens who gained a foothold in the country in what used to be the territory of the northern kingdom of Israel. For a long while even the construction of the Second Temple had to be stopped. When the foundation of this Second Temple was laid, many of those who remembered the Solomonic Temple wept[72] when they contrasted it with the shabby appearance of the Second Temple. The mood of the returnees was best reflected in the following words recorded in the book of Nehemiah which the Septuagint Bible ascribes to Ezra.

---

71. China.
72. Ezra 3:12.

> Behold, we are servants this day; in the land that thou
> gavest to our fathers to eat its fruit and its good gifts, behold, we
> are servants.
>
> *Nehemiah 9:36*

These words describe the position of Palestine not only immediately following the return of the Babylonian exiles, but through almost the entire five centuries of the existence of the Second Jewish Commonwealth. Through this period, with the exception of a brief interval under the Maccabees, Palestine remained in a subservient position, being a province of one or another of the great powers of that day, until it was destroyed by the Roman empire. The ingathering of Jews from a worldwide dispersion depicted in Isaiah 49 never took place after the Babylonian exile. In fact, the present State of Israel represents a far more real fulfillment of certain features of the restoration promise of Isaiah 49.

But even the present State of Israel is a far cry from the picture of a restored nation as portrayed in Isaiah 49. This final and glorious restoration will only take place with the return of Messiah Jesus whom God has preserved and "appointed for a covenant of the people, to raise up the land, to apportion the desolate inheritances, to say to the prisoners, 'Come forth,' to those who are in darkness, 'Show yourselves.'"

3. HIS MISSION TO THE WORLD

> He[73] said, "It is too small a thing that you should become
> my servant to raise up the tribes of Jacob and to restore the
> preserved of Israel; I have appointed you for a light of the
> nations, to become my salvation to the end of the earth.
>
> *Isaiah 49:6*

The second half of the book of Isaiah (Chapters 40-66) manifests a great interest in the salvation of the Gentile nations. A strong cosmopolitan note is struck at the very beginning of the second half of Isaiah.

> And the glory of Jehovah shall be revealed, and all flesh
> shall see it together.
>
> *Isaiah 40:5*

---

73. Jehovah.

The following are additional examples of the prophetic concern in the salvation of the Gentile world.

> Turn to me and be saved, all the ends of the earth! For I am God, and none else. By myself have I sworn, the word is gone out of my mouth in righteousness, and will not return, that to me every knee shall bow, every tongue shall swear.
>
> *Isaiah 45:22-23*

The word "righteousness" in the prophetic writings has assumed, in the course of time, the connotation of salvation. The last part of the above passage means that God's redemptive purpose will surely be accomplished, in consequence of which all nations shall worship Jehovah.

> Jehovah has made bare his holy arm before the eyes of all nations, and all the ends of the earth shall see the salvation of our God.
>
> *Isaiah 52:10*

This prophetic concern in the salvation of the Gentile world will be better understood if we acquaint ourselves with the history of the period to which these utterances were addressed. The defeat of the Babylonian empire in 538 B.C. by Cyrus the Great and the conquest of Pharaonic Egypt in 525 B.C. by Cambyses, the son and successor of Cyrus the Great, marked the beginning of the ascendancy of Aryan civilization. While Hamitic Egyptian and Semitic Mesopotamian civilizations were nearing their end, Indo-European peoples moved up to the forefront of history in the sixth century B.C. It was a century of great intellectual as well as political movements, an age of change and challenge. Armies were on the move, men's minds were astir everywhere. "Everywhere they were waking up out of the traditions of kingships and priests and blood sacrifices and asking the most penetrating questions."[74] "It has long been realized that the sixth century B.C. was an epoch in which a variety of important events took place, not only within the limited field of Old Testament history, nor even within the confines of Near Eastern civilization, but throughout the world. It is the century of Confucius, of Zoroaster, of Buddha. It is also the century of the Ionian (Greek) philosophers."[75]

---

74. H. G. Wells, A SHORT HISTORY OF THE WORLD (A.P. Watt & Son: London, 1938), p.100. By permission of Professor G. P. Wells, F.R.S.
75. Peter R. Ackroyd, EXILE AND RESTORATION (The Westminster Press: Philadelphia, 1968), p.7 Copyright by SCM Press, Ltd., 1968. Used by permission.

Discussing the situation among the Jewish people, one observer states that "the sixth century B.C. was a century of hope renewed. Rebirth followed on ruin, new life on decay. The disaster of the opening years[76] was the opportunity for a new outburst of faith in the future . . .What took place two thousand five hundred years ago among the Jews in Babylon and in Palestine marks out the sixth century B.C. as a certain epoch of the first order in the history of Israel. The century may claim also Zoroaster, Confucius, and the Buddha . . . It was a creative epoch in the history of the world."[77]

Isaiah 40-66 takes cognizance of the new world which was shaping up in the sixth century B.C., a world to be dominated by Aryan peoples until the end of history as we know it, i.e. the end of the age, or the end of the times of the nations. The awareness of this fact may be seen from the following allusions to this new Aryan world.

> Keep silence before me, O islands; let the peoples renew their strength.
>
> *Isaiah 41:1a*

According to Genesis the Aryan peoples descended from Japheth, and the European continent which became the home of the bulk of the Japhetic or Aryan peoples is designated in the Old Testament by the word isles, islands, or coastlands.[78] Commenting on the above passage in Isaiah, the great scholar of Semitics Franz Delitzsch says: "This was the expression commonly employed in the Old Testament to designate the continent of Europe, the solid ground of which is so deeply cut, and so broken up by seas and lakes, that it looks as if it were about to resolve itself into nothing but islands and peninsulas."[79]

When the Suffering Servant of Jehovah is introduced for the first time we have the following references to the Aryan peoples.

---

76. i.e., the destruction of the Judean Kingdom by Nebuchadnezzar in the beginning of the sixth century B.C.
77. D. Winton Thomas, "The Sixth Century B.C.: A Creative Epoch in the History of Israel", art. in JOURNAL OF SEMITIC STUDIES (Manchester University Press: Manchester, England), Vol. VI, No. 1, Spring 1961, p. 46. Used by permission.
78. Genesis 10:5.
79. Franz Delitzsch, THE PROPHECIES OF ISAIAH (Wm. B. Zerdmans Publishing Co.: Grand Rapids, Michigan, 1949), Vol. 1, p. 157.

> He will not become faint or broken till he has established
> justice in the earth; and the islands wait for his instruction.
>
> *Isaiah 42:4*

"The islands wait for his instruction," conveys the idea that there existed among the Aryan peoples a consciousness of need which will make them responsive to the message of the Suffering Servant. There are a number of other passages in the second half of Isaiah addressed to this new Aryan period of world history.[80]

The Old Testament had a message for this emerging new world of the sixth century B.C., the century which saw the rise of Confucius, Zoroaster, Buddha, and the Greek philosophers of Asia Minor. It was a many-faceted message, and its common distinguishing feature was expressed by the word "new." Reference was already made to the New Covenant, the new fellowship between God and man envisaged by Jeremiah. According to Ezekiel a new Israel was to come into existence, a people with a "new heart" and a "new spirit."

> For I will take you from among the nations, and gather you out of all the countries, and will bring you into your own land. Then will I sprinkle clean water upon you, and you shall be clean; from all your filthiness, and from all your idols will I cleanse you. A new heart also will I give you, and a new spirit I will put within you; and I will take out of your flesh the heart of stone and give you a heart of flesh.
>
> *Ezekiel 36:24-26*

In Ezekiel 37 the Israel which receives from God this "new heart" and "new spirit" is a new Israel.

> "Thus says the Lord God: Behold, I will open your graves, and raise you from your graves, O my people; and I will bring you home into the land of Israel. And you shall know that I am Jehovah, when I open your graves and raise you from your graves, O my people. And I will put my spirit within you, and you shall live, and I will place you in your own land; then you shall know that I, Jehovah, have spoken, and I have performed it, says Jehovah."
>
> *Ezekiel 37:12-14*

According to Isaiah the prophecy concerning the mission of the Suffering Servant of Jehovah — for whose instruction there will be a

---

80.   Isaiah 42:10; 49:1; 51:5; 59:18; 66:19.

receptive longing in theAryan world, who is the restorer of Israel and the Savior of the nations — is a new message. Immediately after the Divine introduction of the Messianic Servant of Jehovah the prophet bursts out in the following hymn of joy.

> Sing to Jehovah a new song, His praise from the end of the earth, you navigators of the sea, and its fullness; you islands, and their inhabitants.
>
> *Isaiah 42:10*

Great as the deliverance from Egyptian bondage was, the final restoration of Israel will eclipse the Exodus from Egypt; it will amount to something entirely new.

> Remember not the former things, nor meditate upon those of earlier times. Behold, I work out a new thing; it springs forth now; shall you not know it? I will make a way in the wilderness and rivers in the desert. The beasts of the field will praise me, wild dogs and ostriches; for I give water in the wilderness, streams in the desert, to give drink to my chosen people. The people that I formed for myself, that they may declare my praise.
>
> *Isaiah 43:18-21*

The effect which the new deliverance of Israel will have on the Gentile nations is described in the following words.

> This one will say, I belong to Jehovah; a second will solemnly name the name of Jacob; and a third will inscribe himself to Jehovah, and name the name of Israel with honor.
>
> *Isaiah 44:5*

The restoration of Israel and the conversion of the Gentile nations which will be accomplished by the Servant of Jehovah will usher in a new age, a new era in the history of the world. Even nature will be affected by mankind's spiritual regeneration.

> For behold I create a new heaven and a new earth; and men will not remember the first, nor do they come to one's mind . . . The wolf and the lamb shall feed together, the lion shall eat straw like the ox, and dust shall be the serpent's food.
>
> *Isaiah 65:17-25*

V. IS THE ATONING ASPECT OF ISAIAH'S SUFFERING SERVANT AN ISOLATED CONCEPT?

We saw how in the 42nd Chapter of Isaiah God, speaking through the prophet, introduced the Messianic Servant — "Behold my servant, whom I uphold" — and outlined his Messianic program. In the central division of Isaiah 40-66 we have a body of teachings to the effect that the spiritual part of the Messianic program described in Chapter 42 will be accomplished by the Messiah by way of personal suffering. These prophetic teachings begin in Chapter 49 and reach their climactic point in Chapter 53. We now wish to pose the question whether Isaiah's concept of a Suffering and atoning Messiah is a stray notion in the Old Testament.

1. THE SACRIFICE OF ISAAC. [81]

There are a number of authoritative utterances and certain religious practices in traditional Judaism which are related to the story of the sacrifice of Isaac. They furnish clear evidence of the vicarious and atoning efficacy which traditional Judaism ascribed to this event in the patriarchal history. The Talmud explains the use of a ram's horn in the ritual of New Year's Day as a reminder of the ram which Abraham offered in place of Isaac.[82] The story of the offering up of Isaac forms the portion of Scripture read in the synagogue during the services of the second day of the New Year's festival. Among the Jewish people the New Year's festival initiates the ten day's season of repentance, referred to as "Fearful Days," and culminating in the festival of the Day of Atonement. The following excerpts reflect the teaching of traditional Judaism pertaining to the meaning of the sacrifice of Isaac. It should be noted that instead of "sacrifice" the word "binding" is often used.

Palestinian Targum: "And Abraham prayed in the name of the Word of the Lord, and said, Thou art the Lord who seest, and art not seen. I pray for mercy before Thee, O Lord. It is wholly manifest and known before Thee that in my heart there was no dividing, in

---

81.   Genesis 22:1-18.
82.   Rosh Hashana 16a.

the time that Thou didst command me to offer Isaac my son, and to make him dust and ashes before Thee; but that forthwith I arose in the morning and performed Thy word with joy, and I have fulfilled Thy word. And now I pray for mercies before Thee, O Lord God, that when the children of Isaac offer in the hour of need, thou mayest remember on their behalf the binding of Isaac their father, and remit and forgive their sins and deliver them out of all need."

Commenting on the Biblical statement, "And Abraham called the name of that place "Jehovah will provide", one of the Midrashic expositors declares that Abraham prayed that for the sake of the sacrifice of Isaac God may be filled with compassion towards Isaac's descendants whenever they should fall into sin.[83]

In another Midrashic discussion of the concluding portion of the story of the sacrifice of Isaac, Abraham is said to have besought God to look upon the sacrifice of Isaac as if Isaac's ashes actually lay heaped upon the altar, and that on this account God may grant forgiveness and deliverance to Isaac's descendants whenever they should sin and become afflicted. In His reply God promised to do in accordance with Abraham's plea, provided that the Israelites will on New Year's Day festivals blow the horn. To Abraham's question as to what horn God was referring, God directed his attention to the ram which was caught by its horn in the nearby thicket.[84]

In his exposition of the second part of the above Biblical sentence, "as it is said to this day, 'On the mount of Jehovah it shall be provided' ", Rashi, one of the medieval Jewish commentators, cites one interpretation of this passage to the effect that God will approve of the sacrifice of Isaac as being of the essence of an atonement, bringing to Israel remission from sin and deliverance from its penalty.

If we were to take the position that the above pronouncements merely express the opinions of certain inviduals, the portions from the Prayer Book quoted below bear the unmistakable stamp of authority of the Synagogue, representing traditional Judaism as a whole.

"Sovereign of all worlds! Not because of our righteous acts do

---

83. Genesis R. 56:15.
84. Tanchuma 30:23.

we lay our supplications before Thee, but because of Thine abundant mercies. What are we? What is our life? What is our piety? What our righteousness? . . . Nevertheless, we are Thy people, the children of Thy covenant, the children of Abraham, Thy friend, to whom Thou didst swear on Mount Moriah; the seed of Isaac, his only son, who was bound upon the altar . . . "[85]

"We beseech Thee, O gracious and merciful King, remember and give heed to the Covenant between the Pieces,[86] and let the binding (upon the altar) of his only son appear before Thee, to the welfare of Israel."[87]

"Our God and the God of our fathers, let us be remembered by Thee for good: grant us a visitation of salvation and mercy from Thy heavens, the heavens of old; and remember unto us, O Lord our God, the covenant and lovingkindness and the oath which Thou swearest unto Abraham our father on Mount Moriah: and may the binding with which Abraham our father bound his son Isaac on the altar appear before Thee, how he overbore his compassion in order to perform Thy will with a perfect heart. So may Thy compassion overbear Thine anger against us; in Thy great goodness may the fierceness of Thy wrath turn aside from Thy people, Thy city, and Thine inheritance . . . O remember the binding of Isaac this day in mercy unto his seed."[88]

"Remember the binding of him and be gracious unto his posterity."[89]

2. MOSES

While Moses was on Mount Sinai, where he received from God the laws by which Israel's religious and corporate life was to be governed, the Israelites lapsed into the idolatrous sin of the Golden Calf incident. God's reaction communicated to Moses was to destroy the people of Israel, whom He had delivered from Egyptian bon-

---

85. From the morning prayer as found in the Authorized Daily Prayer Book; English translation by Rev. S. Singer.
86. Referring to the conclusion of the Abrahamic covenant as recorded in Genesis 15:9-21.
87. Prayer recited on Mondays and Thursdays.
88. From the afternoon prayer for New Year's Day.
89. From the evening prayer for the Day of Atonement.

dage only several weeks before, and begin a new nation with Moses. Startled equally by the blasphemous character of his people's sin and by the severity of the Divine judgment, Moses begged to be allowed to perish in Israel's stead.

> On the morrow[90], Moses said to the people, "You have sinned a great sin; and now I will go up to Jehovah[91]; perhaps I can make an atonement for your sin". And Moses returned to Jehovah and said, "Oh, this people have sinned a great sin, and have made for themselves gods of gold. But now, if thou wilt forgive their sin —; and if not, blot me, I pray thee, out of the book which thou hast written."
>
> *Exodus 32: 30-32*

Moses wished to die a vicarious death, the innocent dying in place of the guilty. Alluding to the Wilderness episode the Psalmist has this to say:

> They forgot God their Savior, who had done great things in Egypt. Wondrous works in the land of Ham, and terrible things by the Red Sea. Therefore he said that he would destroy them, had not Moses his chosen one stood in the breach before him, to turn away his wrath from destroying them . . . They angered him also at the waters of Meribah, and it went ill with Moses for their sake.
>
> *Psalm 106: 21-23,32*

Another relapse into idolatry occurred in the region of Beth-Peor in the land of Moab. The Israelites permitted the women of Moab, probably of the neighboring city of Beth-Peor, to entice them to a sacrificial festival in honor of their licentious idol Baal-Peor. God's judgment upon them was swift and severe: twenty-four thousand Israelites lost their lives in consequence of this sin. When Moses died, as the Israelites had reached the gates of the Promised Land, he was buried in the valley opposite Beth-Peor. Rashi states that Moses' grave, which in accordance with a Talmudic reference was brought into existence at the creation of the world, was intentionally prepared in the Beth-Peor area in order that Moses may atone for Israel's sin at Beth-Peor.

---

90. Of the Golden Calf incident.
91. Reestablish contact with God on Mount Sinai.

3. HOSEA

The prophetic message of Hosea derives its extraordinary significance from the fact that it is interwoven with his unfortunate marital experience. His wife Gomer committed adultery, and it is thought she became a temple prostitute, an abominable religious practice adopted by Hosea's native northern Kingdom of Israel from its pagan neighbors. Gomer became the personal property of a male lover. Hosea separated Gomer from himself and the children, but it appears that he continued to love her. God made use use of Hosea's distressing personal experience in order to enable him to gain some insight into the nature of God's love for man.

> And Jehovah said to me, "Go again, love a woman who is beloved of a paramour and is an adulteress, even as Jehovah loves the people of Israel, though they turn to other gods . . .
> *Hosea 3:1*

God's relation to Israel is depicted as that of a husband to his wife. Like Gomer, Israel, too, committed adultery by going after other gods. Like Hosea, God never ceased to love Israel. Gomer's adultery separated her from her husband; Israel's unfaithfulness alienated her from God. Israel's disloyalty to God created a Divine dilemma: her sin separated her from God, and yet God could not stop loving her, as seen from the following passage:

> How shall I give you up, O Ephraim![92] How shall I hand you over,[93] O Israel! . . . My heart recoils within me, my compassion grows warm and tender.
> *Hosea 11:8*

Hosea thus learned from his tragic experience that God suffered because of Israel's betrayal no less than he himself did on account of his wife's adultery. If God is able to love, he must be able to suffer. For suffering is inseparable from love. The adjective "passionate" used to describe the intensity of love conveys the notion of suffering. A God that is apathetic cannot be sympathetic,[94] for sympathy implies the ability to share in somebody else's sufferings.

---

92. Another name for northern Israel.
93. To her enemies.
94. H. Wheeler Robinson, TWO HEBREW PROPHETS (Lutterworth Press, London, 1929) p.23.

If God's love for sinful man does not permit Him to let the sinner go, then His love must be mingled with suffering no less intense than the love itself.

There was something else which Hosea learned from his sorrowful experience. He was instructed by God to buy Gomer back from her paramour whose property she became and give her a place in his house, but not to restore her for the time being to her former marital relationship. Separation of the sinner from his immoral associations is an important step in his reclamation, but since sin is an inward attitude, the sinner must experience an inner, moral cleansing before he can be restored to fellowship with God. During the period of separation from her evil environment, Gomer will have the opportunity to reflect on the enormity of her sinful behavior and repent of the shame and dishonor she brought on her husband and children.

In His determination to win Israel back to Himself, God proposed to deal with her in the same manner outlined for Hosea, as seen from this passage recounted by Hosea himself.

> So I bought her [95] for fifteen sheckels of silver, and for a homer and a half-homer of barley.[96] And I said to her, "You must dwell as mine for many days; you shall not play the harlot, or belong to another man; so will I also be to you. For the children of Israel shall dwell many days without king or prince, without sacrifice or pillar, without ephod or teraphim.[97] Afterward the children of Israel shall return, and seek Jehovah their God, and David their King; and they shall come in fear to Jehovah and to his goodness in the latter days.
>
> *Hosea 3:2-5*

When Gomer fell into sin she became enslaved by it. Under no circumstances could she by herself break the chains of her bondage. Her salvation depended on outside help. She was set free when Hosea paid the price for her liberation. This is recorded that we may know that sinful man cannot redeem himself. Thus, a new landmark has been reached in Biblical revelation, namely, that God suffers when man becomes alienated from Him, and He suffers in the process of pardoning and rehabilitating the transgressor.

---

95. Gomer.
96. A total sum of thirty sheckels of silver, the official Hebrew price for a slave.
97. A prophetic forecast of a period of Jewish history in which the Jewish people will be free of the sin of idolatry, but without the means of access to, and communication with, the God of Biblical revelation.

4. ISAIAH

Another statement testifying to the fact that God is capable of sharing in His people's sufferings is expressed in the following passage in Isaiah:

> In all their affliction he was afflicted, and the angel of his presence saved them; in his love and in his pity he redeemed them; he lifted them up and carried them all the days of old.
>
> *Isaiah 63:9*

5. JEREMIAH

Jeremiah's prophetic ministry extended to the very end of the ancient State of Israel.

"Though he loved his people with passion and pled with them all his life, he failed to convince or move them to repentance . . . [False] prophets and [self-seeking] priests called for his execution. He was stoned, beaten and thrust into the stocks. The King cut up the roll of his prophecies and the people following their formalist leaders rejected his word. With the first captivity under Jehoiakim all the better classes left Jerusalem, but he elected to remain with the refuse. When in the reign of Zedekiah the Chaldeans came down on the city [of Jerusalem] and Jeremiah counselled its surrender, he was again beaten and was flung into a pit to starve to death. When he was freed and the besiegers gave him the opportunity, he would not go over to them. Even when the city had fallen and her captors hearing of his counsel offered him security and a position in Babylonia, he chose instead to share the fortunes of the little remnant left in their ruined land."[98]

Referring to his country's woes he said:

> When I would strengthen myself against sorrow, my heart is sick within me. Hark, the cry of the daughter of my people from a far-off country: 'Is Jehovah not in Zion, is her King not in her?' . . . O that my head were waters, and my eyes a fountain of tears, that I might weep day and night, for the slain of the daughter of my people.
>
> *Jeremiah 8:18-19; 9:1 (8:18-19,23 Heb.)*

---

98. George Adam Smith, JEREMIAH (Hodder and Stoughton, Ltd.,:London), pp.320, 343-344. Used by permission.

Even his own fellow-villagers turned against him. Speaking of their schemes to get rid of him, he says:

> Jehovah made it known to me and I knew it; then thou
> dids't show me their evil deeds. But I was like a gentle lamb led
> to the slaughter; I did not know that it was against me that they
> devised schemes, saying, "Let us destroy the tree with its fruit,
> and let us cut him off from the land of the living, that his name
> be remembered no more".
>
> *Jeremiah 11:18-19*

"He was weighed down with his people's sins; he bore on his heart the full burden of them. He confessed them. The shame which the people did not feel for them, he felt; and he painted the curse upon them in words which prove how deeply the iron had entered his own soul"[99]

> Woe is me because of my hurt! my wound is grievous; but I said,
> "Truly this is my sickness and I must bear it."
>
> *Jeremiah 10:19*

6. EZEKIEL

Ezekiel was the other major prophet of the exilic period. He was commanded by God to lie on his side and in this symbolic manner bear the iniquity of his people.

> "Then lie on your left side, and lay the iniquity of the house
> of Israel[100] upon it; for the number of the days that you lie upon
> it, you shall bear their iniquity ... And when you have com-
> pleted these, lie again on thy right side, and you shall bear the
> iniquity of the house of Judah forty days: forty days I assign
> you, a day for each year."
>
> *Ezekiel 4:4,6*

7. THE GENERATION OF THE BABYLONIAN EXILE

A combination of events made the Jewish people of the Babylo-nian exile period unusually receptive to the message concerning the Suffering Servant. The great Semitic scholar Franz Delitzsch, who was of a firm conviction that the whole book of Isaiah was the work

---

99.   Ibid., pp.345-346.
100. Northern Israel.

of the prophet Isaiah, made the following pertinent observation in his introduction to the second half of the book of Isaiah: "We have admitted that, throughout the whole of the twenty-seven prophecies, the author of chapters 40-66 has the captivity as his fixed standpoint . . . The standpoint of the prophet is the second half of the captivity".[101] Delitzsch also asserts that every prophetic vision of the future must have its roots in, or connection with, the period in which the particular prophetic revelation is made. If it were not so, no part of any prophecy would have been understood either by the prophet or the people who were the immediate recipients of that particular prophecy. It is believed that when Isaiah became convinced that he can count on no sympathetic response to his ministry on the part of either the king or the people, he confined his labors to the small circle of his disciples, as is implied in the following passage:

> Bind up the testimony, seal the teaching among my disciples. I will wait for Jehovah, who is hiding his face from the house of Jacob, and I will hope in him.
>
> *Isaiah 8:16-17*

It was suggested that these disciples of Isaiah published in due course of time the prophet's writings. It stands to reason that the second half of Isaiah (chapters 40-66) was primarily addressed to the people of the Babylonian exile period. It would have been unintelligible had it been directed to any other generation, as seen from the following words containing the prophet's appeal to depart from Babylon aimed at that segment of the exiles who were uncertain of the wisdom of returning to Judea.

> Go forth from Babylon, flee from Chaldea, declare this with a shout of joy, proclaim it, send it forth to the end of the earth; say, "Jehovah has redeemed his servant Jacob!"
>
> *Isaiah 48:20*

Among the exiles in Babylon there was a community of Jews who remained loyal to Israel's spiritual heritage. Jeremiah referred to them as the good figs.[102] These faithful Israelites were burdened with the idea that they were in exile because of the sins of their fathers.

---

101.   Franz Delitzsch, THE PROPHECIES OF ISAIAH ((Wm. B. Eerdmans Publishing Company: Grand Rapids, Mich., 1949), Vol. 2, pp. 132,138.
102.   Jeremiah 24: 1-9.

> Our fathers sinned, and are no more; and we bear their iniquities.
>
> *Lamentations 5:7*

It was the first time in Jewish history when the collective experience of a whole generation gave to that generation the proper insight into the meaning of the Suffering Servant idea.

There was another important factor which made the Suffering Servant concept highly relevant to the situation of the people living towards the end of Babylonian exile. There were two extreme attitudes among the Babylonian exiles. One group was of the opinion that Cyrus, being a Gentile, his decree terminating the Exile could not possibly herald the restoration of Israel as predicted by the prophets. Consequently they were unwilling to pull up stakes and return to Judea. To answer their objections, the prophet assured them that Cyrus is indeed a Divinely appointed agent, and his defeat of the Babylonian world-power was the work of God who used him to facilitate the resettlement of the Jews in the land of their fathers, as seen from the following words:

> I stirred up one from the north, and he has come, from the rising of the sun now who invokes my name, — he shall tread upon rulers as on mortar, as the potter treads clay . . . Who says of Cyrus, "He is my shepherd, and he shall fulfill all my purpose", saying to Jerusalem, "She shall be built, and the temple founded".
>
> *Isaiah 41:25;44:28*

Another segment of the exiles took the very opposite view, namely that Cyrus is indeed the deliverer who will fulfill all of the prophetic promises with regards to the restoration of the Jewish State. To combat this erroneous view, the prophet declared that essential as it is that they depart from Babylon and return to Judea, their full restoration will not be the work of one who is nothing but a military conqueror, who does not even know Jehovah.[103] Israel's final deliverance will be the work of another Deliverer, the One whom God introduces in Chapter 42 as "My servant, whom I uphold, my chosen, in whom my soul delights." He will accomplish God's redemptive purpose in the world, both for Israel and for the Gentiles, but not by force of arms or the clashing of armies. "He will not cry or lift up his voice, or make it heard in the street. A bruised

---

103.   Isaiah 45: 4-5.

reed he will not break, and a dimly burning wick he will not quench."[104]

In conclusion, Isaiah 40-66 reminded the Babylonian exiles that a new period was dawning upon their world. This new world was pregnant with new epoch-making developments. It will culminate according to Isaiah 40-66 and Daniel 2 in the establishment of the Kingdom of God on earth. Upon the threshold of this new Aryan period of world history God has planted a new message: "Behold, I work out a new thing; it springs forth now; shall you not know it?"[105] The new thing is the revelation concerning the Person of the Suffering Servant of Jehovah, the final restorer of Israel, the Savior of the whole world. The story of this Suffering Servant occupies the central place of Isaiah 40-66. He is the central Figure of the ages, the central Figure of history. For His word the nations in the Aryan period will longingly be waiting.[106] The first phase of His mission will be marked by deep humiliation and great suffering for Himself, and seeming failure for His cause. The second phase of His mission will be crowned with the most blessed results: Israel will be spiritually regenerated and gloriously restored as a nation in her own land; the whole Gentile world will be redeemed; and nature, which has suffered on account of man's sin, will be renewed.

In Isaiah 49, this Suffering Servant, who in verses 5, 6, 8 and 9 accomplishes the restoration of Israel, is Himself addressed by God as Israel. When God pressed Abraham into His service he was told that the purpose of this mission is that through his descendants God's salvation may reach all the nations of the earth.[107] But this Divine objective has never been fulfilled by the Jewish people as such. What the Jews as a nation failed to do, the Suffering Servant of Jehovah will accomplish. "He will not fail nor be discouraged — or He will not faint or be broken — till he has established justice in the earth.[108] In a previous chapter we saw that the Messiah has many names, and they are all descriptive, i.e., they describe His character and His mission. He is called Immanuel, Wonderful Counsellor, Mighty God, Prince of Peace. In Isaiah 49 He is called Israel, because through Him Israel's mission to the world will be fully discharged in the "latter days," i.e. at the end of the age.

------

104.   Isaiah 42: 1-3.
105.   Isaiah 43:19.
106.   Isaiah 42:4.
107.   Genesis 12:1-3.
108.   Isaiah 42:4.

CHAPTER 6
IS JESUS OF NAZARETH THE SUFFERING SERVANT OF ISAIAH?

I. The Initial Abasement And Subsequent Exaltation Of The Suffering Servant

II. The Universal Rejection Of The Suffering Servant

III. The Dawn Of A Penitent Faith

IV. The Humiliation Of The Suffering Servant

V. The Resurrection And Triumph Of The Suffering Servant

CHAPTER 6
IS JESUS OF NAZARETH THE SUFFERING SERVANT OF ISAIAH?

In our consideration of the Suffering Servant of Isaiah 53 we have shown that it is impossible to interpret this prophecy as referring to Israel. We cited a multitude of excerpts testifying to the fact that Jewish commentators, ancient and medieval, have, by and large, understood this prophecy as speaking about the Messiah. The question we now wish to ask is, has the prophecy of the Suffering Servant of Isaiah been fulfilled in the life and mission of Jesus of Nazareth? To answer this question we will need to analyze the message of the prophecy of Isaiah 52: 13-15, 53: 1-12. This message can easily be divided into six sections.

I. THE INITIAL ABASEMENT AND SUBSEQUENT EXALTATION OF THE SUFFERING SERVANT

Behold, my servant shall prosper, he shall be exalted and be lifted up and shall be very high. Just as many were appalled at him (so disfigured, his appearance was not human and his form unlike that of the sons of men). So shall he sprinkle many nations: kings shall shut their mouths because of him, for they see what has not been told them, and of that which they had not heard shall they discern the meaning.

Isaiah 52: 13-15

In this first section we have a summary statement of the Messianic career of the Suffering Servant.

"To deal wisely" means to prosper or to be successful. An ancient Rabbinic Midrash has this comment on the opening words of the first section: "This is the King Messiah. He shall be exalted above Abraham . . . He shall be extolled more than Moses . . . And He shall be higher than the ministering angels.[1]

Verse 14 tells us that before His exaltation there will be a period of humiliation. Verses 14 and 15 present a contrast between the depth of his abasement and the height of His glorification. The

---

1. Yalkut Shimoni, part 2, vol. 53,col.3.

effect of His exaltation on the rulers of the earth has already been
mentioned in chapter 49. There, too, the Servant is initially despised
and abhorred. But a change occurs in the second phase of His
mission.

> Kings shall see and arise; princes, and they shall prostrate
> themselves.
>
> *Isaiah 49:7*

The effect of the triumph of the Suffering Servant on the
earth's rulers is described in verse 15 of the first section. Kings, we
are told, will be dumbfounded when they are confronted with the
incredible turn of events in the career of the Suffering Servant. In
part, at least, this portion of the prophecy has found fulfillment in
the Messianic career of Jesus of Nazareth. Executed on a cross like a
common criminal, in the course of time He lifted the world empire
of pagan Rome off its hinges. The cross which symbolized helpless-
ness and defeat, suffering and shame, compassion and mercy,
evoked nothing but contempt in the ancient world. But as this
ancient world approached its end, the sight of the Cross caused
kings to rise from their thrones and princes to prostrate themselves
on the ground. It was a change the ancient world never believed
could happen. It was contrary to its way of thinking and its belief.
Victory through suffering — this went against the very grain of
ancient civilization. It was something the ancient world never heard
of, something which impelled it to rethink the whole question of the
destiny of man and society. It caused a revolutionary upheaval in the
whole fabric of ancient civilization. "For they see what has not been
told them, and that which they had not heard shall they discern the
meaning."

II. THE UNIVERSAL REJECTION OF THE SUFFERING SERVANT

> Who has believed what we have heard, and over whom has
> the arm of Jehovah been revealed? For he sprang up before him
> as a sapling, and like a root-sprout out of dry ground; he had no
> form nor stateliness that we should look at him, and no beauty
> that we should desire him. He was despised and forsaken by
> men: a man of sorrows, and acquainted with sickness: and as
> one from whom men hide their face[2] he was despised, and we
> esteemed him not.
>
> *Isaiah 53:1-3*

---

2.   "From Whom Men Avert Their Gaze", as translated by Christopher R. North, is a
     better rendering of the meaning of the Hebrew text, see his THE SUFFERING
     SERVANT IN DEUTERO-ISAIAH, p. 121.

Who are the speakers who in Isaiah 53: 1 pose the question, "Who has believed what we have heard?" A comparison of verses 1, 5 and 8 leads us to conclude that the speakers in verse 1 are the representatives of a repentant Israel. This, because the same persons who pose the question in verse 1 state in verse 5 that the Suffering Servant was wounded for their transgression, and in verse 8 they declare that he was stricken for the transgressions of my people, and "my people" in the context of verse 8 certainly refers to Israel.

And yet the national identity of the speakers was probably intentionally left vague, in order to convey the thought that the rejection of the Suffering Servant will not be confined to Israel, but it will constitute a universal attitude. "Who has believed what we have heard, and over whom has the arm of Jehovah been revealed?" Only a numerically insignificant remnant of both Jews and Gentiles have believed, those who saw in the message and career of the Suffering Servant the mighty hand of God.

The reason why the world of Jews and Gentiles assumed an attitude of indifference to the Suffering Servant is because He came up from dry ground, i.e., He grew up and lived in the midst of lowly, unpromising, circumstances. There was nothing about His outward appearance and the manner in which He went about accomplishing His mission to arrest people's attention. Already in the first introduction of the Servant we were told that "He will not cry, nor lift up his voice, or make it heard in the street."[3] It was just this absence of pomp, ostentation, splash or glitter in His personality and His mission that generated disbelief and indifference. How all this was fulfilled in the life and work of Jesus of Nazareth may be seen from the following recorded incidents. On a certain Sabbath He spoke in one of the synagogues in his own city of Nazareth. The reaction to His appearance is recorded in the following words.

> Is not this the carpenter's son? Is not his mother called Mary? And are not his brothers James and Joseph and Simon and Judas? And are not all his sisters with us? Where then did this man get all this
>
> *Matthew 13: 55-56*

> Philip found Nathanael, and said to him, "We have found him of whom Moses in the law and also the prophets wrote,

---

3.   Isaiah 42:2.

Jesus of Nazareth, the son of Joseph." Nathanael said to him, "Can anything good come out of Nazareth?"

John 1: 45-46

The world has always admired a conquering hero, one who is riding forth to battle against the oppressor. But the world has little admiration for the one who is meek and lowly, who offers God's forgiveness, and brings salvation from sin. It was not sin that troubled the world at Messiah's first coming, and it is not sin that troubles the world today.

The statement "He was despised and forsaken by men" deserves some comment. In the Hebrew text the word "men" actually means men of rank, rather than men in general. What the prophet is seeking to tell us is that the Suffering Servant found no support for His cause among men of influence. "He had none of the men of any distinction on his side."[4] That this was the experience of Jesus of Nazareth may be seen from the following recorded incident. During one of His visits in Jerusalem an attempt was made by the priesthood and the Pharisees to arrest Him. It was during the Feast of the Tabernacles, which means that Jerusalem was crowded with people who came from all over to celebrate the Feast. Taking advantage of the occasion Jesus was teaching in the Temple. The people who listened to Him were so deeply impressed that to arrest Him might have caused a public disturbance. The following is part of this account in the Gospel of John.

> The officers then went back to the chief priests and Pharisees, who said to them, "Why did you not bring him?" The officers answered, "No man ever spoke like this man." The Pharisees answered them, "Have you also been deceived? Have any of the authorities or Pharisees believed in him. But this crowd,[5] who do not know the law, are accursed."
>
> *John 7:45-49*

"He was despised in particular by the men of influence."

III. THE DAWN OF A PENITENT FAITH

> Surely ours were the sicknesses that he bore, and ours the sorrows he carried; we, however, regarded him stricken, smit-

---

4. Franz Delitzsch, THE PROPHECIES OF ISAIAH (Wm. B. Eerdman's Publishing Company: Grand Rapids, Michigan, 1949), pp. 314.

5. Referring to the rank and file of the people.

> ten of God, and afflicted. But he was wounded for our sins,
> bruised for our iniquities; the chastisement that secured our
> well-being was upon him, and with his wounds we are healed.
> All we like sheep have gone astray; we have turned every one to
> his own way; and Jehovah has caused the iniquity of us all to fall
> on him.
>
> *Isaiah 53: 4-6*

Actually this reversal of the attitude of disbelief belongs in the
last part of chapter 53 as it does not take place until the second phase
of the Suffering Servant's mission. It is possible that it was placed
here in order to show the contrast with the posture of unbelief
described in the preceding passage. Isaiah 52: 13-15, 53: 1-12 is full
of such contrasts. We have here the same vagueness of identity of the
speakers as in the preceding passage of Isaiah 53: 1-3, and for the
same reason. Israel was the first to turn from Him on a national
scale, and Israel will be the first to turn to Him on a national scale;
the acceptance will be as universal as the rejection has been.

IV. THE HUMILIATION OF THE SUFFERING SERVANT

> He was oppressed and he was afflicted, yet he opened not
> his mouth, like a lamb that is led to the slaughter and like a
> sheep that before its shearers is dumb, so he opened not his
> mouth. He was taken away from prison and judgment; and of
> his generation who considered that he was snatched away out of
> the land of the living, stricken for the transgression of my
> people?
>
> *Isaiah 53: 7-8*

The first sentence of the above passage asserts the voluntary
character of Messiah's suffering. It is variously rendered that He
"bowed Himself," that "He was oppressed," that "He was used
violently," that "He was treated tyrannically," and yet He "humbled"
or "submitted" Himself, and took this heavy burden on our account
entirely voluntarily. "When we suffer, how hard we find it to be still!
The flames of resentment — how they leap up in our bosom, and
flush our cheek with angry red! . . . Or if there is silence, it is at times
akin to stoicism, the proud determination not to let men see how we
feel. But the spirit of the Servant is loftier and grander unutterably.
In sublime and magnanimous silence He endures to the uttermost,

sustained by His mighty purpose and by the conviction, Jehovah wills it."[6]

It is amazing how readily the reciting of this passage brings up before us the Figure of Jesus of Nazareth, the patience and silence which marked His behavior when He stood before the Jewish Sanhedrin and the Roman governor Pontius Pilate, and the love He exhibited in the final hours of His agony on the cross. "All the references in the New Testament to the Lamb of God spring from this passage in the book of Isaiah."[7]

The second sentence (verse 8) in our passage describes the trial and death of the Suffering Servant. The first part of this sentence is also rendered in a number of ways. The Hebrew word translated "prison" means primarily violent restraint; the Hebrew word "mishpat" refers to the judicial proceeding to which He was subjected. The meaning of the statement, "He has been taken away from prison and judgment" is that He was carried away by death in circumstances of judicial persecution and hostile oppression.

The second part of verse 8, "and of his generation who considered that he was snatched away out of the land of the living, stricken for the transgression of my people," is also phrased in many ways. The most probable meaning of this statement is, that of the people of His day, who among them poured out a complaint. It is suggested that this represents a prophetic reference to the prevailing Jewish custom, in cases of trial for life, of calling upon all who had anything to say in favor of the accused to come forward and "declare" or "plead" on his behalf. There may be an allusion to this custom in the following passage in the Talmud concerning the trial of Jesus of Nazareth: "On the eve of the Sabbath and the Passover they hung Jesus. And the herald went forth before him for forty days crying, 'Jesus goes to be executed, because he has practised sorcery and seduced Israel and estranged them from God. Let any one who can bring forward any justifying plea for him come and give information concerning it; but no justifying plea was found for him and so he was hung on the eve of the Sabbath and the Passover. Rabbi Ulla said, 'But do you think that he belongs to those for whom a justifying

---

6. James Culross, THE MAN OF SORROWS AND THE JOY THAT WAS SET BEFORE HIM (Drummond Tract Society); quoted by David Baron, THE SERVANT OF JEHOVAH, p. 100.
7. Franz Delitzsch, op. cit., Vol. 2, p. 323.

plea is to be sought? He was a very seducer, and the All-merciful has said, You shall not spare him, nor conceal him.' But the case of Jesus stood differently because he stood near to the Kingdom.[8]

The Jewish Sanhedrin, the Supreme Court among the Jewish people of that day, was guided in their judicial proceedings by a principle that it is their business to save, rather than to destroy, life, if only possible. "That this humane custom of calling upon those who knew anything in favor of the accused to come and declare it, was not observed in the case of Jesus of Nazareth (notwithstanding the above-cited Talmudic legend), and that the proceedings at this hasty mock trial before the Sanhedrin were in flagrant contradiction with the regulations which were supposed to govern their procedure, these are facts of history; but there is this much truth in this Talmudic passage that none dared to appear in His favor; and that in the great crisis when the Messiah of God stood on His trial before the hostile Jewish hierarchy and the politically-minded self-seeking representatives of the then great Gentile world power, no one came forward with a justifying plea on His behalf for fear of the Jewish authorities . . . even His own disciples, who when they witnessed His resurrection became as bold as lions, and willingly laid down their lives for Him, became demoralized with fear and forsook Him and fled."[9]

And of the people of his day, who from among them poured forth a complaint, who whispered a prayer, on His behalf, for (or that) he was cut off from the land of the living, that for the transgression of my people he was stricken. Ellison states that the speaker in this passage is the prophet himself. "Isaiah had doubtless seen that in the Servant's work the chief obstacle and the chief burdens would come from Israel, with whom, as always, the prophet identifies himself. He does not confine the sin to Israel, but he stresses Israel's share."[10]

V. THE DEATH AND BURIAL OF THE SUFFERING SERVANT

And they assigned him his grave with the wicked, and with a rich man in his death, because he had done no wrong and

---

8. Sanhedrin, fol. 43. The statement "because he stood near to the Kingdom," probably refers to the Davidic decent of Jesus of Nazareth.
9. David Baron, Op. Cit., pp. 106-107.
10. H. L. Ellison, THE SERVANT OF JEHOVAH, p. 33.

there was no deceit in his mouth.

Isaiah 53:9

This passage deals with the death and burial of the Suffering Servant. A somewhat better rendering of the statement is this; "And they assigned him his grave with evildoers, but with a rich man in his death." According to Deuteronomy a man sentenced to death by hanging must not be left in this position overnight; he had to be removed from the gallows and buried on the same day on which he was executed.[11] The ancient Jewish historian Josephus of the first century of our era, citing the Mosaic law against blasphemy supplies additional details about the kind of burial given to such persons in the following passage: "He that blasphemes God, let him be stoned; and let him hang upon a tree all that day, and then let him be buried in an ignominious and obscure manner."[12] Since Jesus of Nazareth was accused of blasphemy according to the New Testament record, and confirmed by the above-cited Talmudic passage, He should have received a malefactor's burial. In the normal course of events this is what would have taken place. It is implied in the first part of verse 9: "And they assigned his grave with sinners," i.e. He was marked for a criminal's burial. But in the second part of verse 9 the prophet declares that this was not to happen! It is expressed in these words: "and with a rich man in his death." Incidentally, the word "death" actually means martyrdom or martyr-death.[13] He would have received a malefactor's burial, but since it was a martyr's death that He died, He was actually buried in a rich man's grave. The third part of verse 9 gives the full explanation for what happened or was to happen: "because he had done no wrong, and there was no deceit in his mouth." He was not to be buried like a criminal, because He was no evildoer. He died for the sins of others. With His death, His part in the Divine scheme of man's redemption was finished, and God would not allow any more indignities to be heaped upon Him.

Under what amazing circumstances this portion of the prophecy relating to the death and burial of the Suffering Servant was fulfilled in the death and burial of Messiah Jesus may be seen from the account in the New Testament.

And when evening had come, since it was the day of the Preparation, the day before the Sabbath. That Joseph who was

---

11. Deuteronomy 21: 22-23.
12. Flavius Josephus, ANTIQUITIES OF THE JEWS, Book IV, Chapter VIII, 6.
13. Franz Delitzsch, Op. Cit., Vol. 2, p. 329.

of Arimathea, an honorable member of the council who was also himself looking for the kingdom of God, taking courage, went to Pilate and asked for the body of Jesus. And Pilate wondered that he was already dead; and having summoned the centurion, he inquired of him whether he was already dead. And having ascertained from the centurion, he gave the dead body to Joseph. And he bought linen, and taking him down, he wrapped him in the linen, and put him in a tomb which was hewn out of a rock; and he rolled a stone against the entrance of the tomb. And Mary of Magdala and Mary the mother of Jesus saw where he was laid.

Mark 15: 42-47

Matthew states that this tomb belonged to a man named Joseph, "a rich man from Arimathea, who was also a disciple of Jesus."[14] He was a respected member of the Sanhedrin, and a secret follower and admirer of Jesus of Nazareth. This man of high social standing received permission from the Roman governor to bury the body of Jesus. He had not much time to lose because, as Luke tells us, Sabbath eve was approaching."[15] According to the record in the Gospel of John the body of Jesus was laid in that particular tomb because of the proximity of the tomb to the place of the crucifixion and the need to make haste on account of the approaching Sabbath.

Now in the place where he was crucified there was a garden, and in the garden a new tomb, in which no one had ever been laid. There, therefore, on account of the Jewish day of Preparation, since the tomb was near, they laid Jesus.

John 19: 41-42

Thus it was that men and circumstances were used of God to fulfill the most minute details concerning the death and burial of the Suffering Servant uttered by the prophet centuries before the predicted events had taken place.

VI. THE RESURRECTION AND TRIUMPH OF THE SUFFERING SERVANT

Yet it was the will of Jehovah to bruise him, to put him to grief; when he makes himself an offering for sin, he should see posterity, he should prolong his days, and the purpose of

---

14.   Matthew 27: 57, 60.
15.   Luke 23: 54.

Jehovah should prosper through him. He shall see the fruit of the travail of his soul and be satisfied; by his knowledge shall the righteous one, my servant, make many to be accounted righteous, and he shall bear their iniquities. Therefore I will assign him the many for his portion, and numberless shall be his spoil; because he has poured out his soul to death, and he was numbered with transgressors; yet he bore the sin of many and makes intercession for the transgressors.

Isaiah 53: 10-12

In the first sentence (verse 10) of this final passage we have a restatement of the meaning of the death of the Suffering Servant. Whatever part both Jews and Gentiles were permitted to play in the sufferings and death of the Servant, they were the instruments in the hand of God — "it was the will of Jehovah to bruise him, to put him to grief."

The remainder of the passage is based on the asumption of the resurrection of the Suffering Servant. "When he makes himself an offering for sin, he should see posterity, he should prolong his days." The word posterity is "seed" in the Hebrew text. This takes us back to the Messianic Psalm 22 where we read

Posterity (or a seed) shall serve him.

Psalm 22: 30 (22: 31Heb.)

In consequence of His atoning death He shall see Himself possessed of a large family of followers, a redeemed and regenerated people of both Jews and Gentiles.

The last two sentences (verses 11 and 12) have Jehovah as the speaker. It was Jehovah who introduced the Servant first in Isaiah 42, then, again, in Isaiah 52: 13-15; it is Jehovah who has the last word in the story of the Suffering Servant. The Servant, Jehovah declares, "shall see the fruit of the travail of his soul and be satisfied; through his knowledge shall my righteous servant make many to be accounted righteous, and he shall bear their iniquities."

THE MESSIANIC HOPE IN THE OLD TESTAMENT: CONCLUDING REMARKS

Before concluding our main study of the Messianic Hope in the Old Testament, a few words need to be said about the extra-canonical writings of the Old Testament which flourished in the last two centuries B.C. and the first century A.D. The Messianic Hope holds a prominent place in many of these writings, especially in the Book of Enoch, The Assumption of Moses, the Apocalypse of Baruch and 4 Esra. It was observed by one of the great Jewish scholars that while these writings may have broadened, they have not deepened, the Messianic ideas of the prophets.[16]

In summary, the Old Testament represents the Messianic Person as having a Divine-human origin, and as accomplishing His mission in two stages: (1) As the *Suffering Servant* He liberates man from his enslavement to his sinful nature. Beginning with the account of Adam and Eve whose moral nakedness God caused to be covered with skins secured by shedding innocent blood, the idea of a Suffering Servant is weaved into the warp and woof of the entire Old Testament until it reaches its fullness in the Person of the Suffering Servant of Isaiah 53. (2) As the *Messianic King* He will cause righteousness and peace to spring up in the affairs of men and nations, and He will establish God's Kingdom on earth.

---

16. Joseph Klausner, THE MESSIANIC IDEA IN ISRAEL (The Macmillan Company: New York, 1955), p. 384.

PART TWO

THE MESSIANIC MISSION
OF JESUS OF NAZARETH

*"Think not that I have come to abolish the law and the
prophets; I have come not to abolish them but to fulfill them".*
Matthew 5:17

*"We have found him of whom Moses in the law and also the
prophets wrote, Jesus of Nazareth, the son of Joseph".*
John 1:45

*Nathanael answered him, "Rabbi, you are the Son of God!
You are the King of Israel!"*
John 1:49

CHAPTER

CHAPTER 1
DIVINE SELF-DISCLOSURE
IN THE OLD TESTAMENT

I. God's Presence In The Midst Of His People

II. Angelic Appearances

III. The Covenant

IV. The Son Of God

CHAPTER 1
DIVINE SELF-DISCLOSURE
IN THE OLD TESTAMENT

By the term "Divine self-disclosure" we mean the various manifestations of God's presence in the midst of His people. These manifestations are a recurring phenomenon in the Old Testament period and they reach a culminating point in the Person of Messiah Jesus in whom God became flesh and dwelt in our midst.[1] In the following pages we wish to trace the gradual unfolding of this phenomenon in the Old Testament.

I. GOD'S PRESENCE IN THE MIDST OF HIS PEOPLE

Right after the Sinai Covenant was concluded by which Israel became Jehovah's people, Moses received the following instruction.

> Speak to the people of Israel that they bring me an offering; from every man who gives it willingly you shall take an offering for me . . . And let them make me a sanctuary, that I may dwell in their midst.
> *Exodus 25: 8*

In Leviticus the term "tabernacle" is used in place of "sanctuary."

> If you walk in my statues and observe my commandments and do them. Then I will give you rain in due season, and the land shall yield its increase, and the trees of the field shall yield their fruit . . . And I will set my tabernacle among you, and my soul shall not abhor you. And I will walk among you, and will be your God, and you shall be by people.
> *Leviticus 26: 3-4, 11-12*

In the course of time the question arose in the minds of certain Israelites, does God who created the whole universe really dwell on a certain spot on this earth, in a tabernacle or sanctuary made by

---

1. The Gospel of John 1:14.

human hands? This was the question which King Solomon posed during his dedication of the Temple in Jerusalem erected during his reign.

> But will God indeed dwell on the earth? behold, the heaven and heavens cannot contain thee; how much less this house which I have built!
>
> *1 Kings 8: 27*

But the answer to Solomon's question came even before he uttered it. When the ark containing the two tables of stone put there by Moses in the Wilderness was placed in the "inner sanctuary," the "most holy place" of the Temple, underneath the wings of the cherubim, we are told that a cloud symbolizing the Presence of God filled the sanctuary.[2] It was the same cloud, also called "the glory of Jehovah," that filled the tabernacle in the Wilderness, a cloud by day and a fire by night.[3] The belief that God did indeed dwell in the midst of His people has its source in the conviction that God is a Person, and this truth was rooted in the Biblical account of the creation of man.

> Then God said, Let us make man in our image, after our likeness . . . So God created man in his own image, in the image of God he created him . . . And the Lord God formed man of the dust of the ground, and breathed into his nostrils the breath of life; and man became a living being.
>
> *Genesis 1: 26a - 27; 2:7*

According to the above statement man came into existence as a special creation. Since man is a person and since he was created after God's likeness, it follows that God, too, is a Person, and God "breathed" into man something of His own Personality. From this Biblical concept man reasoned that certain characteristics of personality must be common to God and man. This does not mean that Biblical man considered himself equal to God. God is the Creator, man is the creature; God is holy, man is sinful. God is self-sufficient, — man is not. But the account of man's creation convinced man that man is a person, because God is a Person. In a world divided between a belief in gods of stone statues, and a belief in a God of pure reason, de-

---

2.   1 Kings 8:10-11.
3.   Exodus 40:34-38.

tached and far removed from the earthly sphere, Biblical revelation proclaims a God who is neither the god of materialism nor the God of cold and pure reason, but a living, dynamic Divine Person, deeply involved in the welfare and destiny of the world which He created and which He sustains.

It is by virtue of this common bond of personality that God and man manifest a desire to communicate with each other. This desire underlies man's search after God, a reaching out after Him to whom man is linked by certain common bonds of personality.

> As the heart longs for the water brooks, so longs my soul for thee, O God. My soul thirsts for God, for the living God.
> *Psalm 42:1-2 (42: 2-3 Heb.)*

It is because of certain characteristics of personality shared in common with man that God also discloses a yearning to communicate and commune with man. The program of redemption, set in motion after the all of man, is a Divine determination to reopen the lines of communication which existed prior to man's alienation from God. In the book of Hebrews we are told that in the Biblical period God used many and various ways to communicate with man.[4] We will now consider some of these ways.

II. ANGELIC APPEARANCES

The Hebrew word "angel" means messenger. Angels are God's messengers to man. They appear in the whole Biblical period, both in the Old and New Testament. One of the remarkable features of the angelic appearances in the Old Testament is that the angel frequently speaks of Jehovah in the first person, as if he — the angel — were Jehovah Himself.

When Hagar, Sarah's maidservant, left the house of her mistress and went into the desert, we are told that an angelic messenger appeared and

> The angel of Jehovah said to her, "Return to your mistress, and submit to her." And the angel of Jehovah said to her "I will greatly multiply your seed so that it cannot be numbered for

---

4.   Hebrews 1:1.

multitude." And the angel of Jehovah said to her, "Behold, you are with child, and shall bear a son; you shall call his name Ishmael, because Jehovah has heard your affliction" . . . And she called the name of Jehovah who spoke to her, "Thou God seest me;" for she said, "Have I really seen God and remained alive after seeing him?"

Genesis 16: 9-11, 13

The following is an account of the appearance of three angelic messengers to Abraham. One of the three acted as the spokesman, and he spoke and acted as if he were Jehovah Himself.

And Jehovah appeared to him[5] by the oaks of Mamre, as he sat at the door of the tent in the heat of the day . . . They[6] said to him "Where is Sarah your wife?" And he said, "She is in the tent." And he[7] said, "I will certainly return to you at this time next year, and Sarah your wife shall have a son;" and Sarah heard it in the tent door which was behind him. Now Abraham and Sarah were old and advanced in years; and it had ceased to be with Sarah after the manner of women. So Sarah laughed within herself, saying, "After I have grown old, and my husband is old, shall I have pleasure?" And Jehovah said to Abraham, "Why did Sarah laugh, saying, 'Shall I indeed bear a child, now that I am old?' Is anything too hard for Jehovah?"

Genesis 18: 1, 9-14

The following three passages are taken from angelic appearances in the days of Jacob.

Then the angel of God spoke to me in a dream, saying, "Jacob", and I said, "Here am I!" And he said . . ."I am the God of Bethel,[8] where you anointed a pillar and where you made a vow unto me; now arise, go forth from this land, and return to the land of your birth."

Genesis 31: 11-13

And Jacob was left alone; and there wrestled a man with him until the breaking of the day. When he[9] saw that he did not prevail against him, he touched the hollow of his thigh; and

---

5. Abraham.
6. The three angelic messengers.
7. The spokesman of the angelic messengers.
8. A reference to the Divine revelation granted to Jacob at Bethel.
9. The angelic messenger.

Jacob's thigh was put out of joint as he wrestled with him . . .
And he said unto him, "What is your name?" And he said,
"Jacob." And he said, "Your name shall be called no more Jacob,
but Israel: for you have striven with God and with men, and
have prevailed . . ." And Jacob called the name of the place
Peniel, saying, "For I have seen God face to face, and yet my life
is preserved."

Genesis 32: 24-25, 27-28, 30 (32: 25-26, 28-29, 31 Heb.)

When Jacob pronounced his blessing upon his children just
before he died, he uttered the following words when Joseph approached him with his two sons.

The God before whom my fathers Abraham and Isaac
walked, the God who has shepherded me all life long unto this
day — The angel who has redeemed me from all evil — bless the
lads; and in them let my name and the name of my fathers
Abraham and Isaac be perpetuated; and let them grow into a
multitude in the midst of the earth.

Genesis 48: 15-16

The following angelic appearances took place in the Exodus
period of Israel's history.

And the angel of Jehovah appeared to him[10] in a flame of
fire out of the midst of a bush; and he looked, and, behold, the
bush burned with fire, yet it was not consumed. And Moses said,
"I will turn aside and see this great sight, why the bush is not
burnt. When Jehovah saw that he turned aside to see, God
called to him out of the midst of the bush and said, "Moses,
Moses!" And he said, "Here am I." Then he[11] said "Do not come
near; put off your shoes from your feet, for the place on which
you are standing is holy ground." And he said, "I am the God of
your father, the God of Abraham, the God of Isaac, and the
God of Jacob;" and Moses hid his face, for he was afraid to look at
God.

Exodus 3: 2-6

In the following passage we are told that Jehovah led the Israelites through the wilderness.

---

10. Moses.
11. The angel identified as Jehovah.

> And Jehovah went before them by day in a pillar of cloud to
> lead them along the way, and by night in a pillar of fire to give
> them light, that they might travel by day and night.
>
> *Exodus 13: 21*

In the passage below relating the miraculous deliverance of the
Israelites from the pursuing Egyptians, Jehovah is personified by
the angel.

> Then the angel of God who went before the camp of Israel
> moved and went behind them; and the pillar of cloud moved
> from before them and stood behind them. Intervening between
> the host of Egypt and the host of Israel; and it was a cloud of
> darkness to them, but it gave light by sight to these; so that the one
> came not near the other all night . . . And it came to pass that in
> the morning watch Jehovah looked upon the host of the Egyp-
> tians through the pillar of fire and of cloud and troubled the host
> of the Egyptians.
>
> *Exodus 14: 19-20, 24*

The same phenomenon of personification of Jehovah by
angelic messengers continues in many other situations in the Old
Testament period.[12]

The following passage explains why it is that angels often spoke
and acted as if they were Jehovah Himself.

> "Behold, I send an angel before you, to guard you on the way
> and to bring you into the place which I have prepared. Beware of
> him and obey his voice, provoke him not; for he will not pardon
> your transgressions; for my name is in him."
>
> *Exodus 23: 20-21*

With reference to this angel, Rashi, medieval Jewish commentator,
declares that Rabbinic authorities identify the angel in the above
passage with Metatron. Metatron is the name of the chief of the
angels who according to one Talmudic passage sits in the inmost
dwelling of God, and is the same person as the "Prince of the
Presence", the angel who is the very Face of God.[13] In the Bible a
person's name is identical with that person. It expresses the very

---

12. See, f.e., Joshua 5: 13-15; Judges 2: 1-5; see, especially, Judges 6: 11-24, and
    Judges 13: 2-23.
13. Bab. Chagiga 15a.

essence of that person. The Rabbinic statement, to which Rashi refers in his exposition of the passage in Exodus 23: 21, declares that "His [the angel's] name is like the name of his Master."[14] All of this means one thing: In the Bible, especially in the Old Testament, God frequently takes on the form of angels in order to communicate with man.

III. THE COVENANT

If angelic appearances were one of the ways God used to communicate with man, the Sinai Covenant was a means of His identifying Himself with Israel. The ancient world was full of covenants.[15] Covenants were made between individuals, as for example, the covenant between Jonathan and David, between family clans, and between rulers. But the Sinai Covenant, a covenant between God and a whole people, is something unique even in the ancient world. The covenant idea dominates the whole Bible, Old and New Testament. The Sinai Covenant brought Israel into existence as a people and a religious community. Through the Sinai Covenant God entered into an extraordinary relationship with Israel.

What exactly the Covenant came to mean to Israel may be seen if we realize that it was interpreted in terms of a marriage covenant. In the ancient world marriage was a covenant, and it is the only covenant institution which has come down to us from the ancient world. Israel is often spoken of as God's bride.

> Fear not, for you will not be ashamed; be not confounded, for you will not be put to shame; for you will forget the shame of your youth, and shall not remember the reproach of your widowhood any more. For your Maker is your husband, Jehovah of hosts is his name; and your Redeemer is the Holy one of Israel, the God of the whole earth he is called.
>
> *Isaiah 54: 4-5*

The Hebrew word "Goel" ("redeemer") originally denoted the nearest of kin whose duty it was to redeem, to ransom, to purchase back, the mortgaged land and return it to the original owner who

---

14. Sanh. 38b.
15. George E. Mendenhall, LAW AND COVENANT IN ISRAEL AND THE ANCIENT NEAR EAST (The Biblical Colloqium: Pittsburgh, Pa., 1955).

was forced to part with it through unfortunate circumstances. If an Israelite for the same reason fell into slavery, it was the duty of his nearest kin to "redeem" him, i.e. to pay the ransom money necessary to set him free. The "Goel" was also obligated to avenge the death of the nearest kin. Finally, the "Goel" was duty bound to marry the widow of his nearest kin who left no children in order to save the family name from extinction.[16] Through the conclusion of the Sinai Covenant God became Israel's Redeemer, i.e., her "Goel," her nearest kin, and He was duty bound, as it were, to "redeem" Israel when she got in trouble.

The following are additional excerpts in which Israel is represented as married to God.

> The word of Jehovah came to me saying. "Go and declare in the hearing Jersalem. 'Thus says Jehovah, 'I remember the devotion of your youth, your love as a bride, when you followed me in the wilderness in a land that was not sown."
> *Jeremiah 2: 1-2*

> Can a maiden forget her ornaments, or a bride her attire? yet my people have forgotten me days without number.
> *Jeremiah 2: 32*

Israel had nothing to boast of about her origin. According to the Psalmist, she was of low estate,[17] of little account, few in number, wandering from country to country.[18] Ezekiel likens Israel's beginning to an exposed, castaway, baby girl.

> "And as for your birth, on the day when you were born your navel string was not cut, not were you washed with water to cleanse you, not rubbed with salt, nor swaddled at all. No eye pitied you, to do any of these things unto you, to have compassion upon you; but you were cast out on the open field, for you were abhorred on the day when you were born.
> *Ezekiel 16: 4-5*

It was in this state that God found her. But He picked her up, took her to Himself, nursed her to health and cared for her until she reached puberty.

---

16. See, f.e., Leviticus 25:25; 25:48, 49; Deuteronomy 19: 2-6; Ruth 3:12; 4: 1-9.
17. Psalm 136:23.
18. Psalm 105:12-13.

And when I passed by you, and saw you rolling in your own blood, I said to you in your blood,[19] Live. I have caused you to multiply like the plants in the field; and you grew up and became tall and arrived at full maidenhood;[20] your breasts were formed, and your hair had grown; yet you were [still] naked and bare.[21]

Ezekiel 16: 6-7

Then God took her up again, made her into his bride, lavished upon her His love, and surrounded her with all the honor and wealth at His disposal.

When I passed by you again and looked upon you, behold, you were at the age of love; and I spread my skirt over you, and covered your nakedness;[22] yea I swore unto you,[23] and entered into a covenant with you, says the Lord God, and you became mine. Then I washed you with water, and thoroughly washed away your blood from you, and I anointed you with oil. I clothed you also with broidered work and shod you with leather, I swathed you in fine linen, and I covered you with silk. And I decked you with ornaments, and I put bracelets on your hands, and a chain on your neck. And I put a ring on your nose, and earrings in your ears, and a beautiful crown upon your head."

Ezekiel 16: 8-12

Accordingly, whenever Israel goes after other gods, i.e., if she chooses to follow life-goals which are inconsistent with her destiny as marked out in Biblical revelation, she is called an adulteress, i.e., unfaithful to Jehovah who entered into a covenant relation with her. The speaker in the excerpt below is Jehovah and His words are addressed to Israel.

Plead with your mother, plead, for she is not my wife, and I am not her husband, let her therefore put away her harlotry out of her sight, and her adulteries from between her breasts. Lest I

---

19. The sense of the word "blood" is, probably, that had God not rescued her she would have bled to death.
20. Literally, you came to excellent ornaments, i.e. you acquired excellent beauty.
21. An allusion to the poverty of their state when they were yet strangers in the land of Canaan.
22. A Biblical idiom for marriage (see Ruth 3: 9).
23. An allusion to the marriage vow.

strip her naked, and set her as in the day when she was born,
and make her as a wilderness, and set her like a parched land,
and slay her with thirst . . . For their mother has played the
harlot . . . for she said, 'I will go after my lovers, who give me my
bread and my water, my wool and my flax, my oil and my
drink' . . . And she did not know that it was I who gave her the
grain, the wine, and the oil, and who lavished upon her silver
and gold which they used for Baal.[24]

Hosea 2: 2-3, 5, 8 (2: 4-5, 7, 10 Heb.)

IV. THE SON OF GOD

When Moses was commissioned by God to demand of Pharaoh
to let the Hebrews leave the country, he was given the following
message to be delivered to the Egyptian king.

Thus says Jehovah, "Israel is my son, even my first-born.
And I say to you, 'Let my son go that he may serve me' " . . .

Exodus 4: 22-23

When Israel was a child, then I loved him, and called my
son out of Egypt . . .   I taught Ephraim also to walk, taking
them up by their arms, but they did not know that I healed
them. I drew them with cords of a man, with bands of love; and I
was to them as one that eases the yoke on their jaws, and I bent
down to them and fed them.[25]

Hosea 11: 1, 3-4

In the Nathan prophecy given to King David God promised to
be a Father to David's immediate offspring.[26] While this referred, in
the first place, to Solomon, the promise was by no means limited to
him. God was a Father to Hezekiah and Josiah, no less than to
Solomon who in his old age had proven unfaithful to Jehovah. By
virtue of His Davidic descent the Messianic King bears also this filial

---

24. Baal - the word in Hebrew means a Canaanite god, and also a man who is his
     wife's lord and master.
25. The following are some of the other references in which God is represented as
     Israel's Father: Deuteronomy 32:6, 18; Isaiah 63:16; 64:8; Jeremiah 3:14, 19;
     31:9; Malachi 1:6.
26. See 2 Samuel 7:14.

relationship to God. Not only so, but in Him the Old Testament concept of Divine sonship attains its completion. He is not merely *a* son of God in the sense of the other members of the Davidic line. He is *the* Son of God, as may be seen from the following two psalms both of which are interpreted of the Messiah in Rabbinic writings.

> He shall cry to me, 'Thou art my Father, my God, and the Rock of my salvation.' And I will make him the first-born, the highest of the kings of the earth. My mercy[27] I will keep for him for ever, and my covenant shall stand firm with him.
>
> *Psalm 89: 26-28 (89: 27-29 Heb.)*

In the Midrash, verse 27 of Psalm 89 is interpreted of the Messiah.[28]

> Why do the nations rage, and the peoples plot in vain! The kings of the earth rise in rebellion, and the rulers take counsel together, against Jehovah and against His Messiah (saying) "Let us break their bands asunder, and cast away their cords from us."
>
> He who is enthroned in the heavens laughs, Jehovah mocks at them. Then he will speak to them in his wrath, and terrify them in his fury, (saying). "I have established my king on Zion, my holy hill."
>
> I will declare the decree! Jehovah said to me, "You are my son, today I have begotten you. Ask of me, and I will give the nations for your inheritance, and the ends of the earth shall be your possession. You shall break them with a rod of iron, like a potter's vessel you shall dash them in pieces."
>
> And now, you kings, show yourselves wise; be admonished, you judges of the earth! Serve Jehovah with fear, and rejoice with trembling. Kiss the son,[29] lest he be angry, and you perish in the way; for his anger may easily be kindled; blessed are all they that take refuge in him.
>
> *Psalm 2: 1-12*

Psalm 2 is one of the great Messianic psalms. The invasion by a group of nations of the Judean kingdom in the days of Jehoshafat may have been the historical basis of Psalm 2. The prophetic writer

---

27. The word "chesed" translated "mercy" in the above text is often rendered "grace", "covenant-love.".
28. Exodus R. 19:8.
29. This has reference to the Person to whom Jehovah says in verse 7: "You are my son, today I have begotten you."

may have seen in this event a forerunner of a world-wide revolt of the nations against Jehovah and His Messiah taking place at the end of the age, during the period immediately preceding Messiah's coming. "The Old Testament," Delitzsch declares, "knows of no kingship to which world dominion was promised and to which [Divine] sonship was ascribed (2 Samuel 7:14; Psalm 89:28) save the Davidic. The Psalm celebrates the world-dominion of a king who is a son of David and a Son of God."[30]

There are many references and comments in Rabbinic writings on the Messianic significance of this Psalm. The rise of the nations against Jehovah and His Messiah is applied by one source to the invasion of the Land of Israel by the armies of Gog in the last days of history prior to the appearance of the Messiah as recorded in Ezekiel 38 and 39.[31]

Another source likens the rebellious uprising "against God, and His Messiah" to a robber who stands defiantly behind the palace of the king, and says, "If I shall find the son of the king, I shall lay hold on him, and crucify him, and kill him in a cruel death. But the Holy Spirit mocks at him, 'He that sits in the heavens shall laugh.'[32]

In his introduction to Sanhedrin, chapter 10, Maimonides[33] says: "The prophets and saints have longed for the days of the Messiah, and great has been their desire towards him, for there will be with him the gathering together of the righteous and the administration of goodness, and wisdom, and royal righteousness, with the abundance of his uprightness and the spread of his wisdom, and his approach to God, as it is said: Jehovah said unto me, Thou art my son, today have I begotten thee."

Another reference states that when the hour comes, God speaks to the Messiah about the making of a new covenant, and He says to him: "This day have I begotten thee."[34]

---

30. Franz Delitzsch, BIBLICAL COMMENTARY ON THE PSALMS (Hodder and Stoughton: London, 1894), Vol. 1, p. 118.
31. Berach, 7b; Abod. Zarah 3b; Midrash on Ps. 2.
32. YALKUT, Vol. 2 par. 620, p.90a.
33. Physician and great Talmudic scholar born in Spain in 1135 whose articles of faith have been included in the daily Prayer Book.
34. MIDRASH on Psalm 2:7.

With reference to the statement in Psalm 2:8 (Ask of me, and I will give the nations for your inheritance") we have the following comment in the Talmud: "Our Rabbis have taught us in a Mishna with reference to Messiah who is about to be revealed quickly, that the Holy One, blessed be He, says to him, 'Ask of Me,' for it is said, 'I will declare the decree. Ask of me and I will give nations for thine inheritance.' "[35]

Psalm 2 is divided into four strophes or parts, each consisting of three sentences. The first strophe is an introduction. We find ourselves in the midst of a revolt on the part of ungodly Gentile nations, aiming to eradicate the influence of Biblical religion in the world.

In the second part (verses 4-6), the prophet sees how Jehovah thunders against the rebels in His hot displeasure, and in defiance of the rebellious nations He proclaims the establishment of His Messianic King on David's throne in Jerusalem.

In the third portion, the Messianic King Himself speaks. He declares who He is and what He is to do by virture of a Divine decree. The Hebrew word rendered decree in English signifies a statue or a law. The source of the decree He refers to is Jehovah Himself, it therefore is unshakable. The decree contains a declaration that He, the Messianic King of the Davidic line, is God's Son: "Thou art my Son, today I have begotten thee!" Delitzsch states that as far as Biblical revelation is concerned this Divine decree was first made known to the world in the Nathan Prophecy in which God promised David that He will be a Father to his seed.[36]

By virtue of His sonship, He received from Jehovah sovereignty over the nations of the earth, for the earth and all its fullness belong to Jehovah. He only needs to desire to assume sovereignty over the nations, it is His for the asking. "Ask of me, and I will give the nations for Thy inheritance, and the ends of the earth for thy possession."

The concluding portion of the Psalm (verses 10-12) is recited again by the Psalmist. In the first portion of the Psalm the poetic seer described a rebellion of nations against Jehovah and His Messianic

---

35.   Sukkah 52a.
36.   2 Samuel 7:14; also Psalm 89:27.

King. In the last portion he gives an admonition to the rulers of the nations to serve Jehovah with reverence and to submit to His Messianic King: "Serve Jehovah with fear . . . Kiss the son . . ." The word "kiss" signifies to pay homage. When Samuel installed Saul as king of Israel, he kissed him as an expression of his homage to the newly inaugurated king.[37] Aben Ezra,[38] one of the great Jewish commentators of the Bible, gives the following exposition of the statement "Kiss the Son": "As 'serve Jehovah' refers to God, so 'Kiss the Son' refers to His Messiah; the meaning of 'bar' (used here instead of the usual 'ben' for son) is the same here as in Proverbs 31:1 where the same word 'bar' is used for son." He goes on to say that kissing the king as a sign of homage is a custom practiced among the world's nations.

David Kimchi, another great medieval Jewish expositor of the Bible, interprets "Kiss the Son" as referring to the Messiah and he adds the following comment: "This is the interpretation of our Rabbis of blessed memory."

---

37. 1 Samuel 10:1.
38. Born in Toledo, Spain, in the beginning of 12th century.

CHAPTER 2
THE BIRTH OF JESUS THE MESSIAH

I. "Behold, The Virgin Shall Conceive"

II. Was Messiah's Supranatural Death Necessary?
   1. God Alone Is The Source Of Our Redemption
   2. Messiah — The Second Adam

CHAPTER 2
THE BIRTH OF JESUS THE MESSIAH

Now the birth of Jesus the Messiah[1] took place as follows: When his mother Mary had been betrothed to Joseph, before they came together she was found with child of the Holy Spirit. And Joseph her husband, being a just man, and not willing to expose her, resolved to divorce her privately. But while he was reflecting on these things, behold, an angel of the Lord appeared to him in a dream, saying, "Joseph, son of David, do not be afraid to take Mary as your wife; for that which has been conceived in her is of the Holy Spirit. She will bear a son; and you shall call his name Jesus, for he will save[2] his people from their sins." All this took place that what was spoken by the Lord through the prophet might be fulfilled, saying, "Behold, the virgin shall conceive and bear a son, and they shall call his name Immanuel,"[3] which means "God with us." And Joseph arose from his sleep, and did as the angel of the Lord commanded him, and he took her as his wife. But he knew her not[4] until she gave birth to a son; and he called his name Jesus.

Matthew 1: 18-25

Now in the sixth month[5] the angel Gabriel was sent from God to a city in Galilee, named Nazareth. To a virgin engaged to a man whose name was Joseph, of the house of David; and the virgin's name was Mary. And he came to her and said, "Hail, O favored one, the Lord is with you!" But she was greatly troubled at this statement, and kept pondering what kind of salutation this might be. And the angel said to her, "Do not be afraid, Mary, for you have found favor with God. And behold, you will conceive in your womb and bear a son, and you shall name him Jesus. He will be great, and will be called the Son of the Most High; and the Lord God will give to him the throne of his father David. And he will reign over the house of Jacob forever; and of his kingdom there will be no end." And Mary said to the angel,

---

1. The Hebrew word "Messiah" is used here instead of "Christ."
2. The words "he will save" are derived from Yeshua, the Hebrew name of Jesus.
3. Isaiah 7:14.
4. Had no marital relations.
5. The sixth month since Elizabeth, the mother of John the Baptizer, became pregnant.

"How can this be, since I know not a man?"[6] And the angel said to her, "The Holy Spirit will come upon you, and the power of the Most High will overshadow you, therefore the holy thing which is begotten shall be called the Son of God . . . For with God nothing will be impossible."

Luke 1: 26-35, 37

I. "BEHOLD, THE VIRGIN SHALL CONCEIVE"

Matthew's Gospel concludes the angelic announcement to Joseph concerning the birth of Jesus with the following comment:

All this took place that what was spoken by the Lord through the prophet might be fulfilled, saying, "Behold, the virgin shall conceive and bear a son, and they shall call his name Immanuel," which means 'God with us.'

Matthew 1: 22-23

Was Matthew correct in translating into "virgin" the Hebrew word "almah" used by Isaiah in the Immanuel prophecy? We must say that he was no less correct than the Jewish translators of the Old Testament into Greek who had rendered the word "almah" into "virgin" long before the birth of Jesus. Greek was the language of the civilized world of that day, and the Greek Old Testament, the so-called Septuagint, was the Bible used by Greek-speaking Jews.

In the Hebrew Old Testament there are two words conveying the meaning of "virgin." One is the word "bethulah," the second is the word "almah." According to Franz Delitzsch, "bethulah signifies a maiden living in seclusion in her parents' house and still a long way from matrimony;" "almah," on the other hand, "is applied to one fully mature, and approaching the time of her marriage." Both terms, Delitzsch maintains, can be used of persons who were betrothed, and even of such as were married.[7]

---

6. "I have no husband" — Revised Standard Version; "I am a virgin" — New American Standard Bible.
7. Franz Delitzsch, THE PROPHECIES OF ISAIAH (Wm. B. Eerdmans Publishing Company: Grand Rapids, Michigan, 1949), Vol. 1, p. 217.

> Lament like a virgin girded with sackcloth for the husband
> of her youth.
>
> *Joel 1: 8*

In the Hebrew text of the above passage the person called upon to mourn for the husband of her youth is designated by the noun "bethulah."

According to Cyrus H. Gordon, eminent Jewish scholar in Semitics, "the commonly held view that 'virgin' is Christian, whereas 'young woman' is Jewish[8] is not quite true. The fact is that the Septuagint, which is the Jewish translation made in pre-Christian Alexandria, takes *almah* to mean 'virgin' here. Accordingly, the New Testament follows the Jewish interpretation of Isaiah 7:14. Little purpose would be served in repeating the learned expositions that Hebraists have already contributed in their attempt to clarify the point at issue. It all boils down to this: the distinctive Hebrew word for virgin is *bethulah,* whereas *almah* means a 'young woman' who may be a virgin, but is not necessarily so." Dr. Gordon cites an excerpt from one of the recently discovered Ugarit texts dating back to around 1400 B.C. celebrating the marriage of the male and female lunar deities. In this particular text there is a prediction that the lunar goddess will bear a son. In one sentence the bride is called by a word which is "the exact etymological counterpart of the Hebrew 'almah'; in another sentence she is called by "the etymological counterpart of the Hebrew 'bethulah.' "Therefore", Dr. Gordon concludes, "the New Testament rendering of 'almah' as 'virgin' for Isaiah 7:14 rests on the older Jewish interpretation, which in turn is now borne out for *precisely this annunciation formula* by a text that is not only pre-Isaianic but is pre-Mosaic in the form that we now have it on a clay tablet."[9]

In the Hebrew Old Testament the noun "almah" is used to designate a virgin in the following passages.

> Before he had done speaking, behold, Rebekah, who was
> born to Bethuel the son of Milcah, the wife of Nahor,

---

8. The author means that it is not proper to maintain that to translate 'almah" into "virgin" is a Christian and therefore an incorrect, rendering, whereas, the rendering of "almah"into "young woman" is a Jewish and therefore the correct translation.
9. Cyrus H. Goron, "Almah in Isaiah 7:14", art. in JOURNAL OF BIBLE AND RELIGION, XXI, 2 (Aprill, 1953), p. 106 Used by permission.

Abraham's brother, came out with her water jar upon her
shoulder. The maiden was very fair to look upon, a virgin,
whom no man had known.

Genesis 24: 15-16

In the above passage, we have the Hebrew word "bethulah" in verse
16, which is the "distinctive Hebrew word for virgin" according to
Dr. Gordon. Relating his experience of how he happened to select
Rebekah to be Isaac's wife, Abraham's servant said this:

"I came today to the spring, and said, O Jehovah, the God
of my master Abraham, if now thou wilt prosper the way which
I go. Behold, I am standing by the spring of water; and it shall
come to pass, that when the virgin comes out to draw water, and
I say to her, 'Give me, I pray, a little water from your pitcher to
drink.' And she will say to me, 'Drink, and I will also draw for
your camels,' let her be the woman whom Jehovah has appointed for my master's son."

Genesis 24: 42-44

The word "virgin" in verse 43 is the noun "almah" in the Hebrew
text. Rebekah who in verse 16 is distinctly described as a virgin and
designated by the word "bethulah", is in verse 43 identified by the
word "almah."

Describing how Miriam was instrumental in saving her brother,
the infant Moses, from death, we read the following:

Then his sister said to Pharaoh's daughter, "Shall I go and
call you a nurse from the Hebrew women to nurse the child for
you?" And Pharaoh's daughter said to her, "Go"; so the girl
went and called the child's mother.

Exodus 2: 7-8

The "girl" or "maid" in verse 8 is the English translation of the word
"almah" in the Hebrew text. "Almah" is used here to designate
Miriam, the sister of the baby Moses, who was evidently not married
at that time.

In the Song of Solomon, the word "almah" in the plural occurs
in the following passage.

O that you would kiss me with the kisses of your mouth: for
your love is better than wine. Your anointing oils are fragrant,
your name is oil poured out; therefore do the maidens love you.

Song of Solomon 1: 2-3

The word "maidens" in verse 3 is the Hebrew word "almah" in the plural. It is rightly suggested that the plural of the Hebrew word "almah" rendered "maidens" in the English text could hardly refer to married women.

The same may be said about another passage in the same book in which the Hebrew word "almah" occurs also in the plural.

> There are sixty queens and eighty concubines, and maidens without number.
>
> *Song of Solomon 6:8*

The noun "maidens" being the English rendering of the plural of the Hebrew word "almah" evidently refers to unmarried women.

To summarize, the two words, "bethulah" and "almah," are used in the Old Testament to designate a virgin, a young woman of marriageable age, and even a young married woman. Since the Immanuel prophecy was intended to serve as a sign or proof for King Ahaz, the sign had to make sense, otherwise it could not have been a meaningful sign. Had the word "almah" in the Immanuel prophecy been used to indicate a "virgin," the only sense it would have conveyed was that the future Messianic King would be born out of wedlock, in which case it would have made no sense either to Isaiah or to King Ahaz or to anyone else of that day. In the context of the historical situation during which the Immanuel Prophecy was given, this prophecy brought to Isaiah and his contemporaries a two-fold message. To the Davidic King Ahaz it announced God's judgment upon the Davidic dynasty whose failings were climaxed by the reckless decision of Ahaz to invite Assyrian intervention. The long-range effect of this policy was the destruction of the Judean state and the downfall of the Davidic dynasty. The after-effects of these tragic events upon the Messianic Hope would be well-nigh disastrous. The Messianic Prince, who in accordance with God's promises must spring from David's house, will come at a time when the Davidic line will have been all but extinguished. The disinherited Messianic Prince will not be born in the proud royal city of Jerusalem, but, as indicated by Micah, in Bethlehem, the insignificant birthplace of Jesse, the father of David. Messiah's mother will not be, as she would have been, had the Davidic dynasty remained faithful, a queen residing in the royal palace; instead, she will be just an "almah," some *unnamed and insignificant maiden.* This essentially was the meaning which the word *"almah"* conveyed to Isaiah and his contemporaries, the only meaning which at that particular time could have made sense. The Bethlehem prophecy of Micah and the Immanuel Prophecy of Isaiah combined to stress the element of *humiliation* associated with Messiah's birth, as part of the working out of God's judgment upon Israel — the nation and its Davidic dynasty.

When the angel Gabriel announced to Mary that she was pregnant and that the child she will give birth to will be none other than the long-promised Messiah, she was greatly troubled in her heart and she said,

> "How can this be since I have no husband?"
>
> *Luke 1:34*

We can almost detect the tone of despair in Mary's voice. What will be the reaction of Joseph, the man to whom she was betrothed, when he hears that she is pregnant? But this is not all. If we take into consideration the decree issued by the heathen Roman government ordering a census in the whole Roman empire which made it necessary for Joseph and Mary to go south all the way to Bethlehem to register in the city of their ancestor David; their inability, possibly because of their limited material means, to find in Bethlehem proper accommodations, probably because the town of Bethlehem was crowded with people who came there for the purpose of registration; their selection of a stable to serve as the maternity room when Mary went into labor, and the use of a manger in the stable in place of a crib for the newborn child; finally their decision to flee to Egypt in order to escape the murderous designs of the half-Idumean tyrant Herod who had usurped the throne of the Jewish Kingdom of that day and who was determined to exterminate all potential legitimate rivals to the throne — and we have a set of most humiliating circumstances connected with the birth of the Messianic King which gave to the Immanuel prophecy a fulfillment over and beyond that which Isaiah and his contemporaries were in a position to visualize or comprehend.

But judgment alone is seldom, if ever, God's way with Israel, or with mankind in general. And so the other side of the Immanuel Prophecy contained a message of consolation addressed to the faithful remnant of Isaiah's day. God would not permit man's unfaithfulness to nullify His redemptive purpose. The sinfulness of the nation and the shortcomings of the Davidic dynasty led to the destruction of ancient Israel and the downfall of the Davidic dynasty. But through this Immanuel Israel will be revived and the Davidic dynasty restored to a never-ceasing existence. This, in fulfillment of God's promise to David, as seen in the following passage already cited before.

> "And your house and your kingdom shall be made sure for
> ever before me; your throne shall be established for ever."
>   *2 Samuel 7:16*

It was this Divine promise to King David which formed the basis of the Isaiah prophecy concerning the Messianic King uttered some three centuries later as seen in the passage below which also was quoted before in this work.

> For to us a child is born, to us a son is given; and the
> government will be upon his shoulder, and his name will be
> called "Wonderful Counsellor, Mighty God, Everlasting
> Father, Prince of Peace." Of the increase of his government and
> of peace there will be no end, upon the throne of David, and
> over his kingdom, to establish it, and to uphold it with justice
> and righteousness from this time forth and for evermore; the
> zeal of Jehovah of hosts will do this.
>   *Isaiah 9: 6-7 (9: 5-6 Heb.)*

As to the lowly hamlet of Bethlehem, it became enshrined in the hearts of millions all over the world, in every age and generation, as the little town where the hopes and fears of thousands of years met on the night of Messiah's birth. And Mary, the unnamed and insignificant maiden of Isaiah 7:14, fully aware of her low position ("For He has had regard for the humble state of His handmaid," Luke 1:48), became the most blessed of women; while Mary's son Jesus who from birth on experienced want and poverty, is the Immanuel of Isaiah's prophecy, God with us, the Son of man, the Son of God, who brought man nearer to God than any human being in history.

II. WAS MESSIAH'S SUPRANATURAL BIRTH NECESSARY?

I am using the adjective "supranatural" advisedly for lack of a better term. "Natural" and "supranatural" are human terms just as time is a terrestrial idea. With God everything is natural or everything is supranatural. The conception, the prenatal development and birth of every new life, is a supranatural marvel. And yet, the birth of Jesus the Messiah was different from the birth of any other human being. Why? On this side of heaven we shall probably never know all the considerations in the mind of God who ordained that the birth of Jesus shall be extraordinary and unique. But there is enough in the Biblical text to shed much precious light on this subject, as seen from the following.

1. GOD ALONE IS THE SOURCE OF OUR REDEMPTION

Of the two accounts of the birth of Jesus the one recorded in the Gospel of Matthew is summarized in the opening sentence as follows:

> The book of the genealogy of Jesus the Messiah, the son of David, the son of Abraham
>
> *Matthew 1:1*

This statement immediately links up the birth of the Messiah with the Divine election of Abraham. In the second account of the birth of Jesus, as found in the Gospel of Luke, we are told that to Mary's bewildering question, "How can this be, since I have no husband?" addressed to the angel who declared to her that she was bearing in her womb the life of the Messianic child, the angel, among other things, replied,

> "For with God nothing shall be impossible."
>
> *Luke 1:37*

to which Mary responded in words of complete surrender,

> "Behold, the handmaid of the Lord; be it unto me according to your word."
>
> *Luke 1:38*

The angelic declaration "For with God nothing will be impossible" also connects the birth of Jesus with the story of Abraham. Were these words of the angel intended to direct Mary's attention back to Sarah, Abraham's wife, to whom an angel had spoken the same words when he announced to her that she will give birth to a son?[10] Abraham was seventy-five years old and Sarah sixty-five years when

---

10.   Genesis 18:14.

they arrived in the Promised Land. Upon his departure from Haran God made to Abraham the three-fold promise, namely, that he would be made into a great nation; that the land of Canaan would become his possession; and that through him all nations would be blessed.[11] But Sarah, Abraham's wife, could bear no children. How then could these tremendous Divine promises ever be realized? Abraham and Sarah decided to give, as it were, to God a helping hand. Sarah turned Hagar, her Egyptian slave girl, over to Abraham to become his concubine, with the understanding that the son born of this union shall become Abraham's and Sarah's heir.[12] And so Ishmael was born. Abraham was eighty-six years old when Ishmael was born. How shocked and mystified Abraham was when some thirteen years later God declared to him that not Ishmael, but a son to be born of Sarah, will be his heir.[13] Within one year God's Word was fulfilled, and Sarah gave birth to a son. Abraham was one hundred years old, and Sarah ninety years when Isaac was born.[14] When the announcement was made to Abraham that within one year Sarah will give birth to a son, Sarah ironically laughed within herself, saying, how could she give birth to a child when she was old. Then the angel replied: "Is there anything too hard for Jehovah?"[15] the same words which two millenia later the angel was to say to Mary.

If God was determined that a son born of Sarah shall be Abraham's heir, why did He have to wait twenty-four years? In the Old Testament the answer is found in the following passage.

> Look up to the rock whence you are hewn, and to the hollow of the pit whence you are dug. Look up to Abraham your forefather, and to Sarah who bore you; for he was but one when I called him, and blessed him, and multiplied him.
>
> *Isaiah 51:1-2*

Abraham and Sarah were intentionally kept childless by God until they were "as good as dead," as dead as the rock and the hollow of the pit, as far as their ability to give birth to a child was concerned. This was done to emphasize a fundamental Biblical truth that God's

---

11. Genesis 12:2-3, 7.
12. Genesis 16:1-2.
13. Genesis 17:15-21.
14. Genesis 21:1-7.
15. Genesis 18:13-14.

redemptive purpose which He set in motion with the call of Abraham was to be carried out not by man's power or human ingenuity, but by the power of God alone. *It is God, not man, who is the author of our salvation.* This phenomenon was to be repeated, on a far grander scale, with the birth of the Messiah in whom and through whom God's redemptive plan begun with Abraham was to be fully accomplished. And this child, so miraculously conceived and born, was to be Immanuel, God-with-us, for through Him God's yearning to identify Himself fully with man, manifested in the Old Testament dispensation "in many and various ways," was to attain full realization.

2. MESSIAH – THE SECOND ADAM

To Mary's perplexing question, how could she be pregnant when she had no intimate relations with any man, the angel also said,

> "The Holy Spirit will come upon you, and the power of the Most High will overshadow you; therefore the child to be born will be called holy, the Son of God."
>
> *Luke 1:35*

This angelic reference to the Holy Spirit takes us back to the opening lines of the Biblical creation story.

> In the beginning God created the heavens and the earth. The earth was without form and void, and darkness was upon the face of the deep; and the Spirit of God was moving over the face of the waters.
>
> *Genesis 1: 1-2*

The literal meaning of the word "moving" is "hovering." It is applied to the hovering and brooding of a bird over its young, to warm them, and develop their vital powers. It was this "creative Spirit of God, the principle of all life (Psalm 33:6, 104:30), which worked upon the formless, lifeless mass, separating, quickening, and preparing the living forms, which were called into being by the creative words that followed."[16] It may be of some interest to cite here a Rabbinic

---

16.   C. F. Keil and Franz Delitzsch, THE PENTATEUCH (T. And T. Clark: Edinburgh, n.d.), Vol. 1, p. 49; see also Deuteronomy 32:11.

paraphrase of the above statement in Genesis with reference to the Spirit of God: " 'The Spirit of the Lord was moving over the face of the waters' - this is the Spirit of the King Messiah."[17]

The uniqueness of Messiah's birth was perhaps meant to indicate that He was the Second Adam, the New Adam, with whom and through whom God was bringing into existence a new humanity. We know that "Son of Man," i.e., Son of Adam, was a Messianic title by which Jesus frequently identified Himself. This idea that Jesus represents a new creation is frequently taught by the New Testament writers. Here we will cite only two of these passages.

> Then as one man's[18] trespass led to condemnation for all men, so one man's[19] act of righteousness leads to acquittal and life for all men. For as by one man's disobedience many were made sinners, so by one man's obedience many will be made righteous.
>
> *Romans 5: 18-19*

> The first man was from the earth, a man of dust; the second man is from heaven. As was the man of dust, so are those who are of the dust, and as is the man of heaven, so are those who are of heaven. Just as we have borne the image of the man of dust, we shall also bear the image of the man of heaven.
>
> *1 Corinthians 15: 47-49*

As the supranatural birth of Isaac had as its purpose to give rise to a new and extraordinary nation, a nation which was to stand apart and not be reckoned among the nations,[20] to be used of God in the realization of His redemptive purpose for the world, so was the supranatural birth of the Messiah intended to be the precursor of a new humanity.

> Jesus answered him, "Truly, truly, I say to you, unless one is born anew, he cannot see the kingdom of God".
>
> *John 3:3*

> Therefore, if any one is in the Messiah, he is a new creation; the old has passed away, behold, the new has come.
>
> *2 Corinthians 5:17*

---

17. Genesis R. 2.
18. Referring to Adam.
19. Referring to Messiah Jesus.
20. Numbers 22:9.

ADDENDUM

In Part One of this work we saw how the Messiah is designated in the Old Testament Scriptures by a variety of names, such as "Shiloh," "Immanuel," "Wonderful," "Counsellor" (or "Wonderful Counsellor"), "Mighty God," "Everlasting Father," "Prince of Peace," "Jehovah our Righteousness," etc. All these Messianic titles describe various aspects of His personality and foretell the many facets of His mission. His proper or personal name, the name "Yeshua" ("Jesus"), brings together the various elements contained in all the Messianic titles bestowed upon Him in the Old Testament, for it is in the name of "Yeshua" that man finds his full salvation.

This personal name of the Messiah is not mentioned in the Old Testament. There is, however, a statement in the Old Testament Scriptures which implies that Messiah's personal name would not be revealed until just before His birth, as seen in the opening words of the following great Messianic chapter.

> Listen to me, O coastlands, and hearken, you peoples from afar: Jehovah called me from the womb, from the body of my mother has he made mention of my name.
>
> *Isaiah 49:1*

David Baron, the saintly and scholarly Hebrew Christian of a previous generation, suggested that one of the possible reasons for not disclosing Messiah's personal name until just before His birth was to prevent impostors from assuming this name. In A.D. 132, the man who dragged the Jews of Palestine into a second armed struggle with the mighty Roman empire with frightful consequences for world Jewry, posed as the Messiah by assuming the name "Bar Kochba" ("Son of a Star"), in reference to the Messianic prophecy attributed to Balaam in the following passage.

> I see him, but not now; I behold him, but not nigh: a star shall come forth out of Jacob, and a scepter shall rise out of Israel . . .
>
> *Numbers 24:17*

CHAPTER 3
THE TEACHINGS OF JESUS THE MESSIAH

I. What Did Jesus Claim For His Teachings
   1. Divine Authority
   2. Permanence
   3. Their Divine Origin Can Be Tested Subjectively
   4. Their Divine Origin Can Be Tested Objectively

II. The Teachings Of Jesus Concerning The Fatherhood Of God

III. The Teachings Of Jesus Concerning Man
   1. Man Is Evil But Has A Capacity For Good
   2. Man Can Serve Only One Master
   3. Happiness Does Not Depend On An Abundance Of Things
   4. The Greatest Mosaic Commandment
   5. Messiah's New Commandment

IV. Jesus' View Of Human Sin
   1. Sin Is Bondage
   2. Sin Can Become Unpardonable

V. Jesus' View Of His Mission
   1. He Came To Change Human Lives
   2. He Came To Reveal God's Search For Man
   3. He Came To Establish God's Law

VI. The Kingdom Of God
   1. The Concept Of The Kingdom Of God In The Old Testament
   2. The Concept Of The Kingdom Of God In The New Testament

VII. The Realization Of The Kingdom Of God

VIII. The Return Of Messiah Jesus

IX. The Purpose Of Messiah's Second Coming
   1. The First Stage Of The Messianic Program
   2. The Second Stage Of The Messianic Program
   3. The Third Stage Of The Messianic Program

CHAPTER 3

THE TEACHINGS OF JESUS THE MESSIAH

The discussion in this chapter is concerned with some of the teachings of Messiah Jesus, and only with those attributed directly to Him.

I. WHAT DID JESUS CLAIM FOR HIS TEACHINGS?

1. DIVINE AUTHORITY

> For I did not speak on my own initiative, but the Father himself who sent me has given me commandment, what to say, and what to speak.
>
> *John 12: 49*

2. PERMANENCE

> Heaven and earth will pass away, but my words shall not pass away.
>
> *Matthew 24: 35*

3. THEIR DIVINE ORIGIN CAN BE TESTED SUBJECTIVELY

> Jesus therefore answered them, and said, "My teaching is not mine, but his who sent me. If any man is willing to do his will he shall know of the teaching, whether it is of God or whether I speak of myself."
>
> *John 7: 16-17*

4. THEIR DIVINE ORIGIN CAN BE TESTED OBJECTIVELY

> If I do not do the works of my Father, do not believe me. But if I do them, though you do not believe me, believe the works; that you may know and understand that the Father is in me, and I in the Father.
>
> *John 10: 37-38*

If He did not do the work of God, how are we to explain the never-ceasing influence of Jesus in the last nineteen centuries? In his monumental work, A STUDY OF HISTORY, Toynbee devotes as much space in the index of the last volume to Jesus of Nazareth as to any of the following six historical persons: Plato, Alexander the Great, Julius Caesar, Charlemagne, Mohammed, Napoleon. Years ago a Jewish writer posed the following question concerning the influence of Jesus in world history: "What is it about this man to explain his ascendancy in the world? A multitude of sages, prophets, poets and kings bequeathed to the world their teachings; but only one broke all human bounds. If we examine this question objectively and logically, we must ask again, why did one single soul succeed to such a place of honor? Is he the only jewel in God's treasure house, and are all other souls mere broken pottery fragments?"[1]

In a conversation with General Bertrand on St. Helena Island, Napoleon made the following statement about Messiah Jesus: "It is this which to me is absolute proof of Christ's divinity. I myself was able to inspire masses of men to lay down their lives. But it was necessary for me to be present with them in person in order to ignite in their hearts a holy flame of inspiration with the electric spark of my eyes and the power of the sound of my voice. Undoubtedly, I possess the secret of that magic power capable of urging people forward, but I am unable to transfer this power to others. I could not share this power with any of my generals nor could I perpetuate in the hearts of men a love for me, and through that love to do wonders in them without the intermediating help of the physical and material. The same was true of Caesar and Alexander the Macedonian. In time we will be forgotten, our names will remain mere themes for school children. What a gulf there is between my loneliness and the eternal kingdom of Jesus Christ, who is loved, to whom people pray, and of whom they preach!"[2]

The following passage is from Will Durant's CAESAR AND CHRIST. "We may accept the old belief that the morals of the early Christians were a reproving example to the pagan world. After the weakening of the ancient faiths had removed their frail support

---

1. A. Steinman, in one of the old issues of the Hebrew periodical TKUFAH; quoted by J. I. Landsman, DER WEG (Warsaw), May, 1927.
2. Prof. F. Ferster, CHRIST AND HUMAN LIFE (Munich, 1922), p. 93; quoted by J. I. Landsman In DER WEG (Warsaw), May 1927.

from the moral life, and the attempt of Stoicism at an almost natural ethic had failed with all but the best of men, a new supernatural ethic accomplished . . . the task of regulating the jungle instincts of man into a viable morality. The hope of the coming Kingdom carried with it a belief in a Judge who saw every act, knew man's every thought, and could not be eluded or deceived. To this divine surveillance was added mutual scrutiny: in these little groups [of Christians] sin could with difficulty find a hiding place; . . . Abortion and infanticide, which were decimating pagan society, were forbidden to Christians as the equivalents of murder; in many instances Christians rescued exposed infants, baptized them, and brought them up with the aid of the [Christian] community fund . . . In general, Christianity continued and exaggerated the moral sternness of the embattled Jews. Divorce was allowed only when a pagan wished to annul a marriage with a convert . . . Homosexual practices were condemned with an earnestness rare in antiquity . . . The general picture of Christian morals in this period is one of piety, mutual loyalty, marital fidelity, and a quiet happiness in the possession of a confident faith. The younger Pliny was compelled to report to emperor Trajan that the Christians led peaceful and exemplary lives[3] . . .

"All in all, no more attractive religion has ever been presented to mankind. It offered itself without restriction to all individuals, classes, and nations; it was not limited to one people, like Judaism, nor to the freemen of one state, like the official cults of Greece and Rome. By making all men heirs of Christ's victory over death, Christianity announced the basic equality of men, and made transiently trivial all differences of earthly degree. To the miserable, maimed, bereaved, disheartened, and humiliated it brought a new virtue of compassion, and an ennobling dignity; it gave them the inspiring figure, story, and ethic of Christ; it brightened their lives with the hope of the coming Kingdom, and endless happiness beyond the grave. To even the greatest sinners it promised forgiveness, and their full acceptance into the community of the saved. To minds harassed with the insoluble problems of orgin and destiny, evil and suffering, it brought a system of divinely revealed doctrine in which the simplest soul could find mental rest. To men and

---

3. Will Durant, CEASAR AND CHRIST (Simon and Schuster, Inc.: New York, 1944), pp. 598-599. Copyright 1944 by Will Durant, Reprinted by permission of Simon and Schuster, Inc.

women imprisoned in the prose of poverty and toil it brought the poetry of the sacraments and the Eucharist, a ritual that made every major event of life a vital scene in the moving drama of God and man. Into the moral vacuum of a dying paganism, into the coldness of Stoicism and the corruption of Epicureanism, into a world sick of brutality, cruelty, oppression, and sexual chaos, into a pacified empire that seemed no longer to need the masculine virtues or the gods of war, it brought a new morality of brotherhood, kindliness, decency, and peace."[4]

He never went to college, He never wrote a book. He was a poor carpenter. His public ministry lasted about three-and-a-half years. When the tide of public opinion turned against Him, His followers left Him and fled. One of them turned Him over to His enemies. "He was nailed to a cross between two criminals. His executioners gambled for the only piece of property He had on earth while He was dying — and that was His coat. When He was dead He was taken down and laid in a borrowed grave through the pity of a friend. Nineteen wide centuries have come and gone and today He is the centerpiece of the human race and the leader of the column of progress. I am far within the mark when I say that all the armies that ever marched, and all the navies that were ever built, and all the parliaments that ever sat, and all the kings that ever reigned, put together have not affected the life of man upon this earth as powerfully as has that One Solitary Life."[5]

"If I do not do the works of my Father, do not believe me, believe the works, that you may know and understand that the Father is in me, and I in the Father."

II. THE TEACHINGS OF JESUS CONCERNING THE FATHERHOOD OF GOD

This was one of the central teachings of Messiah Jesus concerning God. He often spoke of God as "my Father" or "the Father." When addressing His followers He referred to God as "Your Father." "Your Father . . . sees," "Your . . . Father knows," "Your . . . Father feeds." The Fatherhood of God is taught in the Old Testa-

---

4.   Ibid., p. 602.
5.   "One Solitary Life," by an Unknown Author.

ment and in post-exilic Jewish writings. But in none of these does the Fatherhood of God hold as prominent a place as in the mind of Jesus. It is said that Jesus restored the reality of God's Fatherhood to man's knowledge. He gathered around Himself men and women from all walks and stations of life and He made them feel they are members of one family with God as their Father. God — He taught — is concerned about the needs of all His creatures.

> "Look at the birds of the air, that they do not sow, neither do they reap, nor gather into barns; and yet your heavenly Father feeds them; are you not worth much more than they?"
>
> *Matthew 6:26*

III. THE TEACHINGS OF JESUS CONCERNING MAN

1. MAN IS EVIL BUT HAS A CAPACITY FOR GOOD

> If you then, being evil, know how to give good gifts to your children, how much more shall your Father who is in heaven give what is good to those who ask him!
>
> *Matthew 7:11*

It is this His firm belief in man's capacity for good that underlies His desire to restore all who have left the path of righteousness and moral uprightness, whether it is the despised and dishonest publican, the woman caught in adultery, or the repentant thief on the cross.

2. MAN CAN SERVE ONLY ONE MASTER

Human life cannot be torn between two conflicting loyalties or passions. We either live for God or for ourselves.

> No one can serve two masters; for either he will hate the one and love the other, or he will hold to one and despise the other; you cannot serve God and Mammon.[6]
>
> *Matthew 6:24*

---

6. Riches, or material things.

3. HAPPINESS DOES NOT DEPEND ON AN ABUNDANCE OF THINGS

> And he said to them, "Beware, and be on guard against every form of greed; for not even when one has an abundance does his life consist of his possessions."
>
> *Luke 12:15*

> For what will a man be profited, if he gains the whole world and forfeits his soul? Or what will a man give in exchange for his soul?
>
> *Matthew 16: 26*

4. THE GREATEST MOSAIC COMMANDMENT

To a question asked of Him what He thought constitutes the greatest commandment in the Law of Moses, Jesus quoted the following statements from Deuteronomy and Leviticus.

> "You shall love Jehovah your God with all your heart, and with all your soul, and with all your mind." This is the great and foremost commandment. And a second is like it, "You shall love your neighbor as yourself." On these two commandments depend the whole Law and the Prophets.
>
> *Matthew 22: 37-40*

Already in the Decalogue, Israel's basic law, man's attitude to God and his moral and social life are implied to be interdependent: a right relationship to our fellow men is determined by our right relationship to God. *God, not man, is the source of human morality.* Israel's failure under the Sinai Covenant generated a conviction in the prophets that for man to live in accordance with God's law the human heart must be cleansed by God.[7]

But the prophets were not the originators of this thought. The germ idea is imbedded in the Pentateuch, in the Decalogue, and in the two commandments concerning our love for God and our love for our fellow men. But whereas in the Law of Moses these two commandments are separated from each other, Jesus brought them

---

7.   Ezekiel 36:25-27; also Jeremiah 31:33 (31:32 Heb.).

together. Thus, He reemphasized the ruling principle of the Decalogue according to which man's attitude to God and his moral and social conduct are inseparable. He did more than this: He reduced the essence of the whole Divine law as found in the Pentateuch to the two commandments about our love for God and for our fellow men, and he implied that in fulfilling God's law man should be motivated by the inner compulsion of love, rather than by the constraint of the law. In the Messianic Manifesto[8] He gave His own definition of what it means to love our neighbor as ourselves.

> And just as you want men to treat you, treat them in the same way.
>
> *Luke 6:31*

> Therefore whatever you want others to do for you, do so for them; for this is the Law and the Prophets.
>
> *Matthew 7: 12*

5. MESSIAH'S NEW COMMANDMENT

When He was about to lay down His life for man's redemption, Messiah Jesus gave to His disciples a new commandment.

> A new commandment I give to you, that you love one another; even as I have loved you, that you also love one another.
>
> *John 13:34*

Men have killed other men in order to save their souls, or in defense of certain ideologies, or because they considered that the good of the state required it. But the true followers of Messiah Jesus are not to shape their attitude to their fellow men by their own ideas. They are to love one another even as He loved them.

> This is my commandment, that you love one another, just as I have loved you. Greater love has no man than this, that one lay down his life for his friends.[9]
>
> *John 15: 12-13*

---

8. The so-called Sermon on the Mount.
9. But Messiah Jesus laid down His life for all, friends and foes.

IV. JESUS' VIEW OF HUMAN SIN

1. SIN IS BONDAGE

> Jesus answered them, truly, truly, I say to you, every one who commits sin is the slave of sin.
>
> *John 8: 34*

This statement applies to the habitual practice of sin. When a man, against his better knowledge, chooses the practice of evil, sin obtains the mastery over his affections and will, and he becomes the slave of that which he chooses.

2. SIN CAN BECOME UNPARDONABLE

Addressing some of them who unreasonably opposed Him, He said:

> If you were blind, you would have no guilt; but now that you say, 'We see', your guilt remains.
>
> *John 9: 41*

and to His disciples, He said:

> If I had not come and spoken to them, they would not have sin,[10] but now they have no excuse for their sin.
>
> *John 15: 22*

Jesus does not refer in these passages to sin in general, for He knows that man is sinful by nature. He is speaking of sin committed deliberately, of human responsibility when one deliberately rejects spiritual and moral light. If such a person continues to resist the light, he will reach in the end a point of no return.

> Whoever blasphemes against the Holy Spirit never has forgiveness, but is guilty of an eternal sin.
>
> *Mark 3: 29*

Sin with such a person has become an inextricable habit of the soul.

---

10. "They would not be guilty of sin."

V. JESUS' VIEW OF HIS MISSION

Before He was born the angel who announced His birth said that His name shall be called Jesus "for it is he who will save his people from their sins."[11] John the Baptizer referred to him as "the lamb of God who takes away the sin of the world."[12] How did His Mission appear to Messiah Jesus Himself?

1. HE CAME TO CHANGE HUMAN LIVES

In the first place, Jesus viewed his mission as aiming to bring about a transformation of human lives as seen from the following two incidents. There was a certain Zaccheus, an Israelite, who was a Roman tax collector. These tax collectors were held in contempt by the Jewish people, not only because they placed themselves at the service of hated, heathen Rome, but also because they were often dishonest and exacted fraudulently more than their due. Zaccheus was of short stature, and when one day he saw Jesus approaching, accompanied by a crowd of people, he climbed up a tree in order to get a good look at Him. The following is a report of this incident.

> When Jesus came to the place, he looked up and said to him, "Zaccheus, hurry and come down, for today I must stay at your house." And he hurried and came down, and received him gladly. And when they saw it, they all began to grumble, saying, "He has gone to be the guest of a man who is a sinner." And Zaccheus stopped and said to the Lord, "Behold, Lord, half of my possessions I will give to the poor, and if I have defrauded anyone of anything, I will give back four times as much." And Jesus said to him, "Today salvation has come to this house, because he, too, is a son of Abraham. For the Son of Man[13] has come to seek and to save that which is lost."
>
> *Luke 19: 5-10*

As a result of Jesus' visit to his house Zaccheus gave up his ill-gotten gains and became morally a changed man.

---

11. Matthew 1:21.
12. John 1:29.
13. One of the Messianic titles by which Jesus frequently identified Himself.

Another example of the saving effect which men and women experienced when their lives were touched by the words and works of Jesus is found in the account of the woman who was spoken of in that particular community as "a sinner." A certain Pharisee[14] by name Simon invited Jesus to his house for dinner. He may have wished to learn more about this new wonder-working "teacher"about whom the Pharisaic religious leaders were so puzzled and mystified. As they were sitting at the table this woman who had led an immoral life entered the dining room. Perhaps she had listened to Jesus and heard him as He issued the invitation to all who are burdened and are heavy-laden to come to Him for rest and peace.[15] It semed to her that His words were especially addressed to her, for the burden of her sinful and unhappy life weighed heavily on her. She brought with her a flask of perfume, commonly worn by Jewish women of that day around the neck, hung down below the breast. She walked straight over to Jesus and stood behind him, at His feet, as He was reclining at the table, the body resting on a couch, and the feet turned away from the table in the direction of the wall. As she stood at His feet, "reverently bending, a shower of tears . . . 'bedewed' His feet. As if surprised, or else afraid to awaken His attention, or defile Him by her tears, she quickly wiped them away with the long tresses of her hair that had fallen down and touched Him, as she bent over His feet. No, not to wash them in such impure waters had she come, but to show such loving gratefulness and reverence as in her [moral] poverty she could, and in her humility she might offer."[16] The reaction of the host to this incident is recorded in the following passage.

> Now when the Pharisee who had invited him saw this, he said to himself , "If this man were a prophet he would know who and what sort of person this woman is who is touching him, that she is a sinner." Jesus answered and said to him "Simon, I have something to say to you ;" and he replied, "Say it, Teacher." "A certain money-lender had two debtors: one owed five hundred denarii and the other fifty. When they were unable to pay, he graciously forgave them both; which of them therefore will love him more?" Simon answered and said, "I suppose the one

---

14. A Traditionalist, a member of strict, "orthodox," Judaism of that day.
15. Matthew 11:28-29.
16. Alfred Edersheim, THE LIFE AND TIMES OF JESUS THE MESSIAH (Longmans, Green, and Co.: London, 1899), Vol. 1, p. 566.

whom he forgave more ;" and he said to him, "You have judged
correctly." And turning toward the woman, He said to Simon,
"Do you see this woman? I entered your house; you gave me no
water for my feet, but she has wet my feet with her tears, and
wiped them with her hair. You gave me no kiss; but she since the
time I came in, has not ceased to kiss my feet. You did not anoint
my head with oil,[17] but she anointed my feet with perfume. For
this reason I say to you, her sins, which are many, have been
forgiven, for she loved much, but he who is forgiven little loves
little." And he said to her, "Your sins have been forgiven." And
those who were reclining at table with him began to say among
themselves, "Who is this man who even forgives sins?" And he
said to the woman, "Your faith has saved you; go in peace."

Luke 7: 39-50

"Undoubtedly, her faith *had* saved her. What she had heard
from His lips, what she knew of Him, she had believed. She had
believed in 'the good tidings of peace' which He had brought, in the
love of God, and His Fatherhood of pity to the most sunken and
needy; in Messiah Jesus, as the Messenger of Reconciliation and
Peace with God in the Kingdom of Heaven which He had so suddenly and unexpectedly opened to her, from out of whose unfolded
golden gates Heaven's light had fallen upon her, Heaven's voices
had come to her."[18]

2. HE CAME TO REVEAL GOD'S SEARCH FOR MAN

The above statement which forms the conclusion of the Zac-
chaeus story presents another aspect of the mission of Jesus. It is
nowhere better illustrated than in the Parable of the Lost Sheep,
the Lost Coin, and the Lost Son.

Now the tax collectors and sinners were all drawing near
to hear him. And the Pharisees and the scribes murmured,
saying, "This man receives sinners and eats with them."

So he told them this parable: "What man of you, having a

---

17. Water for the washing of the feet, a kiss, anointing the head — these were the
common courtesies extended to invited guests.
18. Alfred Edersheim, Op. Cit., Vol. 1, pp. 568-569.

hundred sheep, if he has lost one of them, does not leave the ninety-nine in the wilderness, and go after the one which is lost, until he finds it? And when he has found it, he lays it on his shoulders, rejoicing. And when he comes home, he calls together his friends and his neighbors, saying to them, 'Rejoice with me, for I have found my sheep which was lost.' Even so, I tell you, there will be more joy in heaven over one sinner who repents than over ninety-nine righteous persons who need no repentance.

"Or what woman having ten silver coins, if she loses one coin, does not light a lamp and sweep the house and seek diligently until she finds it? And when she has found it, she calls together her friends and neighbors, saying, 'Rejoice with me, for I have found the coin which I had lost.' Even so, I tell you, there is joy before the angels of God over one sinner who repents."

And he said, "There was a man who had two sons: and the younger of them said to his father, 'Father, give me the share of property that falls to me.' And he divided his living between them. Not many days later, the younger son gathered all he had and took his journey into a far country, and there he squandered his property in loose living. And when he had spent everything, a great famine arose in that country, and he began to be in want. So he went and joined himself to one of the citizens of that country, who sent him into his fields to feed swine. And he would gladly have fed on the pods that the swine ate; and no one gave him anything. But when he came to himself he said, 'How many of my father's hired servants have bread enough and to spare, but I will perish here with hunger! I will arise and go to my father, and I will say to him, "Father, I have sinned against heaven and before you; I am no longer worthy to be called your son; treat me as one of your hired servants."' And he arose and came to his father. But while he was yet at a distance, his father saw him and had compassion, and ran and embraced him and kissed him. And the son said to him, 'Father, I have sinned against heaven and before you; I am no longer worthly to be called your son. But the father said to his servants, 'Bring quickly the best robe, and put it on him; and put a ring on his hand, and shoes on his feet. And bring the fatted calf and kill it, and let us make merry. For this my son was dead, and is alive again; he was lost, and is found; and they began to make merry.

"Now his elder son was in the field; and as he came and drew near to the house, he heard music and dancing. And he called one of the servants and asked what this meant. And he

said to him, 'Your brother has come, and your father has killed
the fatted calf, because he has received him safe and sound.' But
he was angry and refused to go in; his father came out and
entreated him, but he answered his father, 'Lo, these many
years I have served you, and I never disobeyed your command;
yet you never gave me a kid, that I might make merry with my
friends. But when this son of yours came, who has devoured
your living with harlots, you killed for him the fatted calf!" And
he said to him, 'Son you are always with me, and all that is mine
is yours. It was fitting to make merry and be glad, for this your
brother was dead, and is alive; he was lost, and is found.' "

Luke 15: 1-32

The occasion which induced Jesus to give these parables was
the resentment aroused among the Pharisees and scribes by His
solicitous interest in the "publicans and sinners" a class of people
considered then as morally degraded.

Now the tax collectors and sinners were all drawing near
to hear him. And the Pharisees and scribes murmured, saying,
This man receives sinners and eats with them."

Luke 15:1-2

All three parables display certain common features: the loss of an
object or person, a search, or yearning, for the lost object or person,
the joy produced by the finding of the lost object or person.

a. The lost sheep

The distinctive facet of this parable is the utter impossibility of
the sheep of finding its way back after it had strayed from the fold.
The determination of the shepherd to recover the lost sheep is given
in the statement to the effect that the shepherd goes out to look for
the sheep "until he finds it." The condition of the sheep after it was
located may be inferred from the fact that the shepherd had to carry
the sheep back on his shoulders. There it lay in the wilderness with
torn fleece, bruised and emaciated, too weak to stand on its feet.
The joy which the shepherd experienced in finding the sheep may
be seen in the feeling of happiness with which he relates to his
neighbors his recovery of his lost sheep.

b. The lost coin

This parable concerns the case of a poor woman, perhaps a

widow, living in a humble cottage, perhaps with no window, the only light in the cottage coming in from the door. She lost one of the ten pieces of money which she probably had put away for a certain definite purpose. This explains her desperate effort to locate the lost piece of money. She lights a lamp, sweeps the house, searches every corner carefully until she finds it. Having found the lost piece of money, she rushed out to her neighbors who sympathized with her loss to break to them the good news of recovering the lost money.

c. The lost son

The story of the younger of the two sons is exhibited in this parable in several successive scenes. In the first, he requests his father to hand over to him his share of the inheritance, probably under the pretext of starting out in life by himself. Having received his portion of the inheritance he removes himself far away from home in order to be free to do what he pleases. In a short time he spends in wasteful excesses and in riotous living all he had. About that time a severe famine arose in that particular area. He is thus reduced to a state of utter destitution. He reaches the depth of degradation when he, a Jew, and a son of a well-to-do, respectable family, hires himself out as a swineherd to a Gentile owner. His hunger was of such intensity that he has a craving for the pods which the swine ate.

It was this desperation that became the turning-point in moral degradation. In this final scene we see him returning to his senses. In his extremity he began to see clearly how his self-will and folly brought all this ruin upon him. Consequently, he decides to return home, beg his father for forgiveness, and ask him to let him work for him as one of his servants.

Then comes the final scene. The father sights him from a distance, runs to meet him, falls on his neck and covers him with kisses. Overwhelmed by this unexpected manifestation of fatherly love, all the young man could manage to say was: "Father, I have sinned against heaven and before you; I am no longer worthy to be called your son." But the father instructed his servants to place on his body the finest robe, put a ring on his finger, and shoes on his feet; also to kill the fatted calf and make a feast: " For this my son was dead and is alive again; he was lost, and is found."

In the meantime the older brother returned from the field

where he had been busy all day looking after the father's estate. When he approached the family homestead and heard the music and the dancing he was angry and would not come in. His father went out entreating him to come in and participate in the festivities. But he refused saying: "Lo, these many years I have served you, and I never disobeyed your command; yet you never gave me a kid to make merry with my friends. But when this son of yours came, who has devoured your living with harlots, you killed for him the fatted calf." But the father said to him, "Son, you are always with me, and all that is mine is yours. It was fitting to make merry and be glad, for this your brother was dead, and is alive; he was lost, and is found."

The Parable of the Lost Sheep ends with the following words: "Just so, I tell you, there will be more joy in heaven over one sinner who repents than over ninety-nine righteous persons who need no repentance." The Parable of the Lost Coin concludes with the statement: "Just so, I tell you, there is joy before the angels of God over one sinner who repents." The Pharisees are symbolized by the ninety-nine sheep in the first and by the nine pieces of silver — in the second parable. In the third parable they are represented by the older brother. The sinners are symbolized by the lost sheep in the first, by the lost coin in the second, and by the lost son in the third parable. The Pharisees were the super-religious people who occupied the front seats in the synagogue, who would present God with a long list of things which they have done for him and who would pride themselves that they are not like the publicans.

Through these parables Jesus intended to teach the Pharisees and all of us that there is more joy in heaven over the moral recovery of one sinner than over all those self-righteous people who think that all is well with them and they need no repentance. In his resentment, the older brother referred to his fallen brother as "your son." But in his kind and gracious reply, the father gently reminded him that this his son happens to be "your brother." It was needful for the Pharisees of all times to know that however low a person may sink morally, he is still a child of God, a child of the Father in Heaven, never beyond the possibility of recovery, however sinful he may have become.

But this is not all. Like the Lost Sheep which strayed from the fold into the wilderness, man when alienated from God is totally incapable of finding his way back to God unaided; that like the Lost Coin, man when separated from God fails to fulfill the purpose of his existence; that like the Lost Son, he spends his days in wasting his precious God-given resources.

Finally, these precious, exquisite and so true to life, parables would teach us that Jesus came to unfold to us God's stooping love for lost man, His yearning to bring man back to Himself, and to restore him to a position in which he would be able to accomplish his Divinely appointed destiny. "For the Son of Man has come to seek and to save that which is lost."

THE NINETY AND NINE[19]

There were ninety and nine that safely lay
In the shelter of the fold,
But one was out on the hills away,
Far off from the gates of gold —
Away on the mountains wild and bare,
Away from the tender Shepherd's care.
"Lord, Thou hast here Thy ninety and nine;
Are they not enough for Thee?"
But the Shepherd made answer: "This of mine
Has wandered away from me,
And although the road be rough and steep
I go to the desert to find my sheep."
But none of the ransomed ever know
How deep were the waters crossed;
Nor how dark was the night that the Lord passed through
Ere He found His sheep that was lost.
Out in the desert He heard its cry —
Sick and helpless, and ready to die.
"Lord, whence are those blood-drops all the way
That mark out the mountain's track?"
"They were shed for one who had gone astray
Ere the Shepherd could bring him back."
"Lord, whence are thy hands so rent and torn?"
"They are pierced tonight by many a thorn."
But all thro' the mountains, thunder-riven,
And up from the rocky steep,
There arose a glad cry to the gate of heaven,
"Rejoice! I have found my sheep!"
And the angels echoed around the throne,
"Rejoice, for the Lord brings back His own!

---

19.   The world-famous hymn sung by Ira D. Sankey.

3. HE CAME TO ESTABLISH GOD'S LAW

Another goal to His Mission was, according to Jesus Himself, to establish God's law.

> Do not think that I came to abolish the Law or the Prophets;
> I did not come to abolish, but to fulfill.
>
> *Matthew 5:17*

These words uttered in the Messianic Manifesto constitute His first declaration concerning the purpose of His Mission. He came not merely to plead with God to excuse man's moral failures, but rather to establish God's holy law in the hearts and affairs of men. "He came into the world to establish the law, to make it honorable; to stand in the midst of human history as the severest of all moral teachers, embodying the highest ideal of law, and at all costs insisting upon obedience thereto. In that ultimate triumph of the Messiah — when 'He shall see of the travail of His soul and be satisfied! and in those who have been ransomed and redeemed shall find the fulfillment of His highest purpose — He will not lead into the larger life a great host of men and women crippled and incapable, without spiritual power, and defective in moral character. When His work is done in His own, He will present them to His Father without spot or wrinkle or any such thing, perfected with the perfection of his own holiness of character and righteousness of conduct."[20] "Do not think that I came to abolish the Law or the Prophets; I did not come to abolish but to fulfill."

VI. THE KINGDOM OF GOD

1. THE CONCEPT OF THE KINGDOM OF GOD IN THE OLD TESTAMENT

According to the Biblical view, history is moving towards the establishment of God's visible rule on earth. In the Old Testament the term "Kingdom of God" is mentioned in some form in a number

20. G. Campbell Morgan, THE TEACHING OF CHRIST (Fleming H. Revell and Company: New York, 1913), p. 159.

of passages.[21] But the idea of the coming of God's rule on earth pervades the whole of the Old Testament. " . . . The whole [Biblical] history of Israel [is] big with the promise of the world's salvation, and its institutions and promises [are] pointing to the establishment of a universal kingdom of God upon earth by means of the Messiah.[22] Not only so, but "the Old Testament in its different parts is organically connected; and . . . alike the connecting, the impelling, and the final idea of it is that of a universal kingdom of God upon earth."[23] The unfolding of this idea may be traced through the three stages of Israel's Biblical history: the patriarchal, the Mosaic and the prophetic. The first promise made by God to Abraham is concluded with the statement

> And in you and in your seed shall all the families of the
> earth be blessed.
>
> *Genesis 12:3*

The promise was repeated twice to Abraham,[24] renewed to Isaac,[25] and reiterated to Jacob.[26] It was the "planting-ground for the Kingdom of God, whence in the fullness of time and of preparation it would be transplanted into the heathen world."[27] It marked, from the very outset of Israel's history, the nature of her Divinely-appointed mission.

This mission has been restated at the very beginning of the Mosaic stage of Israel's history in the following Divine declaration made just before the Sinai revelation was given.

> You shall be my property from among all nations, for all
> the earth is mine. And you shall be unto me a kingdom of priests
> and a holy nation.
>
> *Exodus 19:5-6*

"As Israel was ideally, so all nations were through their ministry to become really the possession of God: a kingdom of priests, a holy people; for all the earth, as well as Israel, was God's. And the

---

21. See, f.e., Exodus 15:18; Chronicles 13:8; Psalm 22:29-30 (22:28-29 Heb.); 103:19; 145:11-13; Micah 4:7; Obadiah 1:21.

22. Alfred Edersheim, PROPHECY AND HISTORY IN RELATION TO THE MESSIAH (Longmans, Green, and Co.: London, 1885). pp. 2-3.

23. Ibid., p. 31.

24. Genesis 18:18; 22:18.

25. Genesis 26:4.

26. Genesis 28:14.

27. Alfred Edersheim, Op. Cit., p. 44.

realization of this would be the kingdom of God on earth."[28]

The Kingdom of God idea was embodied in the prophetic concept of the Servant of Jehovah. The three main agencies in the Old Testament economy — the prince, the priest, the prophet — and even the people as a whole were, as God's servants, engaged in the task of realizing some aspect of the Kingdom of God. The prince was to execute, in God's name, judgment and dispense justice. The priest was to mediate between a holy God and sinful man. The prophet was to bring to man God's Word.

We have shown in previous chapters how the Messiah was to sum up in Himself Israel's institutions, how he was to merge in His Person the three offices of king, priest and prophet, how He was to fulfill Israel's mission.

"The conception of the Kingdom of God, which to our modern consciousness seems somewhat obscure . . . is one of the fundamental ideas of the Old Testament. It was the pride of Israel, not merely because Israel believed in the privileges it would confer on themselves, but because alone of all nations Israel was capable of believing in the possibility of a covenant between heaven and earth, between God and man, in a welding of Divine purposes with the counsels of earth, and in the fact that, even within the modest boundaries of a small nation, the rule of earthly affairs was not unworthy of God. To be sure, this also constituted Israel's sorrow and source of suffering in the course of history; the limitation not only of its free political and purely human, but even of its religious development; the appointed bitter criticism of a Reality which ever fell short and ever contradicted the Ideal. But in this very sorrow and never-ceasing criticism and earthly lamentation and limitation, Israel became the guide and leader in that infinite striving which, by believing in and seeking after the coming Kingdom of God, and by the final Advent of the Messiah upon earth, would and did join Idea and Reality — the life of God and that of man, heaven and earth. The one prevailing and impelling idea of the Old Testament is the royal reign of God on earth . . . Almost a thousand years before Christ rises the longing cry after the future Kingdom of God — a kingdom which is to conquer and to win all nations, and to plant in Israel righteousness, knowledge, peace and blessing — that Kingdom of God in

---

28.   Ibid., p. 45.

which God, or His Viceregent, the Messiah, is to be King over the whole earth, and all generations are to come up and worship the Lord of Hosts."[29]

2. THE CONCEPT OF THE KINGDOM OF GOD IN THE NEW TESTAMENT

In the New Testament, the Kingdom of God is central in all of Messiah's doings and teachings. "The call of Jesus points back, first to John [the Baptizer] and then, much farther, into the Old Testament."[30] In the Gospel of Matthew, the word "Kingdom,", i.e., the Kingdom of God, is used by Jesus forty-seven times.[31] When He sent out the twelve apostles to announce the near approach of the Messianic Kingdom, Jesus said to them:

> "And as you proceed, preach, saying, 'The kingdom of heaven is at hand.' "
>
> *Matthew 10:7*

When He gained a sufficiently large number of followers to enable Him to send seventy disciples on a mission tour, He instructed them to announce that the Kingdom of God has arrived.

> "And whatever city you enter, and they receive you, eat what is set before you. And heal those in it who are sick, and say to them, 'The kingdom of God has come near to you.' "
>
> *Luke 10:8-9*

The Kingdom of God was the fundamental concept in His parabolic teachings. Of the twenty-nine parables recorded in the New Testament, seventeen make definite mention of the Kingdom of God; in the remaining twelve the Kingdom of God is the dominant thought. G. Campbell Morgan defines the Biblical Kingdom of God idea in three words: "Rule, Realm, Result." The Kingdom of God is the rule of God; the Kingdom of God is the realm or sphere over which God's rule is exercised; the Kingdom of God is the result realized in the realm over which God rules.[32]

---

29. T. Keim, JESU VON NAZARA, Vol. 2, pp. 35, 36; quoted by Alfred Edersheim, Op. Cit., pp. 47-48.
30. Ibid.
31. G. Campbell Morgan, THE TEACHINGS OF CHRIST (Fleming H. Revell Co.: New York, N. Y., 1913), p. 200.
32. Ibid., p. 207.

In the very beginning of His ministry Jesus declared that the Kingdom of God He came to set up on earth is a community of regenerated men and women.

> Truly, truly, I say to you, unless one is born again,[33] he cannot see the Kingdom of God.
>
> *John 3:3*

The same idea was advanced by Him when He said that to enter His Kingdom of God one must rid himself of preconceived ideas.

> At that time the disciples came to Jesus, saying, "Who then is the greatest in the kingdom of heaven?" And having called a child, he placed him in their midst. And said, "Indeed, I say to you, unless you change and become like children, you shall not enter the kingdom of heaven."
>
> *Matthew 18:1-3*

In Phillips' New Testament the words of Jesus are rendered thus: "Unless you change your whole outlook."

When John the Baptizer addressed to Jesus a question which expressed his perplexity over the fact that Jesus had not inaugurated His Messianic mission with a show of outward majesty and crushing force, Jesus — who at the moment when John's messengers arrived was occupied healing the sick and afflicted — told the messengers to say this to John

> Go and tell John what you have seen and heard: the blind receive their sight, the lame walk, the lepers are cleansed, and the deaf hear, the dead are raised up, the poor have the gospel preached to them.
>
> *Luke 7:22*

In His reply to John's messengers Messiah Jesus declares that the citizens of the new community — the Kingdom of God — which He is establishing on earth must *first of all* busy themselves attending to the physical and spiritual needs of the world round about them.

The last time Jesus spoke of the Kingdom of God before His death was when He stood before Pontius Pilate, the Roman gover-

---

33. Or, "from above," referring to a spiritual regeneration of the human individual.

nor into whose hands He was delivered by the Jewish religious
authorities, as recorded in the Gospel of John.

> Pilate, therefore, went into the Praetorium again, and
> summoned Jesus, and said to him, "Are you the king of the
> Jews?" Jesus answered, "Are you saying this of yourself, or did
> others tell you about me?" Pilate answered, "Am I a Jew?" Your
> own nation and chief priests have delivered you to me; what
> have you done?" Jesus aswered, "My kingdom is not of this
> world; if my kingdom were of this world, my followers would be
> fighting so that I might not be delivered up to the Jews; but as it
> is, my kingdom is not from hence."[34]
>
> *John 18:33-36*

Rome conquered the ancient world. But she could not make any of
the subjugated peoples love Rome, nor could her whole military
might bring about the spiritual or moral regeneration of a single
individual in her whole empire. Jesus declared to Pilate that His
Kingdom of God will not be brought in by military power, by
political or diplomatic scheming. "My kingdom is not from hence"
— not by these human methods will it be established. For His is a
Kingdom which consists of men and women who have experienced
in their lives God's transforming power.

VII. THE REALIZATION OF THE KINGDOM OF GOD

> And he said, "The kingdom of God is, as though a man
> should cast seed on the ground. And goes to bed by night and
> gets up by day, and the seed sprouts up and grows — he knows
> not how. The earth produces of itself; first the blade, then the
> ear, then the full grain in the ear."
>
> *Mark 4: 26-28*

> And he said, "To what may we compare the kingdom of
> God? or by what parable shall we illustrate it? It is like a grain of
> mustard seed which when sown upon the ground is the smallest
> of all seeds on the earth. Yet when it is sown, it grows up, and
> becomes larger than all other garden plants, and puts out large
> branches, so that the birds of the air can make their nests in its
> shade."
>
> *Mark 4: 30-32*[35]

---

34. Not from this world, has no such origin or source.
35. See also Matthew 13:31-32; Luke 13:18-19.

He presented to them another parable, saying,"The kingdom of heaven may be compared to a man who sowed good
seed in his field. But while the men slept, his enemy came and
sowed tares[36] among the wheat, and went away. When the blade
sprang up, and put forth the ear, then the tares appeared also.
And the servants of the householder came and said to him, 'Sir,
did you not sow good seed in your field? How then does it have
tares?' And he said to them, 'An enemy has done this!' and the
servants said to him, 'Do you then wish that we should weed them
out?' And he said, 'No, lest in weeding out the tares, you may also
tear up the wheat. Let both grow together till the harvest; and in
the time of the harvest I will say to the reapers, 'First gather up the
tares, and bind them in bundles to burn them; then gather up the
wheat into my barn.' "

Matthew 13: 24-30

The above parables were designed to teach that the kingdom of
God grows by a process of development in the hearts of those who
enter it, compared to the growth of a seed; first the blade, then the
ear, then the full corn in the ear. But side by side with the good
elements of the Kingdom of God, there is also a development of the
opposing forces of evil. In both areas there is a process of development: the good which Jesus plants in the world is wrought out to its
full manifestation, the forces of evil and darkness growing side by
side with the forces of good, until they attain their most awful
completion. *This means that while Jesus tarries, the world will be getting
better in some areas, and worse in other areas.*

We thus see from these three parables that the Kingdom of God
is being realized in stages: each stage ending in a crisis; it is being
established not by a crisis alone, but by a process ending in a crisis;
not by a process of development alone, but by a crisis prepared for
by a process of development. It will not end by a victory of good over
evil, or of evil over good. "It will end by the crisis in human history,
clear, definite, sharp: a crisis in which evil is to be destroyed and
swept out of the world, and good is to be brought to its final
realization and its ultimate triumph."[37]

Notice, that in the last parable cited above, Jesus distinctly
forbade His followers to attempt to root out the evil forces, some-

---

36. Darnel, a weed resembling wheat.
37. G. Campbell Morgan, Op. Cit., p. 225.

thing to which His followers have not always given heed, with disastrous consequences as the inevitable result. The task of the destruction of evil, Messiah Jesus deferred to the time of His return, and reserved this function to Himself alone.

VIII. THE RETURN OF MESSIAH JESUS

The return of Messiah Jesus to set up God's rule on earth will be the last and greatest crisis in the process of the establishment of the Kingdom of God. Dr. Morgan states that Jesus had much more to say about His return than about the cross which awaited Him or the Church, i.e., the community of believers, which was to come into existence following His resurrection.[38] The idea of His return is implied in many of His parabolic teachings, while the crisis which we sense in these parables is precipitated by His reappearance. In the parable of the drag-net,[39] in the parable of the talents,[40] in the parable of the man taking a far journey,[41] in the parable of the marriage-feast,[42] in the parable of the ten virgins who are waiting for the arrival of the bridegroom,[43] in all these it is the return of Messiah Jesus which creates the crisis.

But we also have direct statements by Jesus concerning His return.

> For the Son of Man is going to come in the glory of his Father with his angels; and then he will recompense each one according to his conduct.
> *Matthew 16:27*[44]

The subject of His return forms the contents of the whole Olivet prophecy.[45]

---

38.   Ibid., p. 297.
39.   Matthew 13:47-50.
40.   Matthew 25:14-30.
41.   Mark 13:35-37; see, also, Luke 12:35-40.
42.   Matthew 22:1-14.
43.   Matthew 25:1-13.
44.   See the parallels in Mark and Luke.
45.   Matthew 24:1-51; Mark 13; Luke 21:5-36.

IX. THE PURPOSE OF MESSIAH'S SECOND COMING

> And all the multitude kept silent, and they were listening to Barnabas and Paul as they were relating what signs and wonders God had done through them among the Gentiles. And after they had stopped speaking, James[46] answered, saying, "Brethren, listen to me, Simeon[47] has related how God first concerned himself about taking from among the Gentiles a people for his name.[48] And with this the words of the Prophets agree, just as it is written. 'After these things I will return, and I will rebuild the dwelling of David which has fallen, and I will rebuild its ruins, and I will restore it. In order that the rest of mankind may seek the Lord, and all the Gentiles upon whom my name has been invoked.' "
>
> *Acts 15: 12-17*

The above statement was made by James, one of the leading apostles of the Jerusalem Church, at a meeting which convened to consider a weighty problem. Large numbers of Gentiles were converted as a result of the labors of Paul and Barnabas. Paul did not insist that the Gentile converts adhere to the Mosaic Law. The essence of the Gospel message is that man's salvation is determined by faith in the atoning death of Jesus the Messiah. Certain Hebrew Christians took exception to this position. They felt that the Gentile converts should be asked to submit to circumcision and to observe the Mosaic Law. The Jerusalem Church met to consider this exceedingly important issue on the decision of which the very existence of the Christian Church seemed to depend. Present at this meeting were the apostles and many of the members of the Jerusalem Church. Most, if not all, of those who attended that meeting were Jews. After due deliberations the conference approved the position of Paul and Barnabas, namely, that Gentile converts to the Messianic faith of Jesus should not be required to accept the Mosaic Law.

But this approval did not come until James,who appears to have presided at the meeting, made the statement recorded in Acts 15: 13-17. The full significance of what he said can only be understood if we realize what was behind this controversy. As increasing numbers of Gentiles continued to flock into the Messsianic movement of

---

46. In the Greek original he is identified by his Hebrew name Jacob.
47. Simon Peter.
48. "[To bear and honor] his name" — THE AMPLIFIED NEW TESTAMENT.

Jesus, it was not difficult to foresee that the day was not far off when the whole Messianic movement would become a Gentile movement. Such an anticipation must have appeared quite distressing to Hebrew Christians with a deep attachment to their Jewish heritage. One wonders whether the demand to have Gentile converts adhere to the Mosaic Law may not have been motivated, in part at least, by a desire to slow down the flow of Gentile converts into the Church.

James, who undoubtedly had been aware of these Hebrew Christian anxieties, was led of the Spirit of God to make the remarks cited above with a view of settling the question at issue and also of calming Hebrew Christian fears. But brief as his statement was, it contains nothing less than an outline of the whole Messianic program during the interval between the resurrection and the return of Messiah Jesus. According to James the Messianic program will be accomplished in three periods or stages.

1. THE FIRST STAGE OF THE MESSIANIC PROGRAM

> Simeon has related how God had first concerned himself about taking from among the Gentiles a people for his name.
>
> *Acts 15:14*

The reference to Simon Peter had to do with a statement which he had made at this conference relating how God used him to bring the first Gentile family into the Messianic fold. The Gentile world as a whole will not be converted, we are informed by James, in the first stage of the Messianic program. During this initial phase God is merely calling out a certain number of Gentiles from every nation to become His people. When this process will be completed, the first stage of the Messianic program will be terminated.

2. THE SECOND STAGE OF THE MESSIANIC PROGRAM

> 'After these things I will return, and I will rebuild the dwelling of David which has fallen, and I will rebuild its ruins, and I will restore it.'
>
> *Acts 15:16*

These words are quoted by James from the opening lines of a

Messianic passage in Amos.[49] The only slight variation which James introduced into the passage as found in Amos is this: In the Amos passage it is Jehovah who restores the Davidic dynasty, in the James passage the actual restoration is accomplished by Jehovah acting through the Messiah Jesus on His return. The second phase of the Messianic program begins with the return of Messiah Jesus. In this stage Messiah Jesus restores the dynasty of David of which He is a lineal descendant.

3. THE THIRD STAGE OF THE MESSIANIC PROGRAM

'In order that the rest of mankind may seek the Lord, and all the Gentiles upon whom my name has been invoked.'

Acts 15: 17

This portion of the James statement is also cited from the Amos Messianic passage.[50] As applied to the return of Messiah Jesus, James uses this portion of the Amos passage to state the purpose of restoring the Davidic dynasty: The Davidic dynasty will be restored, and Israel nationally reestablished, *in order that Messiah's salvation may reach the entire Gentile world.* This is the purpose of the return of Messiah Jesus and the substance of the third stage of the Messianic program.

It should be noted that Paul was in full agreement with the James statement. Writing to the Christians in Rome, Paul says:

For I do not want you, brethren, to be uninformed of this mystery, lest you be wise in your own estimation, that a partial hardening has happened to Israel until the fullness of the Gentiles has come in.

Romans 11: 25

By "the fullness of the Gentiles" Paul understands the completion of the process of the partial ingathering of the Gentiles taking place in

---

49.   Amos 9:11-15.
50.   Amos 9:12.

the first stage of the Messianic program. The reference to the "partial hardening" of Israel means by implication that in the first stage of the Messianic program there will be a partial ingathering of Jews as well as a partial ingathering of Gentiles. This prophetic utterance by Paul made in the first century has been literally fulfilled to the present time. There are today many thousands of Jewish followers of Messiah Jesus all over the world, including the State of Israel. The full ingathering of the Jewish people will be accomplished in the second phase with the return of Messiah Jesus.

> And thus all Israel — Paul continues — will be saved.
>
> *Romans 11: 26*

As the partial ingathering of Jews commenced before the partial ingathering of Gentiles in the first stage of the Messianic program, so also will the full ingathering of Jews in the second stage of the Messianic program precede the full ingathering of Gentiles to take place in the third stage of the Messianic program.

One may now ask, why does the Messianic program have to be accomplished in three stages? Could not Israel and the Gentiles have been gathered in all at once? The reason for this is that in the first century of our era neither Israel as a nation, nor the Gentile world as a whole, were ready for the Messianic message of Jesus. Paul declared that Messiah Jesus came into the world in the fullness of time.[51] By this he meant that the world into which Messiah Jesus came had been prepared historically for His coming. This process of preparation was of a negative and a positive character. On the negative side there was the rise and fall of the three world empires mentioned in Daniel 2, and the grave shortcomings of the Roman empire, the fourth world power of Daniel 2, already manifest in the first century of our era. If we add to this the moral bankruptcy of ancient paganism and the impotence of Greek philosophy — we have a picture of the failure of the ancient world in the religious, moral, intellectual, political and economic areas. On the other hand, the undermining of ancient paganism wrought by Greek philosophy and the unification of the ancient world accomplished by the Greek language and Roman military power and administrative ability — were the positive elements in the preparation of the Gentile world for the first advent of Messiah Jesus.

---

51. Galatians 4:4.

A process of preparation was also proceeding in the Jewish world. The miserable internal history of the ancient Jewish state, its eventual collapse which the Old Testament writers attribute to the transgressions of the people, high and low; the equally sorry record of the short-lived Maccabean state marked by dissentions, divisions, turmoil, cruelties and bloodshed — these were the negative factors in the preparation of the Jewish people for Messiah's coming. On the positive side, we can list the increasing knowledge of the Old Testament writings, the growth of an apocalyptic literature in the centuries following the return from the Babylonian exile, and a deepened understanding by the Jewish people of their destiny as the people of God and of their mission to the world.

We must never lose sight of the fact that Biblical revelation — Old and New Testament — aims to reach all mankind. "Go you therefore, and make disciples of all nations."[52] "Go you into all the world, and preach the Gospel to the whole creation."[53] "And that repentance and remission of sins should be preached in his name unto all the nations, beginning with Jerusalem."[54] Israel's main function in the ages before the first coming of Messiah Jesus was to receive and preserve God's revelation. The main function of the Christian Church between the first and second coming of Messiah Jesus is to deliver this revelation to all mankind.

But the world into which Messiah Jesus came was the relatively small then known civilized world of the Mediterranean coast-lands. Beyond the frontiers of that world lay the vast stretches of the continent of Asia, Africa and Europe, with their teeming millions of Mongolians, Hindu, Negro, Germanic and Slavic races — most of them in a semi-barbaric state. Of the existence of this larger world the nations of the Mediterranean coast-lands knew little or nothing. The American continent was totally unknown until the end of the fifteenth century. For the peoples of this larger world to be in a position to respond one way or another to the Gospel message required many centuries of time. Similarly, while thousands of Jews rallied to the banner of Jesus, the Jewish people as a whole were no more ready to enter upon their Divinely-appointed mission in the

---

52. Matthew 28:19.
53. Mark 16:15.
54. Luke 24:47.

first century than ancient Israel in the days of the first Temple was
prepared to live in accordance with the Law of Moses, or to respond
to the prophetic message of the Old Testament.

Since primitive peoples are not in a position to receive the
Biblical message of human redemption, the first stage of the Messianic program was destined to last long enough for the whole
unknown inhabited part of the earth to be discovered, and for all
nations to reach that stage in their intellectual development to be in a
position to respond for or against the God of Biblical revelation.

Several days before His crucifixion Jesus was asked by His
disciples about the time of His second coming. He refused to give
them a definite date, but He did describe to them certain main
events which would help the followers of Jesus to know whether or
not His return is near at hand. One of these events is the propaga-
tion of the Gospel message in the whole inhabited earth.

> And this gospel of the kingdom[55] shall be preached in the
> whole world[56] for a witness to all the nations, and then shall the
> end[57] come.
>
> *Matthew 24: 14*

It is only now, in the present generation, that the Gospel message is
reaching the whole inhabited earth, and every nation in existence is
in a position to decide for or against the message of Messiah Jesus.

---

55. The Good News of the Messianic Kingdom of God.
56. In the whole inhabited earth.
57. The end of the first stage of the Messianic program.

CHAPTER 4
THE DEATH OF JESUS THE MESSIAH

   I.   The Baptism Of Jesus

  II.   The Temptation In The Wilderness

 III.   The Brazen Serpent

  IV.   Jesus Went To The Cross Willingly

   V.   The First Advance And Direct Disclosure Of His Death

  VI.   The Second Advance And Direct Disclosure Of His Death

 VII.   The Third Advance And Direct Disclosure Of His Death

VIII.   The Fourth Advance And Direct Disclosure Of His Death

  IX.   The Fifth Advance And Direct Disclosure Of His Death

CHAPTER 4
THE DEATH OF JESUS THE MESSIAH

Was the death of Jesus a mere incident in His life? Was it something that just happened? Did He become a martyr to a righteous cause? Was His death a sacrifice of a holy life brought about by sinful men? Was it a natural climax between good and evil? The New Testament declares that Jesus came to die, that He had known in advance that He came to die, that His death was for all mankind, that it was the instrument of accomplishing His mission. In the following pages we will endeavor to show that the New Testament writers derived this information from Jesus Himself.

I. THE BAPTISM OF JESUS

Under the relatively mild and humane reign of Augustus the Jews fared comparatively well in the Roman empire and in Palestine which was then a province of the empire. Their condition worsened considerably upon the accession of Tiberius who, though personally indifferent to all religion, was particularly hostile to Jews and Judaism. Under the various governors, who, as the emperor's representatives, ruled Palestine, conditions were often quite harsh. Reckless disregard of Jewish feelings, malicious insults, exactions, judicial murders without even the formality of a legal process, and cruelty characterized the period of the governorship of Pontius Pilate in whose days the crucifixion of Jesus took place.[1]

Nor were the people happy about the men who held chief spiritual rule over them. The occupancy of the high priesthood was frequently changed by the Roman governors, and appointees to this highest spiritual office of the land were frequently selected with a view of serving the interests of Rome, or its rapacious governors, rather than those of the people. In the days of the ministry of Jesus

---

1. Alfred Edersheim, THE LIFE AND TIMES OF JESUS THE MESSIAH (Longmans, Green, and Co.: London, 1899), Vol. 1, p. 262.

the high priest was a certain Caiaphas who, it appears, administered the office of the high priesthood together with his father-in-law Annas who had been deposed after serving nine years in the high priesthood. And while the members of the Annas family were not charged with the same gross immoralities of the other high priests of that period, they are included in the woes pronounced in the Talmud on the corrupt high priests.[2]

It was in this atmosphere of political and religious distress that Yochanan Ha-Matbil — John the Baptizer — the son of the godly priest Zechariah and his saintly wife Elizabeth, raised the cry that the coming of the Kingdom of God was near at hand. In general, the "Kingdom of God," or the "Kingdom of Heaven," meant to the Jews of that day the coming of God's rule on earth and its full manifestation with the appearance of the Messiah. Overwhelmed by a sense of an impending catastrophe and the sinfulness of the nation John called upon the people to repent and he offered the rite of baptism in the waters of the Jordan as the symbol or expression of their repentance. His activities were first centered in "the wilderness of Judea," i.e., the desolate region around the mouth of the Jordan; soon afterwards we see him in the district of Bethabara, further up the Jordan river.

The baptism of John the Baptizer was not an altogether new idea in Israel. Washing one's body and one's clothes was one of the requirements which every Israelite had to comply with when he or she contracted ritual defilement.[3] Heathen converts to the faith of Israel had to be baptized. But all these situations of baptismal washings applied to individuals only. John the Baptizer called on all the people to submit to the waters of his baptism. There is one significant episode which took place at the very beginning of Israel's national history in which the nation as a whole underwent a symbolic baptism and which may have formed the precedent for the activities of John the Baptizer. Just before the Mount Sinai revelation and in preparation for the Sinai Covenant Moses received the following Divine instruction.

> And Jehovah said to Moses, "Go to the people and conse-
> crate them today and tomorrow, and let them wash their gar-

---

2. Pes. 57a.
3. Of the many references in the Law of Moses, see, f.e., Leviticus 11:25, 28; 16:4; 17:5; 22:6; Numbers 8:7 and chapter 19.

> ments. And be ready by the third day; for on the third day
> Jehovah will come down upon Mount Sinai in the sight of all
> the people . . . So Moses went down from the mountain to the
> people, and consecrated the people; and they washed their gar-
> ments. And he said to the people, "Be ready by the third day; do
> not go near a woman."
>
> *Exodus 19:10-11, 14*

That this purification included their bodies as well as their clothes
may be seen from the prohibition of marital relations during this
period of preparation, and also from the following incident in the
history of Jacob.

> God said to Jacob, "Arise, go up to Bethel, and dwell there;
> and make there an altar to the God who appeared to you when
> you fled from your brother Esau." So Jacob said to his house-
> hold and to all who were with him, "Put away the foreign gods
> that are among you, and purify yourselves, and change your
> garments. Then let us arise and go up to Bethel, that I may
> make there an altar to the God who answered me in the day of
> my distress and has been with me wherever I have gone."
>
> *Genesis 35:1-3*

It was therefore reasonable that as Israel underwent a symbolic
baptism in preparation for their entry into the Sinai Covenant, even
so should Israel submit to another symbolic baptism in preparation
for the New Covenant.[4]

To Jesus the spiritual movement to which John the Baptizer
gave birth was clearly the work of God,[5] and the news of his activities
became to Jesus the signal from His Heavenly Father to initiate His
public ministry. Filled with these thoughts, Jesus presented Himself
one day at the scene of the baptismal waters with the intention of
submitting to the rite of baptism. This took place after all the people
had already been baptized on that particular day.[6] A private meeting
must have taken place between Jesus and John. We are told that

---

4. Maimonides, the Jewish medieval physician, philosopher and Talmudic scholar, traces the origin of the baptism of Gentile converts to Judaism to the above
   passage of Exodus 19:10, 14 (See, Hilc. Issurey Biah 13:3; Yad Ha'Ch., Vol. 2, p.
   142b.). According to the Midrash Siphre on Numbers, p. 30b, ed. Weiss,
   baptism was one of the three things by which Israel was admitted into the Sinai
   Covenant.
5. Matthew 21: 25.
6. Luke 3: 21.

John sought to prevent Jesus from being baptized, since this baptism symbolized repentance from sin. What transpired there is described in the following passage.

> Then Jesus arrived from Galilee at the Jordan coming to John, to be baptized by him. But John tried to prevent him, saying, "I have need to be baptized by you, and do you come to me?" But Jesus answering said to him, "Permit it at this time; for in this way it is fitting for us to fulfill all righteousness;" then he permitted him. And after being baptized, Jesus went up immediately from the water: and behold, the heavens were opened, and he saw the Spirit of God descending as a dove, and coming upon him. And behold a voice out of the heavens, saying, "This is my beloved Son, in whom I am well pleased."
>
> *Matthew 3: 13-17*

The Gospel of Mark begins its account of the ministry of Jesus with the opening message from Isaiah 40:

> The beginning of the gospel of Jesus the Messiah, the Son of God. As it is written in Isaiah the prophet, "Behold, I send my messenger before your face, who shall prepare your way. The voice of one crying in the wilderness, Make ready the way of Jehovah, make his path straight." John the Baptizer appeared in the wilderness proclaiming a baptism of repentance for the forgiveness of sins.
>
> *Mark 1: 1-4*

The above statement shows that the work of John the Baptizer was regarded as preparing the way for the Messianic mission of Jesus, and this, in fulfillment of the statement in Isaiah 40. In a previous chapter it was mentioned that Isaiah 40 is the opening portion of the second half of the book of Isaiah in which the description of the Suffering Servant holds a most prominent place. The words, "in whom I am well pleased," uttered by the Heavenly Voice as Jesus emerged from the baptismal waters, are taken from the first sentence of Isaiah 42: "Behold, my servant . . . in whom my soul delights," which statement was —we said— interpreted of the Messiah by the ancient Targum of Jonathan.

These considerations suggest that Jesus entered upon His ministry in the awareness of doing the work of the Suffering Servant of Isaiah. As a matter of fact, at a later point in His ministry He expressly applied to Himself one of the statements from Isaiah 53.

> For I tell you, that this which is written must be fulfilled in
> me, "And he was classed among transgressors;"[7] for that which
> refers to me has its fulfillment.
>
> *Luke 22: 37*

We are also told that as Jesus emerged from the baptismal waters, the Spirit of God in the form of a dove descended and alighted on Him. The dove was a visible, symbolic, representation of the anointing of Jesus to His Messianic office. We recall that the word "Messiah" has the meaning of having been anointed and that much stress is laid by Isaiah on the fact that the Messiah will be anointed for His work with the fullness of the Spirit of God.

As to why a dove was singled out to represent the Spirit of God, the following considerations appear to offer a satisfactory explanation. In the first place, the dove came to represent the emblem of Israel.[8] The appearance of the dove symbolizing the Holy Spirit would then suggest that it is through Jesus, the ideal Israelite and Israel's Messiah, that Israel's mission in the world would be accomplished.

In the second place, the descent of the dove takes us back to the Biblical account of the Great Flood. The Flood is represented in Genesis as having come upon the world as a Divine judgment upon a wicked generation. Wishing to ascertain how much the Flood waters had receded, Noah sent out first a raven, then a dove. The return of the dove with an olive leaf in its mouth indicated to Noah that the Flood waters had receded considerably. The sight of the olive leaf signified the end of God's judgment upon the world of Noah's day, and His offer of forgiveness to mankind.

Thus, the two phenomena which appeared as Jesus emerged from Jordan's baptismal waters contained the two chief aspects of the Messianic program: God's judgment upon human wickedness, and His offer of pardon through the atoning death of the Messiah who came to fulfill Israel's mission.

---

7. Quoted from Isaiah 53:12.
8. Midrash on Song 1:15; Sanh. 95a; Ber. R. 39; Yalkut on Ps. 55:7; etc.

II. THE TEMPTATION IN THE WILDERNESS[9]

The sublime experience at the baptism of Jesus was quickly followed by a time of severe testing, as related in the account of the Temptation in the wilderness. Two ways by which to accomplish His mission presented themselves to Him in the course of this Temptation. One was the way men have always chosen: the way of ambition, self-seeking, self-glory, and power — the way of the world, the devil, and the flesh. Jesus resolutely rejected this way. The path He chose was that of self-denial, the one which His Heavenly Father marked out for Him to follow, the path which was inevitably to set Him in irreconcilable conflict with the expectations of those in whose midst He was to labor.

III. THE BRAZEN SERPENT

The earliest allusions to His death were made by Jesus at the very beginning of His public ministry, and recorded in the account of the first cleansing of the Temple,[10] and when He was interviewed by Nicodemus.[11] With reference to the Messianic expectations of the Jewish people of the first century of our era, including the followers of Jesus prior to His Resurrection, the uppermost thing in their mind was the national restoration of Israel. This national hope grew in intensity in proportion to the increasing oppression from the heathen Roman power occupying their native land. Thus it happened that the national ingredient of the Messianic hope eclipsed that other aspect of Messiah's mission which had to do with man's moral life and his ultimate destiny. Jesus never ignored the national element of Israel's Messianic hope. But if His mission was to accomplish its purpose, the unbalanced and un-Biblical views of His contemporaries had to be corrected. Accordingly, to those who had ears to hear and were willing to learn He unfolded, step by step, the spiritual side of Messiah's work as found in the Old Testament. His first recorded effort in this direction took place during His meeting with Nicodemus, and for this purpose He selected the brazen serpent incident in the Wilderness phase of Israel's history.

---

9.   Matthew 4:1-11; Mark 1:12-13; Luke 4:1-13.
10.   John 2:13-22.
11.   John 3:1-15

Because Edom refused permission to pass through its territory, the Israelites were obliged to go around the land of Edom and proceed in the direction of the Gulf of Akabah through the deep depression of the Arabah. The low-lying plain of Arabah is intensely hot, desolate, bare of vegetation, and often devoid of drinking water. It was this Arabah which best fitted the description by Moses as "that great and terrible wilderness."[12] During this passage the Israelites became despondent and began to murmur against God and Moses. In punishment for this they were bitten by fiery serpents, of which this part of the wilderness has an abundance, and many of them died. The name "fiery serpents" is derived from the fiery-red spots on their skin. The Israelites repented and pleaded with Moses to intercede with God on their behalf. In response to Moses' prayer God instructed him to make a serpent of brass or copper and set it up on a pole. Any Israelite who was bitten by a fiery serpent was instructed to approach the pole and look up to the brazen serpent. If he did so, he escaped death and became well.[13]

The meaning attached to the brazen serpent incident by Jewish tradition may be seen from the following excerpts.

> He, who lifted up his heart to the name of the Memra[14] of Jehovah, lived.
> *Targum Pseudo-Jonathan on Numbers 21:8-9*

> And Moses made a serpent of brass, and set it in a place aloft. And it was that every one that was bitten with the serpent, and lifted his face in prayer unto His Father who is in Heaven, and looked unto the brazen serpent, he was healed.
> *Jerusalem Targum on Numbers 21:8-9*

Similarly, the author of the Apocryphal WISDOM OF SOLOMON, declares that the brazen serpent was to the bitten Israelites

> A token of salvation to remind them of the commandment of thy law. For the one who turned toward it was saved not because of what he saw. But because of thee, who is the preserver of all.
> *WISDOM OF SOLOMON 16:6-7*

---

12.   Deuteronomy 1:19
13.   Numbers 21:4-9.
14.   "Memra" — the Word of God.

The Mishnah has the following:

> "But could the serpent slay or the serpent keep alive? It is rather to teach you that as the Israelites directed their thoughts on high and kept their hearts in subjection to their Father in Heaven, they were healed; otherwise they pined away."
>
> *Rosh Ha-Shanah 3:8*

The Yalkut[15] reasons that the brazen serpent incident teaches that the dead shall live again. "Behold, if God made it that, through the similitude of the serpent which brought death, the dying should be restored to life, how much more shall He, who is Life, restore the dead to life."[16]

"Here lies the true interpretation of what Jesus taught. If the uplifted serpent, as symbol, brought life to the believing look which was fixed upon the giving, pardoning love of God, then, in the truest sense, shall the uplifted Son of Man give true life to everyone that believes, looking up in Him to the giving and forgiving love of God, which His Son came to bring, to declare, and to manifest."[17]

The Jerusalem Targum cited above sees some relation between the fiery serpents which bit the Israelites in the Wilderness and the Serpent which persuaded Adam and Eve to break God's commandment. Thus, the brazen serpent set up by Moses, upon God's instruction, upon a pole represents the Evil one who was destined to be defeated by the Messiah, the Second Adam, in fulfillment of God's promise to Eve. To Nicodemus who came to inquire from Jesus about the how and when of the restoration of the Davidic Kingdom, Jesus said that Messiah must ascend a cross before He mounts a throne.

> And as Moses lifted up the serpent in the wilderness, even so must the Son of Man be lifted up. That whoever believes in him may have eternal life.
>
> *John 3:14-15*

---

15.   A Haggadic compilation of expositional teachings on the various books of the Old Testament said to have originated in the early part of the 13th century, though it probably contains older material.

16.   Yalkut, Vol. 1, p. 240c.

17.   Alfred Edersheim, Op. Cit., Vol. 1, p. 388.

IV.   JESUS WENT TO THE CROSS WILLINGLY

Not only did Messiah Jesus know from the very commencement of His Messianic mission that His death constituted a necessary element of the Messianic mission, He went to the cross of His own free will.

> I am the good shepherd; the good shepherd lays down his life for the sheep . . . For this reason the Father loves me, because I lay down my life that I may take it again. No one takes it away from me, but I lay it down of my own accord; I have power to lay it down, and I have power to take it again; this charge I have received from my Father.
>
> *John 10: 11, 17-18*

V. THE FIRST ADVANCE AND DIRECT DISCLOSURE OF HIS DEATH

> Now when Jesus came into the district of Caesarea Philippi, he began asking his disciples, saying, "Who do people say that the Son of Man is?" And they said, "Some say John the Baptizer; some, Elijah; and others, Jeremiah, or one of the prophets." He said to them, "But who do you say that I am?" And Simon Peter answered and said, "You are the Messiah, the Son of the living God."
>
> *Matthew 16:13-16*[18]

What led to the question as to who the people thought Jesus might be was an incident related in the beginning of the same chapter in Matthew's Gospel and which manifested an ever-widening gulf between Jesus and Jewish religious leadership of His day. This incident is recorded in the following passage.

> And the Pharisees and Sadducees came up, and testing him asked him to show them a sign from heaven. But He answered and said to them, "When it is evening, you say, 'It will be fair weather, for the sky is red.' And in the morning, 'There will be a storm today, for the sky is red and threatening;' do you know how to discern the appearance of the sky, but cannot discern the signs of the times? An evil and adulterous generation seeks after

---

18.   See parallels in Mark 8: 27-29; Luke 9: 18-20.

a sign; and a sign will not be given it, except the sign of Jonah;"
and he left them and went away.

Matthew 16; 1-4

The Pharisees were the traditionalists of that day. They accepted the Old Testament Scriptures as the Word of God, but they added to it the teachings passed on to them by tradition. The Sadducees were the "liberals." They rejected the supernatural element in religion, they did not believe in a resurrection, to them religion was not much more than an ethical code. The Pharisees added to, the Sadducees subtracted from, the Mosaic revelation. The Pharisees were the party of the people. The Sadducees were the party of the rich. The Pharisees cherished the hope of the coming of a Messianic Person, the Sadducees were content with the present, and suspicious and apprehensive of any change that might disturb the status quo and their privileged position. In their opposition to Jesus they were chiefly motivated by a fear that His activities might lead to civil disturbances and retaliation by the Roman authorities.

The Messiah expected by the Pharisees, and hence by the Majority of the Jewish people of the first century of our era, was first of all a political Messiah. He was to usher in God's rule by defeating Israel's enemies, i.e., the Roman empire, and setting up a glorified version of the Davidic Kingdom. The whole demeanor and activities of Jesus showed Him to be so much unlike the Messiah of Pharisaic expectations. True, as the statements by the apostles cited above indicated, Jesus was generally regarded as an extraordinary personality. He was classed with some of the ancient prophets. And He wrought miracles which could not be explained away. He was going about doing good, feeding the hungry, healing the sick and speaking words of peace and encouragement to those in sorrow and heavy-laden. But what about the political restoration of the Davidic kingdom which according to Pharisaic ideas was the first and chief item on the agenda of the Messianic program? Were the Pharisaic notions wrong? This could not possibly be, seeing that the Pharisees were the teachers and interpreters of the Mosaic revelation. Hence, the Pharisees concluded that Jesus could not be the true Messiah. As to His miracles, they attributed them to His alliance with evil powers.[19] Had not Moses warned Israel against miracle-working false prophets?[20] And so, soon after the second miracle of the

---

19.   Matthew 12:24.
20.   Deuteronomy 13:1-3.

feeding of the multitude,[21] a group of Pharisees and Sadducees came to Jesus and challenged Him to prove His Messiahship by some extraordinary, supernatural phenomenon directly from heaven. This request was not made in good faith, but merely to test Him.

The attitude of the religious leaders to Jesus proved that they failed to learn the lessons from their own history, or the history of the ancient world of which the Jewish people were then a part. In the centuries from their entry into the Promised Land under Joshua until the Babylonian exile the Jews had an independent national existence. The history of that period is recorded in the Old Testament writings, and what a deplorable record it is! When we turn from Jewish to Gentile history we meet with the same state of affairs. The lot of the rank and file of the people in the various countries of the ancient world was no different when ruled by their native, than by alien, despots. And did Greece fare any better, that remarkable people with its democracy, liberty and brilliant intellectual powers? The world "Failure" stands inscribed in large letters over the history of the ancient world, Jewish and Gentile.

But the Jewish religious leaders of the first century also failed to grasp the main thrust of God's redemptive purpose as unfolded in the Old Testament. Did not Jeremiah on the eve of the destruction of the first Jewish state, speak of the dawn of a new age in which Israel will be placed in a new relationship to God when God's law will be inscribed on their hearts rather than on scrolls of parchment?[22] Did not Ezekiel, in the same period, indicate that Israel's moral cleansing and a change of heart will constitute the distinguishing feature of her national restoration?[23] It was exactly this Messianic Kingdom of God of Old Testament prophecy that Jesus came to establish. It was the Gospel — the Good News — of this Kingdom that He was preaching, a kingdom composed of spiritually regenerated men and women.[24] He declared that if we seek first this kind of Kingdom, God's rule in our hearts, all other things will be added to us.[25]

---

21. Matthew 15:32-39.
22. Jeremiah 31:31-34 (31:30-33 Heb.).
23. Ezekiel 36:24-27.
24. John 3:3.
25. Matthew 6:33.

The state of mind and attitude of the religious leaders at this late stage of His ministry — only months before His Crucifixion — served as a reminder to Jesus of the need to initiate the disciples into the full meaning of His death. Matthew states that from that time on Jesus began to teach His disciples about the significance of His death. There are three direct statements made by Jesus during this period concerning His approaching death. The first was uttered in the region of Caesarea Philippi.

> From that time Jesus the Messiah began to show his disciples that he must go to Jerusalem, and suffer many things from the elders and chief priests and scribes, and be killed, and be raised up on the third day.
>
> *Matthew 16:21*[26]

Notice the word "must". He *must* go to Jerusalem and die. This "must" expresses an inward necessity, and this inward necessity was for Jesus identical with the will of God recorded on the pages of Holy Writ centuries before He came. "We have seen already that from the beginning our Lord's sense of His own vocation and destiny was essentially related to that of the [Suffering] Servant of the Lord in the Book of Isaiah, and it is there that the ultimate source of the "must" is to be found." This will of God for a career of suffering and death was for Jesus a primary necessity; "it belongs, in however vague and undefined a form, to our Lord's consciousness of what He is and what He is called to do." As soon as His disciples confessed Him to be the Messiah He began to teach them the doctrine of the Suffering Messiah. "The necessity of His death is not a dreary, incomprehensible something that He is compelled to reckon with by untoward circumstances; for Him it is given, so to speak, with the very conception of His person and His work. When He unfolds Messiahship it contains death. This was the first and last thing He taught about it, the first and last thing He wished His disciples to learn . . . The necessity to suffer and die, which was involved in His vocation, and the dim sense of which belonged to His very being, so that without it He would not have been what He was, was now beginning to take definite shape in His mind. As events made plain the forces with which He had to deal, He could see more clearly how this [Divine] necessity would work itself out."[27]

---

26. See, the parallels in Mark and Luke.
27. James Denny, THE DEATH OF CHRIST (Eaton and Mains: New York, N. Y., n.d.), pp.31-32.

VI. THE SECOND ADVANCE AND DIRECT DISCLOSURE
OF HIS DEATH

The second time He spoke explicitly about His death was after the healing of the epileptic boy.

> And while they were gathering together in Galilee, Jesus said to them, "The Son of Man is going to be delivered into the hands of men. And they will kill him and he will be raised again on the third day;" and they[28] were deeply grieved.
>
> *Matthew 17: 22-23*[29]

VII. THE THIRD ADVANCE AND DIRECT DISLOSURE
OF HIS DEATH

> And they were on the road, going up to Jerusalem, and Jesus was walking on ahead of them; and they[30] were amazed, and those who followed were fearful; and again he took the twelve aside and began to tell them what was going to happen to him. Saying, "Behold, we are going up to Jerusalem, and the Son of Man will be delivered up to the chief priests and the scribes; and they will condemn him to death, and will deliver him up to the Gentiles. And they will mock him and spit upon him, and scourge him, and kill him, and three days later He will rise again."
>
> *Mark 10: 32-34*

Directly before this third statement concerning His death Peter made some remark about the apostles having left everything — home and business — when they chose to follow Jesus. In reply to this observation Jesus spoke of eternal life and other rewards which await them in the future Messianic Kingdom.[31] These thoughts of the glories of the Messianic Kingdom might have so preoccupied their minds as to render them forgetful of the fearful present soon to unfold itself before them. It was therefore needful for Messiah Jesus to remind them that there is no Messianic King unless He is

---

28. His disciples.
29. See the parallels in Mark and Luke.
30. The disciples.
31. Mark 10:28-30 and its parallels in Matthew and Luke.

also a Savior, no Crown without a Cross. Incidentally, this is the first recorded instance to the effect that the Gentiles were to have a part in putting the Messiah to death. In Luke's version of this prediction we also have the significant mention by Jesus that all this will happen in fulfillment of Old Testament Scriptures.[32]

VIII. THE FOURTH ADVANCE AND DIRECT DISCLOSURE OF HIS DEATH

And James and John, the two sons of Zebedee, came up to him, saying to him, "Teacher, we want you to do for us whatever we ask of you." And he said to them, "What do you want me to do for you?" And they said to him, "Grant that we may sit in your glory,[33] one on your right, and one on your left." But Jesus said to them, "You do not know what you are asking for; are you able to drink the cup that I drink, or to be baptized with the baptism[34] with which I am baptized?" And they said to him, "We are able;" and Jesus said to them, "The cup that I drink you shall drink; and you shall be baptized with the baptism with which I am baptized.[35] But to sit on my right or on my left, this is not mine to give; but it is for those for whom it has been prepared." And hearing this, the ten began to feel indignant toward James and John. And calling them to himself, Jesus said to them, "You know that those who are recognized as rulers of the Gentiles lord it over them; and their great men exercise authority over them. But it is not so among you, but whoever wishes to become great among you shall be your servant. And whoever wishes to be first among you shall be slave of all. For even the Son of Man did not come to be served, but to serve, and to give His life a ransom for many."

Mark 10: 35-45[36]

That the apostles needed a reminder that a Cross must come before the Crown was demonstrated by the incident recorded above. James and John[37] were related to Jesus and, together with Simon Peter,

---

32. Luke 18:31.
33. Messianic Kingdom.
34. Referring to His forthcoming crucifixion the full meaning of which they as yet failed to grasp.
35. A prophetic allusion to the persecutions which the followers of Jesus were destined to experience.
36. See the Matthew parallel.
37. Jacob and Yochanan — their Hebrew names.

they stood quite close to Him. This may explain the frankness with which they presented their request. Jesus administered to them a tender rebuke. He told them that among His followers greatness should consist of a readiness to serve others, even as He, the Messiah, came not to be served, but to serve, and to give His life a ransom for many.

Humanly speaking, had this incident not taken place, there would have been no explicit reference by Jesus to the *atoning* character of His death — until the Last Supper event. In the New Testament, as well as the Old, some of the greatest theological doctrines came about in response to certain historical exigencies. It is therefore a precarious undertaking to make certain assumptions on the basis of silence in the Biblical record. The casual, matter-of-fact, manner in which the statement about giving His life a ransom for many was made only goes to show how deep-seated a conviction the atoning nature of His death must have been with Messiah Jesus.

The word "ransom" is the English translation of the word "lutron" in the Greek text. In the Greek Old Testament "lutron" is used to render the meaning of four different Hebrew words conveying the notion of atonement and redemption. Two of these words are "kipper" and "padhah." It has been suggested[38] that Jesus might have pondered over the substance of Psalm 49 in which both words "kipper" and "padhah" occur. The following is a passage from this Psalm.

> Hear this, all peoples, give ear all inhabitants of the world. Both low and high, rich and poor together. My mouth shall utter wisdom, the meditation of my heart shall be understanding. I will incline my ear to a proverb, I will open my riddle to the music of the lyre.

> Why should I fear in times of trouble, when the iniquity of my persecutors surrounds me. Even of them who trust in their wealth and boast of the abundance of their riches? Truly no man can ransom himself, or give to God the price of his life. (For the ransom of his life is costly and he must let it alone for ever). That he should continue to live on for ever, and never see the pit.

---

38. Ritschl, in RECHTE. U. VERSÖHNUNG, Vol. 2, p. 69 ff.; see, James Denney, Op. Cit., p. 44.

Yea, he shall see that even the wise die, the fool and the stupid alike must perish and leave their wealth to others. Their graves are their homes for ever, their dwelling places to all generations, though they call lands by their own name. But man cannot abide in his splendor, he is like the beasts that perish. This is the fate of those who have foolish confidence and the end of those who are pleased with their portion. Like sheep they are appointed for Hades; death shall be their shepherd; straight to the grave they descend, and their form shall waste away; Hades shall be their home. But God will ransom my soul from the power of Hades, for he shall receive me.

Psalm 49: 1-15 (49:2-16 Heb.)

"Truly no man can ransom himself," the Psalmist declares, "or give to God the price of his life . . . But God will ransom my soul from the power of Hades." How God will do this, was now declared by Jesus: "For the Son of Man did not come to be served, but to serve, and to give his life a ransom for many."

IX. THE FIFTH ADVANCE AND DIRECT DISCLOSURE OF HIS DEATH

Now there were certain Greeks[39] among those who were going up to worship at the feast.[40] These therefore came to Philip, who was from Bethsaida of Galilee, and began to ask him, saying, "Sir, we wish to see Jesus." Philip came and told Andrew; Andrew came, and Philip, and they told Jesus. And Jesus answered them, saying, "The hour has come for the Son of Man to be glorified.[41] Truly, truly, I say to you, unless a grain of wheat falls into the earth and dies, it remains by itself alone, but if it dies, it bears much fruit. He who loves his life loses it; and he who hates his life in this world shall keep it to life eternal. If any one serves me, let him follow me; and where I am, there shall my servant also be; if any one serves me, the Father will honor him. Now my soul has become troubled; and what shall I say? Father, save me from this hour: but for this purpose I came to this hour. Father, glorify thy name;" there came therefore a voice out of heaven: "I have both glorified, and will glorify it again."[42] The multitude therefore, who stood by and heard it,

---

39. Greek proselytes to Judaism.
40. Passover.
41. His exaltation through His death.
42. The meaning of this Heavenly voice is: as God has already been glorified through Messiah's active life and work, so shall He be glorified through His sufferings and death.

were saying that it had thundered; others were saying, "An angel has spoken to him." Jesus answered and said, "This voice has not come for my sake, but for your sakes. Now judgment is upon this world; now the ruler of this world[43] shall be cast out. And I, if I be lifted up from the earth, will draw all men to myself." But he was saying this to indicate the kind of death by which he was to die.

John 12: 20-33

The incident related above took place on the third day of Passion Week, probably towards the end of the day on which Jesus had brought His public ministry to a close. The Greeks, Gentile proselytes to Judaism, who came to attend the Passover celebration, probably listened to Jesus as He was teaching in the Temple. They addressed a request to one of the apostles to arrange for them an interview with Jesus. The sight of these Greeks was a reminder to Jesus of the "other sheep," the Gentiles, who also need to be gathered into Messiah's Kingdom. At the beginning of His public ministry He declared to Nicodemus — a spokesman for the Jews — that before He ascends the throne of His father David He must be lifted up on a cross, even as the serpent was lifted up by Moses in the wilderness "that whoever believes may in him have eternal life."[44] At the end of His public ministry, at this meeting with representatives of the Gentiles, He speaks again of His death as the means of redemption, not only of the Jews, but of the whole world. "And I, if I be lifted up from the earth, will draw all men to myself."

"As we see these 'Greeks' approaching, the beginning of Messiah's History seems re-enacted at its close. Not now in the stable of Bethlehem, but in the Temple, are the 'wise men,' the representatives of the Gentile world, offering their homage to the Messiah . . . The hour of decision was about to strike. Not merely as the Messiah of Israel, but in His world-wide bearing as 'the Son of Man,' was He about to be glorified by receiving the homage of the Gentile world, of which the symbol and the firstfruits were now before Him. But only in one way could He thus be glorified: by dying for the salvation of the world, and so opening the Kingdom of Heaven to all believers. On a thousand hills was the glorious harvest to tremble in the golden sunlight; but the corn of wheat falling into the ground, must, as it

---

43.   A reference to Satan.
44.   John 3:15.

falls, die, burst its envelope, and so spring into a very manifoldness of life. Otherwise would it have remained alone . . .

"Yet, He was not unconscious of the awful realities which this involved. He was true Man, and His Human Soul was troubled in view of it: True Man, therefore He felt it; True Man, therefore He spoke it . . . Truly Man, but also truly more than Man — and hence both the expressed desire, and at the same time the victory over that desire: "What shall I say, 'Father, save me from this hour? But for this cause came I into this hour.' " And the seeming discord is resolved, as both the Human and the Divine in the Son — faith and sight — join in glorious accord: "Father, glorify Thy Name.'"[45]

45.   Alfred Edersheim, Op. Cit., Vol. 2, pp. 391-392.

CHAPTER 5
THE DEATH OF JESUS IN THE LIGHT OF
ISRAEL'S EXODUS FROM EGYPT

THE DEATH OF JESUS IN THE LIGHT OF ISRAEL'S EXODUS FROM EGYPT

The next day he[1] saw Jesus coming toward him, and said, "Behold, the Lamb of God, who takes away the sin of the world!"

John 1:29

Clean out the old leaven that you may be a new lump,[2] as you really are unleavened, for Christ, our Passover lamb, has been sacrified.

1 Corinthians 5:7

You know that you were ransomed from the futile ways inherited from your fathers, not with perishable things such as silver or gold. But with the precious blood of Christ, like that of a lamb without blemish or spot.

1 Peter 1:18-19

The above statements show how the New Testament associates the death of Jesus with the sacrifice of the Passover lamb. This, in turn, suggests that Israel's exodus from Egypt, together with the Passover event which preceded it and the Wilderness experiences which followed it, are capable of illuminating much of the meaning of the death of Jesus.

I. THE PASSOVER EVENT

1. THE INSTITUTION OF THE FIRST PASSOVER

Whether or not the Passover was a transformation of an annual shepherd-festival celebrated by the early Semites when they would

---

1. i.e., John the Baptizer.
2. i.e., unleavened, or uncontaminated, dough.

dedicate the first-born of their flock of sheep or goats,[3] the Exodus Passover marked Israel's birth into nationhood. It came into existence on the eve of the departure of the Hebrews from Egypt, and it had a two-fold goal, as seen from the following statement.

> Therefore say to the people of Israel, "I am Jehovah, and I will bring you out from under the burdens of the Egyptians, and I will deliver you from their bondage, and I will redeem you with an outstretched arm and with great judgments. And I will take you for me for a people, and I will be your God; and you shall know that I am Jehovah your God who has brought you out from under the burdens of the Egyptians. And I will bring you into the land which I swore to give to Abraham, to Isaac, and to Jacob; and I will give it to you for a heritage: I am Jehovah."
>
> *Exodus 6:6-8*

The immediate objective of the Exodus was to liberate the Hebrews from Egyptian bondage. In order that the Hebrews may enter into possession of the land which God had promised to their ancestors it was imperative to free them from Egyptian servitude. For a people to become a nation, they need a country of their own, just as children need a home if they are to grow into mature men and women. But the ultimate purpose of their deliverance from Egyptian bondage was that Jehovah may become their God. "And I will take you for me for a people, and I will be your God."

From history, however, we know that the generation which departed from Egypt never attained the goal of their deliverance from Egypt; not only did Jehovah not become their God, they were not even permitted to enter the Promised Land, and were left to perish in the Wilderness. The generation which grew up in the Wilderness did enter the Promised Land, but they were told in advance by Moses that while the Promised Land is their permanent inheritance, their continued occupancy of their land will be determined by their loyalty to Jehovah, i.e., by whether or not Jehovah becomes their God. Jehovah did not become ancient Israel's God. Therefore, the people of the northern kingdom of Israel went into Assyrian captivity in 722 B.C., and the people of the southern kingdom of Judah were deported into the Babylonian exile around

---

3. Martin Buber, MOSES (Harper Brothers: New York, Harper Torchbook Edition 1958), pp. 69-73.

the end of the sixth century B.C. In less than forty years after the death of Messiah Jesus the Land of Israel was again laid in ruins, this time—by the Romans; and the Jewish people were sent into a world-wide dispersion which lasted some nineteen centuries. It is obvious, then, that Jehovah did not become Israel's God, and therefore the ultimate objective of the Exodus from Egypt was not realized in Jewish history. Why this was so may be known from an examination of the teachings embodied in the institution of the first Passover at the time of the Exodus from Egypt.

As observed in Egypt, the first Passover consisted of three elements: the lamb, the unleavened bread, and the bitter herbs.

2. THE PASSOVER LAMB

The lamb had to be a male, like the burnt offerings instituted later on in the Wilderness,[4] as it was taking the place of the first-born Israelite male. It had to be free of blemish or injury. As man's substitute the sacrificial lamb had to symbolize moral perfection. The killing of the Passover lamb constituted a sacrifice in the Biblical sense of the word.

> And it shall come to pass, when your children shall say to you, "What do you mean by this service?" You shall say, "It is the sacrifice of Jehovah's Passover, who passed over the houses of the people of Israel in Egypt, when he slew the Egyptians but spared our houses."
>
> *Exodus 12: 26-27*

The word "sacrifice" used in the above passage is the Hebrew noun "zevach," a word never used in the Old Testament to indicate mere killing, but always applied to the killing of a sacrificial animal. The killing of the Passover lamb was the first kind of sacrifice enjoined upon the Hebrews when they were in the process of becoming God's covenant people, i.e., of entering as a people into a covenant relationship with God. The Passover lamb was a unique sacrifice. It was instituted in Egypt, before the promulgation of the Mosaic Code and before the formal conclusion of the Sinai Covenant. It had certain features common to both the sin-offerings and peace-

---

4.   Leviticus 1:3, 11.

offerings. Like the peace-offering, the Passover sacrifice was eaten by the offerers. The peace-offering signified the state of peace, or communion and fellowship, between the Deity and the offerer. But this state of peace was made possible by the shedding of blood. Shedding and manipulation of blood always signified expiation or atonement.

> For the life of the flesh is in the blood and I have given it to you upon the altar to make an atonement for your souls; for it is the blood which makes an atonement for the soul.
>
> *Leviticus 17: 11*

The blood of the Egyptian Passover was applied to the door lintel and doorposts, these taking the place of the altar.

That the offering of the Passover lamb was an atoning sacrifice is confirmed by the additional fact that hyssop was used to apply the blood to the door lintel and doorposts.

> You shall take a bunch of hyssop and dip it in the blood which is in the basin, and touch the lintel and the two doorposts with the blood which is in the basin. . .
>
> *Exodus 12: 22*

Hyssop figures everywhere in the Mosaic Code as the instrument by which ritual purification was effected, and was closely associated with the idea of atonement.[5] When David cried to God for forgiveness on account of his sin with Bathsheba, he pleaded in the following words:

> Purge me with hyssop, and I shall be clean; wash me, and I shall be whiter than snow.
>
> *Psalm 51: 7 (51:9 Heb.)*

The death of the firstborn was a judgment not only on the Egyptians but also on the heathen religion of Egypt, and was aimed against the Egyptian belief that their deified king is in control of their present life and of the afterlife. The firstborn human male represented human life, the firstborn animal male signified animal life and also that by which human life is sustained. The judgment of

---

5. See, Leviticus 14:4, 6, 51-52; Numbers 19:18-19.

the death of the firstborn male, human and animal, was to demonstrate to the Egyptians that not Pharaoh their king, but Jehovah is the author of all life, the creator and sustainer of human life.

> For I will pass through the land of Egypt this night, and I will smite all the firstborn in the land of Egypt, both man and beast; and on all the gods of Egypt I will execute judgment: I am Jehovah.
>
> *Exodus 12: 12*

The Hebrews were not spared because they were morally superior than the Egyptians. As a matter of fact, they were not morally superior than the Egyptians, and they were practising many of the Egyptian abominations.[6] It was the atoning blood of the Passover lamb which shielded the Hebrews from God's judgment.

> For Jehovah will pass through to smite the Egyptians, and when he sees the blood on the lintel and on the two doorposts, Jehovah will pass over the door, and will not allow the destroyer to enter your houses to smite you.
>
> *Exodus 12: 23*

Reference was already made to the fact that the door lintel and doorposts were used in place of an altar on which the blood of sacrificial animals was being sprinkled. But if this were the only reason, the blood of the Passover sacrifice could have been applied to the inside, instead to the outside of the house. The above passage supplies the added reason for this commandment: when God sees the blood on the door lintel and doorposts, He will not allow death to enter the houses of the Hebrews. But the destroying angel did not need to see the blood on the door lintel and doorposts in order to know which houses are occupied by the Hebrews. The full explanation for the instruction to paint the blood on the outside of the house is found in the following passage:

> And the blood[7] shall be a sign for you, upon the houses where you are; and when I see the blood, I will pass over you, and no plague shall fall upon you to destroy you, when I smite the land of Egypt.
>
> *Exodus 12: 13*

---

6. See, Joshua 24:14; Ezekiel 20:7-8.
7. Of the Passover sacrifice.

"And the blood shall be a sign for you." The blood of the Passover sacrifice, when applied to the outside of their houses, shall be a sign for the Hebrews. The sign was a Divine declaration that all men, Hebrews as well as Egyptians, are morally unclean, that sin alienates all men from God, and that alienation from God means spiritual death; and that only the sacrifice of a morally perfect life, as symbolized by the lamb without blemish, can beget in man a new life from God, a spiritually regenerated life.

The Hebrews were warned not to leave their houses during the night when God brings upon the Egyptians the judgment of the death of the firstborn.

> And none of you shall go out of the door of his house until the morning.
>
> *Exodus 12: 22*

During the awful night when Divine judgment was raging all over Egypt, the Israelites were safe only inside their houses. Egypt represented the world outside of God, the world of sin and darkness. Such a world is under God's judgment, and there is safety only for those who are sheltered by the Divinely-instituted atonement.

3. THE UNLEAVENED BREAD

The Egyptians became so distressed and terrified in the wake of the death of the firstborn that they prevailed on the Hebrews to leave the country at once. This hasty departure left the Hebrews no time to bake bread for the long journey. Consequently, they prepared the dough for bread, but were unable to leaven it, and they took this unleavened dough with them. On their first stop at Succoth they made flat, thin, cakes out of this unleavened dough and used them instead of bread. In Hebrew these flat unleavened cakes are called Matzah in the singular and Matzoth in the plural.

> And the Egyptians were urgent with the people, that they might send them out of the land in haste; for they said, "We are all dead men." So the people took their dough before it was leavened, their kneading bowls being bound up in their clothes on their shoulders . . . And the people of Israel journeyed from Rameses to Succoth . . . And they baked unleavened cakes of the dough which they brought out of Egypt, for it was not

leavened; because they were thrust out of Egypt, and could not tarry, neither had they prepared for themselves any provisions.

Exodus 12: 33-34, 37, 39

But what had its origin in sheer necessity became memorialized in subsequent history. Future Passovers were to be observed by the eating of unleavened bread for seven days, which season assumed the name of the feast of Unleavened Bread, while the Passover Feast, strictly speaking, designates the celebration taking place in the evening of the 14th day of the month of Nisan.

> "Seven days you shall eat unleavened bread; on the first day you shall put away leaven out of your houses, for if any one eats what is leavened, from the first day until the seventh day, that person shall be cut off from Israel . . . In the first month, on the fourteenth day of the month in the evening, you shall eat unleavened bread, until the twenty-first day of the month at evening. For seven days no leaven shall be found in your houses . . . You shall eat nothing leavened; in all your dwellings you shall eat unleavened bread."
>
> *Exodus 12: 15, 18-20*

The meaning of the commandment to eat unleavened bread is derived from the fact that leaven is a ferment, i.e. a substance capable of producing fermentation by breaking down, or decomposing, complex substances, as, for example, the souring of milk. In the religious or theological sense leaven symbolizes moral decomposition or moral corruption.[8] As the sacrifice of the Passover lamb signified that Israel's national life had its beginning in a moral cleansing, the eating of unleavened bread during the seven days suggested that her national existence must be marked by her continued freedom from moral corruption.

4. THE BITTER HERBS

This was the third element of the Passover service. The Passover lamb was to be eaten with unleavened bread and with bitter herbs.

---

8. THE SONCINO PENTATEUCH, edited by the Chief Rabbi of Great Britain (The Soncino Press: London, 1938), p. 256.

They shall eat the flesh[9] that night, roasted in fire, with
unleavened bread and bitter herbs they shall eat it.

Exodus 12: 8

The eating of bitter herbs was intended to perpetuate the memory
of the severity of the Egyptian bondage.

5. *THE PERMANENT RELEVANCE OF THE PASSOVER EVENT*

And when you come to the land which Jehovah will give
you, according as he has promised, you shall keep this service.
And when your children shall say to you, "What do you mean by
this service?" You shall say, "It is the sacrifice of Jehovah's
Passover, who passed over the houses of the people of Israel in
Egypt, when he smote the Egyptians and delivered our
houses . . ." And you shall tell your son on that day, "It is
because of what Jehovah did for me when I came out of Egypt."

Exodus 12: 25-27, 13:8

While the annual celebration of the Passover served to com-
memorate the deliverance from Egyptian bondage, its equally
important object was to impress on succeeding generations the
transcendent relevance of the Passover event. The people of every
generation must relive the event and so appropriate it as if they
themselves had experienced the Egyptian bondage and the deliverance from it.

The Biblical period of Jewish history, marked by repeated
episodes of Jewish apostasy from the God of Biblical revelation, has
finally brought conviction to the Jewish people in the post-Biblical
period that the Passover event was prophetic of a future, full, and
permanent redemption, a conviction which had already been expressed in the long ago in the prophetic writings of the Old Testament. These insights into the real meaning of the Passover event
found expression in the many Messianic passages incorporated in
the Haggada, i.e., the story of the Passover, recited annually at the
Passover Service. The following are a few excerpts.

---

9. Of the lamb.

> Have compassion, we beseech Thee, O Eternal, our God!
> on Thy people Israel, upon Jerusalem Thy city, on Zion the
> dwelling place of Thy glory, on the kingdom of the house of
> David Thine anointed, and on the great and holy house which is
> called by Thy name.[10]
> And do Thou rebuild Jerusalem, the holy city, speedily.
> Blessed art Thou, O Eternal, who in His mercy will rebuild
> Jerusalem. Amen.

Another Messianic element in the Passover Service is bound up
with the coming of Elijah as Messiah's forerunner. A special cup of
wine is placed on the Passover table for Elijah, and following the
drinking of the third cup of wine the door is opened and Elijah is
invited in.

At the conclusion of the Passover Service a parable entitled
"The Only Kid" is recited or sung. It is a symbolic presentation of
certain great events in Jewish and world history, of the rise and fall
of the four world powers of Daniel 2, of the great wars at the end of
the Age, of the final triumph of God over the ungodly forces of the
world, of the restoration of Israel, and the establishment of God's
Kingdom on earth.

II. THE TIMING OF MESSIAH'S DEATH

Jesus of Nazareth was as truly the Son of Man as He was the Son
of God. When He put on the robes of flesh, He became subjected to
certain human limitations. Because it was necessary that He be truly
and fully man, certain types of knowledge were withheld from Him
during the earthly phase of His ministry. With reference to the exact
day of His return He said this:

> But of that day and hour no one knows, not even the angels
> of heaven, nor the Son,[11] but the Father alone.
>
> *Matthew 24:36*

---

10. An allusion to the Temple.
11. Referring to Himself.

We have shown that from the very beginning Jesus had known that to die for man's redemption was an essential part of His Messianic mission. But there is no recorded evidence that He had advance knowledge of the exact time of His death until two days before the Passover.

> And it happened that when Jesus had finished all these words,[12] he said to his disciples. "You know that after two days comes the Passover, and the Son of Man will be delivered up to be crucified."
>
> *Matthew 26: 1-2*[13]

> Now before the feast of the Passover, Jesus knowing that his hour had come that he should depart out of this world to the Father, having loved his own who were in the world, he loved them to the end.
>
> *John 13:1*

While the religious leaders grouped around the High Priest had for some time entertained ideas of doing away with Jesus, they at first did not plan to carry out their designs during the Passover season. During the Passover festivities Jerusalem was crowded with people from many parts of the world. His triumphal entry into Jerusalem on Palm Sunday and His daily appearances in the Temple must have drawn large numbers of people to Jesus. The leaders were fearful of precipitating a riot if they were to execute their scheme during the Passover season.

> Now it was two days before the Passover and the feast of Unleavened Bread; and the chief priests and scribes were seeking how to seize him by stealth and kill him. For they said, "Not during the feast, lest there be a tumult of the people."
>
> *Mark 14:1-2*

> Now the feast of Unleavened bread which is called the Passover was drawing near. And the chief priests and the scribes were seeking how to put him to death; for they were afraid of the people.
>
> *Luke 22:1-2*

---

12. Referring to the so-called Olivet prophetic discourse.
13. See, also, Matthew 26:6-12; Mark 14:3-8.

It was Judas Iscariot, for some time a disaffected disciple of Jesus, that solved the dilemma of the opponents of Jesus. Being one of the twelve apostles and knowing beforehand the scheduled activities and movements of the apostolic group, he went to the enemies of Jesus and presented to them a plan of how to lay hold of Jesus without inciting a public disturbance.

> And Satan entered into Judas called Iscariot, who was of the number of the twelve. And he went away and conferred with the chief priest and officers how he might deliver him up to them. And they were glad and agreed to give him money. And he consented and began seeking a good opportunity to deliver him up to them in the absence of the multitude.
>
> *Luke 22:3-6*[14]

And so, contrary to the intentions of Jewish religious leadership, Messiah Jesus did die during the Passover season. I am persuaded that this took place by the overruling hand of Providence, because of the intimate relationship between the Passover event and the Messianic mission of Jesus. In the discussion which follows we shall endeavor to show what this relationship is.

III. THE NEW EXODUS

When the fall of ancient Israel became a certainty, there sprang up a large number of God-inspired prophetic utterances which declared that the rise of the new Israel will be equivalent to a new Exodus which in its importance will surpass the first Exodus. Two of these references are given below.

> Thus says Jehovah, who makes a way in the sea, a path in the mighty waters. Who brings forth chariot and horse, army and warrior; they lie down, they cannot rise, they are extinguished, quenched like a wick:[15] "Remember not the former things, nor consider the things of old. Behold, I am doing a new

---

14. See, also, Mark 14:10-11.
15. A reference to the miraculous event of the Sea of Reeds ("Red Sea").

thing; now it springs forth, do you not perceive it? I will make a way in the wilderness and rivers in the desert. The wild beasts will honor me, the jackals and the ostriches; for I give water in the wilderness, rivers in the desert, to give drink to my chosen people. The people whom I formed for myself that they might declare my praise."

Isaiah 43:16-21

"Therefore, behold the days are coming, says Jehovah, when it shall no longer be said, 'As Jehovah lives who brought up the people of Israel out of the land of Egypt.' But 'As Jehovah lives who brought up the people of Israel out of the north country and out of all the countries where he had driven them'; for I will bring them back to their own land which I gave to their fathers."

Jeremiah 16:14-15

However, the history of the Jewish community, which sprang up after the Babylonian exile was terminated, proved that this Second Jewish Commonwealth was not a fulfillment of the new Exodus as promised by the prophets, as seen from the following excerpts.

Behold, we are servants this day; in the land which thou gavest to our fathers to enjoy its fruit and its good gifts, behold, we are servants.[16]

Nehemiah 9:36

Jehovah, thou hast been favorable to thy land; thou hast brought back the captivity of Jacob. Thou hast forgiven the iniquity of thy people, thou hast covered all their sin — (Selah). Thou hast withdrawn all thy wrath; Thou hast turned thyself from the fierceness of thy anger.

Restore us again, O God of our salvation, and cause thy indignation toward us to cease. Wilt thou be angry with us forever? Wilt thou prolong thy anger to all generations? Wilt thou not revive us again, that thy people may rejoice in thee? Cause us to see thy grace, O Jehovah, and grant us thy salvation.

Psalm 85:1-7 (85:2-8 Heb.)[17]

---

16. This statement reflects the subordinate position of the Second Jewish Commonwealth with the exception of the brief Maccabean period.

17. This Psalm written in the post-Babylonian period reveals the state of mind of the Second Jewish Commonwealth, a far cry from the new Exodus restoration promises of the prophets.

The same impression is imparted to us by the writings of the three post-exilic prophets — Haggai, Zechariah and Malachi. We do not find there any suggestion that the Second Commonwealth represents the new Exodus restoration. In fact, Zechariah envisions another invasion of the Land of Israel.[18]

IV. JESUS BRINGS ABOUT THE NEW EXODUS

1. A PROPHET LIKE UNTO MOSES

Shortly before his death Moses made, among other things, the following statement to the Israelites as they were preparing to cross into the Promised Land

> Jehovah your God will raise up for you a prophet like me from among you, from your brethren — him you shall heed — Just as you desired of Jehovah your God at Horeb on the day of the assembly, when you said, 'Let me not hear again the voice of Jehovah my God, or see this great fire any more, lest I die.' And Jehovah said to me, 'They have rightly said all that they have spoken. I will raise up from them a prophet like you from among their brethren; and I will put my words in his mouth, and he shall speak to them all that I command him. And whoever will not give heed to my words which he shall speak in my name, I myself will require it of him."
>
> *Deuteronomy 18:15-19*

From the above we see that one of the distinguishing marks of the prophet like unto Moses whom God was to raise up was that like Moses he will be a mediator between God and Israel. As one reads the Gospels one is amazed to find the many resemblances between the mission of Moses and that of Jesus. Both Moses and Jesus were threatened with destruction at their birth. From the waters of the Red Sea Moses led Israel into the Wilderness where they sojourned for forty years. After emerging from the waters of the Jordan Jesus went into the Wilderness where for forty days He was exposed to wild beasts and suffered hunger.[19] The Scripture passages which

---

18. Zechariah 12 and 13.
19. Matthew 4:1-11; Mark 1:12-13; Luke 4:1-13.

Jesus used to repel Satan's assaults on Him in the Wilderness were all taken from Deuteronomy,[20] thus proving how much the mind and heart of Jesus were preoccupied with the Wilderness experiences of Israel.

2. JESUS – THE NEW DELIVERER

The terms "release," "deliverance" and "liberty" which expressed the goal of the first Exodus became familiar and oft recurring words in the vocabulary of Jesus, as seen from the following incidents.

> And he came to Nazareth, where he had been brought up; and he went to the synagogue, as his custom was, on the Sabbath day; and he stood and read. And there was given to him the book of the prophet Isaiah; he opened the book and found the place where it was written: "The Spirit of the Lord is upon me, because he has anointed me to preach good news[21] to the poor; he has sent me to proclaim release to the captives and recovering of sight to the blind, to set at liberty those who are oppressed. To proclaim the acceptable year of the Lord." And he closed the book, and gave it back to the attendant, and sat down; and the eyes of all in the synagogue were fixed on him. And he began to say to them "Today this scripture has been fulfilled in your hearing."
>
> *Luke 4:16-21*

When criticized by a synagogue official for having healed on the Sabbath a woman who had been disabled for some eighteen years, Jesus said to him.

> You hypocrites! Does not each of you on the Sabbath untie his ox or his ass from the manger, and lead it away to water it? And ought not this woman, a daughter of Abraham whom Satan bound for eighteen years, be loosed from this bond on the Sabbath day?"
>
> *Luke 13:15-16*

---

20.   Deuteronomy 8:3; 6:16; 6:13.
21.   "Good news" — the Gospel.

He breaks the chains of slavery of the demon-possessed; He restores sight to the physically and spiritually blind; He brings health for the sick in body and soul; He gives self-respect to the despised and outcast; He offers relief to those upon whom Rabbinism had placed burdens of religious observances too heavy to bear.[22] These are some of the benefits of the new Exodus bestowed by the Second Moses.[23]

3. THE MEDIATOR OF A NEW REVELATION

The Sermon on the Mount is another instance of the New Exodus aspect of the Messianic mission of Jesus. The Ten Beatitudes with which the Sermon on the Mount opens constitute the Ten Commandments of Messiah's new revelation written on tables of flesh of the human heart rather than on stone.

Seeing the crowds, he went up on the mountain, and when he sat down his disciples came to him. And he opened his mouth and taught them, saying:

"Blessed are the poor in spirit, for theirs is the kingdom of heaven.

"Blessed are those who mourn, for they shall be comforted.

"Blessed are the meek, for they shall inherit the earth.

"Blessed are those who hunger and thirst for righteousness, for they shall be satisfied.

"Blessed are the merciful, for they shall obtain mercy.

"Blessed are the pure in heart, for they shall see God.

"Blessed are the peacemakers, for they shall be called sons of God.

---

22.   Matthew 11:28, 23:4.
23.   See, F. W. Dillistone, THE SIGNIFICANCE OF THE CROSS (The Westminster Press; Philadelphia, 1944), p. 40.

"Blessed are those who are persecuted for righteousness sake, for theirs is the kingdom of heaven.

"Blessed are you when men revile you and persecute you and utter all kinds of evil against you falsely on my account. Rejoice and be glad, for your reward is great in heaven, for so men persecuted the prophets who were before you . . .

"You have heard that it was said to the men of old, 'You shall not kill; and whoever kills shall be liable to judgment.' But I say to you that every one who is angry with his brother shall be liable to judgment; whoever insults his brother shall be liable to the council, and whoever says 'You fool!' shall be liable to the hell of fire . . .[24]

"You have heard that it was said, 'You shall not commit adultery! But I say to you that every one who looks at a woman lustfully has already committed adultery with her in his heart . . .

"You have heard that it was said, 'You shall love your neighbor and hate your enemy.' [25] But I say to you, Love your enemies and pray for those who persecute you. So that you may be sons of your Father who is in heaven; for he makes his sun rise on the evil and on the good, and sends rain on the just and on the unjust.

Matthew 5:1-11, 21-22, 27-28, 43-45

---

24. "You have heard that it was said to the people in the old days 'Thou shalt not murder,' and anyone who does so must stand his trial. But I say to you that anyone who is angry with his brother must stand his trial; anyone who contemptuously calls his brother a fool must face the supreme court; and anyone who looks down on his brother as a lost soul is himself heading straight for the fire of destruction" — J. B. Phillips, THE NEW TESTAMENT IN MODERN ENGLISH.

25. To my knowledge, a representative instance in the Mosaic Law to which the injunction to hate your enemy may refer is found in Deuteronomy 23: 3-6 and is aimed at the Ammonites and Moabites because of the hostility which they displayed towards the Israelites in the Wilderness. However, it is the spirit of intolerance of traditional Rabbinism to which the statement "hate your enemies" applies. A good illustration of it is the *Birkath ha-minim* inserted into the Shemoneh Esreh prayers around A.D. 100 and containing a curse pronounced upon Jewish followers of Jesus. See, also, Maimonides, on MANSLAUGHTER, chps. 4 and 13 — a fitting illustration of Rabbinic religious intolerance.

V. FROM MOSES TO ELIJAH TO JESUS THE MESSIAH

We have seen in a previous chapter how on a number of occasions Jesus threw out indirect hints of His death as being an essential element of His Messianic mission. Knowing that the Jewish people expected primarily a political Messiah, His intention must have been to put off a direct confrontation of His disciples with the subject of His forthcoming death until they had sufficient time to get to know Him better and to learn from Him the real nature of Biblical Messianism. Nevertheless, when after more than two and a half years had passed He made His first direct disclosure of His approaching death in Jerusalem, He precipitated a crisis among His disciples. Not being able, prior to His resurrection, to visualize how His dying would accomplish the Messianic program, the disciples were confused and bewildered. Their feelings were expressed by Peter when he said: "God forbid, Lord! This shall never happen to you."[26]

About a week had passed since that incident. Then He took three of the most representative of the apostolic band — Peter, James and John — "and led them to a high mountain apart."[27] Since this took place in the region of Caesarea Philippi, the most northern part of Jewish habitation, it is believed that the mountain to which Jesus and the three apostles repaired was the snow-covered Mount Hermon. From the statement by Luke that when they had reached a certain area on this "high mountain," Peter and the other two apostles were drowsy,[28] it appears that it must have been night when they had reached their destination on one of the peaks of Mount Hermon. What transpired there is described by all three synoptic Gospels. We are citing the account by Luke, as it seems to be the most complete.

> Now about eight days after these sayings he took with him Peter, John and James, and went up to the mountain to pray. And as he was praying, the appearance of his countenance was altered, and his raiment became dazzling white. And behold, two men talked with him, Moses and Elijah. Who appeared in glory and spoke of his departure, which he was to accomplish at Jerusalem. Now Peter and those who were with him were heavy

---

26.   Matthew 16:22.
27.   Matthew 17:1.
28.   Luke 9:32.

with sleep but kept awake, and they saw his[29] glory and the two men who stood with him. And as the men were parting from him, Peter said to Jesus, "Master, it is well that we are here; let us make three booths, one for you and one for Moses and one for Elijah," not knowing what he said. As he said this, a cloud came and overshadowed them; and they were afraid as they entered the cloud. And a voice came out of the cloud, saying, "This is my Son, my Chosen; listen to him!" And when the voice had spoken, Jesus was found alone; and they kept silence and told no one in those days anything of what they had seen.[30]

Luke 9:28-36[31]

Some thirty years later, writing to a group of Christians, Peter refers to this experience in the following passage.

For we did not follow cleverly devised myths when we made known to you the power and coming of our Lord Jesus Christ, but we were eyewitnesses of his majesty. For when he received honor and glory from God the Father and the voice was borne to him by the Majestic Glory, "This is my beloved Son, with whom I am well pleased." We heard this voice borne from heaven, for we were with him on the holy mountain.

2 Peter 1:16-18

What was the significance of the presence of Moses and Elijah on the Mount of Transfiguration? We are told that Moses and Elijah spoke to Jesus about His approaching decease which He was to accomplish in Jerusalem. The word "decease" is in the original Greek "exodos," the English "exodus." The "exodus" about which Moses and Elijah had spoken to Jesus referred not merely to His decease, but to the purpose of His decease, including His resurrection and ascension, by which He was to accomplish a new Exodus for which the Egyptian Exodus was a type and a pledge.

But surely Jesus had no need of being made aware of the purpose of His decease. He had known it all along, and it was this first disclosure by Him of the purpose of His exodus that precipitated a crisis in the attitude of His followers to Him, which crisis induced Him to take their three representatives to a mountain

---

29. Referring to Jesus.
30. According to Matthew and Mark, it was Jesus Himself who instructed them not to speak about this experience until after His resurection.
31. See, also, Matthew 17:1-9; Mark 9:2-9.

retreat to pray. Whenever a critical point was reached in the earthly ministry of Jesus, Heaven intervened. It was so at His baptism (Matthew 3:16-17; Mark 1:10-11; Luke 3:21-22). It was so also when tested by Satan.

> Then the devil left him; and behold, angels came and ministered to him.
>
> *Matthew 4:11 (Mark 1:13)*

Heaven's intervention came again at the end of His teaching ministry, on the occasion of His interview by the visiting Greeks (John 12:28); and finally before His arrest while He was in the agony of prayer in Gethsemane.

> "Father, if thou art willing, remove this cup from me; nevertheless not my will, but thine, be done." And there appeared to him an angel from heaven, strengthening him
>
> *Luke 22:42-43*

In Luke's account of the Mount of Transfiguration experience we are told that Jesus' purpose in the retreat to the mountain was to pray. "Although the text does not expressly state it, we can scarcely doubt, that he prayed with them, and still less, that He prayed for them . . . And, with deep reverence be it said, for Himself also did Jesus pray. For, as the pale moonlight shone on the fields of snow in the deep passes of Hermon, so did the light of the coming night shine on the cold glitter of Death in the near future. He needed prayer, that in it His Soul might be calm and still-perfect, in the unruffled quiet of His Self-Surrender, the absolute rest of His Faith, and the victory of His sacrificial Obedience."[32] The Heavenly Vision on the Mount of Transfiguration was God's answer to His prayer.

The presence of Moses and Elijah on the Mount of Transfiguration had a two-fold purpose. In the first place, it was to teach the three apostles that the "exodus" of Jesus, i.e., His death and resurrection, are in full accord with the Messianic thrust of the Law as represented by Moses, and prophecy as represented by Elijah. Moses' transgression in the Wilderness was not the only — and

---

32. Alfred Edersheim, THE LIFE AND TIMES OF JESUS THE MESSIAH (Longmans, Green, and Co.: London, 1899), Vol. 1, pp. 95-96.

probably not the main — reason why he was prevented by God from entering the Promised Land. Moses' failure to lead Israel into the Promised Land symbolically presaged the eventual failure of the Sinai Covenant mediated by Moses to bring the purpose of Israel's Exodus from Egypt to a full consummation. As he stood on the threshold of the destruction of the Judean State at the beginning of the sixth century B.C., Jeremiah stressed the failure of the Sinai Covenant and he foretold its replacement by a new covenant (Jeremiah 31:31-34, 31:30-33 Heb.).

In the days of Elijah the process of paganization of northern Israel was hastened by the activities of Jezebel, a pagan woman of foreign birth and the wife of King Ahab. For a long time Elijah had striven to recall northern Israel to a renewed allegiance to the Sinai Covenant. Queen Jezebel destroyed many of the true prophets and she vowed to do away with Elijah, their leader. In the wake of this threat to his life Elijah fled southward, and he finally made his way to Mount Horeb where the Sinai Covenant had been inaugurated. The following is a description of Elijah's experience at Mount Sinai.

> And there he came to a cave,[33] and lodged there; and behold, the word of Jehovah came to him, and he said to him, "What are you doing here, Elijah?" He said, "I have been very jealous for Jehovah, the God of hosts; for the people of Israel have forsaken thy covenant, thrown down thy alters, and slain thy prophets with the sword;[34] and I, even I only, am left; and they seek my life, to take it away." And he,[35] said, "Go forth, and stand upon the mount before Jehovah." And behold, Jehovah passed by, and a great and strong wind rent the mountains, and broke in pieces the rocks before Jehovah, but Jehovah was not in the wind; and after the wind an earthquake, but Jehovah was not in the earthquake. And after the earthquake a fire, but Jehovah was not in the fire; and after the fire a still small voice. And when Elijah heard it, he wrapped his face in his mantle and went out and stood at the entrance of the cave; and behold, there came a voice to him, and said, "What are you doing here,

---

33. This "cave" is thought to be the place on Mount Sinai where Moses received a special revelation following the Golden Calf incident — Exodus 33:21.
34. A reference to the destruction by Jezebel of the disciples of the true prophets, or members of the prophetic school who remained loyal to Jehovah.
35. i.e., God.

Elijah?" He said, "I have been very jealous for Jehovah, the God
of hosts; for the people of Israel have forsaken thy covenant,
thrown down thy altars, and slain thy prophets with the sword;
and I, even I only, am left; and they seek my life, to take it away."
And Jehovah said to him, "Go, return on your way to the
wilderness of Damascus; and when you arrive, you shall anoint
Hazael to be king over Syria. And Jehu the son of Nimshi you
shall anoint to be king over Israel; and Elisha the son of Shaphat
of Abelmeholah you shall anoint to be prophet in your place.
And him who escapes from the sword of Hazael shall Jehu slay;
and him who escapes from the sword of Jehu shall Elisha slay.
Yet I will leave seven thousand in Israel, all the knees that have
not bowed to Baal, and every mouth that has not kissed him."

1 Kings 19: 9-18

While the text does not state Elijah's reason for going to Mount
Sinai, there is little doubt that he was motivated by a desire for a
Divine revelation which would reaffirm the validity of the Sinai
Covenant and promise God's intervention in reimposing the Covenant on northern Israel. Whatever the statement that God was not in
the storm, earthquake and fire may mean, it probably was intended
to impress on Elijah the fact that the objectives of the Sinai Covenant
will not be attained by the instrumentality of judgment as represented by the physical phenomena of storm, earthquake and fire,
the very same phenomena which attended the original Sinai revelation after the exodus from Egypt. There is no question that the
entire Divine manifestation granted to Elijah — the question, "What
are you doing here, Elijah?", God's absence in the storm, earthquake
and fire, and His presence in the still small voice — constituted
another milestone in Biblical revelation, and a preparation for
Jeremiah's promise of the New Covenant which would engrave
God's law on human hearts rather than on tables of stone.

The other purpose of the presence of Moses and Elijah on the
Mount of Transfiguration was to re-assure the Lord Jesus Himself.
The basis of this reassurance was the implication that the Messianic
mission of Jesus will be carried out through a remnant. The idea of a
remnant goes back all the way to the Wilderness period of Israel's
history. Only those Israelites who were less than twenty years old
when they left Egypt were permitted to enter the Promised Land
and thus attain the goal of their liberation from Egypt. All others
were intentionally left to die in the Wilderness.

But it was in the days of Elijah when for the first time the
concept of God's redemptive purpose being realized through a

remnant came to the fore. At Mount Sinai Elijah learned that while the doom of northern Israel was sealed, a remnant will be saved.

> "Yet I will leave seven thousand in Israel, all the knees that have not bowed to Baal, and every mouth that has not kissed him."
>
> *1 Kings 19:18*

The prophet Isaiah grasped the full significance of the role which the faithful remnant was destined to play. To Isaiah the remnant is the holy seed.[36] The following is one of the well-known statements by Isaiah concerning the remnant.

> A remnant will return, the remnant of Jacob, to the mighty God. For though your people Israel be as the sand of the sea, only a remnant of them will return . . .
>
> *Isaiah 10:21-22a*

The apostle Paul may have had in mind the lesson of the Mount of Transfiguration vision when he made the following statement.

> I ask, then, has God rejected his people?[37] By no means! I myself am an Israelite, a descendant of Abraham, a member of the tribe of Benjamin. God has not rejected his people whom he foreknew; do you not know what the scripture says of Elijah, how he pleads with God against Israel? "Lord, they have killed thy prophets, they have demolished thy altars, and I alone am left, and they seek my life." But what is God's reply to him? "I have kept for myself seven thousand men who have not bowed the knee to Baal." So too at the present time there is a remnant, chosen by grace.
>
> *Romans 11:1-5*

To summarize, the presence on the Mount of Transfiguration of Moses the Lawgiver and Elijah, the Representative of Old Testament prophecy and Messiah's Forerunner, had as its purpose, first, to reaffirm the fact that the Messiah came to complete the Sinai revelation and to fulfill Old Testament prophecy ("I came not to destroy the law and the prophets, but to complete"); second to assure both Jesus and the apostles that the goal of Messiah's first advent would be achieved by a remnant.

---

36. Isaiah 6:13.
37. Because they failed to acknowledge, on a national level, Jesus as the Messiah?

VI. MESSIAH JESUS INITIATES THE NEW COVENANT

It was said that "when an Israelite thought of a covenant he thought of a sacrifice."[38] The Abrahamic Covenant was concluded with a sacrifice.[39] The Sinai Covenant was made by means of a sacrifice.[40] In Part One of this work we have seen how the Suffering Servant of Jehovah was introduced to us not only as the Mediator, but as the embodiment, of the New Covenant,[41] and as the One who pours out His life as the sacrifice of the New Covenant.[42]

Hours before His arrest Messiah Jesus sat down with His apostles to celebrate the Passover in the city of Jerusalem, in a room pre-arranged for this purpose. The Passover as it was brought into existence in Egypt was a family festival. During the days of the Temple the Passover Service was centered around the lamb which was sacrificed in the Temple. Therefore only those who went to Jerusalem to offer up the sacrifice of the lamb observed the Passover in accordance with Biblical regulations. This means that in the days of the Temple the Passover was chiefly celebrated by men, as only men were required to make their appearance in the Temple on the three great annual festivals. How the many Jews living at some distance from Palestine in the days of the Second Temple observed the Passover is not clearly known. With the destruction of the Temple and the cessation of the sacrifices, the Passover reverted to its original family character.

The Passover Service as celebrated in the days of Jesus did not differ much from the way in which it is being celebrated by the Jewish people today, except, of course, for the absence of the Passover lamb. At the opening of the Passover Service the host recited the customary Kiddush prayer in which he gave thanks for the wine. At the present time a cup is filled for each individual seated at the table. Among Oriental Jews the host alone fills the first cup and after reciting the Kiddush blessing he drinks from it and passes it around.

---

38.   F.C.N. Hicks, THE FULLNESS OF SACRIFICE (S.P.C.K.: London, 1953), p. 22.
39.   Genesis 15:9-21.
40.   Exodus 24: 3-9.
41.   Isaiah 42: 1-6b.
42.   Isaiah 53.

Each of the celebrants at the table would pour a little from the host's cup into his own cup and drink it. It appears that this was the procedure followed by Jesus.[43]

Next took place the first washing of the hands. There were two handwashings. In the first one, the host alone washed his hands. It was at this point that Jesus, who as the host, or celebrant, rose from the table to wash His hands, performed the washing of the disciples' feet. This act of self-abasement and the words addressed to the disciples as reported in Luke's and John's Gospel were connected with a dispute which arose among the disciples about who should occupy the chief seat at the table next to Jesus. By His deed and the accompanying statement He endeavored to teach them that in His Messianic Kingdom self-effacement and service to others are the distinguishing mark of true greatness.

> A dispute also arose among them, which of them was to be regarded as the greatest. And he said to them, "The kings of the Gentiles exercise lordship over them; and those in authority over them are called benefactors."But not so with you;rather let the greatest among you become as the youngest, and the leader as one who serves. For which is the greater, one who sits at table or one who serves? Is it not the one who sits at table? But I am among you as one who serves."
>
> *Luke 22:24-27*

> When he had washed their feet, and taken his garments and resumed his place, he said to them, "Do you know what I have done to you? You call me Teacher and Lord; and you are right, for so I am. If I then, your Lord and Teacher, have washed your feet, you also ought to wash one another's feet. For I have given you an example, that you also should do as I have done to you. Truly, truly I say to you, a servant is not greater than his master; nor is he who is sent greater than he who sent him. If you know these things, blessed are you if you do them."
>
> *John 13: 12-17*

Presently, the Passover dishes were brought to the table. The head of the company would dip some of the bitter herbs into salt-water or vinegar, utter a blessing, partake of them and then pass

---

43.   See Alfred Edersheim, Op. Cit., Vol. 2, p. 496. See also Elias Newman, THE JEWISH PASSOVER AND THE CHRISTIAN LORD'S SUPPER (The Zion Society For Israel: Minneapolis, Minnesota, 1947), p.13.

them to each of the company. Next, he would break one of the unleavened cakes — the middle of the three cakes according to the present ritual — of which half was put aside for after supper. This is called the Aphikomen. The head of the company then lifts the plate containing the remaining unleavened cakes and recites the following: "This is the bread of affliction which our fathers ate in the land of Egypt. All that are hungry, come and eat; all that are needy, come, keep the Passover." After the destruction of the Land of Israel, and the dispersion of the Jews by the Romans, the following sentence was added: "This year here, next year in the land of Israel; this year bondsmen, next year free!" Now, the second cup is filled with wine, and the youngest in the company is instructed to make formal inquiry as to the meaning of the various observances of the Passover Service. In reply, the father or head of the company recites the Passover story. When this is finished, the host takes up, in succession, the dish containing the Passover lamb, the one with the unleavened cakes, and that with the bitter herbs, briefly expounding the meaning of each. Then the first part of the Hallel composed of Psalms 113 and 114 is recited or sung. The second cup is then drunk. This ends the first part of the Passover Service.

The second part begins by all washing their hands. The head of the company then breaks the unleavened cakes on the plate, recites a prayer of thanks, and distributes the broken pieces to each of the company. At the present, each member of the company eats first a piece of unleavened bread, then some of the bitter herbs dipped in Charoseth,[44] and lastly two small pieces of unleavened bread between which a piece of radish has been placed. But there is a statement in the book containing the ritual of the Passover Service that in the days of the Second Temple the "sop," or the two small pieces of unleavened bread, contained also a piece of the Passover lamb with the bitter herbs. It is believed that this was the "sop" which Jesus handed out to the apostles, Judas Iscariot being the first to receive it, since he obviously occupied the chief place next to Jesus. For all practical purposes the "sop," containing, as it did then, the three main ingredients of the Passover Service represented the Passover meal. After the eating of the Passover lamb, the Passover meal was considered as finished. The third cup was filled with wine. Grace, or the blessing after the meal, was recited, after which the third cup was drunk.

44. Made of nuts and fruits pounded together and mixed with vinegar.

It was at this juncture, after the grace following the meal, that Jesus the Messiah instituted what became the "Lord's Supper" or "Holy Communion," the most sacred rite in the Messianic faith of Jesus. The following are the New Testament reports of what had taken place.

> Now as they were eating, Jesus took bread, and blessed, and broke it, and gave it to the disciples and said, "Take, eat; this is my body." And he took a cup, and when he had given thanks he gave it to them, saying, "Drink of it, all of you. For this is my blood of the covenant, which is poured out for many for the forgiveness of sins."
>
> *Matthew 26: 26-28*

> And as they were eating, he took bread, and blessed, and broke it, and gave it to them, and said, "Take; this is my body." And he took a cup, and when he had given thanks he gave it to them, and they all drank of it. And he said to them, "This is my blood of the covenant, which is poured out for many."
>
> *Mark 14: 22-24*

> And when the hour came, he sat at table, and the apostles with him. And he said to them, "I have earnestly desired to eat this Passover with you before I suffer . . ." And he took a cup, and when he had given thanks he said, "Take this, and divide it among yourselves . . ." And he took bread, and when he had given thanks he broke it and gave it to them, saying, "This is my body." And likewise the cup after supper, saying, "This cup which is poured out for you is the new covenant in my blood."
>
> *Luke 22: 14-15, 17, 19-20*

The account in Luke's Gospel is quite important, since it supplies certain details not present in the two other accounts. The statement in verse 17, "And he took a cup, and when he had given thanks he said, 'Take this, and divide it among yourselves'", refers to the first of the four cups of wine which are drunk during the Passover Service at different intervals. Then, in verse 20, we read this: "And likewise the cup after supper, saying, 'This cup which is poured out for you is the new covenant in my blood.' " "After supper" means after the Passover meal. Both the Matthew and Mark accounts state that He had given thanks in connection with this cup of wine which Luke tells us was drunk after supper. This was the third cup which is drunk following the recitation of grace after the meal. Paul refers to it as the cup of blessing.[45] This, because, like the first cup, the third cup also required a special blessing, and because it was drunk after the recitation of grace after the meal. In verse 19 Luke tells us, "And he took bread, and when he had given thanks he broke it and gave it to them, saying, 'This is my body.' " And right after this statement Luke declares, "And likewise the cup after supper, saying, 'This cup which is poured out for you is the new covenant in my blood.' " In other words, the bread and the cup of wine were both used after supper. The statement that He had given thanks in connection with the bread also refers to the reciting of grace after the meal, for thanks for the bread had already been given in the beginning of the Passover meal immediately after the second handwashing.

When the Passover lamb was the main dish, no food was allowed after the meal was finished. Since the cessation of the Temple sacrifices the Jewish people conclude the Passover Service with the eating of a piece of the broken-off middle Matzah called the Aphikomen or the after-dish. It was at this junction that the "Lord's Supper" was instituted. It seems that Messiah Jesus anticipated, as it were, the present Jewish practice of eating the Aphikomen. Following the grace after the meal, He took a piece of unleavened bread, broke it, distributed it among the apostles and said, "Take, eat, this is my body." Likewise he took the third cup of wine, and He passed it around among the apostles, accompanied by the words, "Drink of it, all of you. For this is my blood of the covenant which is poured out for many for the forgiveness of sins." In Luke's account, the last portion is worded thus: "This cup which is poured out for you is the new covenant in my blood."[46] In making the Sinai covenant Moses sprinkled the blood of slain animals upon the people. The drinking of the wine symbolizing Messiah's shed blood suggests that the blood of the new covenant was not to be sprinkled upon man's exterior, but — whatever it means — it must become part of our inner lives. "Drink of it, all of you."

We are told in the Gospel records that after this they sang a hymn. This refers to the second half of the Hallel appointed for reciting or singing at the conclusion of the Passover Service and the

---

45. 1 Corinthians 10:16.
46. This probably has reference to the "new covenant" promised by Jeremiah in Jer. 31: 31-34 (31: 30-33 Heb.).

drinking of the last cup of wine. The second half of the Hallel consists of Psalms 115, 116, 117 and 118. The following is a passage from the last of these Psalms which may have reflected something of the state of mind of Jesus during those momentous hours as He was preparing to lay down His life.

> I shall not die, but live, and declare the works of Jehovah. Jehovah has chastened me sorely, but he has not given me over to death . . . The stone which the builders rejected has become the head stone of the corner. This is Jehovah's doing; it is marvellous in our eyes. This is the day which Jehovah has made; let us rejoice and be glad in it.
>
> *Psalm 118: 17-18, 22-24*

With these words ringing in their ears, Jesus and the eleven apostles left the "Upper Room," went out into the dark of the night and arrived at "a place called Gethsemane." There He was arrested, brought before the Jewish religious leaders, charged with blasphemy, accused falsely that He had said that He will destroy the Temple,[47] pronounced guilty of death, and finally handed over to the Roman governor Pontius Pilate for execution on the grounds that He was a political agitator, forbidding the people to pay taxes to the Roman government and pretending to be a king. About nine o'clock in the morning of the 15th day of Nisan, the first day of the Feast of Unleavened Bread, Jesus was placed on a cross by a detachment of Roman soldiers. Two common criminals were executed at the same time, one on His right, and one on His left.

Jesus died six hours after He had been put on the cross. Three hours before He expired darkness fell over the whole land and an earthquake took place. At the end of the three hours the Veil of the Temple was torn from top to bottom.[48] The Veil separated the Most Holy Place from the Holy Place and the remainder of the Temple. The High Priest was the only person who entered the Most Holy Place, and this only once a year, on the Day of Atonement, to offer the blood of atonement for the sins of the whole nation.

Can this New Testament account be verified historically? There are four independent testimonies, all relating the occurrence of certain happenings in Jerusalem and/or the Sanctuary about this

---

47.   Matthew 26: 59-61; 27:39-40.
48.   Matthew 27:45,50-51; Mark 15:33, 37-38; Luke 23:44-45.

time and recorded by Tacitus, the pagan Roman historian of the first century;[49] by the Jewish historian Flavius Josephus — also of the first century of our era;[50] the Gospel according to the Hebrews, of the first century of our era and used by the two Hebrew Christian sects of Ebionites and Nazarenes; and the Talmud.

In the days of the Second Temple there was a custom to fasten a red-colored strip of wool to the head of the goat which was to be sent away into the wilderness on the Day of Atonement. When this red ribbon became white, it was a sign that God had forgiven Israel's sins. There is a statement in the Talmud that "forty years before the second Temple was destroyed . . . the red wool did not become white." The same passage informs us that the gates of the Temple which had been previously closed swung open of their own accord. This was regarded as a portent of the coming destruction of the Temple.[51] Forty years before the destruction of the Temple coincides exactly with the year of the crucifixion of Jesus of Nazareth.

Whether or not the events described in the various documents referred to above were related to the earthquake mentioned in the New Testament as having occurred during the final three hours while Jesus was hanging on the cross, the tearing of the Veil of the Most Holy Place suggested that the death of the Messiah has removed the barrier between God and man, and made God accessible to all people, both Jews and Gentiles.

When Jesus was placed on the cross, an inscription was nailed to the cross containing the political aspect of the crime with which He was charged and for which He was crucified. The inscription was in Hebrew, Latin and Greek, and it read: "Jesus of Nazareth, the King of the Jews."[52] Latin represented the political sphere, Greek — the intellectual sphere of the Gentile world of the first century of our era; while Hebrew represented the Jewish people. Thus, the religious representatives of the Jewish world and the political and intellectual representatives of the Gentile world joined hands in placing Jesus on the cross. But Hebrew is also the language of the Old Testament in which in centuries past Jehovah of Biblical revelation

---

49. THE HISTORIES OF TACITUS, V. 13.
50. THE JEWISH WAR, Book VI, 5.3.
51. Yoma 29b.
52. Matthew 27:37: Mark 15:26: John 19:19-210.

spelled out His redemptive purpose for the world. Back of the
combined efforts of Jews and Gentiles in the crucifixion of Jesus
there was the hand of God who used man's wilfulness and human
failure in order to save mankind from itself. For He who was nailed
to the cross is none other than the Son of God, the Son of Man, the
Son of Abraham, the Son of David.

> "For truly in this city[53] there were gathered together
> against thy holy servant Jesus, whom thou didst anoint, both
> Herod and Pontius Pilate, along with the Gentiles and the
> peoples of Israel. To do whatever thy hand and thy purpose pre-
> destined to take place."
>
> *Acts 4: 27-28*

---

53. Jerusalem.

CHAPTER 6
THE UNIVERSAL AND PERMANENT VALIDITY
OF THE DEATH OF JESUS

CHAPTER 6
THE UNIVERSAL AND PERMANENT VALIDITY OF THE DEATH OF JESUS

In the preceding chapter we considered the death of Jesus in the light of Israel's Exodus from Egypt. We now wish to discuss the universal and permanent meaning of His death.

I. WAS MESSIAH'S DEATH REALLY NECESSARY?

Notwithstanding the contemporary decline of the sense of sin, man is aware today as much as ever that not all is well with his soul. He remains conscious of the futility of his life, of his enslavement by degrading habits, of the corruption of his nature which causes him to do the things which he should not and not to do the things which he should; moreover, even at this juncture of history man is not entirely indifferent to the consequences which his misconduct creates in the lives of others. "It is the moral evil of individuals which is the ultimate cause of sufferings involved in war or bad social conditions."[1] "Man himself has been and is the responsible agent for much of the actual suffering of history."[2]

But is it not possible for man to change things by mere penitence, apart from Messiah's saving death on the Cross? Any person seeking to solve the problem of sin in his life will discover, if he is honest with himself, that he is engaged in an impossible task. He will, in the first place, find that he simply lacks the power to bring about a regeneration of his nature. He will also realize that he is unable to undo the evils which his immoral behavior has brought upon others. King David committed adultery with Bathsheba, the wife of Uriah, an officer in the Israel army. To cover up his adultery by marrying Bathsheba, David arranged to have Uriah placed in the front line of

---

1. H. Wheeler Robinson, SUFFERING HUMAN AND DIVINE (The Mcmillan Co.: New York, 1939), p. 76.
2. Ibid., p. 104.

a battle then raging between the opposing armies of Israel and one of her enemies. David's scheme worked out fully when Uriah was killed in enemy action. His marriage to Bathsheba may have helped to conceal his adultery. But what about Uriah's death which David indirectly brought about? Did David's subsequent repentance restore Uriah to life? Did it cancel out the sorrow and shame which David inflicted on a whole family?

Throughout history there has been a universal recognition that for civilized society and ordered human life to be possible, evildoers must be punished. The Bible attributes to God the origin of the principle of retribution and the imposition upon man of the duty to enforce it.[3] But experience has shown that human enforcement of this principle does not solve man's crime against his fellow men. A university professor who is engaged in valuable research work is held up one day on his way to his laboratory and killed. If the killer is sentenced to death and executed, does his punishment fit his crime? To assume that it does, is to take the position that the murderer's life was of equal worth to society as the life of the professor. If the murderer is sentenced to life imprisonment, will his conscience, if he has any left, acquiesce in the fact that while his own life has been spared, his victim is dead? And how shall man apply the principle of retribution in a case of mass murders, such as was committed by the Nazis? Has the execution of a number of leading Nazis atoned for the death of millions of their victims? "No right-minded man will ever forgive himself for his own wrong-doing; ought he to believe that a holy God can dismiss sin more lightly than he does himself?"[4]

This world is God's world: He made it and He sustains it. We must never lose sight of the fact that human sin is primarily sin against God.[5] Can He afford to be indifferent to the wreckage and ruin with which man's path through history has been littered? It is true that when God gave to man the freedom of choice He made it possible for man to be immoral, so that in a sense God is partly responsible for the existence of evil in the world.

> "I form the light and create darkness; I make peace and create evil: I Jehovah do all these things."
>
> *Isaiah 45:7*

---

3. Genesis 9:5-6.
4. A. Wheeler Robinson, Op. Cit., p. 176.
5. Psalm 51:4 (51:6 Heb.).

But man's freedom to choose does not lessen the measure of the responsibility for how he uses his freedom of choice. How then should God deal with the problem of sin? It is the clear teaching of the entire New Testament that the death of Jesus the Messiah is God's answer to the problem of human sin.

II. THE DEATH OF JESUS
REPRESENTS THE CULMINATION OF MORAL EVIL

The death of Jesus was no isolated eruption of human sin, as may be seen from the following parable spoken by Jesus shortly before His death.

> "There was a householder who planted a vineyard, and set a hedge around it, and dug a wine press in it, and built a tower, and let it out to tenants, and went into another country. When the season of fruit drew near, he sent his servants to the tenants to get his fruit. And the tenants took his servants and beat one, killed another, and stoned another. Again he sent other servants, more than the first; and they did the same to them. Afterward he sent his son to them, saying, 'They will respect my son.' But when the tenants saw the son, they said to themselves, 'This is the heir; come, let us kill him and have his inheritance.' And they took him and cast him out of the vineyard, and killed him."

Matthew 21:33-39

This parable is a modification of a similar parable in Isaiah where the vineyard represents Israel. The Isaiah parable concludes with God's decision to punish Israel by making their land a waste. The servants, sent to the tenants in the New Testament parable, are the prophets of Israel, God's messengers sent to Israel at various periods of her history.[6] In the New Testament parable some of these messengers from God were mistreated, others including the king's son, were killed. In actual history, Israel's prophets from Moses on met with hostility on the part of the people or their leaders. Moses would have fared badly if not for the threat of Divine intervention on his behalf; Elijah fled for his life; Jeremiah was almost done to death.

---

6.   2 Chronicles 36: 15-16.

In a real sense the whole earth is God's vineyard.[7] Bad as things were in Israel, the moral state of the Gentile world was even worse.[8] The death of Jesus the Son of God was the combined action of Jews and Gentiles.[9] "The sins of men actually crucified Jesus — the sins of [the vested interests of] Jewish religious leadership of the first century, the sin of Judas who betrayed Him, the sin of Peter who denied Him, the sin of Pontius Pilate, who found injustice easier than justice, the sin of Roman soldiers who added mocking to His scourging and crucifixion. These are our sins as much as theirs — jealousy, prejudice, disloyalty, time-serving, pitilessness — though the consequences are not so clearly seen when we are the sinners."[10] The death of Messiah Jesus was the concentration and culmination of the sin of all mankind.

III. THE DEATH OF JESUS REVEALS GOD'S CORRECTIVE JUSTICE

Whom[11] he[12] had established . . . as an expiation by his blood . . . for the demonstration of his [corrective] justice.
Romans 3:25

"The retribution that awaits, or rather, that accompanies, sin has nothing arbitrary about it, either in its infliction or its remission. As Emerson puts it, 'Crime and punishment grow out of one stem. Punishment is a fruit that unsuspected ripens within the flower of the pleasure which conceals it.' "[13] "It is difficult to believe that God . . . is indifferent to [man's] refusal to obey His will. To imagine Him as unconcerned when disobeyed is in effect to make Him count His own will as a thing of no account, to make Him false to this own self and disloyal to the eternal verities which are Himself. A God who remained unmoved when men defied that will which is perfect righteousness would not be a moral God . . . A God who could create a universe that His will might be done therein and then be su-

---

7. "For all the earth (i.e., all nations) is mine." Exodus 19:5.
8. Romans 1:18-32.
9. Acts 4:27.
10. H. Wheeler Robinson, Op. Cit., p. 65.
11. i.e., Jesus the Messiah.
12. i.e., God.
13. H. Wheeler Robinson, Op. Cit., p. 181.

premely indifferent when that will was disregarded, would indeed be a strange being devoid of rationality."[14]

As extreme developments in atmospheric conditions of the earth bring about violent disturbances designed to restore the equilibrium, so does man's disobedience of God's will become a disturbing factor in the overall Divine purpose for mankind. Man was given life by God in order to fulfill God's purpose. Through disobedience man nullifies God's purpose in his life. Man therefore forfeits the right — let alone the reason — to retain the life received from God. Hence God said to Adam that on the day when he transgresses God's will, he shall die.[15] Death is man's separation from God. For Adam his separation from God was symbolically expressed when he was driven out from God's presence.[16]

> The soul that sins, it shall die.
>
> *Ezekiel 18:4* [17]

The same truth was conveyed by the ritual of laying of hands by the Israelite on the head of the animal which he brought for sacrifice, thus indicating that the offerer retains his life by virture of the transfer of his sins onto the sacrificial animal.[18]

IV. HOW DID GOD CLEAR THE SINNER PRIOR TO THE DEATH OF JESUS?

> But now the righteousness of God has been manifested apart from the law, although the law and the prophets bear witness to it. Even the righteousness of God through faith in Jesus Christ for all who believe; for there is no distinction. Since

---

14. Bertrand R. Brasnett, THE SUFFERING OF THE IMPASSIBLE GOD (S P C K: London, 1928), p. 8. Used by permission.
15. Genesis 3:17.
16. Genesis 3:24.
17. See also Jeremiah 31:30 (31:29 Heb.).
18. See, especially, the ritual of the Day of Atonement which may be considered the culminating point of the whole Levitical sacrificial system. On that occasion the high priest, acting as the representative of the whole people, laid his hands on the head of one of the two goats and confessed the sins of the people. Leviticus 16:6-22.

all have sinned and fall short of the glory of God.[19] They are jus-
tified as a pure gift by his grace through the redemption which is
in Christ Jesus. Whom God had established beforehand as an expiation by his blood, to be received by faith; for the demonstration of his justice, because of the tolerance shown, in the forbearance of God, to sins done in former times. To prove at the present
time that he himself is righteous and that he justifies him who has
faith in Jesus.

Romans 3:21-26

1. *"THE RIGHTEOUSNESS OF GOD"*

But now the righteousness of God has been manifested.
Romans 3:21a

The apostle Paul was confronted with the question that if the
death of Messiah Jesus is God's way of saving men, how were men
saved, or how did God deal with the problem of human sin, in the
centuries prior to the coming of Jesus? The above passage in Paul's
Letter to the Christians in Rome constitutes his answer. The "righteousness of God" has here the same connotation as in Romans 1:17
where it refers to God's way of saving man through the death and
resurrection of Jesus. The idea inherent in the word "righteousness"
as used by the apostle Paul in Romans 1:17 and in Romans 3:21a is
taken over from the Old Testament. It occurs there in the Piel form
of the verb on five occasions[20] signifying "to declare just;" and twelve
times in the Hiphil form where it signifies in eleven passages to
"declare just judicially," and in the twelfth passage where its meaning
is to "make one just."[21]

We saw in Part One of this work how "righteousness" is associated with the Person of the Messiah in the Old Testament. Of
David, the earthly progenitor of the Messiah, it was said:

---

19. The meaning of this parenthetical statement is that sin is man's failure to obey
     God's will and consequently to become all that God meant for him to become.
20. Job 32:2; 33:32; Jeremiah 3:11; Ezekiel 16:51, 52.
21. Exodus 23:7; Deuteronomy 25:1; 2 Samuel 15:4; 1 Kings 8:32; 2 Chronicles
     6:23; Job 27:5; Psalm 82:3; Proverbs 17:15; Isaiah 1:8, 5:23; 53: 11; Daniel
     12:3.

> David reigned over all Israel; and David executed justice
> and righteousness unto all his people.
>
> *2 Samuel 8:15*

A conviction had been gained by the people of the Old Testament
that Messiah, the Second David, will establish a kingdom based on
righteousness, a renewal and extension of the Davidic rule.

In the course of time a gradual merging took place of the two
ideas: "justice" or "righteousness," and "salvation" or the extension
of help to those who are weak and helpless. This may be seen in
God's concern for the stranger, the fatherless and the widow.[22] In
the prophetic writings the "righteousness" of God is often used in
the sense of God's faithfulness to His saving purpose. This is especially true of Isaiah 40-66 where "righteousness acquired the meaning of God's faithfulness to His redemptive promises and is often
used interchangeably with the word "salvation." Speaking of Cyrus,
the prophet declares in God's name

> "I have raised him up in righteousness, and I will make
> straight all his ways; he shall build my city and set my exiles free
> not for price or reward," says Jehovah of hosts.
>
> *Isaiah 45:13*

The word "righteousness" in this passage has the meaning of God's
faithfulness to His promise to restore Israel from the Babylonian
exile.

> Hearken to me, you stubborn of heart, you who are far
> from righteousness. I bring near my righteousness, it is not far
> off, and my salvation will not tarry; I will put my salvation in
> Zion, for Israel my glory.
>
> *Isaiah 46:12-13*

Here "righteousness" means salvation or deliverance.[23]

As Israel grew in experience and in self-reflection, she gained
the conviction that all her troubles stem from her disobedience,
from her failure to live in accordance with God's will.

---

22.   "He executes justice for the fatherless and the widow, and loves the sojourner,
giving him food and clothing." Deuteronomy 10:18. See, also, Deut. 14:28-29;
27:19.
23.   See, also Isaiah 51:4-5; 56:1-2.

> Who gave up Jacob to the spoiler, and Israel to the robbers?
> Is it not Jehovah, against whom we have sinned, in whose ways
> they would not walk, and whose law they would not obey?
>
> *Isaiah 42:24*

To fulfill the purpose for which she was brought into existence
Israel had to become a holy people.

> And Jehovah said to Moses. Speak to all the congregation of
> the people of Israel, and say to them, You shall be holy; for I
> Jehovah your God am holy.
>
> *Leviticus 19:1-2*[24]

But Israel never became a holy people.

> We have all become like one who is unclean, and all our
> righteous deeds are like a polluted garment.
>
> *Isaiah 64:6 (64:5 Heb.)*

Not only so, but Israel came to realize that she could never become a
holy people by her own means.

> Can the Ethiopian change his skin or the leopard his spots?
> Then can you also do good who are accustomed to do evil.
>
> *Jeremiah 13:23*

The conclusion to which Israel arrived was that their righteousness
as well as their salvation can come only from God.

> In Jehovah shall all the seed of Israel become righteous,
> and shall glory.
>
> *Isaiah 45:25*

> I will greatly rejoice in Jehovah, my soul shall exult in my
> God; for he has clothed me with the garments of salvation, he has
> covered me with the robe of righteousness, as a bridegroom
> decks himself with a garland, and a bride adorns herself with her
> jewels.
>
> *Isaiah 61:10*

To the question, how will God accomplish this spiritual change

---

24.   See also Exodus 19:4-6.

in Israel, Isaiah gave the answer in his description of the Suffering
Servant.

> By his knowledge shall the righteous one, my servant, make
> many to be accounted righteous; and he shall bear their ini-
> quities.
>
> *Isaiah 53:11*

It is this "righteousness of God", with which the saints of the Old
Testament have been longing to be invested, that became manifested through the atoning death of Jesus the Messiah as a free gift
from God for all who will appropriate it by faith.

2. *"APART FROM THE LAW"*

> But now the righteousness of God has been manifested
> apart from the law, although the law and the prophets bear
> witness to it.
>
> *Romans 3:21*

God's way of saving man through Jesus the Messiah is, Paul
declares, "apart from the law." What Paul means by "apart from the
law" he explains a little further on by citing the case of Abraham.[25]
We are reminded by the apostle that Abraham was "put right" with
God centuries before the Mosaic Law was given and even before he
was circumcised. Is this Divine way of redeeming man through
Messiah's death something new? It is new in the sense in which the
covenant promised by God through Jeremiah is a "new covenant,"
i.e., it will be unlike the Sinai Covenant.[26] But it is not something
which was altoghether unknown in the Old Testament period. For
Abraham was "declared just", i.e., was put right with God, long
before the promulgation of the Sinai Covenant, and simply on the
basis of his trust in God's Word.

While God's way of saving man through Messiah's death is
"apart from the [Mosaic] law", "the law and the prophets bear
witness to it", i.e., both the Mosaic Law through the Levitical sacrifices, and the prophets through the Messianic predictions, pointed
in the direction of the redemption through the Messiah.

---

25. Romans 4:1-13; Genesis 15:6.
26. Jeremiah 31:31-34 (31:30-33 Heb.).

3. THE DEATH OF MESSIAH JESUS IS A SUBSTITUTIONARY DEATH

> They are justified . . . through the redemption which is in Christ Jesus. Whom God had established . . . as an expiation by his blood . . . But God shows his love for us in that while we were yet sinners Christ died for us.
>
> *Romans 3:24-25; 5:8*

It was a custom under Pontius Pilate, the Roman governor of the Judean province, to release a Jewish prisoner during the Passover feast. It was a good political gesture designed to win for Rome the goodwill of the populace. Having gained the conviction that Jesus had done nothing to justify a death sentence, Pilate was seeking for a pretext to set Him free. The crowd assembled outside the governor's palace reminded Pilate of the custom of setting a prisoner free. He then asked them, which of two prisoners they would desire him to release: Barabbas, or Jesus called the Messiah. Pilate must have felt that they will surely ask for the release of Jesus. Pilate's scheme might have worked, for there is evidence in the Gospel records that the cry to release Barabbas was the result of the urgings of the high priests, the elders and those bound to them economically. Even so, their efforts might have failed if not for the deep disillusionment experienced by the people who thronged Jerusalem at the Passover celebration and who expected Jesus to inaugurate the Messianic Kingdom which to them was chiefly a glorified political kingdom. These disappointed hopes must have produced a "backlash" reaction which was fully exploited by the religious authorities, the deadly enemies of Jesus.

This Barabbas, who was set free in place of Jesus had been involved in some insurrection during which he committed murder. Whether he was a plain gangster or he committed violence from political motives, he may have gained some popularity among certain elements of the populace. Someone composed a story about this Barabbas which may well reflect the true state of mind of the imprisoned convict.[27] According to this storyteller, Barabbas and the two gangsters who were crucified together with Jesus belonged to the same criminal gang, and the three were sentenced to die on the

---

27.   DER WEG (Warsaw, Poland), March-April, 1939.

cross. Knowing that the hour of his execution was drawing near, Barabbas was agitated and paced the floor of his cell during the last night of his imprisonment. He knew of the custom to release a prisoner during the Passover season. But will the people call for his release? Whether it was wishful thinking or not, Barabbas had some hopes that the people will ask for his release. He was not unaware of having gained some popularity among the people.

Not being able to sleep, Barabbas heard of some commotion outside of the prison cell. From bits of overheard conversation among the guards he learned that the occasion of the commotion was the arrest of Jesus of Nazareth. This bit of news threw Barabbas into a state of alarm and despondency. Surely the people will clamor for the release of the miracle working Rabbi from Galilee who went about feeding the hungry, healing the sick and comforting the sorrowful. Suddenly he heard the steps of one of the guards approaching his cell door. His end has now come — Barabbas thought. He was certain that the guard was coming to take him out to the place of the execution. Then the door of his cell came open, and at the entrance there stood the officer of the prison guard. "Barabbas, get out, you are free!," the officer shouted. "Free!" stammered the murderer. "That is impossible!" The officer came near him, placed his hand on his trembling shoulder and pointing with his finger in the direction of the cell door, he said to him: "You are free, Barabbas, Jesus of Nazareth dies today in your place on the cross which was prepared for you.!"

> Him who knew no sin he made to be sin for our sake, so that in him we might become the righteousness of God.
>
> *2 Corinthians 5:21*

> You know that you were ransomed from the futile ways inherited from your fathers, not with perishable things such as silver or gold. But with the precious blood of Christ, like that of a lamb without blemish or spot.
>
> *1 Peter 1: 18-19*

The question may be asked, since our sin is primarily sin against God, is it right for a third party to suffer the consequences? The Biblical answer to this objection is that Jesus was not a third party. It was God the Father, against whom we have sinned, who through Jesus on the Cross of Calvary took our sin upon Himself and suffered our shame and our death.

All this is from God, who through Christ reconciled us to

himself and gave us the ministry of reconciliation. That is, God
was in Christ reconciling the world to himself . . .

2 Corinthians 5: 18-19

From the beginning to the end, the New Testament teaches that God
the Father is the author of salvation through Jesus the Messiah.

For God so loved the world that he gave his only Son, that
whoever believes in him should not perish but have eternal
life.[28]

John 3:16

4. MESSIAH'S DEATH WAS FOREORDAINED

Whom God had established beforehand as a means of
expiation through his blood, to be appropriated by faith; for the
demonstration of his justice, on account of the tolerance shown,
during the forbearance of God, to sins done in former times. To
prove at the present time that while he himself is just he can
justify him who believes in Jesus.

Romans 3:25-26

For thousands of years myriads of sinners enjoyed impunity.
With the exception certain isolated acts of judgments Divine righteousness appeared almost as non-existent. Men sinned but continued
to live and even to reach a hoary old age. In the remarkable statement cited above the apostle Paul brings to a climax his answer to the
question, how God was dealing with the problem of human sin
before the death of Jesus if His death is the only way of saving man.
The Cross, Paul says, is no Divine afterthought. In all eternity before
the creation of man God had foreknown that man will disobey His
will. If notwithstanding His foreknowledge, God nevertheless
created man, it is because He had a predetermined plan to save man
from the effects of his disobedience. What was predetermined in
eternity in the mind of God, became a reality in history through the
death of Jesus on Calvary's Cross. Man's redemption "expresses the

---

28.   See also the following references: Matthew 10:40; 15:24; Mark 9:37; Luke 9:48;
      10:1; John 4:34; 5:23,24, 30, 36; 6:29; 38:40, 44, 57; 7:16, 28-29; 8:16, 18, 26,
      29, 42; 9:4; 11:42, 44-45, 49; 13:16, 20; 14:24; 15:21; 16:5; 17:3; 18:21, 23, 25;
      20:21; Romans 3:24-25; 5:8, 10;1 Corinthians 1:30; 2 Corinthians 5:18-19; 1
      Peter 1:3; 1 John 4:10; etc., etc.

original design and final purpose of God" which "has come to a full and perfect manifestation in the death of Jesus on the hill of Calvary."[29]

> He[30] was destined before the foundation of the world but was made manifest at the end of the times for your sake.
>
> *1 Peter 1:20*

The Levitical sacrifices had no power to atone for sins.[31] It was the faithfulness of the Israelites to the Law of Moses, with the Levitical sacrificial system at its center, which atoned for their sins, because both the Law of Moses and the Prophets pointed to the Messiah, the perfect sacrifice, the lamb of God that was destined to take away the sin of the world.

As to the heathen, that great mass of mankind which stood outside the Old Testament revelation, they had the moral law, the so-called Noachian Laws of the Rabbis, which ultimately was also derived from God. In the centuries before the advent of Jesus, the heathen were judged in accordance with whether or not they were obedient to the moral law. But the heathen, too, were conscious of their failure to fulfill the moral law, and they were groping and searching for the "Unknown God,"[32] and were longingly waiting for the coming of a Redeemer,

> And the islands wait for his law.
>
> *Isaiah 42:4*

who would bring them a higher revelation, who through His death will draw men unto Himself,[33] who will engrave God's law on human hearts.[34]

Thus the death of Jesus proved that God was never indifferent to human transgression, that in the ages prior to Messiah's advent He could forgive sins with a view to the coming substitutionary and

---

29. F. W. Dillistone, THE SIGNIFICANCE OF THE CROSS (The Westminster Press: Philadelphia, 1944), p. 229.
30. i.e., Jesus
31. Micah 6:6-7; Hebrews 10:4.
32. The Book of Acts 17:22-23.
33. The Gospel of John 12:32.
34. Jeremiah 31:33 (31:32 Heb.).

atoning death of the Messiah, that therefore even then He could forgive sins without compromising with His holy nature.

V. THE DEATH OF JESUS MAKES MAN'S NEW BIRTH POSSIBLE

During His visit in Jerusalem at the beginning of His Messianic mission, Jesus was interviewed by a certain prominent member of the Pharisaic party. We mentioned his name in an earlier chapter, but we omitted from our discussion the weighty matters which were brought up during that interview. The reference to Nicodemus as "a ruler of the Jews" is interpreted to mean that he held a high position in the religious sphere; he may possibly have been a member of the Religious Council, the so-called Sanhedrin.[35] What Nicodemus had heard about Jesus so far must have conflicted with some of his Pharisaic notions about the Messiah. He therefore decided to bring his difficulties directly to Jesus.

> There was a man of the Pharisees, named Nicodemus, a ruler of the Jews. This man came to Jesus by night and said to him, "Rabbi, we know that you are a teacher come from God; for no one can do these signs that you do, unless God be with him." Jesus answered him, "Truly, truly, I say to you, unless one is born anew, he cannot see the kingdom of God." Nicodemus said to him, "How can a man be born when he is old? Can he enter a second time into his mother's womb and be born?" Jesus said to him, "Truly, truly, I say to you, unless one is born of water and the Spirit, he cannot enter the kingdom of God. That which is born of the flesh is flesh, and that which is born of the Spirit is spirit."

> *John 3:1-6*

We undoubtedly have in this account by the apostle John only the gist of what had been said during this interview. The atmosphere of those days was heavily charged with anticipations of the coming of Messiah. To the Jews of that day, when the Land of Israel was under Roman domination, the Kingdom of God which they associated with Messiah's advent was little more than an expanded Israelitish kingdom occupying a dominating position in the world. Jesus was well acquainted with these un-Biblical Jewish Messianic ideas. To Him, as

---

35. See, also, John 7:50 .

well as to the prophets of the Old Testament, the Kingdom of God
meant not the preeminence of Israel but the rule of God in the
hearts of men everywhere, Jews and Gentiles. It is for the coming of
this kind of Kingdom of God that His followers were to pray.

> Our Father who art in heaven, hallowed be thy name. Thy
> kingdom come, thy will be done on earth as it is in heaven.
>   *Matthew 6:9-10*

Startling as the words of Jesus may have sounded to
Nicodemus, and revolutionary as they may sound even to us today,
the ideas expressed by the words "born anew," "water" and the
"spirit," as used by Jesus in this conversation with Nicodemus, were
Old Testament ideas. Mention has already been made in a previous
chapter that when dealing with the subject of Israel's restoration the
prophets declared that God was going to do something new in the
history of Israel and the world. The word "new" is used by all three
major prophets. The following passage in Ezekiel may have formed
the background for the words of Jesus concerning the new birth.

> For I will take you from the nations, and gather you from
> all the countries, and bring you into your own land. I will *sprinkle
> clean water* upon you, and you shall be clean from all your
> uncleannesses and from all your idols I will cleanse you. A *new*
> heart I will give you, and a *new* spirit I will put within you; and I
> will take out of your flesh the heart of stone and give you a heart
> of flesh. And I will put my spirit within you, and cause you to
> walk in my statutes and be careful to observe my ordinances.
>   *Ezekiel 36:24-27*

In the days of the Temple sacrifices, a Gentile wishing to enter
the Kingdom of God, i.e., to become an Israelite, had to comply with
three requirements: circumcision, baptism, and a sacrifice. A
woman had to be baptized and bring a sacrifice.[36] Such a proselyte
was considered as "a little child just born."[37] He had to cut himself
off from his past, his country, and his relatives.

Notice, however, that the Gentile proselyte was considered a
newborn child *after* he had taken the "yoke of the kingdom," after he

---

36. Maimonides, Hilkh. Issurey Biah 13:5; Ber. 47b; Kerith, 9a; Yebam. 45b, 46a
     and b, 48b, 76a, and other passages.
37. Yebamoth 22a, 48b, 97b.

had embraced the religion of Judaism. The new birth of which Jesus had spoken takes place *before* one can enter the Kingdom of God.

> Truly, truly, I say to you, unless one is born anew, he cannot see the Kingdom of God.
>
> *John 3:3*

This idea may be something foreign to Rabbinic Judaism, but it is not foreign to Biblical Judaism. For according to the Bible a Jew is not one who is born of Jewish parents, or a Jewish mother, but one who enters the Covenant of Abraham, and the Jewish male child does not enter the Abrahamic Covenant until he is eight days old. "Jesus lays emphasis on the need of a second birth for every man, Jew and Gentile alike, who would see the Kingdom of God. No earthly privileges would make for a man, and no earthly disadvantages would make against him. Not because he was born a Jew should one enter, not because he was born a Gentile should one be shut out. Every man must, and any man might, be completely made a new man — made over again — to be fit to share the Kingdom, and God alone can do that. The consequence of the second birth is therefore Divine sonship, the partaking of the very life of God . . . The Kingdom of God is the Kingdom of *sons of God*, a spiritual kingdom of filial love, of desire after God, of obedience to His will, of men who share God's own nature."[38]

Shaken out of his Rabbinic complacent belief according to which every Jew who adheres to the Rabbinic religious code will have a share in the Messianic Kingdom,[39] Nicodemus asked

> How can a man be born when he is old? Can he enter a second time into his mother's womb and be born?
>
> *John 3:4*

Can a man start all over from the beginning when his character is already set, can he overthrow all he had been in the past? In posing this question, Nicodemus thought of the new birth in terms of what man could or should do; he failed to realize that this second birth is the work of God. What Jesus meant was not a mere new beginning, but a *different* beginning. For "that which is born of the flesh[40] is

---

38. George Reith, THE GOSPEL ACCORDING TO ST. JOHN (T. & T. Clark: Edinburgh, 1889): reprinted in 1926, Vol. 1, pp. 45-46.
39. Sanh. 10:1.
40. "Flesh" here refers to unredeemed and unregenerated human nature.

flesh, and that which is born of the Spirit is spirit."[41] "Man may rise to high possibilities — mental, even moral: self-development, self-improvement, self-restraint, submission to a grand idea or a higher law, refined moral egotism, aesthetic, even moral truism,"[42] but all this will fail in the end. How else are we to account for the failure of Greek philosophy and all other intellectual movements of antiquity to change the ancient world? How are we to explain the miserable performance of the French Revolution — and of the Communist Revolution of our own day? "That which is born of the flesh, is flesh."

The new birth which Jesus was speaking of is the work of God.

> Truly, truly, I say to you, unless one is born of water and the Spirit, he cannot enter the kingdom of God.
>
> *John 3:5*

To be "born of water and the Spirit" indicates the two stages of the new life which man may appropriate. The first, represented by baptism, is the stage of repentance, it amounts to a break with one's past, with old habits, old attitudes, the old way of life; the water of baptism symbolizes the washing away of our sins, while our immersion beneath the baptismal waters signifies the death of the old human nature. The "Spirit" is the new animating Divine principle which from now on energizes our life.

Once man says *Yes* to what had taken place on Calvary's Cross, the Spirit of God begins to work in our hearts and produces the regeneration of our nature.

> We know that our old self was crucified with him so that the sinful body might be rendered powerless, and we might no longer be enslaved to sin. For he who has died is freed from sin.
>
> *Romans 6:6-7*

> Therefore, if any one is in Christ he is a new creation; the old has passed away, behold, the new has come.
>
> *2 Corinthians 5:17*

---

41. John 3:6
42. Alfred Edersheim, THE LIFE AND TIMES OF JESUS THE MESSIAH (Longmans Green, and Co.: London, 1899), Vol. 1, p. 385

> I have been crucified with Christ; it is no longer I who live, but Christ who lives in me; and the life I now live in the flesh I live by faith in the Son of God, who loved me and gave himself for me.
>
> *Galatian 2:20*

> Put to death therefore what is earthly in you: immorality, impurity, passion, evil desire, and covetousness, which is idolatry . . . In these you once walked, when you lived in them. But now put them all away: anger, wrath, malice, slander, and foul talk from your mouth. Do not lie to one another, seeing that you have put off the old nature with its practices. And have put on the new nature, which is being renewed in knowledge after the image of its Creator.
>
> *Colossians 3:5, 7-10*

This writer has never ceased to marvel at the effects of the transforming power of Christian conversion in the lives of people — irrespective of racial, national, social or economic background. Christian coversion is the never-ceasing Divine miracle in the world. There is something desperately wrong with a follower of Jesus the Messiah if the world cannot tell him apart from others. True followers of Jesus are likened to branches growing out of the vine, Jesus Himself being the vine.

> I am the true vine, and my Father is the vinedresser. Every branch of mine that bears no fruit, he takes away, and every branch that does bear fruit he prunes, that it may bear more fruit . . . I am the vine, you are the branches, he who abides in me, and I in him, he it is that bears much fruit, for apart from me you can do nothing . . . By this is my Father glorified, that you bear much fruit, and so prove to be my disciples.
>
> *John 15:1-2, 5, 8*

VI. MAN MUST DECIDE FOR OR AGAINST JESUS

> But now the righteousness of God has been manifested . . . through *faith* in Jesus Christ for all who *believe* . . . They are justified by his grace as a *gift*, through the redemption which is in Christ Jesus. Whom God had established beforehand as an expiation by his blood, to be *received by faith*.
>
> *Romans 3:21, 22, 24-25*

Man's redemption through the atoning death of Jesus is God's gift to man. But man must make the decision whether or not to receive the gift. The death of Jesus is the objective part of our redemption, it was accomplished at a certain time and a certain place. But man is not redeemed until what was done on the Cross of Calvary becomes subjective within him. "The Crucifixion of Jesus confronts the soul of man with a searching dilemma, with the necessity of finally making up his mind. For it means one of two things. Either it means that *that* sort of believing about God, *that* sort of living, even when it is at its maximal point of purity and devotion, is so fantastically false, so utterly wide of the truth, that it cannot stand up to the forces which actually dominate the world, but is doomed to be stamped out by them . . . Or, on the other hand, it means that it is so true, so firmly rooted in fact, that it can afford to accept seemingly utter defeat, knowing that the victory, God's victory, is in the end with it. One of two things; the Crucifixion of Jesus is either a great, grim, hoarse, derisive shout of *No* to the proposition that God is love . . ., or it is a firm, steady, undefeated *Yes* . . . Who then is to decide which it is? The strange thing is — though it is not strange in view of the personal nature of God's dealing with us — the individual man must decide, must answer the question. And if the right answer be given, it is not the less of the inspiration of God because it is the man's own answer. The [affirmative] conviction that stirs deep within a man's mind and heart . . . is only possible because God has put Christ and [His] Cross at a fork in [man's] road where the challenge of the Cross can no longer be avoided, [and] has given [to man] a nature capable of discerning, in its presence, this final dilemma of our personal life — either to believe in and commit oneself to the God of Jesus Christ, or to conclude that human existence is . . . in spite of all the incidental fine things that are in it, a meaningless waste of effort and suffering, ending in a silence of universal death."[43]

VII. THE DEATH OF JESUS AND THE PROBLEM OF HUMAN SUFFERING

1. "MY GOD, MY GOD, WHY HAST THOU FORSAKEN ME?"

The above words uttered by Jesus from the Cross minutes before He

---

43.   Herbert H. Farmer, TOWARDS BELIEF IN GOD (S C M Press: London, 1943), pp. 124-125 Used by permission.

died were taken from the opening statement in Psalm 22. It is thought that the intense sorrow and grief reflected in this Psalm describe an episode in David's life when he was haunted and driven from place to place by the murderous hatred of King Saul. The startling correspondence between the sufferings of the person in this Psalm 22 and those of Jesus on the Cross may be seen by comparing certain excerpts from both accounts.

> My God, my God, why hast thou forsaken me? Why art thou so far from helping me, from the words of my groaning? . . . All who see me mock at me, they make mouths at me, they wag their heads: "He commited his cause to Jehovah: let him deliver him, let him rescue him, for he delights in him!" . . .

> Yea, dogs are round about me; a company of evildoers encircle me; they have pierced my hands and feet — I can count all my bones — They stare and gloat over me. They divide my garments among them, and for my raiment they cast lots.
> *Psalm 22:1, 7-8, 16-18 (22:2, 8-9, 17-19 Heb.)*[44]

> And when they came to a place called Golgotha (which means the place of a skull). They[45] offered him wine to drink, mingled with gall; but when he tasted it, he would not drink it. And when they had crucified him, they divided his garments among them by casting lots. Then they sat down and kept watch over him there . . . And those who passed by derided him, wagging their heads. And saying . . . "If you are the Son of God, come down from the cross." So also the chief priest, with the scribes and elders, mocked him, saying. "He saved others; he cannot save himself; he is the King of Israel; let him come down from the cross, and we will believe in him. He trusts in God; let God deliver him now, if he desires him, for he said, 'I am the Son of God.' "
> *Matthew 27:33-36, 39-43*

"My God, my God, why hast thou forsaken me?" Human sinfulness alienates man from God and creates an ever-widening gulf between them. The further on one continues on his life's path without God, the more blunted becomes his sense of sin and his awareness of his need of God's presence. It is not so with the man of

---

44. One of the Jewish Midrashim interprets the sufferings depicted in this Psalm as referring to the Suffering Messiah (Yalkut on Isaiah 60).
45. i.e., the Roman soldiers

God. The longer he lives in God's presence, the deeper is his sorrow when anything happens which mars his communion with God. No human beings on this earth lived nearer to God than Jesus of Nazareth. When only twelve years old he already felt the urge to be about His Heavenly Father's business. "In God He lived, moved and had His being." The very air He breathed was holy and Divine.

When He ascended the Cross He became "the lamb of God, who takes away the sin of the world." It was on the Cross that His identification with the collective sin of mankind became full and complete. "He who knew no sin became sin in our stead," and He experienced the full measure of alienation which sin effects between God and the sinner. To His holy nature this alienation from His Heavenly Father, however brief may have been its duration, caused anguish of soul beyond human comprehension. Its sting was sharper than the crown of thorns piercing His flesh and all the bodily torture of the Cross. And it must have been the intensity of this spiritual suffering which wrung out of Him the cry "My God, my God, why has thou forsaken me?"

2. "CROSS-BEARING" SUFFERING

Excluding sufferings which human folly brings upon man, human sufferings may be divided into two groups. In one belong sufferings incurred by man in the process of striving for a worthy cause or for what may be deemed to be a worthy cause. In the New Testament terminology this kind of suffering may be called "cross-bearing" suffering.

> And he[46] said to all, "If any man would come after me, let him deny himself and take up his cross daily and follow me."
> *Luke 9:23*

In the Psalms and the prophetic writings there are frequent references to the sufferings which the wicked inflicted on the righteous.[47]

---

46. i.e., Jesus.
47. See, f.e., Habakkuk 1:4. The references in the Psalms are too numerous to cite here.

In the Old Testament period the men of God often suffered on account of their faith.

> They were stoned, they were sawn in two, they were tempted, they were killed with the sword; they went about in skins of sheep and goats, destitute, afflicted, ill-treated. Of whom the world was unworthy, wandering over deserts and mountains, and in dens and caves of the earth.
>
> *Hebrews 11:37-38*

In the New Testament period, the apostles, the early disciples, and Christian martyrs of all ages have discovered in due course of time the meaning of cross-bearing. Jesus had warned His disciples that the world — Jews and Gentiles — will hate them because it hates Him.

> If the world hates you, know that it has hated me before it hated you. If you were of the world,[48] the world would love its own: but because you are not of the world, but I chose you out of the world, therefore the world hates you . . . They will put you out of the synagogues; indeed, the hour is coming when whoever kills you will think he is offering service to God.
>
> *John 15:18-19; 16:2*

There is a Satanic element in every hostility to the cause of Jesus.

> For we are not contending against flesh and blood,[49] but against the principalities, against the powers, against the world rulers of this present darkness, against the spiritual hosts of wickedness in the heavenly places.
>
> *Ephesians 6:12*

But there is yet another aspect to this cross-bearing type of suffering. Writing to the Colossian Christians about the sufferings which he experienced in the course of his ministry, Paul says this:

> Now I rejoice in my sufferings for your sake, and in my flesh I complete what is lacking in Messiah's afflictions for the sake of his body, the church.[50]
>
> *Colossians 1:24*

---

48. i.e., the world hostile to the God of Biblical revelation.
49. i.e., mere flesh and blood.
50. The church is often referred to in the New Testament as the body of the Messiah.

The meaning of the above statement is brought out more fully in the
Amplified New Testament.

> [Even] now I rejoice in the midst of my sufferings on your
> behalf. And in my own person I am making up whatever is still
> lacking and remains to be completed on our part of Messiah's
> afflictions, for the sake of His body, which is the Church.
>
> *Colossians 1:24*

What the above statement implies is that the true follower of Jesus is
the instrument through which Messiah's sufferings continue as an
ongoing process for the sake of the redemption of the world. Not
only does the disciple of Jesus receive a new nature: but, even as he
formerly added to the ruin and sorrow of the world, he now has an
opportunity, through his own cross-bearing, to undo, in part at least,
the damage wrought in his pre-Christian days, and to work towards
the reconstruction of the world.

3. "PURPOSELESS" SUFFERING

There is a second class of sufferings which to our limited human
reason seems purposeless. Included among these are incurable
diseases, and deformities of new-born children which bring their
lives to a premature end or leave them maimed and disabled for the
rest of their life. These afflictions men often find hardest to bear.
They appear to serve no useful purpose.

There is also in our present culture a peculiar attitude to the
dying person. In the past most people died at home and were
surrounded to the last moment by their loved ones. In these days we
do not want people to die in our homes. We shove them off to
hospitals and nursing homes where they spend their last days, attended by strangers and surrounded by medical equipment. In their
final hours these people are deprived of the company of those who
were part and parcel of their lives and of their world. At a time when
they are in their greatest need of consolation and strength which the
presence of loved ones could afford they are left to depart from this
world deserted and alone.

We are assured in the Bible that in Messiah Jesus God will never
forsake us. When earth's joys grow dim and its glories pass away;
when in us and around us we see nothing but change and decay;

when human helpers fail and human comforts flee — God, the Help of the helpless, He who never changes, abides with us to the very end, and takes us safely across to the opposite shore.[51]

Of special relevance is the following passage from the book of Hebrews in the New Testament.

> For we do not have a high priest who is unable to sympathize with our weaknesses, but one who in every respect has been tried[52] as we are, yet without sinning . . . Although he was a Son,[53] he learned obedience through what he suffered. And being made perfect he became the source of eternal salvation to all who obey him.
>
> *Hebrews 4:15; 5:8-9*

To learn obedience means, in the above text, to learn to do God's will while living under human limitations. As the Son of God Jesus always lived in harmony with God's will, both in His pre-incarnate state and after He returned to heaven. But to live in accordance with God's will in human circumstances, and under human conditions, often involves suffering. This kind of obedience Jesus could practice only by becoming man, and by experiencing human suffering. It is through sharing our common lot that Jesus became "perfect," i.e., completely human. And it is because of this that He is able to sympathize with our infirmities.

Whatever may be the source or nature of our suffering, we need never feel alone and forsaken. Jesus the Son of God and the Son of man, He who is the "man of sorrows" and "acquainted with grief," who for our sake endured the agony of the Cross, this Jesus is always by our side, to succor and to comfort. "Lo, I am with you always, to the end of the age" (Matthew 28:20).

> For I am sure that neither death, nor life, nor angels, nor principalities, nor things present, nor things to come, nor powers. Nor heights, nor depth, nor anything else in all creation,

---

51. Adapted from the hymn "Abide with me: fast falls the eventide," from Henry Francis Lyte.
52. This is the true sense of the word "tempted" in the text. See, *The Epistle To The Hebrews* by A. B. Davidson.
53. Referring to Messiah's Divine sonship.

will be able to separate us from the love of God in Messiah Jesus
our Lord.

Romans 8:38-39

When I survey the wondrous Cross
On which the Prince of Glory died,
My richest gain I count but loss,
And pour contempt on all my pride.

Forbid, O God, that I should boast,
Save in the death of Christ my Lord:
All the vain things that charm me most,
I sacrifice them to his blood.

See, from his head, his hands, his feet,
Sorrow and love flow mingled down:
Did ever such love and sorrow meet,
Or thorns compose so rich a crown?

Were the whole realm of nature mine,
That were a present far too small;
Love so amazing, so Divine,
Demands my soul, my life, my all.

Isaac Watts

PART THREE

LIFE AFTER DEATH

"If a man die, shall he live again?"
Job 14:14

CHAPTER 1
THE RESURRECTION HOPE IN THE OLD TESTAMENT

I. Non-Biblical Ideas About Death And The Hereafter
   1. Extinction After Death
   2. Sheol — The Hebrew Realm Of The Dead
      a. Sheol is not synonymous with the grave
      b. Sheol is described under a variety of terms
      c. All people, both righteous and wicked, go to Sheol
   3. Divine Retribution Takes Place Here And Now

II. The Struggle Of The Old Testament Against Non-Biblical Ideas Concerning Death And The Hereafter
   1. The Conflict Between The Non-Biblical Ideas And The Facts Of Life
   2. The Progressive Unfolding Of Biblical Truth
      a. The doctrine of God
      b. The doctrine of man
      c. The doctrine of human life
      d. The doctrine of man's death
   3. For The Righteous Death Means No Separation From God

III. The Immortality Of The Individual
   1. The Emergence Of The Individual To A Place Of Prominence
   2. The Fall And Restoration Of Israel Advanced The Resurrection Hope
   3. The Resurrection Hope In Relation To The Messianic Hope

CHAPTER 1
THE RESSURECTION HOPE IN THE OLD TESTAMENT

In the 15th chapter of his First Letter to the Corinthian Christians the apostle Paul declares that if Jesus was not raised from the dead, the Christian message is worthless. How true! For if Jesus did not rise from the dead, then He was not the Son of God; and if He was not the Son of God, He may have died for a worthy cause, but His death has no redeeming value and power such as is attributed to it in the New Testament. Morever, if Jesus did not rise from the dead, man has no assurance of a ressurection after death, and, consequently human life is deprived of any meaningful purpose. But does the Bible really teach a resurrection from the dead, and, if so, did Jesus really rise from the dead? This is the subject to which the chapters which follow are devoted. But first let us turn our attention to the doctrine of the ressurection in the Old Testament.

I. NON-BIBLICAL IDEAS ABOUT DEATH AND THE HEREAFTER

There are in the Old Testament a number of expressions about death and the hereafter which represent ideas which the Hebrews inherited through their ancestors from their Mesopotamian homeland. These ideas do not constitute Biblical teachings, but they made an important contribution to the gradual unfolding of the thought of the Old Testament concerning death and the hereafter.

1. EXTINCTION AFTER DEATH

Certain statements in the Old Testament declare that death is the end of man's whole history.

> "Look away from me, that I may know gladness, before I depart and be no more!"
>
> *Psalm 39:13 (39:14 Heb.)*

> "Why dost thou not pardon my transgression and take my iniquity? For now I shall lie in the earth; thou wilt seek me, but I shall not be."

"For there is hope for a tree, if it be cut down, that it will sprout again, and that its shoots will not cease . . . But man dies, and is laid low; man breathes his last, and where is he? As waters fail from a lake, and a river wastes away and dries up. So man lies down and rises not again; til the heavens are no more he will not awake, or be roused out of his sleep . . . If a man die, shall he live again?"

Job 7:21; 14:7,10-12, 14a

For the fate of the sons of men and the fate of beasts is the same; as one dies, so dies the other; they all have the same breath, and man has no advantage over the beasts; for all is vanity. All go to one place; all are from the dust, and all turn to dust again. Who knows whether the spirit of man goes upward and the spirit of the beast goes down to the earth? So I saw that there is nothing better than that a man should enjoy his work, for that is his lot; who can bring him to see what will be after him?

Ecclesiastes 3:19-22

The above are a few isolated voices representing moods and feelings of despondency which may assail any of us in the dark hours of our life. They do not reflect the thought, teaching or faith of the Old Testament. Where there is belief in God, belief in some existence after death is natural. That the Hewbrews held firmly to a belief in a hereafter may be seen from the well-established notions about a realm of the dead, and the widespread use of the arts of necromancy, forbidden by the Law of Moses and denounced by the prophets.[1]

2. SHEOL – THE HEBREW REALM OF THE DEAD

Sheol is the place to which, according to Hebrew belief, men go after death. The name occurs in all three divisions of the Old Testament. Its derivation is uncertain. The Babylonians used a similarly-sounding word Su-alu as one of their names to designate the under-world. The Hebrew word Sheol is thought to come from a root meaning a gape, yawn, or hollow subterranean place.[2]

---

1. Leviticus 19:31; Deuteronomy 18:11; 1 Samuel 28:9; Isaiah 8:19.
2. William Gesenius, A HEBREW AND ENGLISH LEXICON OF THE OLD TESTAMENT, English Translations (Houghton, Mifflin and Company: Boston, 1897).

a. Sheol is not synonymous with the grave

Jacob speaks of going down to Sheol to join his son Joseph whose supposed death he mourned but of whose burial he knew nothing. Expressions, such as to be "gathered to one's people," to "be gathered to one's fathers," to "go to one's fathers," to "sleep with one's fathers." are used of the death of certain persons, such as Abraham, Jacob, Aaron, Moses, David, and others, whose resting place was far removed from their ancestral graves.[3]

b. Sheol is described under a variety of terms

Pit;[4] Shachath;[5] the lower parts of the earth;[6] Abaddon or Destruction;[7] the place of silence;[8] a land of darkness and the shadow of death;[9] a monster with an open mouth;[10] a prison with gates and bar;[11] a place unvisited by God's wonders.[12]

c. All people, both righteous and wicked, go to Sheol

Truly no man can ransom himself[13] . . . That he should continue to live on for ever, and never see the Pit.

What man can live and never see death? who can deliver his soul from the power of Sheol?
Psalm 49:7,9 (49:8, 10 Heb.); 89:48 (89:49 Heb.)

There the wicked cease from troubling, and there the weary are at rest. There the prisoners are at ease together; they hear not the voice of the taskmaster. The small and the great are there, and the slave is free from his master.
Job 3:17-19

---

3. Genesis 15:15; 25:8, 17; 49:33; Numbers 20:24; 31:2; Deuteronomy 32:50; 1 Kings 2:10.
4. Bor — Psalm 28:1; 30:3 (30:4 Heb.); Proverbs 1:12; Isaiah 38:18, etc.
5. Job 33:24; Psalm 55:23 (55:24 Heb.); etc.
6. Isaiah 44:23; Ezekiel 26:20; etc.
7. Job 26:6; 28:22; Proverbs 15:11.
8. Psalm 94:17; 115:17.
9. Job 10:21-22; Psalm 143:3; Lamentations 3:6.
10. Isaiah 5:14.
11. Job 17:16; 38:17.
12. Psalm 88:10-12 (88:11-13 Heb.).
13. or a brother.

d. All dead are separated from God.

> For in death there is no remembrance of thee; in Sheol who can give thee praise?

> What profit is there in my death, if I go down to the Pit? will the dust praise thee? will it tell of thy faithfulness?
> *Psalm 6:5 (6:6 Heb.): 30:9 (30:10 Heb.)*

> Dost thou work wonders for the dead? do the shades rise up to praise thee? Is thy lovingkindness declared in the grave, or thy faithfulness in Abaddon?[14] Are thy wonders known in the darkness, or thy saving help in the land of forgetfulness?

> The dead do not praise Jehovah, nor do any that go down into silence.
> *Psalm 88:10-12 (88:11-13); 115:17*

The following is a prayer of praise of king Hezekiah after he had recovered from his sickness.

> I said, in the noontide of my days I must depart; I am consigned to the gates of Sheol for the rest of my years. I said, I shall not see Jehovah in the land of the living; I shall look upon man no more among the inhabitants of the world . . . Lo, it was for my welfare that I had great bitterness; but thou hast held back my life from the pit of destruction, for thou hast cast all my sins behind thy back. For Sheol cannot thank thee, death cannot praise thee: those who go down to the Pit cannot hope for thy faithfulness.
> *Isaiah 38:10-11, 17-18*

Samuel, the man of God, is in Sheol, Saul, whom God had rejected, is in the same place.[15] "To the Old Testament saint this life on earth was a brief but happy visit paid to the Lord; but death summoned the visitor away, and it came to an end. This is always the significant element in the popular view of death, that it severed the relation between the person and God."[16]

---

14. One of the names of Sheol or Hades.
15. 1 Samuel 28:3-19.
16. A.B. Davidson, THE THEOLOGY OF THE OLD TESTAMENT (T. & T. Clark, Edinburgh: Eighth Impression, 1952), p. 503.

3. *DIVINE RETRIBUTION TAKES PLACE HERE AND NOW*

As long as the Hebrews adhered to the idea that Sheol was a neutral place, that it was the final destination of all people, good and bad, that all relations between Sheol's denizens and God were severed — it was inevitable that they should expect that the rewarding of the righteous and the punishment of the wicked must take place here and now. These beliefs find expression in the following representative passages.

> Fret not yourself because of the wicked, be not envious of wrongdoers! For they will soon fade like the grass, and wither like the green herb. Trust in Jehovah, and do good; so you will dwell in the land, and enjoy security. Take delight in Jehovah, and he will give you the desires of your heart . . . Be still before Jehovah, and wait patiently for him; fret not yourself over him who prospers in his way, over the man who carries out evil devices! . . . For the wicked shall be cut off; but those who wait for Jehovah shall possess the land. Yet a little while, and the wicked will be no more; though you look well at his place, he will not be there.
>
> *Psalm 37:1-4,7,9-10*

The following is a piece of advice by Zophar given to the upright Job, whose spiritual anguish was as intense as his physical sufferings because he was at a loss to understand why God permitted so much evil to come upon him. Zophar's words illustrate the fallacy of a belief quite prevalent in those days that all human suffering — including that of Job — is the result of the sufferer's past misconduct, and that the righteous and those that mend their ways are always rewarded, and the wicked are always recompensed in this life.

> "Know then that God exacts of you less than your guilt deserves . . . If iniquity is in your hand, put it far away, and let not wickedness dwell in your tents. Surely then you will lift up your face without blemish; you will be secure, and will not fear. You will forget your misery; you will remember it as waters that have passed away. And your life will be brighter than the noonday; its darkness will be like the morning . . . But the eyes of the wicked will fail."
>
> *Job 11:6b, 14-17, 20a*

II. THE STRUGGLE OF THE OLD TESTAMENT
AGAINST NON-BIBLICAL IDEAS
CONCERNING DEATH AND THE HEREAFTER

In the course of time the popular notions concerning death and the hereafter were discredited and, finally, overthrown. Among the factors which contributed to their decline were: the lack of correspondence between those notions and the facts of life as experienced and observed by the people of the Old Testament; the progressive unfolding of Biblical concepts; the place of prominence which the individual Israelite gained in the life of the nation. In the process of this struggle the saints of the Old Testament discovered truths which lay buried in the heart of the Old Testament from its very beginning.

1. THE CONFLICT BETWEEN THE NON-BIBLICAL IDEAS AND THE FACTS OF LIFE

This conflict was raging especially around popular notions concerning divine retribution. Men became increasingly aware that good people often suffer — and bad people often prosper — throughout their lives. The realization of these facts caused much uneasiness to the saints of the Old Testament.

> Why dost thou stand afar off, Jehovah? why dost thou hide thyself in times of trouble? In arrogance the wicked hotly pursues the poor . . . In the pride of his countenance the wicked does not seek him;[17] all his thoughts are, "There is no God." His ways prosper at all times . . . He thinks in his heart, "I shall not be moved; throughout all generations I shall not meet adversity."
>
> *Psalm 10:1-2a, 4-5a, 6*

> But as for me, my feet had almost stumbled, my steps had well nigh slipped. For I was envious of the arrogant, when I saw the prosperity of the wicked. For they have no pangs; their bodies are sound and sleek. They are not in trouble as other men are; they are not stricken like other men. Therefore pride is their necklace; violence covers them as a garment. Their eyes swell out with fatness, their hearts overflow with follies. They

---

17. God.

scoff and speak with malice; loftily they threaten oppression. They set their mouths against the heavens, and their tongue struts through the earth. Therefore the people turn and praise them; and find no fault in them. And they say, "How can God know? is there knowledge in the Most High?"

Psalm 73:2-11

"Why do the wicked live, reach old age, and grow mighty in power? Their children are established in their presence, and their offspring before their eyes. Their houses are safe from fear, and no rod of God is upon them . . . They spend their days in prosperity, and in peace they go down to Sheol. They say to God, 'Depart from us! we do not desire the knowledge of thy ways. What is the Almighty, that we should serve him? and what profit do we get if we pray to him?' "

Job 21:7-9, 13-15

Righteous art thou, O Jehovah, when I complain to thee; yet I would plead my cause before thee; why does the way of the wicked prosper? why do all who are treacherous thrive?

Jeremiah 12:1

2. THE PROGRESSIVE UNFOLDING OF BIBLICAL TRUTH

The emergence of the Biblical hope of immortality was largely due to an increasing understanding of the distinctive Biblical doctrines concerning God, man, human life, and human death, and the growing appreciation of the tremendous implications inherent in the covenant relationship which God established with Abraham and with all who share in the faith of Abraham.

a. The doctrine of God

The possession of a definite and ethical doctrine of God was something peculiar to Israel among all nations of antiquity. "The Accadian hymns, the Zoroastrian books, the poetry and philosophy of the Greeks, show us how moral ideas grew in other races, how the Ethnic[18] belief in the Divine was purified and elevated, and how it made a nearer approach to monotheism as the thought of evil deepened into the sense of sin. But before Israel there is no instance

---

18. Refers to nations outside of Israel.

of a people with a distinct and consistent faith in one God, the Creator of all; righteous in Himself and caring for righteousness; above the world, yet in it; visiting men, and coming into fellowship with them. And outside of Israel there is no instance of a monotheism growing steadily through the various stages of the people's history in purity and completeness, and in access to the national and individual conscience."[19]

"The monotheistic movement in Israel was one of continuous progress through incessant conflict, until a result was reached of incalculable value to humanity. That result was a faith in God singularly comprehensive, sublime, and practical, — a faith which rested, not on speculation and reasoning, but on a conviction of God having directly revealed Himself to the spirits of men, and which, while ignoring metaphysical theorizing, ascribed to God all metaphysical as well as moral perfections; a faith which, in spite of its simplicity, so apprehended the relationship of God to nature as neither to confound them like pantheism, nor to separate them like deism, but to assert both the immanence and the transcendence of the divine; a faith in a living and personal God, the Almighty and sole Creator, preserver, and ruler of the world; a faith, especially, in a God, holy in all His ways and righteous in all His works, who was directing and guiding human affairs to a destination worthy of His own character; and therefore an essentially ethical, elevating, and hopeful faith."[20]

b. The doctrine of man

Man, according to the Old Testament, is related to the lower creatures on one hand, and to God on the other hand. Like the lower creatures, man is flesh, with all the weaknesses and limitations inherent in this part of his nature, consisting, in common with the lower creatures, of matter and the divine principle of life.[21] It is through the agency of this Divine principle of life that both animals and human beings are animated.[22]

---

19.   Steward D.F. Salmond, THE CHRISTIAN DOCTRINE OF IMMORTALITY (T. & T. Clark: Edinburgh, 1895), p. 191.
20.   R. Flint, Encyclopedia Britannica, Vol. 23, p. 239; quoted by D.F. Salmond, Op. Cit., pp. 191-192.
21.   Expressed in the Bible as dust or earth and spirit or breath — Genesis 1:30; 2:7; 6:17; 7:15.
22.   Psalm 104:30.

But the distinction between man and the lower creatures is deeper than their kinship. The lower creatures spring into existence by divine command, and as the direct product of matter under the operation of the Divine principle of life.[23] Man, on the other hand, comes into being by an immediate act of God.[24] Man, therefore, is a special creation of God, made in His image, created as a free moral personality. He is superior to nature and destined to exercise dominion over nature. He is created for fellowship with God.

c. The doctrine of human life

The uniqueness of man's origin determined the unique character of his destiny, i.e., his life and death. Man is a special creation, meant to live in the nearness of God's presence.

> And I will make my abode among you . . . And I will walk among you, and will be your God, and you shall be my people.
> *Leviticus 26: 11a, 12*

> "Therefore choose life, that you and your descendants may live. Loving Jehovah your God, obeying his voice, and cleaving to him; for that means life to you and length of days, that you may dwell in the land which Jehovah swore to your fathers, to Abraham, to Isaac, and to Jacob, to give them."
> *Deuteronomy 30: 19b-20*

Notice the statement, "loving Jehovah your God, obeying his voice, and cleaving to him; for that means life to you and length of days."

> I say to Jehovah, "Thou art my Lord; I have no good apart from thee." . . . Jehovah is my chosen portion and my cup . . . Thou dost show me the path of life; in thy presence there is fullness of joy, in thy right hand are pleasures for evermore.
> *Psalm 16:2, 5a, 11*

d. The doctrine of man's death

As soon as we enter the sphere of the Old Testament we encounter the doctrine that death is the consequence of sin. To the original man God said:

---

23. Genesis 1:24; 2:19.
24. Genesis 1:26-27.

> But of the tree of the knowledge of good and evil you shall
> not eat, for in the day that you eat of it you shall die.
>
> *Genesis 2:17*

Adam's sin consisted not in the eating from the forbidden tree, but in disobedience. On the day he disobeyed, his close fellowship with God was broken, and death claimed him for its own. In accordance with the Old Testament view of human life, as life lived in communion with God, Adam died morally and spiritually on the day of his transgression. For Adam was neither inherently mortal, nor inherently immortal. From the statement in Genesis 2:17 we infer that had Adam remained in his original state of close communion with God the life he was given would have flowed on uninterruptedly.

This concept of death is not something which had crept into the Old Testament from some alien source. It is an inseparable part of the thought and teaching of the Old Testament. There are in the Old Testament certain statements in which death is considered as man's natural experience. But these utterances do not intend to imply that man was originally destined for death; they merely take cognizance of the fact that death is *now* man's lot, that it has, so to speak, become "naturalized."[25]

The link between *sin and death* is emphasized in the Mosaic Law pertaining to coming in contact with a dead person. Any individual who touches a corpse is considered defiled for seven days, and he must comply with the prescribed rules for purification. All those who find themselves in a house in which a person died, and if someone just happened to enter such a house, are considered as ritually unclean. Touching a grave defiles a person. The house in which a person died, and all its furnishings are considered defiled. The person who touches a person that had been in contact with a corpse also became defiled. Any person who thus became defiled and who failed to comply with the regulations pertaining to their purification "shall be cut off from Israel."[26]

The connection between sin and death is also indicated in the following sentence:

---

25. A.B. Davidson, Op. Cit., p. 523.
26. Numbers 19:11-22; see, also, Leviticus 21:1, 11; Numbers 5:2-3; 9:6-10.

When he[27] incurred guilt through Baal, he died.

Hosea 13:1b

According to the Biblical record, the idolatry of Northern Israel dates back to the beginning of its existence as a separate national state. Its statehood was destroyed two hundred years later. But Hosea dates Northern Israel's national death from the beginning of its idolatry. Evidently, Hosea believed that Northern Israel "died" when it became separated from Jehovah, Israel's God.

In the Old Testament all sin results in separation from God. Death is the most serious consequence of sin; hence death is the most permanent severance from God. It is the completion of a process of separation from God which begins during life. In the New Testament we are told that Jesus the Messiah who knew no sin was made by God to be sin for us.[28] It was this sin of the human race which Jesus took upon Himself that gave Him a sense of separation from God. And it was this consciousness of severance from God that constituted the most agonizing element in the death of Jesus, and which was reflected in His cry from the Cross: "My God, my God, why has thou forsaken me?"[29]

3. FOR THE RIGHTEOUS DEATH MEANS NO SEPARATION FROM GOD

Since according to the Old Testament the "good" of life is fellowship with God, therefore, in view of the Old Testament, immortality is a permanent maintenance of this fellowship with God. The emphasis in the Old Testament is not on mere subsistence — this idea was never questioned — but subsistence in fellowship with God; not the mere continuance of life as such, but continuance of life in the nearness of God's presence, in communion with Him. On the other hand, death is not the mere cessation of life as we know it, but severance of man's fellowship with God. Thus, the Old Testament concept of life as life in fellowship with God was in conflict with the un-Biblical view that every death means separation from God's fellowship. In the manner in which this conflict was resolved lies the

---

27. Northern Israel.
28. Second Letter to the Corinthians 5:21.
29. The Gospel of Matthew 27:46; Mark 15:34.

contribution of the Old Testament to the subject of human immortality, as shown in the following representative passages.

a. Psalm 73

The psalmist declares how the continued prosperity of the wicked and the adversity of the righteous had been a source of much concern to him and a challenge to his faith in God.

> But as for me, my feet had almost stumbled, my steps had well nigh slipped. For I was envious of the arrogant, when I saw the prosperity of the wicked. All in vain have I kept my heart clean and washed my hands in innocence.
>
> *73:2-3, 13*

He sought the meaning of this problem, and found none. And so he repaired to God's sanctuary, and there in communion with God he received the answer.

> But when I thought how to understand this, it seemed to me a wearisome task. Until I went into the sanctuary of God; then I perceived their end.
>
> *73:16-17*

The solution of his problem — he discovered — lies in man's relation to God. The wicked are separated from Him in life, they will be more completely separated from Him in death.

> For lo, those who are far from thee shall perish; thou dost put an end to those who are false to thee.
>
> *73:27*

But the righteous are ever close to God. In this consists their felicity. Even after death their relation to God remains unchanged.

> Nevertheless I am continually with thee; thou dost hold my right hand. Thou dost guide me with thy counsel, and afterward thou wilt receive me to glory . . . My flesh and my heart may fail, but God is the strength of my heart and my portion for ever
>
> *73:23-24, 26*

"The future is dark to him, but it is illuminated by the assured confidence, that his way beyond the grave will lead, not downwards, but upwards, . . . and that the issue of his earthly existence will be a glorious solution of the riddle."[30]

b. Psalm 49

The problem of man's final destiny is carried a step further in this Psalm. The psalmist begins by stating that he has an important message for all mankind.

> Hear this, all peoples! give ear, all inhabitants of the world.
> Both low and high, rich and poor together!
>
> *49:1-2 (49:2-3 Heb.)*

He is well aware that all men die, this is mankind's universal fate.

> Yea, he shall see that even the wise die, the fool and the stupid alike must perish and leave their wealth to others.
>
> *49:10 (49:11 Heb.)*

But at death the separate destinies of the righteous and the wicked, the godly and the ungodly, become manifest. Those who trust in their wealth, who live by the material things only, go to Sheol, Sheol becomes their home.

> Like sheep they are appointed for Sheol; Death shall be their shepherd; straight to the grave they descend, and their form shall waste away; Sheol shall be their home.
>
> *49:14 (49:15 Heb.)*

Those, however, whose lives were God-oriented, God takes to Himself.

> But God will ransom my soul from the power of Sheol, for he will receive me.
>
> *49:15 (49:16 Heb.)*

The phrase "he will receive me" or "he will take me" used here and in Psalm 73:24 takes us back to the story of Enoch in Genesis:

---

30. Franz Delitzsch, BIBLICAL COMMENTARY ON THE PSALMS (Hodder and Stoughton: London, 1888), Vol. 2, p. 368.

> Enoch walked with God; and he was not, for God took him.
>
> *Genesis 5:24*

Enoch and Elijah[31] are the two persons in the Old Testament period who, having by-passed death, were received by God. "The translations of Enoch and Elijah were hints that pointed away beyond the cheerless notion that the way of all led down to the depths of Hades."[32]

The ideas set forth in these two psalms presented a challenge to the popular notion according to which all people at death go to Sheol. They constitute an important milestone in the unfolding of the Biblical doctrine of human immortality. They express the conviction that human destiny beyond the grave is determined entirely by our relation to God. For those who live apart from God, death remains death. Those who in this life abide in God's presence, are taken up into His presence at the time of death.[33]

c. Job

Like Abraham, Job also was tested. He had everything that any godly man in the patriarchal period could possibly desire: health, wealth, many children, and an honorable place in the community. He was a religious man. Even in God's estimate he was upright and a man of integrity.[34]

But Satan questioned the motives for Job's religiousity.

> Then Satan answered Jehovah, "Does Job fear God for nought? Hast thou not put a hedge about him and his house and all that he has, on every side? Thou hast blessed the work of his hands, and his possessions have increased in the land. But put forth thy hand now, and touch all that he has, and he will curse thee to thy face."
>
> *Job 1:9-11*

What Satan meant was that when all goes well with us it is not

31. 2 Kings 2:11.
32. Franz Delitzsch, Op. Cit., Vol. 2, p. 137.
33. A.B. Davidson, Op. Cit., p. 464.
34. Job 1:8.

difficult to be religious. God accepted Satan's challenge and gave him permission to touch all Job had but to spare him personally. Within a short time Job's children died, and he lost all his possessions. Yet Job remained steadfast in his attitude to God.

But Satan was not satisfied. If only God would permit him to break down Job's health, he was certain that Job would renounce his faith. Satan received permission to do this also. Job was stricken with a loathsome disease. He was covered with sores from the sole of his feet to the crown of his head.[35] Because of his physical condition he was compelled to leave the place of his residence, and take up abode outside of his town, on a dung-hill, or a mound of ashes, or probably a heap of refuse. In those days one's relation to God was linked up with one's association with his community. To be severed from one's people meant to be cut off from fellowship with God. These beliefs were shared even by Job's three friends, men of wealth and worth, who came from distant places to mourn with him in his bereaved state. According to them, the severity of the calamities which befell Job testified of his exceeding sinfulness.

While Job never regarded himself as being without sin,[36] he was nevertheless convinced in his heart of his essential uprightness. He refused to accept his friends' view that God would not have permitted these calamities to come upon him if he had not been guilty.

> Far be it from me to say that you are right; till I die I will not put away my integrity from me. I hold fast my righteousness, and will not let it go; my heart does not reproach me for any of my days.
>
> *Job 27:5-6*[37]

But if Job was upright in his heart, and righteous in his dealings with his fellow men, why did God permit these evils to come upon him? This question was gnawing at his heart. Are there areas in a man's life which remain altogether outside of God's sovereign power and control? This fear, though unuttered, may have been at the bottom of his sufferings.[38] He perhaps felt that "the firm moorings

---

35. Job 2:7.
36. Job 14:4.
37. See, also, chapter 31.
38. H.L. Ellison, FROM TRAGEDY TO TRIUMPH (The Paternoster Press: London, 1958), p. 118.

of his life have vanished; that the ship of his life is adrift on the dark ocean, without chart, without light, being carried he knows not where."[39]

It is to this deep and concealed fear, often common to men of all times and places, that God addresses Himself in dealing with Job. The essence of God's communication is that it is impossible for man to know all of God's ways apart from Divine revelation. Moreover, Job's friends were rebuked by God for attributing Job's sufferings to his sinfulness — and this is probably one of the purposes of the book of Job.[40] Job was fully vindicated. Most important of all, he was allowed to gain a higher concept of God and human destiny.

> I had heard of thee[41] by the hearing of the ear, but now my eye sees thee. Therefore I despise myself, and repent in dust and ashes.
>
> *Job 42:5-6*

In the previous part of his life Job's knowledge of God was derived from what others had told him, but now he knows God from personal experience. He learned that God alone is the Unchanging One, while all earthly things are transient. Furthermore, "in the hour of Job's greatest desperation he had been driven to the hope of life beyond the grave."[42]

> For I know that my Redeemer lives, and at last he will stand upon the earth. And after my skin has been thus destroyed, then from my flesh[43] I shall see God. Whom I shall see on my side, and my eyes shall behold, and not another . . .
>
> *Job 19:25-27*

---

39. Ibid., p. 31.
40. Chapters 38-41.
41. i.e., God.
42. H. L. Ellison, Op. Cit., p. 127.
43. or without my flesh.

III. THE IMMORTALITY OF THE INDIVIDUAL

1. THE EMERGENCE OF THE INDIVIDUAL TO A PLACE OF PROMINENCE

Among ancient peoples the individual was submerged in the family, tribe, or nation. This condition prevailed also in Israel. The Sinai Covenant was made with the nation. The prophets addressed themselves to the nation or the State. The individual remained in the background. He shared in the blessings of the nation, and he suffered in its reverses. When he contemplated death he consoled himself with the thought of continuing to live in his children; he had his immortality in the ongoing life and work of the Israelite theocracy.

> Children or the building of a city perpetuate a man's name.
> *The Wisdom of Sirach 40:19a*

Nevertheless, the individual in Israel was never completely submerged. The Abrahamic Covenant, and even the Sinai Covenant, contained definite individualistic features, which needed only time to develop more fully. The idea of individual responsibility was inculcated throughout the pre-exilic period of Israel's national history. To Moses who offered to take upon himself the punishment due to the people for the sin committed in the Golden Calf incident, God said:

> "Whoever has sinned against me, him will I blot out of my book."
> *Exodus 32:33*

This principle became incorporated in the Law of Moses.

> "The fathers shall not be put to death for the children, nor shall the children be put to death for the fathers; every man shall be put to death for his own sin."
> *Deuteronomy 24:16*

Of Amaziah, king of Judah, we are told that when he ascended the throne and gained full control of his kingdom he executed the murderers of his father.

> But he did not put to death the children of the murderers;
> according to what is written in the book of the law of Moses,
> where Jehovah commanded, "The fathers shall not be put to
> death for the children, or the children be put to death for the
> fathers; but every man shall die for his own sin."
>
> *2 Kings 14:6*[44]

As the individual became increasingly conscious of his own
worth and dignity and of the meaning of personal life, he began to
claim a more conspicuous place for himself. His spirit struggled
"against the idea of being poured out into the general stream of the
spirit of mankind or even of the people of God."[45]

The real change came with the fall of the Judean State at the
beginning of the sixth century B.C. The individual Israelite lost the
sheltering undergirding of the State. He now faced God and the
world alone, as an individual. Religion assumed an increasingly
personal character. With this shift of religious emphasis from the
nation to the individual, the death of the individual became a
troublesome question. It took on a fresh urgency which required a
new solution. The answer was extracted from the prophetic teachings in connection with the fall and restoration of Israel.

2. THE FALL AND RESTORATION OF ISRAEL ADVANCED THE RESURRECTION HOPE

The hope of immortality was — as we saw in the previous
section — firmly established in the Psalms and in Job. In the prophetic writings the doctrine of immortality advanced into the doctrine of
the resurrection of the dead. Two elements contributed to the
further unfolding of the Old Testament doctrine of the hereafter.
One was the fall of the State; the other, the new prominence gained
by the individual in Israel. The fall of both of the northern and
southern components of Israel was likened to death, and its
restoration was described in terms of a resurrection.

> "Come, let us return to Jehovah; for he has torn, that he
> may heal us; he has stricken, and he will bind us up. After two

---

44.   See, also, Jeremiah 31:29-30 (31:28-29 Heb.); Ezekiel 18:4,20.
45.   A.B. Davidson, Op. Cit., p. 408.

days he will revive us; on the third day he will raise us up, that we may live before him."

Hosea 6:1-2

In the above words Hosea promises to Northern Israel the certainty of a speedy revival if she will return to God in true repentance. "The words primarily hold out nothing more than the quickening of Israel out of its death-like state of rejection from the face of God, and that in a very short period after its conversion to the Lord." But the passage may be counted among the prophetic utterances containing the germ of the hope of a resurrection of the dead.[46] Hosea's statement is interpreted in the Targum as referring to the resurrection from the dead.

Hosea's words were meant for Northern Israel, before she was struck down in the latter part of the eighth century B.C. The same hope of a national resurrection is contained in a prophetic message by Ezekiel addressed to the exiles in Babylon in the sixth century B.C.

> The hand of Jehovah was upon me, and he brought me out by the Spirit of Jehovah, and set me down in the midst of the valley; it was full of bones. And he led me round among them; and behold, there were very many upon the valley; and lo, they were very dry. And he said to me, "Son of man, can these bones live?" And I answered, "O Lord Jehovah, thou knowest." Again he said to me, "Prophesy to these bones and say to them, O dry bones, hear the word of Jehovah. Thus says the Lord Jehovah to these bones: Behold, I will cause breath to enter you and you shall live. And I will lay sinews upon you, and will cause flesh to come upon you, and cover you with skin, and put breath in you, and you shall live; and you shall know that I am Jehovah."
>
> Then he said to me, "Son of man, these bones are the whole house of Israel; Behold, they say, 'Our bones are dried up, and our hope is lost; we are clean cut off.' Therefore prophesy, and say to them, Thus says Jehovah God: Behold, I will open your graves, and raise you from your graves, O my people; and I will bring you home into the land of Israel. And you shall know that I am Jehovah, when I open your graves, and raise you from your graves, O my people. And I will put my Spirit within you,

---

46. C.F. Keil, HOSEA, in THE TWELVE MINOR PROPHETS (T. & T. Clark: Edinburgh, 1868), Vol. 1, p. 96.

and you shall live, and I will place you in your own land; then
you shall know that I, Jehovah, have spoken, and I have done it,
says Jehovah."

Ezekiel 37:1-6, 11-14

While the above pronouncements by Hosea and Ezekiel meant
no more than a national restoration of Israel, they did focus the
attention of the faithful Israelites on the hope of the resurrection of
the individual. This hope was articulated in the writings of Isaiah, in
connection with the return of the remnant from the Babylonian
exile. While praising God for their delivery, the returnees pour out a
plaintive prayer in which they bemoan their small numbers and the
depopulated state of the country.[47]

"What avails it to have been pardoned, to have regained the
Holy Land and the face of God, if the dear dead are left behind in
graves of exile, and all the living must soon pass into that captivity,[48]
from which there is no return. It must have been thoughts like these,
which led to the expression of one of the most abrupt and powerful
of the few hopes of the resurrection from the dead which the Old
Testament contains. This hope, which lightens up chap. 35:7,8,
bursts through again — without logical connection with the context
— in vv. 14-19 of chap. 26."[49]

Thy dead shall live, their bodies shall rise, O dwellers in the
dust, awake and sing for joy! For thy dew is the dew of light, and
on the land of the shades[50] thou[51] wilt let it fall.

Isaiah 26:19

"This is the resurrection of its individual members to a community
which is already restored, the recovery by Israel of her dead men
and women from their separate graves, each with his own freshness
and beauty, in that glorious morning when the Sun of
Righteousness shall arise, with healing under His wings — Thy dew,
O Lord!"[52]

---

47.   Isaiah 26:15-18.
48.   death.
49.   George Adam Smith, THE BOOK OF ISAIAH (Harper & Brothers: New
      York, 1927), Vol. 1, p. 464.
50.   the realm of the dead.
51.   i.e., God.
52.   George Adam Smith, THE BOOK OF ISAIAH (Harper & Brothers: New
      York, 1927), Vol. 1, p. 469.

Attempts have been made — Smith declares — to trace this hope of the resurrection in the Old Testament to foreign influences experienced in the Babylonian exile. Whatever these influences may have been, the origin of Israel's hope of a resurrection was her own religious experience, while the occasion which gave rise to the expression of the hope was the disappointment of the returned Remnant with its meager numbers and the depopulated state of the country. "A restoration of the State or community was not enough: the heart of Israel wanted back in their numbers her dead sons and daughters."[53]

3. THE RESURRECTION HOPE IN RELATION TO THE MESSIANIC HOPE

In Daniel the Messianic idea occupies a most prominent place in the Old Testament. Its first prophetic utterance deals with events which are to take place in the "latter days." It was indicated in a previous chapter that this phrase refers to events which take place at the "end" of history when the kingdom of God is fully and firmly established in this world, and when the whole earth comes under God's rule. In the twelfth chapter of Daniel we have the following statement about the resurrection.

> "At that time shall arise Michael, the great prince who has charge of your people. And there shall be a time of trouble, such as never has been since there was a nation till that time; but at that time your people shall be delivered, every one whose name shall be found written in the book. And many of those who sleep in the dust of the earth shall awake, some to everlasting life; and some to shame and everlasting contempt."
>
> *Daniel 12:1-2*

Here is a resurrection with moral implications. It takes place at the greatest crisis in the history of Israel and in the history of the world. It does not mean that the resurrection here referred to is limited to Israel. Our text is merely concerned with the Israel phase of the resurrection. Those Israelites who shall rise from the dead are

---

53. Ibid., pp. 469-470.

divided into two groups. One of them, the godly Israelites, will rise to everlasting life; the ungodly Israelites will rise to "shame and everlasting contempt." We need not infer from this passage that both these groups will rise in the same chronological period. It is a resurrection of individuals, and a resurrection with clear moral overtones.

Another instance in which the hope of the resurrection is linked with the Messianic hope is found in Isaiah.

> On this mountain Jehovah of hosts will make for all peoples a feast of fat things, a feast of wine on the lees, of fat things full of marrow, of wine on the lees well refined. And he will destroy on this mountain the covering that is cast over all peoples, the veil that is spread over all nations. He will swallow up death for ever, and the Lord God will wipe away tears from all faces, and the reproach of his people he will take away from all the earth; for Jehovah has spoken. It will be said on that day, "Lo, this is our God; we have waited for him, that he might save us. This is Jehovah; we have waited for him; let us be glad and rejoice in his salvation."
>
> *Isaiah 25:6-9*[54]

The feast referred to in chapter 25 is a spiritual feast. All nations participate in it. The cause for this world-wide rejoicing is recorded in the next sentence: God removed the veil, i.e., the spiritual blindness, which was spread over the nations of the earth; death was abolished, and sorrow and suffering ceased. "He will swallow up death for ever, and the Lord God will wipe away tears from all faces." While all this is taking place on earth, it is an earth which has been transformed into heaven. The wall of partition between God and man has been removed; this is the day for which the world has been waiting.

---

54. The above prophetic passage in Isaiah has been Messianically interpreted in the following Rabbinic writings: Moed Q. 28 b; Yalkut I, 190 d; Yalkut II, 56c; Exodus R. 30; Deuteronomy R. 2; Tanchuma 99: 1, citing Isaiah 25:9.

CHAPTER 2
THE RESURRECTION HOPE IN THE
INTER-TESTAMENTAL PERIOD

CHAPTER 2
THE RESURRECTION HOPE
IN THE INTER-TESTAMENTAL PERIOD

By "inter-Testamental period" we mean the centuries between the close of the Old Testament and the opening of the New Testament periods. The Jewish writings produced in this period which were not incorporated in the Hebrew Bible are collectively known as the Apocrypha and the Pseudepigrapha. In its wider sense the Apocrypha includes the Pseudepigrapha, and together they represent a body of writings extending approximately from 200 B.C. to A.D. 100. The compilers of the Hebrew Bible did not include these writings in the Canon of the Hebrew Bible. This, because they did not view these writings as containing the inspired Word of God in the same sense as they regarded the writings of the Hebrew Old Testament.

The importance of this extra-canonical literature rests in the fact that it reflects, among other things, the religious thoughts and convictions of a large, important and articulate segment of Jews. It was stated that the influence of these writings upon the bulk of the Jewish people at that period was even greater than that of the Pharisees who were the founders of Rabbinic traditionalism.[1] The authors of this religious literature, some of whom assumed the names of Old Testament writers as their own pseudonyms, are dealing with a variety of subjects, such as, the concept of God, the nature of the Messiah, the postion of Israel, the Messianic Kingdom, the destiny of the individual, and the hereafter. For our purpose we are solely interested in what they had to say about life after death.

A perusal of this literature reveals that the resurrection hope is a settled conviction in many of these extra-canonical writings. This fact stems from the enhanced importance which the individual Jew assumed in this period, and from the deeper understanding of the contents of the Old Testament writings gained by the Jewish people

---

1. W.O.E. Oesterley and G.H. Box, A SHORT HISTORY OF RABBINICAL AND MEDIEVAL JUDAISM, pp. 30f.

in the years after their return from the Babylonian exile. Several excerpts from these extra-canonical writings follow:

I. THE RESURRECTION HOPE IN THE BOOK OF ENOCH

And it came to pass after this that his name during his lifetime was raised aloft to that Son of Man and to the Lord of Spirits from amongst those who dwell on the earth. And he was raised aloft on the chariots of the spirit and his name vanished among them. And from that day I was no longer numbered amongst them; and he sat me between the two winds, between the north and the west, where the angels took the cords to measure for me the place for the elect and righteous. And there I saw the first fathers and the righteous who from the beginning dwell in that place.

Enoch 70:1-4[2]

II. THE RESURRECTION HOPE IN 2 ESDRAS

Wherefore this is the word concerning them: First of all they see with great exaltion the glory of him who taketh them to himself; and they will rest in seven orders. The first order[3] (of rejoicing) is that they strove with much toil to overcome the evil imagination formed with them, that it might not lead them astray from life unto death. The second, in that they see the entanglement wherein the souls of the ungodly wander, and the punishment that awaiteth them. The third order is in their seeing the testimony which he that formed them hath borne unto them, that in their lifetime they have kept the law which was given them in trust. The fourth is in knowing the rest they will now enjoy, gathered together in their store-chambers, and guarded by the angels in deep repose; and knowing also the glory that awaiteth them at the last. The fifth is in their exulting at the way in which they will gain the future inheritance; furthermore, in seeing the strait and toilsome (way) from which they have been freed, and the broad way which they will begin to receive in enjoyment and immortality. The sixth order is, when

2. In the above excerpt Enoch, who according to the brief statement in the book of Genesis ascended to heaven without tasting death, relates how he saw angels who were given cords to measure off places for the righteous in paradise. The above text is from THE BOOK OF ENOCH by R. H. Charles published by Oxford University Press (London: 1912). The above passage in Enoch dates from the first half of the 1st century B.C.
3. "Order" here is used to indicate state of mind.

it will be shown unto them how their countenance will begin to shine as the sun, and how they will begin to be made like unto the light of the stars, from henceforth incorruptible. The seventh order, which surpasseth all the aforesaid, is in that they will exult with confidence, and put their trust without being confounded, and rejoice without being afraid; for they hasten to see the face of him whom they served in life, and from whom they begin to receive their reward in glory.

2 Esdras 7:90-98[4]

III. THE RESURRECTION HOPE IN WISDOM OF SOLOMON

For God created man to be immortal, and made him to be an image of his own eternity. Nevertheless through envy of the devil came death into the world: and they that do hold of his side do find it.[5] But the souls of the righteous are in the hand of God, and there shall no torment touch them. In the sight of the unwise they seemed to die: and their departure is taken for misery. And their going from us, to be utter destruction: but they are in peace. For though they be punished in the sight of men, yet is their hope full of immortality. And having been a little chastened, they shall be greatly rewarded: for God proved them, and found them worthy for himself. As gold in the furnace hath he tried them, and received them as a burnt offering. And in the time of their visitation they shall shine, and run to and fro like sparks among the stubble. They shall judge the nations, and have dominion over the people, and their Lord shall reign for ever.

Wisdom of Solomon 2:23-24; 3:1-8[6]

IV. THE RESURRECTION HOPE IN 2 MACCABEES

The passages from 2 Maccabees cited below form part of an account of the martyrdom of the seven brothers and their mother which took place during the religious persecution unleashed by Antiochus Epiphanes who, in the interest of cultural uniformity, was determined to destroy the Jewish religion which was the source of Jewish national distinctiveness. One by one the seven brothers and their mother chose death rather than to break the Law of Moses.

---

4. The above and remaining excerpts in this group are from THE APOCRYPHA, edited by Henry Wace, 2 vols., published by John Murray (London: 1888). The above passage is estimated as having been written in the second half of the 1st century of our era.
5. They who follow the devil experience death.
6. The above passage is dated from the early part of the 1st century, B.C.

After the first son was tortured to death, they put the second son to death also. But before he died he said this to the king:

> Thou like a fury takest us out of this present life, but the king of the world will raise us up, who have died for his laws, unto everlasting life.
>
> 2 Maccabees 7:9

Following this the third and fourth sons were also murdered upon their refusal to forsake the religion of their fathers. Before his death, the fourth son said this to the king:

> It is good, being put to death by men, to look for hope from God to be raised up again by him: as for thee, thou shalt have no resurrection to life.
>
> 2 Maccabees 7:14

Their noble mother not only witnessed the terrible death of her seven sons, and in the end she too was put to death, but she called upon each and every one of them to be strong in the Lord and be ready to die rather than to prove unfaithful to the God of their forefathers. The following are her words:

> I cannot tell how ye came into my womb; for I neither gave you breath no life, neither was it I that formed the members of every one of you. But doubtless the Creator of the world, who formed the generation of man, and arranged the beginning of all things, will also of his own mercy give you breath and life again, as ye now regard not your own selves for his laws' sake.
>
> 2 Maccabees 7:22-23

Before the youngest boy was executed, the king sought to persuade the mother to get the boy to change his mind. But the mother rejected the king's suggestion, and she encouraged her last son to stand firm in the following words:

> I beseech thee, my son, look upon the heaven, and the earth, and all that is therein, and consider that God made them of things that were not; and so was mankind made likewise. Fear not this tormentor, but, being worthy of thy brethren, take thy death, that I may receive thee again in mercy with thy brethren.
>
> 2 Maccabees 7:28-29[7]

---

7. 2 MACCABEES is dated from the last quarter of the 2nd century B.C.

CHAPTER 3
THE RESURRECTION OF JESUS THE MESSIAH

I. The Witness of Paul

II. The Witness Of The Gospels
1. The Empty Tomb
2. The Post-Resurrection Appearings Of The Risen Jesus

III. Naturalistic Or Semi-Naturalistic Theories Of The Resurrection Of Jesus
1. The Swoon And Theft Theories
2. The Mythological Theory
3. The Subjective Vision Theory
4. An Easter Faith Without The Easter Fact

CHAPTER 3
THE RESURRECTION OF JESUS THE MESSIAH

Competent students of the New Testament are in full agreement that if not for what was believed to have taken place on the first Easter Sunday morning there would have been no Christian message, no Christian faith, no Christian Church. It is not even certain that the name of Jesus of Nazareth would have been recorded in history if not for the belief in His Resurrection. Whatever may be our position, we need to explain to ourselves the reason for the incredible transformation effected in the lives of the disciples of Jesus so soon after His death. On the day when He was placed on the cross, His followers' faith in Him as Israel's predicted Messiah was broken, and the hopes and expectations which they associated with Him were dashed to the ground. "And they all forsook him and fled."[1] Several weeks later their attitude and behaviour had changed so completely that we can scarcely believe that we are dealing with the same people. Sadness gave place to joy, fear — to courage, weakness — to strength. Whereas immediately after the crucifixion they hid themselves behind locked doors, they now faced fearlessly the religious authorities who condemned their Master, calling upon them to repent, and declaring to them that there is no salvation outside of Messiah Jesus.[2] Before the first century drew to a close the Messianic movement of Jesus was firmly established in the world of that day, and while many of the followers of Jesus died a martyr's death, no amount of repression could stem the spread of the new faith. And from that day to this it has remained the most dynamic spiritual movement in the world. In the following chapters we wish, first, to ascertain what are the facts in the story of the resurrection of Jesus; then, what is the significance of these facts.

I. THE WITNESS OF PAUL

Paul's writings furnish the earliest documentary evidence of the belief in the resurrection of Jesus. In his First Letter to the Thes-

---

1. The Gospel of Mark 15:50.
2. The book of Acts 4:1-12.

salonians, said to have been written in A.D. 51, he refers to the resurrection of Jesus in a casual manner, which goes to show how soon belief in the resurrection of Jesus had become an integral element in the Christian faith.

> But we would not have you ignorant, brethren, concerning those who are asleep, that you may not grieve as others do who have no hope. For since we believe that Jesus died and rose again, even so, through Jesus, God will bring with him those who have fallen asleep.[3]
>
> *1 Thessalonians 4:13-14*

In the First Letter to the Christians in Corinth, written several years later, Paul is dealing with the subject of the resurrection in general. In this connection he mentions the following facts about the resurrection of Jesus.

> Now I would remind you, brethren, in what terms I preached to you the gospel, which you received, in which you stand. By which you are saved, if you hold it fast — unless you believed in vain. For I delivered to you as of first importance what I also received, that Christ died for our sins in accordance with the Scriptures. That he was buried, that he was raised on the third day in accordance with the Scriptures. And that he appeared to Cephas,[4] then to the twelve. Then he appeared to more than five hundred brethren, most of whom are still alive, though some have fallen asleep. Then he appeared to James, then to all the apostles. Last of all, as to one untimely born, he appeared also to me.
>
> *1 Corinthians 15:1-8*

In the first century of our era the Greeks held certain beliefs about the immortality of the soul, but, unlike the Jews, they did not believe in a bodily resurrection. When Paul addressed a Greek audience in Athens he met with ridicule when he mentioned the resurrection of Jesus.[5] It appears that certain members of the church in the Greek city of Corinth could not reconcile themselves to the belief in a bodily resurrection. In his letter Paul declares to them that the resurrection of Christ is the heart of the Christian message.

---

3. The word "sleep" is used by Paul to denote the sleep of death.
4. Peter.
5. Acts 17:30-32.

> Now if Christ is preached as raised from the dead, how can some of you say that there is no resurrection of the dead? But if there is no resurrection of the dead, then Christ has not been raised. If Christ has not been raised, then our preaching is in vain and your faith is in vain.
>
> *1 Corinthians 15:12-14*

He reminds them that the story of the Resurrection of Christ was foremost in his preaching when he was in their midst.[6] Then he enumerates the main facts in the resurrection story. These facts concern two chief events. One of these had to do with the discovery of the empty tomb ("that Christ died . . ., "that he was buried," "that he was raised on the third day")[7]; the second event referred to the various post-resurrection appearings of Christ ("that he appeared to Cephas, then to the twelve, then . . . to more than five hundred brethren . . . then . . . to James, then to all the apostles, last of all . . . to me").[8]

Since Paul did not become a follower of Messiah Jesus until a year or so after the crucifixion, how did he get to know about the empty tomb and the post-resurrection appearings? In the beginning of chapter 15 of his Letter he tells the Corinthians that he received this information. In another Letter, written to the Galatian Christians, he states that he received his information about the resurrection of Jesus directly from Peter and James.

> Then after three years I went up to Jerusalem to visit Cephas, and remained with him fifteen days. But I saw none of the other apostles except James, the Lord's brother.
>
> *Galatians 1:18-19*

His appearing to Paul was the last of the post-resurrection appearings of Jesus.

> Last of all, as to one untimely born, he appeared also to me.
>
> *1 Corinthians 15:8*

The account of Jesus' appearing to Paul is related in three different parts of the book of Acts.[9] This appearing resulted in Paul's conver-

---

6. I Corinthians 15:3.
7. I Corinthians 15:3-4.
8. I Corinthians 15:5-8.
9. Acts 9:1-19; 22:1-16; 26:1-18.

sion, and Paul describes his conversion "as one untimely born," by which he means that his conversion was sudden, brought about by his experience on the Damascus road.

II. THE WITNESS OF THE GOSPELS

1. THE EMPTY TOMB

All four Gospels report that on the morning of the first day of the week, i.e., on the third day after the crucifixion, certain women went to the tomb to anoint the dead body of Jesus. As they arrived at the tomb they found the big stone which had been placed at its entrance rolled away, the tomb was empty, and they saw a man dressed in a white robe who informed them that Messiah Jesus had risen from the dead. Stunned and bewildered they ran from the place in fear and trembling.

And when evening had come, since it was the day of Preparation, that is, the day before the Sabbath. Joseph of Arimathea, a respected member of the council, who was also himself looking for the kingdom of God, took courage and went to Pilate, and asked for the body of Jesus. And Pilate wondered if he were already dead; and summoning the centurion, he asked him whether he was already dead. And when he learned from the centurion that he was dead, he granted the body to Joseph. And he bought a linen shroud, and taking him down, wrapped him in the linen shroud, and laid him in a tomb which had been hewn out of the rock;[10] and he rolled a stone against the door of the tomb. Mary Magdalene and Mary the mother of Jesus saw where he was laid.

And when the Sabbath was past, Mary Magdalene, and Mary the mother of James, and Salome, bought spices, so that they might go and anoint him. And very early on the first day of the week they went to the tomb when the sun had risen. And they were saying to one another, "Who will roll away the stone for us from the door of the tomb?" And looking up, they saw that the stone was rolled back; for it was very large. And enter-

---

10. Apparently this was the family tomb of Joseph of Arimathea.

ing the tomb, they saw a young man sitting on the right side, dressed in a white robe; and they were amazed. And he said to them, "Do not be amazed; you seek Jesus of Nazareth, who was crucified; he has risen, he is not here; see the place where they laid him. But go, tell his disciples and Peter that he is going before you to Galilee; there you will see him, as he told you." And they went out and fled from the tomb; for trembling and astonishment had come upon them; and they said nothing to any one, for they were afraid.

Mark 15:42-47; 16:1-8

When the news about the empty tomb reached the disciples, the whole thing sounded to them like an "idle tale."[11] But Peter and John ran quickly to the burial place. Upon entering the tomb they found the grave clothes lying apparently undisturbed, i.e., they retained the shape of the body around which they were wrapped; while the napkin which had been placed around the head lay rolled up, by itself, separately. The condition of the grave clothes impressed the two disciples greatly, for it must have appeared to them as if the body of Jesus had simply slipped out of the grave clothes.[12]

Matthew's Gospel informs us that when the report of the empty tomb had reached the religious authorities they planted a rumor that the disciples of Jesus had stolen the body. This rumor which circulated for years indirectly confirmed the veracity of the story of the empty tomb. Actually, no detail connected with the resurrection of Jesus is better attested than the fact of the empty grave.[13]

2. THE POST-RESURRECTION APPEARINGS OF THE RISEN JESUS

The empty tomb in itself would have never given rise to the belief that Jesus had risen from the dead. The disciples would have undoubtedly accused the enemies of Jesus of having removed the body. *The appearings of Jesus following upon the discovery of the empty tomb produced the certainty of His bodily Resurrection.* These appearings

---

11.   Luke 24:11.
12.   Luke 24;12; John 20:3-7.
13.   John Mackintosh Shaw, THE RESURRECTION OF CHRIST (T. & T. Clark: Edinburgh, 1920), p. 59.

took place in the space of forty days. He showed Himself to different people, in different places, and on different occasions. Not all of His appearings are recorded in each of the four Gospels. The Gospel of Mark merely mentions one appearing, but describes none. Each of the remaining three Gospel writers describe only those appearings which contained certain features of special interest to them, or which may have been omitted by the other Gospel writers.

Matthew records two appearings, one to the women who came to anoint the dead body, and one to the eleven apostles.[14] Luke reports three appearings in his Gospel — one to two disciples on the road to Emmaus,[15] one to Peter,[16] and one to the eleven apostles[17] — and one appearing recorded in the book of Acts.[18] John relates four appearings: one to Mary Magdalene,[19] one to the disciples when one of them, Thomas, was away,[20] one a week later, also to the disciples, when this same Thomas was with them,[21] and one by the Sea of Tiberias.[22]

III. NATURALISTIC OR SEMI-NATURALISTIC THEORIES OF THE RESURRECTION OF JESUS

1. THE SWOON AND THEFT THEORIES

According to the swoon theory Jesus never really died on the cross. He remained in a state of suspended animation and revived in the sepulcher. If this was the case, we should immediately ask, what became of Him in the post-crucifixion period of His life? Why did He so completely vanish from the earthly scene? Furthermore, the Jesus whom the apostles and five hundred of His followers had seen

---

14.   Matthew 28:1-10, 16-20.
15.   Luke 24:13-32.
16.   Luke 24:34.
17.   Luke 24:36-51.
18.   Acts 1:4-11.
19.   John 20:14-17.
20.   John 20:19-23.
21.   John 20:24-29.
22.   John 21:1-23.

on several occasions following the resurrection was the same Jesus they had known before the crucifixion, and yet not exactly the same. The disciples were impressed with the profound changes in the bodily state of the risen Jesus. These and other considerations are of such an insuperable character that the swoon theory is now hopelessly discredited.

The case against the theft theory is no less formidable. According to this theory the disciples had removed the body of Jesus. This, incidentally, was the oldest attempt of the opponents of Christianity to account for the disappearance of the body of Jesus. As mentioned before, this claim indirectly proves the fact of the empty tomb. Actually, the fact of the empty tomb appears to have been a universal assumption.[23] The many variations of this hypothesis testify to its inability to stand up against the known facts. Its fatal defect is the impossibility to account for the radical overnight change which had taken place in the attitude of the followers of Jesus, which attitude persisted indefinitely. That a multitude of people would adhere for years to come to a story which they knew all along to be a lie, and to be willing to die a violent death for it, is something which defies all rules of probability.

2. THE MYTHOLOGICAL THEORY

The proponents of this theory suggest that the belief in the resurrection of Jesus was derived from certain myths in the East connected with the death and resurrection stories of the pagan gods Attis, Adonis, and Osiris. It is maintained that these myths passed into Christianity by way of Judaism. However, there are several considerations which prove the untenableness of this hypothesis. The death and resurrection myths of Attis, Adonis, and Osiris were poetical renderings of natural phenomena connected with the yearly decay and revival of vegetation. They were annual festivals held in the spring and celebrating the sun's victory over winter. The resurrection of Jesus was commemorated among the early Christians every Sunday. There is not the slightest valid ideolgical correla-

---

23.   Frank Morison, WHO MOVED THE STONE? (Barnes & Noble, Inc.: New York, 1962), University Paperbacks, p. 111.

tion between the fact and significance of the resurrection of Jesus and the above-mentioned pagan myths.

Referring to certain pagan myths which are said to incorporate the idea of a resurrection, Moore states that "Christianity knew its savior and redeemer not as some god whose history was contained in a myth filled with rude, primitive, and even offensive elements, as were the stories of Attis, of Osiris, and, to a degree, of Dionysus. Such myths required violent interpretation to make them acceptable to enlightened minds. On the contrary, the Christian savior had lived and associated with men, whose minds and senses had apprehended his person, acts, and character. These witnesses had transmitted their knowledge directly, and they had testified that the life of Jesus corresponded to his teachings. Jesus was then a historical, not a mythical being. No remote or foul myth obtruded itself on the Christian believer; his faith was founded on positive, historical, and acceptable facts."[24]

Furthermore, Judaism of the first century believed in a bodily resurrection connected with the Universal Day of Judgment, while post-Biblical Judaism of the first century entertained no belief in a death and resurrection of the Messiah. This accounts for the marked difficulty experienced by the apostles in grasping the meaning of Christ's intimations of His forthcoming death. They simply did not associate in their minds and in their religious ideas death with the Messiah. Peter's reaction reflected the feeling of all of them when, in response to Christ's first clear declaration concerning His approaching death, he exclaimed: "God forbid, Lord! This shall never happen to you."[25] This also explains the attitude of skepticism and unbelief exhibited by the disciples when the first news of the resurrection had reached them. One of them, Thomas, after having been informed that Jesus had appeared to the apostles on the first Sunday evening, when he happened to be away, said defiantly: "Unless I see in his hands the print of the nails, and place my finger in the mark of the nails, and place my hand in his side,[26] I will not believe."[27]

---

24. Clifford Herschel Moore, THE RELIGIOUS THOUGHT OF THE GREEKS (Harvard Univesity Press: Cambridge, Mass., 1916), p. 357.
25. Matthew 16:22; Mark 8:32.
26. Pierced by the soldiers to ascertain that he had already died.
27. John 20:25.

3. THE SUBJECTIVE VISION THEORY

According to the advocates of this theory the appearings of the risen Jesus were mental hallucinations generated in the disciples at a time when they found themselves in a state of deep emotional disturbance. They thought they saw Him, because they longed to see Him.[28] The serious flaw in this theory is that the condition or conditions which must exist for hallucinations to occur are entirely absent in the New Testament narratives. It is true that before His crucifixion Jesus had spoken to His disciples of His resurrection.[29] But these intimations made no impression on the disciples simply because a resurrection implied death. They could not grasp the reason or purpose for the Messiah's death, and to the last minute the whole idea sounded unreal to them.[30] They could not link up their Messianic expectations with a dying Messiah. The two disciples who after the crucifixion returned home from Jerusalem were sad and unhappy because the crucifixion was contrary to all their Messianic hopes. To the risen Jesus who appeared on the road beside them and whom they failed to recognize until they arrived home, they spoke of this

"Jesus of Nazareth, who was a prophet mighty in deed and word before God and all the people. And how our chief priests and rulers delivered him up to be condemned to death, and crucified him. But we had hoped that he was the one to redeem Israel."

Luke 24:19-21

The disciples of Jesus did not look for a resurrection because till the last minute they could not make themselves believe that the Messiah of Israel would permit Himself to be killed.

Another serious weakness of this notion of mental hallucina-

---

28. The proponents of this theory are the following: E. Renan, APOTRES, Engl. Trans., 1869; D. F. Strauss, NEW LIFE OF JESUS, Engl. Trans., 1865; C. Weizsacker, APOSTOLIC AGE, 1897-1899; A. Harnack, HISTORY OF DOGMA, Engl. Trans., 1904; A. Meyer, DIE AUFERSTEHUNG CHRISTI, 1905; P. W. Schmiedel, art. "Resurrection and Ascension Narratives", in Encyclopedia Biblica; etc., etc.
29. Matthew 16:21; 17:9, 22:23; 20:18-19; 26:32, etc., and parallels.
30. Mark 9:9-10.

tions is that the risen Jesus was seen by different people, under differing circumstances, and in several locations. At one time He was seen by over five hundred of His followers at once. The following passage will show how utterly impossible it is to find any evidence of hallucinations in the New Testament resurrection narratives.

> As they were saying this[31], Jesus himself stood among them. But they were startled and frightened, and supposed that they saw a spirit. And he said to them, "Why are you troubled, and why do questionings[32] rise in your heart? See my hands, and my feet, that it is I myself; handle me, and see, for a spirit has not flesh and bones as you see that I have."
>
> *Luke 24:36-40*

The above realistic resurrection scene is not an isolated incident, rather it is representative of the nature of the appearings of the risen Jesus as recorded in the New Testament. The women take hold of his feet;[33] Thomas is invited to feel with his hands the nail prints in His hands and feet, and the scar in His pierced side;[34] on the shore of the Sea of Tiberias the risen Jesus invites the seven disciples to have breakfast.[35]

So certain were the disciples that they had witnessed the bodily Resurrection of Jesus that to declare to the world the fact of the Messiah's resurrection they considered to be their life's mission. When Peter called upon the disciples to select one of their number to the office of an apostle, to fill the vacancy made by the defection of Judas, he described the function of an apostle as that of "a witness to his resurrection."[36] This was their story until the end of their earthly ministry, and for their conviction of the truth of their story they were willing to pay with their lives. In the very first chapter of the fourth Gospel, written some time between A.D. 69 and A.D. 90, the apostle John declares the Messiah to be the embodiment of God who took up His abode among men. He was "full of grace and truth; we beheld his glory, glory as of the only Son from the Father . . . And

---

31. This statement refers to the report concerning the risen Jesus brought to the apostles by the two disciples from Emmaus.
32. Relative to the veracity and reality of the news of His resurrection.
33. Matthew 28:9; John 20:17.
34. John 20:26-27.
35. John 21:9-13.
36. Acts 1:15-22.

from his fullness have we all received, grace upon grace. No one has ever seen God; the only Son, who is in the bosom of the Father, he has made him known."[37] And he concludes his description of the Messiah's ministry with two chapters devoted to various incidents connected with the resurrection of Jesus.

The following words were written by Paul in A.D. 64, about 30 years after his conversion, from prison where he waited to be executed. Writing to Timothy, his spiritual son, Paul says:

> You then, my son, be strong in the grace that is in Messiah Jesus. And what you have heard from me before many witnesses entrust to faithful men who will be able to teach others also . . . Remember Jesus the Messiah, risen from the dead, descended from David, as preached in my gospel. The gospel for which I am suffering and wearing fetters like a criminal; but the word of God is not fettered . . . For I am already on the point of being sacrificed; the time of my departure has come. I have fought the good fight, I have finished the race, I have kept the faith. Henceforth there is laid up for me the crown of righteousness, which the Lord, the righteous judge, will award to me on that Day, and not only to me but also to all who have loved his appearing.
>
> *2 Timothy 2:1-2, 8-9; 4:6-8*

Likewise Peter, when sensing approaching death, reminds his Christian readers that the basic things of their faith rest on a sure foundation:

> For we did not follow cleverly devised myths when we made known to you the power and coming of our Lord Jesus the Messiah, but we were eyewitnesses of his majesty.
>
> *2 Peter 1:16*

4. AN EASTER FAITH WITHOUT THE EASTER FACT

There is a group of writers who take the position that the Easter faith could be divorced from the Easter fact. They assert that the Easter faith can retain its abiding relevance without the Easter fact,

---

37. John 1:14, 16, 18.

i.e., without accepting a belief in the bodily resurrection of Jesus. Thus, Keim suggested that the body of Jesus remained in the tomb but His living spirit communicated to the disciples that He is alive.[38]

Streeter, who some years later restated Keim's basic position, maintained that the post-resurrection appearings of Jesus were visions caused by the living spirit of Jesus, the purpose of which was to convince His disciples of His victory over death.[39] That the spirit of Jesus survived, there was no need of visions to convince the disciples. They all believed in the resurrection of the dead, and this involved a belief in the survival of man's spirit or soul after death. Another serious flaw in the vision theory is this: if the post-resurrection appearings of Jesus were visions caused by the spirit of Jesus after the crucifixion, and since all the New Testament narratives affirm that the resurrection of Jesus was a bodily resurrection, it follows that the spirit of Jesus induced the disciples, and through them the entire Christian church, to believe a lie.

Harnack, another opponent of the belief in the bodily resurrection of Jesus, avers that none of the opponents had seen the risen Jesus. He scouts the idea that the Easter faith must rest on a foundation of historical evidence. The essential thing, according to him, about the Easter faith is that Jesus was triumphant over death.[40]

Sanday contends that with the disciples of Jesus belief in the bodily resurrection was an essential thing. Being Pharisaic Jews, a bodily resurrection was the only alternative open to them for believing in life after death at all. They thus transferred to the New Testament the "nature miracles" which gathered around certain great personalities in the Old Testament. It was through the medium of minds dominated by such ideas that the declaration that Jesus was alive was made to the world.[41] "I know" — Sanday declared — "that the suggestions I have made will come with a shock to the great mass of Christians; but in the end I believe that they will be thankfully welcomed. What they would mean is that the greatest of all stumbling blocks to the modern mind is removed, and that the

---

38.   T. Keim, JESUS OF NAZARA, Engl. Trns., 6 vols., 1873-1883.
39.   B. H. Streeter, FOUNDATIONS, 1912.
40.   A. Harnack, WHAT IS CHRISTIANITY?, 1904 p. 163; HISTORY OF DOGMA, Vol. 1, pp. 85-87; see John Mackintosh Shaw, Op. Cit., pp. 188-189.
41.   W. Sanday, MIRACLES, 1911. See John Mackintosh Shaw, Op. Cit., p. 195.

beautiful regularity that we see around us now has been, and will be, the law of the divine action from the beginning to the end of time."[42]

This writer can fully sympathize with all who stand outside of Biblical revelation and who for reasons of their own find themselves unable to accept the New Testament affirmation of the bodily Resurrection of Christ. But he finds it difficult to have any sympathy with the position of those who appear to stand with one foot on Biblical ground and with the other outside of it. There is only one answer for people in this group, the one given by Paul to the Christians in Corinth, and which expresses the firm conviction of the whole New Testament.

> Now if the Messiah is preached as raised from the dead, how can some of you say that there is no resurrection of the dead? But if there is no resurrection of the dead, then the Messiah has not been raised. If the Messiah has not been raised, then our preaching is in vain and your faith is in vain.
>
> *1 Corinthians 15:12-14*

---

42. W. Sanday, BISHOP GORE'S CHALLENGE TO CRITICISM, 1914, p. 30. Quoted by John Mackintosh Shaw, Op. Cit., p. 198.

CHAPTER 4
OBJECTIONS TO THE RESURRECTION OF
JESUS THE MESSIAH

I. The Failure Of The Risen Messiah To Show Himself To His Opponents

II. Is The Bodily Resurrection Of Jesus A Violation Of Natural Law?
   1. Present-Day Scientific View Of Nature
   2. The Biblical View Of Nature
      a. God is the Creator of the world
      b. God conserves and sustains Nature
      c. Nature reflects God's wisdom
      d. The regularity, orderliness and uniformity of Nature
   3. Miracles
      a. The essence of miracles in the Bible
      b. The purpose of miracles

III. Objections To The Resurrection Of Jesus The Messiah: Concluding Observations

CHAPTER 4
OBJECTIONS TO THE RESURRECTION OF JESUS THE MESSIAH

Among the objections to the bodily Resurrection of Jesus discussed in the preceding chapter, there are two which deserve serious consideration. One of these has to do with the failure of the Risen Messiah to show Himself to his opponents; the other is based on the assumption that a bodily resurrection is a violation of natural law. In this chapter we will examine both of these issues.

I. THE FAILURE OF THE RISEN MESSIAH TO SHOW HIMSELF TO HIS OPPONENTS

One of those to raise this question was Celsus, a Roman opponent of Christianity who lived in the second century of our era.[1] The apostles were aware of this problem as seen from this statement by Simon Peter speaking on behalf of the several hundred of the disciples of Jesus who had seen the Risen Jesus.

> And we are witnesses to all that he did both in the country of the Jews and Jerusalem; they put him to death by hanging him on a tree. But God raised him on the third day and made him manifest. Not to all the people but to us who were chosen by God as witnesses, who ate and drank with him after he rose from the dead.
>
> *Acts 10:39-41*

The answer to this question may be found in Biblical revelation. In the marvelous history of Israel no generation has witnessed the hand of God in its destiny in the same measure as did the people of the Exodus period. They were liberated from the yoke of the most powerful empire of that day. They walked safely across the Sea of Reeds leaving the pursuing Egyptians buried beneath its waters. Day by day, on their passage through the Wilderness, they experienced God's protection and care. But none of these things generated in the

---

1. See Origen, Contra Celsum, II, 63.

hearts of these people a genuine trust in God. In the end, God called them a wicked and a faithless generation, unfit for entry into the Promised Land.

> And Jehovah said to Moses, "How long will this people despise me? and how long will they not believe in me, in spite of all the signs which I have wrought among them? . . . But truly, as I live, and as all the earth shall be filled with the glory of Jehovah. None of the men, who have seen my glory and my signs which I wrought in Egypt and in the wilderness, and yet have put me to the proof these ten times and have not hearkened to my voice. Shall see the land which I swore to give to their fathers; and none of those who despised me shall see it . . . I, Jehovah, have spoken; surely this will I do to all this wicked congregation that are gathered together against me: in this wilderness they shall come to a full end, and there they shall die."
> *Numbers 14:11, 21-23, 35*

The miraculous delivery from Egyptian bondage and the crossing of the Sea of Reeds were experienced not by a few, but by all the people. Nevertheless, the majority of that generation was condemned by God to die in the Wilderness. It should be noted that those who defend their disbelief in the Resurrection of Jesus on the ground that He showed Himself only to His followers and not to His opponents, refuse also to accept the veracity of the Exodus stories in spite of the fact that those events were witnessed not by a few but by all the people. Obviously, miracles alone do not necessarily produce genuine faith in God's Word in people who are ill-disposed. Biblically speaking, refusal to believe in God's Word is a moral, not an intellectual, issue. It was for this same reason that Jesus refused to perform miracles in order to win followers.[2] And in a revealing parable dealing with certain aspects of the hereafter, he makes Abraham say that if one refused to believe God's revealed Word, he would not believe even if some one were raised from the dead.[3]

II. IS THE BODILY RESURRECTION OF JESUS A VIOLATION OF NATURAL LAW

In the previous chapter we presented a discussion of the various

---

2. See Mark 8:11-12; Matthew 12:38-42; John 6:26.
3. Luke 16:19-31.

theories seeking to interpret the bodily resurrection of Jesus by naturalistic or seminaturalistic means. Common to all proponents of such theories is a repugnance of the idea of a bodily resurrection. A bodily resurrection, they assert, is contrary to the operation of the laws of Nature, and therefore is unacceptable to the modern mind. The fault with all such thinking stems from two sources. In the first place, at no time do we know all about the workings of Nature, and, as will be shown below, certain of the assumptions about the physical universe which were valid a generation ago have been found wanting in our lifetime. Second, to view the bodily Resurrection of Jesus as a violation of natural law is to betray a lack of knowledge about the Biblical view of Nature.

1. PRESENT-DAY SCIENTIFIC VIEW OF NATURE

In 1925 a competent observer made the following statement: "No man of science could subscribe without qualification to Galileo's beliefs, or to Newton's beliefs, or to all his own scientific beliefs of ten years ago."[4] Thirty-nine years later we are told that only prejudice or ignorance of the true state of affairs will induce one to speak of present-day science as static and infallible.[5] "By the end of the nineteenth century," another observer informs us, "the elementary substance was assumed to be the atom of 'matter' with its fixed mass, and the elementary process, the motion formulated in the equations of dynamics . . . Nineteenth-century science took the motion of matter as the ultimate process and form of energy. To-day periodic energy has become more basic than 'matter'; hence our science is no longer, strictly speaking, 'materialistic' . . . Hence our science is no longer, like Newton's, 'mechanical' . . . Matter and energy are mutually convertible, and in place of the principles maintaining their separate conservations, there is the broader principle of the conservation of matter-energy."[6]

---

4. Alfred North Whitehead, SCIENCE AND THE MODERN WORLD (The Macmillan Company: New York, 1925), p. 255.
5. Philip Edgcombe Hughes, CHRISTIANITY AND THE PROBLEM OF ORIGINS (Presbyterian and Reformed Publishing Company: Philadelphia, Pa., 1964), p.35.
6. John Herman Randall, Jr., "Early Twentieth-Century Currents of Thought," in CHAPTERS IN WESTERN CIVILIZATIONS (Columbia University Press: New York, 1960), Vol. 2, pp. 348, 354.

For a long time, the atom was considered to be the final inde-structible unit of matter. Then in 1911 Rutherford worked out a new theory of the structure of the atom. According to his findings the atom consists of two distinct parts, a positively charged atomic nucleus, surrounded by one or more negatively charged electrons which revolve around the nucleus like the planets around the sun. The nucleus, it was learned, consists of two kinds of elementary particles, positively charged protons, and neutrons which are parti-cles of approximately the same mass as protons but they are elec-trically neutral. The proton is simply the hydrogen nucleus. Thus, electrons, protons, and neutrons became the new fundamental building stones of all matter.[7]

However, subsequent experiments with cosmic radiation and by means of big-tension accelerating equipment succeeded in the production of nuclear transmutations. The first such successful experiment resulted in the transmutation of the nucleus of lithium into that of helium. This opened up a new field of research of nuclear physics proper. Using increasingly more powerful accelerat-ing machines, new elementary particles have been produced which are extremely unstable. These experiments have "shown that the [elementary] particles can be created from other particles or simply from the kinetic energy[8] of such particles, and they can again disin-tegrate into other particles. Actually the experiments have shown the complete mutability of matter. All the elementary particles can, at sufficiently high energies, be transmuted into other particles, or they can simply be created from kinetic energy and can be annihilat-ed into energy, for instance into radiation. Therefore, we have here actually the final proof for the unity of matter. All the elementary particles are made of the same substance, which we may call energy or universal matter; they are just different forms in which matter can appear."[9] Heisenberg, the Director of the Max Planck Institute for Atomic Physics, stated that "a clear distinction between matter and force can no longer be made in this part of physics."[10]

Modern scientific thought is therefore assuming the position

---

7. Werner Heiserberg, PHYSICS AND PHILOSOPHY (Harper & Brothers: New York, 1958), pp. 151, 156.
8. Kinetic energy — energy associated with motion.
9. Ibid., p. 160.
10. Ibid.

that energy is the substance of the universe. This new concept of matter actually means that the "material world has an immaterial substructure."[11] It has also been suggested that the old division between organic and inorganic substance may no longer be valid, and that the word 'living' can perhaps be applied to everything found in the world.[12]

"It is hardly surprising that this revolution in physical theory and concepts has provoked an immense amount of philosophizing, both about the new picture of the world suggested, and about the very nature of the scientific enterprise itself. On the one hand, speculative cosmologies have been erected,[13] only to crumble with some new discovery or change in theory. On the other, both philosophers and scientists have undertaken a careful and critical analysis of the function and nature of scientific theory in general, and of the mathematical formulations in particular. The older view that Newtonian science was a direct reading of the structure of nature is no longer tenable. Scientific theory and concepts, it is only too apparent, develop and change in time; and he would be hardy to-day who maintained that any of the present ideas express 'the way things really are.' "[14]

" . . . we must admit as certain the truth that the absolute can never finally be grasped by the researcher. The absolute represents an ideal goal which is always ahead of us and which we can never reach . . . Science cannot solve the ultimate mystery of nature. And that is because, in the last analysis, we ourselves are part of nature and therefore part of the mystery that we are trying to solve."[15]

" . . . never before has science, for all its amazing advances, been in such a state of indeterminancy and flux. Modern scientists, like scientists of former generations, can only seek to find theories and formulations to fit that small portion of the over-all picture which they are able to observe . . . The perplexities posed by recent re-

---

11. Philip Edgcombe Hughes, Op. Cit., p. 3.
12. A.M. Low, SCIENCE LOOKS AHEAD, 1942, p. 242. See H. Wheeler Robinson, INSPIRATION AND REVELATION IN THE OLD TESTAMENT (Oxford University Press: London, 1946), p. 14.
13. Cosmology — science or theory about the nature of the universe.
14. John Herman Randall, Jr., Op. Cit., Vol. 2, p. 357.
15. Max Planck, WHERE IS SCIENCE GOING? (W.W. Norton & Co., Inc.: New York, 1932), pp. 199-200, 217.

search are such that theological terminology is being introduced into the sacred preserves of science in order to assist towards an interpretation of things."[16] Speaking of the relationship between religion and science in the modern world, Whitehead says: "Religion is the vision of something which stands beyond, behind, and within, the passing flux of immediate things; something which is real, and yet waiting to be realized; something which is a remote possibility, and yet the greatest of present facts; something that gives meaning to all that passes, and yet eludes apprehension . . . The fact of the religious vision, and its history of persistent expansion, is our one ground for optimism. Apart from it, human life is a flash of occasional enjoyments lighting up a mass of pain and misery, a bagatelle of transient experiences."[17]

2. THE BIBLICAL VIEW OF NATURE

As with the belief in immortality, the Biblical view of Nature held by the Hebrews was determined by their Biblical view of God. For our purpose we will review this subject under the following headings.

a. God is the Creator of the world

This truth is declared in the opening two chapters in Genesis, the first book of the Bible. God, we read there, is the Creator of the whole universe, and everything which is in it, both inanimate and animate matter. Though the Creator of Nature, God is a Person; He is not mixed up with Nature, or identified with it. He is above Nature and Nature's Lord, Everything in or about Nature is under God's constant control. This is the message of the whole Bible and not only of the first two chapters of Genesis.

> Lift up your eyes on high and see: who created these?

> "I am Jehovah, who made all things, who stretched out the heavens alone, who spread out the earth - who was with me?"
> *Isaiah 40:26a; 44:24b*

---

16.   Philip Edgcumbe Hughes, Op. Cit., p. 34.
17.   Alfred North Whitehead, Op. Cit., pp. 267-268.

b. God conserves and sustains Nature

He causes the mists to rise, the lightnings to break forth, the rain to come down, the winds to blow.[18] He makes the grass to grow, He feeds the beasts of the field, and the birds of the air.[19] All living beings look to Him for their sustenance.[20] Continuation of life on earth depends on God.[21]

> Thou art Jehovah, thou alone; thou hast made heaven, the heaven of heavens with all their host, the earth and all that is on it, the seas and all that is in them; and thou preservest all of them . . .
>
> *Nehemiah 9:6*

c. Nature reflects God's wisdom

In creating the world God followed a definite and intelligent plan. Wisdom was by God's side in the process of the creation of the world. "Then I[22] was beside him, like a master workman."[23] By divine wisdom the heavens were established, the foundations of the earth were marked out, the mountains were shaped, and the sea given its bounds.[24]

d. The regularity, orderliness, and uniformity of Nature

Nature functions in an orderly, regular, and uniform way, in harmony with certain well-established laws. These laws are referred to in the Bible as commands, decrees, ordinances, or covenants.

> While the earth remains, seedtime and harvest, cold and heat, summer and winter, day and night, shall not cease.
>
> *Genesis 8:22*

" . . . who[25] gives the rain in its season, the autumn rain and

---

18.   Jeremiah 10:13.
19.   Psalm 147:8-9.
20.   Psalm 145:15.
21.   Psalm 104:29-30; Job 34:14-15.
22.   Wisdom.
23.   Proverbs 8:30.
24.   Proverbs 8:22-29.
25.   God.

the spring rain, and keeps for us the weeks appointed for the harvest."

Jeremiah 5:24

Thus says Jehovah, who gives the sun for light by day and the fixed order of the moon and the stars for light by night, who stirs up the sea so that its waves roar — Jehovah of hosts is his name.

Jeremiah 31:35 (31:34 Heb.)

"Thus says Jehovah: If you can break my covenant with the day and my covenant with the night, so that day and night will not come at their appointed time."

Jeremiah 33:20

"Or who shut in the sea with doors, . . . and prescribed bounds for it . . . and said 'Thus far shall you come, and no farther . . . ?' "[26]

Job 38:8-11

Whitehead states that modern science was born in Europe. It could not have had its origin in any other part of the world. This, because the idea of the Order of Things and the Order of Nature, and the thought that every occurrence can be correlated with another occurrence which preceded it, ideas inherent in the Biblical view of God and Nature, were impressed on European minds by medieval scholasticism.[27] "It is quite clear to me, then" says Baillie, "that modern science could not have come into being until the ancient pagan conception of the natural world had given place to the Christian. The reason why ancient science was so little observational, and hardly at all experimental, was that in holding so fast to the intelligibility of the world it failed to do justice to its contingency. Hardly was any Greek scientist able to rid himself of his pagan preconceptions concerning the course which the world-process must inevitably follow. It would follow, they all believed, a cyclical course, and some of them even thought they knew the length of time that each cycle would take to accomplish itself. The spectacle of nature was like a continuous performance at a cinema show . . . What Christianity did was, as it were, to roll the circle of time flat. The rectilinear conception of time, which we all now take for

---

26. God addressing Job.
27. Alfred North Whitehead, Op. Cit., pp. 4, 5, 16, 17.

granted, was introduced into western thought by Christianity."[28]

3. MIRACLES

There are three chief terms in the Old Testament used to denote the word "miracle": *oth* or sign, *mopheth* which means portent, and *niphlaoth* or wonders. In general, *niplaoth* (wonders) describes a miracle in the sense in which the word "miracle" is used in the English language, but not with the implication of a sharp division between the natural and supernatural. *Oth* (sign) and *mopheth* (portent), closely related to each other, pertain to the purpose which the miracle is designed to accomplish.

a. The essence of miracles in the Bible

The root word from which *niphlaoth* (wonders) is derived conveys the meaning of being separate, distinct, unique. Hence, it refers to a person, condition or an event, of a unique, or outstanding character.

It is used to describe God's activities in the sphere of creation.

> "Ah Lord God! It is thou who hast made the heavens and the earth by thy great power and by thy outstretched arm! Nothing is too *wondrous* for thee."
>
> *Jeremiah 32:17*

It serves to describe God's sustaining activities in Nature, embracing such natural phenomena as thunder, rain, snow, and the mystery of childbirth.

> "God thunders *wondrously* with his voice; he does great things which we cannot comprehend. For to the snow he says, 'Fall on the earth'; and to the shower and rain, 'Be strong'."
>
> *Job 37:5-6*

> I praise thee, for thou art fearful and *wonderful; wonderful* are thy works! Thou knowest me right well. My frame was not

---

28. John Baillie, NATURAL SCIENCE AND THE SPIRITUAL LIFE (Oxford University Press: London, 1951), pp. 25-26.

> hidden from thee, when I was being made in secret . . . Thy eyes
> beheld my unformed substance . . .
>
> *Psalm 139:14-16*

The word *wonders* is used to refer to God's providential care in human history. God makes use of natural forces to save Israel from the Egyptians.

> Thou didst blow with thy wind, the sea covered them;[29] they sank as lead in the mighty waters. "Who is like thee, O Jehovah, among the gods? Who is like thee, majestic in holiness, terrible in glorious deeds, doing *wonders*?"
>
> *Exodus 15:10-11*

God's creative and sustaining activities in Nature and history described by the word *wonders* have the following characteristic features.

(1) There is no sharp division between what we call "natural" and "supernatural." In the Bible one is as much miraculous as the other. All creation is a miracle.

(2) Miraculous deeds are wrought by God directly or through man acting as God's agent.

(3) Miracles are at times thought of as special creative acts of God, as for example, when the earth clave asunder and swallowed up those implicated in the Korah rebellion in the Wilderness.[30]

b. The purpose of miracles

The words *oth* (sign) and *mopheth* (portent) pertain to that aspect of the miracle which constitutes its purpose. Miracles are designed to exhibit God's character or to teach certain truths about God. Miracles are never worked by God except for a great cause and a religious purpose. Miracles in the Bible are practically confined to four great periods in Biblical history: (1) The redemption of Israel from Egypt, the passage through the Wilderness and the entry into the Promised Land; (2) The period of Elijah and Elisha which was

---

29. the Egyptians.
30. Numbers 16:28-30.

marked by an intense conflict between Biblical religion and heathenism; (3) The Babylonian exile when Biblical religion once again clashed with heathenism in the days of Daniel; (4) The planting of the Messianic faith of the New Testament when miracles reappeared to attest the Messiahship of Jesus.[31]

"Israel is itself a miracle, a *wonder*, through the divine providence."[32] Israel's history has been a remarkable display of miraculous action, in accordance with repeated promises in the Old Testament, as for example, in the following passage.

> And he said, "Behold, I make a covenant: before all your people I will do *wonders*, such as have not been wrought in all the earth or in any nation; and all the people among whom you are shall see the work of Jehovah; for it is a terrible thing that I will do with you."
>
> *Exodus 34:10*

> Thus says Jehovah, who gives the sun for light by day and the fixed order of the moon and the stars for light by night, who stirs up the sea so that its waves roar — Jehovah of hosts is his name: "If this fixed order departs from before me, says Jehovah, then shall the descendants of Israel cease from being a nation before me for ever."
>
> *Jeremiah 31:35-36 (31:34-35 Heb.)*

Jewish history is a literal and amazing fulfillment of Biblical prophecy. There is not another nation in all of human history which has survived for so long inspite of the fact that during half of its history it was scattered all over the world, without a country of its own. "I remember," declares the Russian philosopher Nicolas Berdyaev, "how the materialist interpretation of history, when I attempted in my youth to verify it by applying it to the destinies of peoples, broke down in the case of the Jews, where destiny seemed absolutely inexplicable from the materialist standpoint. And, indeed, according to the materialistic and positivist criterion, this people ought long ago to have perished. Its survival is a mysterious and wonderful phenomenon demonstrating that the life of this people is governed

---

31. John D. Davis, THE WESTMINSTER DICTIONARY OF THE BIBLE, Revised and Rewritten by Henry Snyder Gehman (The Westminster Press: Philadelphia, 1944), art. "miracle", p. 399.
32. H. Wheeler Robinson, Op. Cit., p. 45.

by a special predetermination, transcending the process of adaption expounded by the materialistic interpretation of history. The survival of the Jews, their resistance to destruction, their endurance under absolutely peculiar conditions and the fateful role played by them in history; all these point to the particular and mysterious foundations of their destiny."[33]

In concluding our discussion of the relationship of the bodily resurrection of Jesus to natural law, we might say that should modern science ever succeed in bringing a dead person back to life, we would take pride in man's accomplishments, and not be in the least disturbed that such a feat may be viewed as a breach of natural law. As a matter of fact, whenever in these days we place a space body in orbit we break natural law, in this instance the law of gravity. Why then should we deny to God the privilege of superseding the very laws which He, and He alone, created, and especially when He is doing this in the interest of human welfare?

But it is not necessary to infer that in performing what we consider miraculous deeds God breaks natural law. It is far more reasonable to assume that when He created this vast universe and made laws by which to sustain and regulate it, God left Himself means or provisions by which to accomplish, in accordance with His foreknowledge, His beneficent and redemptive purposes in human destiny.[34] Moreover, in harmony with Biblical teaching — both of the Old Testament and the New Testament — it is quite permissible to view the Resurrection of Jesus Christ as a new creative act of God.

This writer is affiliated with a large group of scientists, among whom are physicists, chemists, biologists, engineers, and doctors of medicine, many of whom occupy distinguished teaching positions in colleges and universities. All of them accept as true facts the Virgin Birth and the Resurrection of Jesus the Messiah as reported in the New Testament. The excerpts below are from the writings of two representatives of the scientific world belonging to a previous gen-

33. Nicolas Berdyaev, THE MEANING OF HISTORY (Charles Scribner's Sons: New York, 1936), pp. 86-87.
34. When an ambulance truck passes through a red light on the way to extinguish a fire or to land a sick person in the hospital, it follows a law which comes into operation under extraordinary circumstances and which temporarily sets aside the "normal" traffic law.

eration. Dr. Ambrose Fleming was professor of electrical Engineering in the University of London, honorary fellow of St. John's College, Cambridge, recipient of the Faraday Medal in 1928, to whom extended space is devoted in the fourteenth edition of the Encyclopedia Britannica on account of his important research work in physics. He was recognized as one of England's outstanding scientists. Speaking of the Resurrection of Jesus this is what Professor Fleming said: "Let me invite you to study at your leisure the records in the four Gospels of these events, and you will see that nothing in the certainly ascertained facts or principles of science forbids belief in these miracles. If that study is pursued with what eminent lawyers have called a willing mind, it will engender a deep assurance that the Christian Church is not founded on fictions, or nourished on delusions, or, as St. Peter calls them, 'cunningly devised fables,' but on historical and actual events, which, however strange they may be, are indeed the greatest events which have ever happened in the history of the world."[35]

Dr. Howard A. Kelly was one of the "big Four" who, with Osler, Halstead and Welch, had made Johns Hopkins Hospital and School of Medicine world-famous. Dr. Kelly was for thirty years professor of gynecological surgery in the Johns Hopkins University, fellow of the Royal College of Surgeons of Edinburgh, and the author of standard textbooks on gynecology. I had the great privilege of meeting Dr. Kelly in his home, shortly after he was retired from Johns Hopkins University and when I was just beginning practicing medicine. Referring to the Virgin Birth of Jesus as recorded in the Gospel of Luke, Dr. Kelly says, "Luke, the first Christian doctor, his calling being much in evidence in the medical terms he so often uses, was a true scientist, saturated with the spirit of his profession, careful and accurate as an investigator, and fully cognizant of the vital importance of the facts he was about to relate."[36]

"The Virgin Birth," Dr. Kelly says, "is a fact fully established by competent testimony and abundant collateral evidences, believed by men all through the ages as a necessary factor in their salvation secured by an ever-living, ever-acting Savior, viewed with wonder by

35. Ambrose Fleming, MIRACLES AND SCIENCE — THE RESURRECTION OF CHRIST (Religious Tract Society: London, 1917), p. 15. Used by permission of Lutterworth Press.
36. Howard A. Kelly, A SCIENTIFIC MAN AND THE BIBLE (The Sunday School Times: Philadelphia, 1926), pp. 87-88. Used by permission of Harper & Row, Publishers.

angels in Heaven and acknowledged by God the Father. To deny the Virgin Birth because of its miraculous nature is to deny the validity of all Scripture, which is but a continuous series of revelations of the mind and acts of God, and as such is miraculous throughout."[37]

Speaking of the resurrection of Jesus, Dr. Kelly writes: "The doctrine of the Resurrection runs as a mighty undercurrent through the Old Testament Scriptures . . . As we turn from the last chapters of the Gospels to the Acts and the Epistles, we become conscious of a new and mighty unknown force released and at work in the world. So evident is this that even the unbelieving world has testified to its presence ever since Christ's departure, while at the same time there has been one continuous futile series of efforts of that unbelieving world to discover a substitute for it . . . What then does the resurrection mean to me? A clear hope vested in my risen Savior which I could not have, had Christ never risen from the dead; my justification before the bar of eternal justice so that I shall not come into judgment, through Christ's victory over death; my inclusion from henceforth among the witnesses of his resurrection; my burial with Christ, my resurrection with Him, and my life's interests henceforth in seeking those things that are above where Christ is seated at the right hand of God."[38]

III. OBJECTIONS TO THE RESURRECTION OF JESUS THE MESSIAH: CONCLUDING OBSERVATIONS

In the early part of 1968 the Harvard-Radcliffe Christian Fellowship and the Harvard-Radcliffe Discussion Group were joint sponsors of a discussion program featuring an address by Dr. J. N. D. Anderson, dean of the faculty of law in the University of London. The subject of Dr. Anderson's address was: "The Resurrection Of Jesus Christ." The chairman of that meeting was Dr. Armand Nicholi, a psychiatrist connected with the University Health Services in Harvard Medical School. In introducing Dr. Anderson, the chairman said: "Our speaker is a scholar of international repute and

---

37. Ibid., p. 94.
38. Ibid., pp. 125, 128-129, 133-134.

one eminently qualified to deal with the subject of evidence. He is one of the world's leading authorities on Islamic law, and is now visiting professor at the Harvard Law School. He is dean of the faculty of law in the University of London, chairman of the department of Oriental law at the School of Oriental and African Studies, and director of the Institute of Advanced Legal Studies in the University of London." The following is Dr. Anderson's address:

Our chairman has reminded us that men's and women's faith and beliefs are often based on prejudice, instinct, upbringing, and feeling, rather than on reason and evidence. But it is with the aspect of *evidence* for Christianity that we are now concerned. The resurrection of Jesus Christ from the dead has always been regarded as a pivotal point in Christianity. St. Paul wrote long ago, "If Christ be not risen, then is our preaching meaningless, and your faith worthless," "More than that," he said, "we ourselves, we apostles, are found false witnesses to God." So I imagine that everyone in this lecture room would agree that it is clearly a matter of great importance to try to make up one's mind about the Easter story — whether it's fact or whether it's fable. But many people would say, "Obviously this is of great importance but how can it be done? It all happened so long ago. How can we come to any considered conviction about it today?"

There are at least two ways one can set about this. The first way — the way we will follow — is examination of the historical evidence, to try to make up one's mind whether it is early and more or less contemporary and whether it is convincing, or whether it is susceptible to rationalistic interpretation. The other approach would be experimentation — putting the risen Christ to the test in one's own life and the lives of other people.

I shall try to consider this matter not in the manner of the preacher or the theologian, which I make no pretensions to be, but in the manner of a lawyer, which I do attempt to be. Now, on what evidence does the Easter story rest? It rests primarily on the written testimony of six men whom we commonly call Matthew, Mark, Luke, John, Peter, and Paul.

The question is continually asked, Is there no contemporary documentary evidence from non-Christian sources on this subject? And the answer, I think, is that substantially speaking there is none. There is a letter from the younger Pliny to the Emperor Trajan about the year A.D. 110 in which he makes a reference to the origins of Christianity and the early Christian community. There is a very short and passing reference to Jesus of Nazareth and his crucifixion under Pontius Pilate in the writings of Tacitus the Roman historian about the year 115. And there are a number of references, many of them disputed, in the writings of Josephus, who wrote between about 70 and 95. But the references to the origins of Christianity in Josephus, if you accept them as original (as some of them probably are), are meager in the extreme and make no statement on the resurrection. This is not surprising, for if one accepts the gospel records it is perfectly plain that the risen Christ made no attempt whatever to appear to his enemies or his opponents, to put them to confusion, but deliberately showed himself alive after his passion to witnesses chosen by him, and sent them to bear testimony to the rest of humanity.

But when we turn to the New Testament documents the matter is very different. There are abundant references both to the empty tomb and the resurrection appearances and to the effect of the resurrection on the primitive Church. It is perhaps not always realized what considerable strides modern scholarship has taken in fixing beyond any reasonable doubt, to my mind at least, the early date of a great many of the New Testament documents; modern scholarship has really excluded, I think, the extravagantly late date attributed to some New Testament documents not so many years ago. I myself am fully convinced that the New Testament writers were not left to their unaided resources but were given divine aid; but naturally, in this attempt to assess the evidence of the resurrection in a more or less legal manner, I'm not taking that for granted in any way. Nor will you expect me to deal with the precise dates and authenticity of the different New Testament documents. It's not my subject, and I wouldn't presume to deal with it; anyway, it would take far too long. But as a basis for any research of this subject we must briefly examine some of the witnesses.

For our first witness I will call the Apostle Paul. If you will look sometime at the fifteenth chapter of First Corinthians, you will find there a most complete list of the resurrection appearances to be found in any one place in the New Testament. As far as I am aware, the vast majority of reputable scholars considers First Corinthians a genuine document of the Apostle Paul. And there seems no real doubt about the date — that it was written within a year or two of A.D. 55, or even earlier.

If you look at that chapter carefully you will see that the Apostle says he had already given an account by word of mouth, to the very people to whom he was writing, of what he was now committing to paper. This probably takes us back to the year 49, when he paid his first visit to Corinth. As a matter of fact, he states in this chapter that he had himself received what he passed on to others. That, I suppose, takes us back to his visit to Jerusalem, about which he tells us in the first chapter of the epistle to the Galatians, when he spent fifteen days with Simon Peter and also saw James, the Lord's brother. In point of fact, in First Corinthians 15 we have an account of a private interview of the risen Christ with both Peter and James. And that, I suppose, would take us back to about the year 40 — to within ten years of the event.

But whether or not you accept that little bit of reasoning, in this list of the resurrection appearances Paul the Apostle specifically tells us that the Risen Christ appeared on one occasion to 500 brethren at once, and he says that, at the time when he wrote, the majority at least of these 500 witnesses were still alive. So there is our first bit of evidence — a document acknowledged by almost everyone to be written by the Apostle Paul, acknowledged to be written about the year 55, and stating positively that, at the time it was written, the majority of 500 witnesses to the resurrection were still living.

For our second witness we'll call Mark, the writer of the second Gospel. Suggestions have been made that an Aramaic version of the Gospel may have been in circulation at a very early date. Be that as it may, almost everyone accepts Mark as a very early and primitive authority. Most scholars, I believe, accept the statement of one of the earliest Fathers of the Christian Church that Mark was Peter's interpreter; in other words, that Mark's Gospel is substantially a written account of the oral testimony of Simon Peter. And in this very primitive document we find another independent reference to the resurrection appearances and — more important — probably the earliest account of the women's visit to the empty tomb on the first Easter morning.

For our third witness we'll call the writer of the third Gospel and the Acts of the Apostles, conceded by the great majority of scholars to be Luke, "the beloved physician," as St. Paul named him. Sir William Ramsey and others have shown what an accurate historian this writer was in such matters as disputed points in the accounts of the missionary journeys and the titles given to Roman officials whom St. Paul met in the course of those journeys. In these two documents,

Luke and Acts, you find another independent account of the resurrection appearances, and of the women's visit on the first Easter
morning to the empty tomb — and also what I think is the earliest
account of the apostolic preaching in Jerusalem based on the resurrection, going back, we are told, to the day of Pentecost.

Now, we have considered the credentials of three of the witnesses. I'm not going to deal with the other three, not because I don't
accept them as equally authoritative but because time forbids. I have
chosen these three because there is a substantial degree of critical
agreement with regard to the points I've put before you. How then
are we to deal with this testimony? It seems to go right back to the
first generation of Christians. In fact, I would say that beyond any
reasonable doubt whatever, it goes back to the first generation of
Christians. It goes back at the very least to the time of the Pauline
epistles, the earlier Pauline epistles. How is one to deal with it?

The most drastic way of dismissing the evidence would be to say
that these stories were mere fabrications, that they were pure lies.
But, so far as I know, not a single critic today would take such an
attitude. In fact, it would really be an impossible position. Think of
the number of witnesses, over 500. Think of the character of the
witnesses, men and women who gave the world the highest ethical
teaching it has ever known, and who even on the testimony of their
enemies lived it out in their lives. Think of the psychological absur-
dity of picturing a little band of defeated cowards cowering in an
upper room one day and a few days later transformed into a company that no persecution could silence — and then attempting to
attribute this dramatic change to nothing more convincing than a
miserable fabrication they were trying to foist upon the world. That
simply wouldn't make sense.

Others might say, No, we wouldn't call these stories lies, but let's
call them legends; that's a kinder word. And of course, if it had been
possible to date the Gospels two or three hundred years after the
event (I hardly need remind you that the attempt to do that has been
made by a wealth of scholars and that it has quite definitely failed),
then it might have been possible for legends of this sort to develop.
But it seems to me almost meaningless to talk about legends when
you're dealing with the eyewitnesses themselves.

Besides, if you examine these stories you find they don't really
look like legends. To a legend-monger it would have been a great
temptation to invent some story as to how the resurrection took

place, or some incident in which the risen Christ appeared to put his opponents to confusion; but we find no such attempt. What legend-monger would have made the first resurrection appearance to Mary Magdalene, a woman of no great standing in the Christian Church? Wouldn't any legend-monger have made the first appearance to Simon Peter the leading apostle, or John the beloved disciple, or — still more likely, perhaps — to Mary the mother of our Lord? Why to Mary Magdalene?

And who can read about the appearance to Mary Magdalene, or the incident where the risen Christ joined two disciples on an afternoon walk to Emmaus, or the time when Peter and John raced each other to the tomb — who can read these stories and really think they're legend? They are far too dignified and restrained; they are far too true to life and psychology. The difference between them and the sort of stories you find in the apocryphal gospels of but two or three centuries later is a difference almost between heaven and earth. No, as far as I know, no one today suggests that these stories are either lies or legends, just like that.

All the attempts to explain the Easter story and the resurrection appearances that I've seen are marked by a rather interesting phenomenon. The critics, first of all, isolate the stories of the empty tomb and attempt to explain them on a variety of ingenious hypotheses, and then they turn to the ressurection appearances and dismiss them as some form of psychological or pathological experience — no doubt vivid and convincing on the subjective level to the apostles, who certainly believed in the resurrection, but, according to the critics, with no objective foundation.

Well, let us consider the question of the empty tomb. The earliest attempt to explain away the empty tomb can be found in St. Matthew's Gospel. There we are told that the Jewish leaders gave money to the guards to say that the apostles had come by night and stolen away the body and had no doubt disposed of it somewhere. But so far as I know, no one today suggests that the apostles did that. I am aware, of course, of a recent book entitled *The Passover Plot*, which comes back to that particular solution in a rather different way. I'd prefer to deal with that comprehensively a little later. But that the apostles as we know them came and stole the body really would be an impossible view in view of both ethics and psychology. To imagine that they just foisted a miserable deception on the world simply wouldn't fit in with their life and teaching and all we know of them. And it couldn't begin to explain this dramatic change of the little band of defeated cowards into witnesses whom no persecution could silence.

No, better than that would be the suggestion that the body was removed by orders of the high priest or by orders of the Roman governor, or conceivably by Joseph of Arimathea, the owner of the sepulcher. Quite apart from anything else that may be said about those three suggestions, which we'll take together to save time, the crucial point as I see it is this: Within seven short weeks — if the records are to be believed at all, and I cannot see any possible reason for Christian writers to have invented that difficult gap of seven weeks — within seven short weeks Jerusalem was seething with the preaching of the resurrection. The apostles were preaching it up and down the city. The chief priests were very much upset about it. They said that the apostles were trying to bring this man's blood upon them. They were being accused of having crucified the Lord of glory. And they were prepared to go to almost any lengths to nip this dangerous heresy in the bud. Well, then, if the body had been moved by their orders, then, when the apostles started preaching the resurrection up and down the city, why didn't they issue an official denial? Why didn't they say, "That's nonsense. The body was moved at our orders." If that wouldn't have convinced people, why didn't they call as witnesses those who took the body away? If that wouldn't have sufficed, why didn't they point people to its final resting place? And if *that* wouldn't have sufficed, why didn't they produce the body? Surely they could have exploded Christianity once and for all. Why didn't they do it?

To me there's only one answer: They couldn't, because they didn't know where the body was. The same argument would apply to the Roman governor. He too was upset about this strange teaching. If he had had the body moved, it seems incredible that he wouldn't have informed the chief priests when they were so upset. And that would bring us back to the question, Why didn't they explode the whole story?

Well, what about Joseph of Arimathea? I think my answer would be that the critics really can't have it both ways. They have a choice. On the one hand, they can accept what the New Testament says about Joseph, that he was a secret disciple, in which case it is unlikely that he would remove the body without consulting the apostles first — and incredible that he wouldn't have told them afterwards, when the preaching of the resurrection was echoing up and down the lanes and alleys of the city. That would bring us back to the idea that the apostles were foisting a miserable deception on the world.

The other view critics can choose to take about Joseph of Arimathea — apart from the suggestion in *The Passover Plot* — is that he was a pious Jew who put the body in his sepulcher so that it wouldn't hang on the cross on the Sabbath day. In that case it's unlikely that he would have moved the body without consulting the chief priests first, and it is fantastic to suggest that he wouldn't have told them afterward, when they were so upset about this heresy. In that case, why didn't they call Joseph as a witness? Why didn't they issue an official denial?

Another suggestion about the empty tomb was espoused by one of the theological teachers at Cambridge, England, in the days of my own youth and innocence in that university. It runs somewhat like this: The women were Galileans and strangers in Jerusalem; they didn't know their way about the city very well. They saw their Master buried in the half-light of the evening, when their eyes were blinded with tears, and they went to the tomb in the half-light of the morning. According to this theory they missed their way and went to the wrong sepulcher. A young man happened to be hanging about and, guessing what they wanted, said to them, "You seek Jesus of Nazareth. He is not here [pointing to the tomb they were looking at]. Behold the place where they laid him [pointing to another tomb]." But the women got frightened and ran away. Subsequently they decided that the young man was an angel proclaiming the resurrection of their Master.

That's very ingenious, but I don't think it stands up to investigation. To begin with, it's based on accepting the beginning and the end of what the young man is recorded to have said and leaving out the most important part, the middle; and for that I can see no scholarly justification whatever. For we are told that what the young man said is, "You seek Jesus of Nazareth. He is not here. *He is risen.* Behold the place where they laid him" — which changes the whole meaning, of course.

However, even if you think that it's justifiable to deal with his statement the other way, it's not really as easy as it might seem — as those who put forward this theory themselves admit. For if the women went straight back to the apostles and told them, why didn't the apostles do one of two things: either go and check up on the facts for themselves or start preaching the resurrection at once? Unless you ignore the whole tenor of the New Testament documents, they didn't start preaching for another seven weeks. As I've already said, I cannot see any possible motive for Christian writers to have invented that seven-week gap. So we're asked to believe that the women didn't tell the apostles this story for quite a long time. Why not? Because the apostles had supposedly run away to Galilee. Why? Well, because Jerusalem was not a very healthful place for Christians just then. But we're not told why the apostles were so particularly ungallant that they ran away and left their wives and sisters and mothers behind. We're asked to believe that the men went down to Galilee and left the women in Jerusalem, and that the women stayed in Jerusalem for some weeks for no apparent reason. It was only when the apostles came back from Galilee already convinced by some mystical experience that their Master was still alive — only then, supposedly, that the women told them about the visit to the tomb. Then the apostles put two and two together, made seven or eight out of it, and proclaimed the resurrection.

Frankly, I don't find that convincing. On that basis, I suppose the body of our Lord would still have lain where it had always lain, in Joseph's tomb. The chief priests must have know where that was, or if not they could have found out very easily. So they could have exploded the whole story by saying, "This is nonsense. If you don't believe us, come and see."

There is another explanation of the empty tomb, first put forward by a man named Venturini a couple of centuries or so ago. It has been resuscitated in recent years in a slightly different form by a heterodox group of Muslims called the Ahmadiya, who used to have their main headquarters at a place called Qadian and who have their English headquarters in a part of London called Putney. On two occasions they've invited me to go and address them. Their explanation runs like this: Christ was indeed nailed to the cross. He suffered terribly from shock, loss of blood, and pain, and he swooned away; but he didn't actually die. Medical knowledge was not very great at that time, and the apostles thought he was dead. We are told, are we not, that Pilate was surprised that he was dead already. The explanation assertedly is that he was taken down from the cross in a state of swoon by those who wrongly believed him to be dead, and laid in sepulcher. And the cool restfulness of the sepulcher so far revived him that he was eventually able to issue forth from the grave. His ignorant disciples couldn't believe that this was a mere resuscitation. They insisted it was a resurrection from the dead.

Well, again, it's very ingenious. But it won't stand up to investigation. To begin with, steps were taken — it seems — to make quite sure that Jesus was dead; that surely is the meaning of the spear-thrust in his side. But suppose for argument's sake that he was not quite dead. Do you really believe that lying for hour after hour with no medical attention in a rock-hewn tomb in Palestine at Easter, when it's quite cold at night, would so far have revived him, instead of proving the inevitable end to his flickering life, that he would have been able to loose himself from yards of grave-clothes weighted with pounds of spices, roll away a stone that three women felt incapable of tackling, and walk miles on wounded feet? The skeptic Strauss, you know, quite exploded that theory, to my mind, when he wrote that it would have been impossible for a being who had crept sick and faint out of a sepulcher, needing bandaging, sustenance, and attention, to convince his disciples that he was the risen Lord of Life, an impression which lay at the foundation of their future ministry. Such a resuscitation could by no means have changed their reverence into worship.

So much for the empty tomb, except for two quick points. The first is this: Have you noticed that the references to the empty tomb all come in the Gospels, which were written to give the Christian community the facts they wanted to know? In the public preaching to those who were not believers, as recorded in the Acts of the Apostles, there is an enormous emphasis on the fact of the resurrection but not a single reference to the empty tomb. Now, why? To me there is only one answer: There was no point in arguing about the empty tomb. Everyone, friend and opponent, knew that it was empty. The only questions worth arguing about were why it was empty and what its emptiness proved.

The second point is this: I've been talking all this time about the *empty* tomb, but it seems that it wasn't really empty. You remember the account in John's Gospel of how Mary Magdalene ran and called Peter and John and how the two men set out to the tomb. John, the younger, ran on quicker than Peter and came first to the tomb. He stooped down, "peeped" inside (which I believe is the literal meaning of the Greek), and saw the linen clothes and the napkin that had been about the head. And then Simon Peter came along and, characteristically, blundered straight in, followed by John; and they took note of the linen clothes and the napkin, which was not lying with the linen clothes but was apart, wrapped into one place. The Greek there seems to suggest that the linen clothes were lying, not strewn about the tomb, but where the body had been, and that there was a gap where the neck of Christ had lain — and that the napkin which had been about his head was not with the linen clothes but apart and wrapped in its own place, which I suppose means still done up, as though the body had simply withdrawn itself. We are told that when John saw that, he needed no further testimony from man or angel; he saw and believed, and his testimony has come down to us.

So much then for the empty tomb, which seems to me to be an exceedingly important bit of evidence, in fact, a basic piece of evidence. But equally important, I don't think you can dismiss the resurrection appearances as just some form of hallucination or psychological or pathological experience. Now, I'm no doctor. Our chairman this evening is a psychiatrist, and I'd much rather leave this part of the presentation to him. But let me just say that I understand from medical friends that hallucinary experiences commonly conform to certain rules that simply don't apply in this case.

To begin with, only certain types of persons have experiences like this — the type we call high-strung people. But I do not see how you can categorize witnesses to the resurrection as any one or two psychological types. Again, I'm told that experiences of this sort are highly individualistic, because they are naturally linked to the subconscious mind and to the past lives of the persons who experience them. So two different people will not have identical hallucinations. But in this case 500 are recorded as having had the same experience on one occasion, eleven on another, ten on another, and seven on another. And there were groups, too. It doesn't look purely subjective; it looks as if these experiences had some objective foundation.

Again, I am told that experiences of this sort commonly concern some expected event. A mother whose son runs away to sea always believes that he will come home, and she lights a lamp each evening to welcome him home. One day she imagines she sees him walk in at the door. But here the evidence is overwhelming that the disciples were not expecting any such thing. They ought to have been, but they weren't.

Again, I am told that experiences of this sort commonly occur in suitable circumstances with suitable surroundings. But analyze the resurrection appearances: one at the tomb in the early morning; one during the afternoon walk into the country; one or two private interviews in the full light of day; one in an upper room in the evening; one at the lake-side in the early morning; and so on.

Finally, I am told that experiences of this sort commonly recur over a very considerable period, either getting more and more frequent until there is some crisis, or less and less frequent until they die away. But in this case 500 people claim to have had at least one such experience. A number claim to have had several such experiences within a period of forty days. And at the end of those forty days these experiences seem to have come to a sudden end. Not one of these men or women claims to have had such an experience again. I am aware that the Apostle Paul some years later claims to have seen a vision of the risen Christ in heaven on the road to Damascus. I have no doubt that he did have it, but I suggest that there was a fundamental difference between the vision and the experiences of the forty days during which the risen Christ came in and went out among the disciples.

Nor do I think you can explain these alleged appearances by the phenomenon of modern spiritism. Here I'm certainly no expert, but you certainly can't find one medium who was present on each occasion, nor can you find the usual little band of earnest seekers after the supernatural. And the One who appeared seems to have been very different from alleged spirit emanations. He could be clearly seen in broad daylight, recognized with some difficulty (it seems), and he could invite a finger to explore the print of the nails.

Nor do I think that these stories are adequately explained by the theory of the mere spiritual survival of Christ. It seems to me that the evidence goes much further than that. The evidence is that his spirit came back to his mutilated human body, which was somehow transformed — transformed into something that I can only call a spiritual body. If you ask me what a spiritual body is like, I must say frankly that I don't know. But we live in a world of three dimensions, and there are lots of other things we don't know. The evidence seems to point to the fact that this body could withdraw itself from the graveclothes, could apparently pass through closed doors, could appear and disappear, and yet could be recognized with some difficulty, could be clearly seen and distinctly heard, and could invite, as I said, a finger to explore the print of the nails.

Now just a word, if I may, about that recent book called *The*

Passover Plot. It's an ingenious book, but I must say that I find it wholly unconvincing. It is an attempt to explain the whole story of the crucifixion and resurrection, written by a Jew who has great respect for Jesus of Nazareth but who excludes even the possibility of his deity without any examination of this in the book at all. He believes that Christ himself believed he was the Messiah foretold in the Old Testament Scriptures and that he very largely interpreted his messiahship in terms of the passages about the suffering servant in the latter part of Isaiah. And the author of *The Passover Plot* believes that Christ deliberately set to work to fulfill those prophecies by suffering an apparent death, and something that might be regarded as a resurrection. Jesus is said to have very carefully kept the secret of what he intended to do from the twelve apostles, who knew nothing about it whatever, and to have confided his plan only to Joseph of Arimathea and to one or two others in Jerusalem — that he plotted it all; that he virtually provoked the betrayal; that it was arranged that one of the people in the plot should put a sponge to the reed, and put it to his lips, containing a substance which would cause him to swoon away; that Joseph would then go and ask for the body, alleging that it was dead when it was not dead; that the body should be nursed and looked after and that Christ should be revived; but that this plan was frustrated by the spear-thrust in his side. The author imagines that the persons in the plot managed to resuscitate Jesus of Nazareth for a period of about half an hour, that he was able to give messages to his disciples, but that he then died and they disposed of his body somewhere. Then they tried to pass on his messages to the apostles, who knew nothing about this, and the apostles made a whole series of mistakes which led them to a belief in a resurrection.

Never in my life have I read a book which took some bits of evidence and rejected others on such a subjective basis. Many incidents in the Gospels are accepted just because they fit this theory; others are rejected because they don't. Occasionally an attempt is made to give an objective basis, but time and again it's purely subjective. I find the elements in the plot wholly unconvincing — the utter secrecy from the twelve, and the supposed provocation of the betrayal, for example; and I cannot see what would have been the result had the alleged plot succeeded. What would have happened if Christ had apparently come back to life? Would he then have told the disciples? What would he have gained? I cannot believe that this story in any way explains the resurrection appearances, which allegedly refer to an entirely different person. Surely the apostles would not have made so gigantic a mistake as that. And I cannot see how the conspirators would have kept it secret after it had all failed, and would never have shared it with the other apostles.

There's a phenomenon in the world today called the Christian Church. It can be traced back in history to the region of Palestine in the first century. To what does it owe its origin? The New Testament — its documents of association, as a lawyer would call them — makes the unequivocal statement that the Church owed its origin to the resurrection of its founder from the dead. Is there really any other theory that fits the facts?

Much the same can be said about the phenomenon of the Christian Sunday, which can be traced back in much the same way. We need to remember that almost all of the first Christians were convinced Jews who were fanatically attached to the Jewish Sabbath. What would have prompted them to change that to the first day of the week? It would have required something pretty significant. In fact, it took the resurrection to make them do it. Much the same argument could be used about the festival of Easter.

What about the success of the early Church? Our Lord himself had had a big following in Galilee but a very small following in Jerusalem. We are told, however, that the apostles made thousands of converts in Jerusalem, many of them from among the circle of the priests. They did it by preaching the resurrection. And they did it within a short walk of Joseph's tomb. Anyone who listened to them could have walked to the tomb and back between luncheon and what the English call afternoon tea. Do you really believe they would have made all those converts if the tomb hadn't been empty?

What about the apostles? What was it that changed Peter from one who three times denied his Master before servants to someone who defied the chief priests? We are told that the risen Christ appeared to Peter, and he was never the same man again. What changed James, the unbelieving brother of our Lord during the days of his ministry, so that he became the president or bishop of the Jerusalem church a few years later? We are told that the risen Christ appeared to James, and he then wrote about his human relative as the Lord of glory. Or what about Paul the persecutor, who was in the inner councils of the chief priests? Do you believe he would have become Paul the apostle without checking up on whether the tomb was empty? Why, he must have *known* the tomb was empty, but he didn't know until the vision on the road to Damascus *why* it was empty.

What about the very strong evidence that Christ himself foretold his resurrection, though the disciples simply couldn't understand it? Not so very long ago there was in England a young man barrister, or what you would call a trial lawyer, by the name of Frank Morison. He was an unbeliever. For years he promised himself that one day he would write a book to disprove the resurrection finally and forever. At last he got the leisure. He was an honest man and did the necessary study. Eventually, he wrote a book that you can buy as a paperback, WHO MOVED THE STONE? Starting from the most critical possible approach to the New Testament documents he concludes *inter alia* that you can explain the trial and the conviction of Jesus only on the basis that he himself had foretold his death and resurrection.

What about that awkward seven weeks' gap to which I have already referred? How can you really explain it in any other way except by that fact that the apostles were completely absorbed for the first forty days by their intermittent interviews with their risen Lord, and that they then waited for another ten days at his command until the Holy Spirit came?

What about Christian experience all down the ages? And the multitude of men and women — rich and poor, reprobate and respectable, learned and ignorant — who have found in the risen Christ their joy and peace and certainty?

And what about the One who rose? Even if someone were to take the attitude, "I can't help it; however strong the evidence may be, I will never believe that Tom Smith could be dead for a large number of hours and then come alive again," would that apply to the One of whom we are speaking? Why, he was unique — unique in his teaching, unique in his miracles, unique in his claims, unique in his personality, unique in his sinlessness. Quite apart from the resurrection there is most excellent evidence to me at least, that he wasn't just a man but God incarnate. Is it incredible that such a One should rise again? To me the incredible thing is that such a One as he should die for us men and for our salvation.

I have been dealing with the historical evidence for the resurrection. No doubt you could hire a lawyer to do it very much better than I've done it. But I can only say that I wholeheartedly believe in what I've been saying. And I suppose that, for the individual, the final evidence of the resurrection — I don't mean the most important evidence but the concluding evidence — is the evidence of personal experience. I'm not referring to some weird mystical experience of the risen Christ apprehended by the senses. I am saying only that all through the ages, and still today, men and women have come to faith in Christ and through him in God through the evidence for the resurrection, and that their faith has been authenticated in daily life. This experience has been true down the ages; it's true today. I've traveled a good deal and have lived in a number of different countries, and I've seen it happen time and again. I can only say that I for one am thoroughly convinced.[39]

39. J.N.D. Anderson, "The Resurrection of Jesus Christ,", art. in CHRISTIANITY TODAY (Washington, D.C.), March 29, 1968; copyright 1968 by CHRISTIANITY TODAY, reprinted by permission.

CHAPTER 5
MAN'S DESTINY IN THE LIGHT OF THE
RESURRECTION OF JESUS THE MESSIAH

CHAPTER 5
MAN'S DESTINY IN THE LIGHT OF THE RESURRECTION OF JESUS THE MESSIAH

I. A BODILY RESURRECTION OR A MERE SURVIVAL OF THE SOUL?

The heart of the Christian message was, and is, the Resurrection of Jesus the Messiah. The Gentile world in which the story of the resurrection was first proclaimed was a world ruled politically by Rome and swayed intellectually by Greek thought. The opposition in this world to the Christian message was aimed chiefly at the resurrection story. Not that the world of that day was antagonistic to a belief in a hereafter. Greek ideas about the hereafter had a long tradition and were centered in a belief in the survival of the soul. But a resurrection was something foreign to Greek thinking, and, what is more important, it was something against which the Greeks became conditioned by their traditional views of the human body.

Under the influence of the Orphic sects which sprang up in the Greek states and colonies in the second half of the sixth century B.C., the cult of the Greeks received an elaborate doctrinal system. According to Orphic teachings, the soul was originally Divine and immortal. The body was considered the seat of evil and the tomb of the soul. An integral part of Orphic theology was the belief in the transmigration of souls. All souls are reincarnated into one body after another. During these successive births and deaths the sins of the past are expiated. The last separation of the soul from the body constitutes its complete deliverance and final salvation.[1]

These Orphic ideas received full and final elaboration in Plato's dialogues. Plato retained the belief of the transmigration of the

---

1. John Baillie, AND THE LIFE EVERLASTING (Charles Scribner's Sons: New York, 1933), pp. 128-132.

souls. The souls of men who followed after gluttony, drunkenness, and wantonness pass into asses and other animals of a like nature; those of the unjust, the tyrannous and the violent — into wolves, hawks, and kites; and the souls of those who practiced civil and sacral virtues which they acquired by habit, instead of by way of philosophic contemplation and discipline, will pass after death into bees, wasps or ants, or into the bodies of just and moderate men.[2]

As in the Orphic system, Plato considered the body the soul's prison house.[3] The follower of philosophy must learn to mistrust the bodily senses and bodily desires, fears and passions, and rise above these.[4] He must free his soul from bodily concerns.[5] The body is a hindrance — certainly no help — in the philosopher's desire after knowledge. He acquires the truth, not through the bodily senses, but through philosophic contemplation. In his quest for truth and knowledge the philosophic sage dishonors the body, i.e., his soul runs away from the body and withdraws into herself.[6] By thus separating himself from the body, the philosophic sage attains to purification.[7] Death frees the sage from the chains of the body. He looks forward to death with much joy because only after death will he find wisdom in all its purity.[8]

The message of the resurrection of Jesus met these ideas in a head-on collision. The followers of Jesus refused to concede an essential antagonism between the body and the soul. They frowned upon ideas which tended to debase the body. They affirmed the Biblical hope of the redemption of the body as well as of the soul. They regarded man's final bliss to be not a disembodied state but a newly glorified bodily existence similar to that of the risen Messiah.

> Even while in our present body we sigh, longing to put over
> it our heavenly dwelling. Sure that, when we have put it on, we
> shall never be found discarnate. For we who are in this "tent"
> sigh under our burden, unwilling to take it off, yet wishing to

---

2. Phaedo, 81-82, B. Jowett, THE DIALOGUES OF PLATO (Random House: New York, 1937), Vol. 1, pp. 466-467.
3. Phaedo, 83.
4. Ibid.
5. Phaedo, 64.
6. Phaedo, 65.
7. Phaedo, 67.
8. Phaedo, 68.

put our heavenly body over it, so that all that is mortal may be absorbed in Life.

2 Corinthians 5:2-4[9]

In his discussion of the belief in the immortality of the soul versus the resurrection of the body, Niebuhr asserts that "all the plausible and implausible proofs for the immortality of the soul are efforts on the part of the human mind to master and to control the consummation of life. They all try to prove in one way or another that an eternal element in the nature of man is worthy and capable of survival beyond death."[10] The concept of the immortality of the soul which does not include a bodily resurrection tends "to deny the meaningfulness of the historical unity of body and soul" and therefore to deny also any meaningful significance to the historical existence of human life whether on the individual or collective level. It is an attempt to destroy the social and historical meaning of life for the sake of affirming man's ability to defy death by his own strength.[11]

This question is of great importance to the problem of the destiny of the human individual. The predicament of the individual stems from his twofold relationship to the historical community of which he is a part. On one hand, he helps build it and is deeply involved in its ongoing existence; on the other hand, the brief duration of his earthly life leaves his tasks unfinished, and his aspirations not fully satisfied. "Every individual is a Moses who perishes outside the promised land." If he takes his involvement in society at all seriously he cannot remain indifferent to its fate after his departure.[12]

There are three possible ways out of this dilemma of the individual. One of them represents the materialistic approach to life. This philosophy denies the existence of any life after death. Immortality is ascribed to the community, and this is supposed to compensate for the brevity of the individual life. The grandeur and majesty of the historical community are said to be the fulfillment of the individual's aspirations. What about those many individuals who are

---

9. The Twentieth Century New Testament translation.
10. Reinhold Niebuhr, THE NATURE AND DESTINY OF MAN (Charles Scribner's Sons: New York, 1943), Vol. 2, p. 295.
11. Ibid., pp. 295-296.
12. Ibid., p. 308.

cut off in the midst of the years, before they had a chance to contribute their share to the life of the community? Of what conceivable value is this imaginary immortality of society to those who for one reason or another are struck down in the bloom of life? The final effect of the materialistic philosophy is to absorb the individual into the life of the community, and eventually to depersonalize him.

At the other extreme is the purely other-worldly concept. It views the individual life as an end in itself. The reality of historical, i.e., earthly, existence is annulled or minimized. The completion of life takes place in heaven alone. "Reformation theology is on the whole defective in failing to preserve the Biblical conception of the end; and modern Barthian eschatology accentuates this defect. It pays little attention to a possible meaning of history as a continuum and speaks of eschatology in terms of eternity which impinges upon every moment of time."[13]

Niebuhr points out that neither the utopian nor the purely other-worldly conceptions are the adequate answer to the individual's paradoxical relation to his earthly existence. On one hand, his life is meaningless apart from his organic connection with, and his involvement in, a historical community; on the other hand, he experiences no conscious personal fulfillment even in the highest achievements of history.[14]

The concept of a bodily resurrection is the Biblical answer to the plight of individual existence, even as the idea of a general resurrection is the Biblical soution to the problem of history. This idea, bringing individuals back to share in the final triumph at the completion of history, does full justice to the individual life, without which the historical existence of society is incomplete; it also does full justice to the entire course of human history, without which the life of the individual is incomplete.[15]

The "body" denotes the total human personality as expressed by life in the human body. The idea of a bodily resurrection is more individual and more social in its connotations than the concept of mere immortality or survival of the soul. It is more individual,

---

13. Ibid., p. 309, note 12.
14. Ibid., p. 312.
15. Ibid., p. 311.

because it affirms eternal significance not for some impersonal "mind," "reason," or "soul," but for the total human personality. The hope of the resurrection means that human life with be emancipated from its finiteness, and consequently from the anxieties and fears which flow from human finiteness.

The hope of the resurrection is also more social because it implies that the social expressions of man's life will participate in the completion of history. It asserts that history will not be destroyed, but proceed to its divinely ordained successful consummation. It invests with deep significance the struggles in which men engage to perfect earthly existence and to preserve what is pure and noble in earthly life.[16]

As long as the earth will continue to exist man's destiny will remain inseparable from the earth. This is the teaching of the Old Testament, it is the teaching of the Lord Jesus in the Gospels, and it is the teaching of the apostles. To the Thessalonian Christians who thought that the return of the Lord Jesus might take place in their lifetime and were concerned that their departed loved ones will not be around to participate in the Kingdom of God which the returning Christ would set up on earth, the apostle Paul sent the following message.

> But we would not have you ignorant, brethren, concerning those who are asleep [i.e., who died], that you may not grieve as others do who have no hope. For since we believe that Jesus died and rose again, even so, through Jesus, God will bring with him those who have fallen asleep [i.e., who died]. For this we declare to you by the word of the Lord, that we who are alive, who are left until the coming of the Lord, shall not precede [into His presence] those who have fallen asleep. For the Lord himself will descend from heaven with a cry of command, with the shout of the archangel, and with the blast of the trumpet of God; and the dead in Christ will rise first. Then we who are alive, who are left, shall be caught up together with them in the clouds to meet the Lord in the air; and so we shall always be with the Lord. Therefore comfort one another with these words.
>
> *1 Thessalonians 4:13-18*

---

16. See also, Reinhold Niebuhr, BEYOND TRAGEDY (Charles Scribner's Sons: New York, 1937), chapter entitled "The Fulfillment of Life."

To be in heaven means to be with the Lord Jesus and where He is. Upon His return to earth Jesus the Messiah will bring back with Him the righteous men and women of the Old Testament period, and the true Christians of the New Testament period. These, together with the true Christians who will be alive on this earth at His return, and a redeemed Israel, will be used by Him in the task of the regeneration of mankind and of the transformation of the earth into what it was always meant to be — an extension of heaven.

II. THE RESURRECTION OF MESSIAH JESUS BEGINS IN US NOW A NEW LIFE

Eternal life is not merely the uninterrupted continuation of our present life. According to the New Testament, *it is a new kind of life,* and this new life can begin in us now. This is made possible because the resurrection of the Messiah is viewed as the creation of a new humanity.

> The first man was from the earth, a man of dust; the second man[17] is from heaven. As was the man of dust, so are those who are of the dust; and as is the man of heaven, so are those who are of heaven. Just as we have borne the image of the man of dust, we shall also bear the image of the man of heaven.
>
> *1 Corinthians 15:47-49*

How does this new life begin in us? The answer is that if we repent of our sinful past, and we surrender our life to Messiah Jesus, our carnal nature loses its dominating influence over us. At the same time, the life-giving Spirit of the Messiah begins in us a new life.

> Truly, truly, I say to you, he who hears my word and believes him who sent me, has eternal life . . . And this is eternal life, that they know thee the only true God, and Jesus the Messiah whom thou hast sent.
>
> *John 5:24a; 17:3*

And you were buried with him[18] in baptism, in which you

---

17. Referring to Messiah Jesus.
18. Messiah Jesus.

were also raised with him through faith in the working of God, who raised him from the dead. And you, who were dead in trespasses and the uncircumcision of your flesh, God made alive together with him, having forgiven us all our trespasses.

Colossians 2:12-13

Therefore, if any one is in the Messiah, he is a new creation; the old has passed away, behold, the new has come.

2 Corinthians 5:17

I have been crucified with the Messiah; it is no longer I who live, but the Messiah who lives in me; and the life I now live in the flesh I live by faith in the Son of God, who loved me and gave himself for me.

Galations 2:20

This concept, that the eternal life which comes to us as a result of the resurrection of the Messiah is a new kind of life and that this new life begins in us now, is pregnant with tremendous moral implications.

If then you have been raised with the Messiah, seek the things that are above, where the Messiah is, seated at the right hand of God. Set your minds on things that are above, not on things that are on earth . . . Put to death, therefore, what is earthly in you: immorality, impurity, passion, evil desire, and covetousness, which is idolatry . . . In these you once walked, when you lived in them. But now put them all away: anger, wrath, malice, slander, and foul talk from your mouth. Do not lie to one another, seeing that you have put off the old nature with its practices. And have put on the new nature, which is being renewed after the image of its creator.

Colossians 3:1-2,5, 7-10

The human body, downgraded and debased in Greek Orphic and philosophic thought, has in the New Testament assumed an exalted position.

Do you not know that your body is a temple of the Holy Spirit within you, which you have from God? You are not your own. You were bought with a price; so glorify God in your body.

1 Corinthians 6:19-20

III. THE RESURRECTION OF MESSIAH JESUS IS THE ASSURANCE OF OUR OWN RESURRECTION

> But the glorious fact is that the Messiah did rise from the dead; he has become the very first to rise of all who sleep the sleep of death. As death entered the world through a man, [19] so has rising from the dead come to us through a man! [20] As members of a sinful race all men die: as members of the Messiah of God all men shall be raised to life, each in his proper order, with the Messiah the very first, and after him all who belong to him when he comes.
>
> *1 Corinthians 15: 20-23* [21]

We said above that eternal life which the resurrection of Messiah Jesus brings to us begins in us now, on this side of the grave. This is our spiritual resurrection. The same God who begins in us this spiritual resurrection will grant us our bodily resurrection after death.

> But if the Messiah lives in you, [then although your natural] body is dead by reason of sin and guilt, the spirit is alive because of [the] righteousness [that He imputes to you]. And if the Spirit of Him who raised up Jesus from the dead dwells in you, [then] He who raised up Messiah Jesus from the dead will also restore to life your mortal bodies through His Spirit Who dwells in you.
>
> *Romans 8: 10-11* [22]

Not only so, but this same indwelling Spirit which one day will raise our bodies from the dead is already at work in us. Through its influence our earthly nature is becoming subordinated to our spiritual nature.

> So we do not lose heart; though our outer nature is wasting away, our inner nature is being renewed every day.
>
> *2 Corinthians 4: 16*

---

19.   i.e., through Adam.
20.   i.e., through the Messiah.
21.   Phillips' Translation.
22.   The Amplified New Testament.

CONCLUSION

With this we bring to a close our discussion of this terribly important question concerning human destiny, "If a man dies, shall he live again?" The answer to this question as given by the Bible is an unequivocal "Yes". This Biblical affirmation has its roots deep in the Old Testament, in the doctrine that man was created in God's image to live in fellowship with God, a fellowship which death and the grave have no power to break. This Old Testament affirmation finds its full realization in the resurrection of Jesus the Messiah.

"Although recent advances in genetics, surgery, agriculture, space exploration, and other scientific fields lead some to speculate that man will one day be able to control his own destiny, the brutal reign of death reminds every man of his ultimate fate. He is surrounded by evidence of physical and spiritual death. Physical death overtakes him through war, violence, catastrophe, accident, disease, or the [natural] deterioration of the body. Spiritual death is seen in man's egocentric existence lived in rebellion against his Creator, his failure to dwell in peace with his fellows, his inability to master his passions and live up to the demands of his own conscience. Dwelling in spiritual darkness and facing an inevitable grave, man can find no way out of his predicament. Then in the providence of God the darkness is pierced by the light-bringing words of Jesus Christ: 'Because I live, you shall live also.' And on the Sunday after His Friday crucifixion, Jesus Christ, true to His promise, burst the bonds of death. His resurrection is announced by God's messengers at the empty tomb: 'He is not here - he is risen!'

"The triumphant resurrection of Jesus Christ, together with His vicarious death on the cross, is the heart of the Gospel. In the cross is seen the greatness of God's love for rebellious man. In the resurrection is demonstrated God's power over sin and death. Without the resurrection, life is absurd and men have absolutely no hope; but because of it, life has eternal meaning, and men who believe are assured a victorious present and a glorious future."[23]

---

23.   From an editorial in CHRISTIANITY TODAY, April 12, 1968; copyright 1968 by CHRISTIANITY TODAY. Used by permission.

THE MESSIANIC HOPE: A SUMMARY

The Biblical Messianic Hope is God's redemptive purpose for the human individual, for society as a whole, and for man's earthly habitat.

I. THE REDEMPTION OF THE HUMAN INDIVUDUAL

The Messianic Hope has its roots in the Biblical concept of God and of human destiny. It is a hope grounded in the Biblical affirmation of a holy, righteous, loving and personal God, who of His own free will entered into a unique covenant relationship with man. Man was created for fellowship with this eternal Divine Person. It is a fellowship which was not intended to be interrupted by man's physical death.

Man — every human being — must freely decide for or against this relationship with God. To decide for it, is life — eternal life; to decide against it, is death — eternal death, as seen from the passage below, though it was addressed first to Israel collectively.

"I call heaven and earth to witness against you this day,
that I have set before you life and death, blessing and curse;
therefore choose life, that you and your descendants may live."
Deuteronomy 30:19

To acquire this life in eternal fellowship with God involves a new, a spiritual, birth.

Jesus answered him, "Truly, truly, I say to you, unless one
is born anew, he cannot see the kingdom of God."
John 3:3

Like physical birth, this spiritual birth means a new beginning. And yet, physical birth is not entirely a new beginning, since we bring with us some of the physical features and certain mental traits of our ancestors. The spiritual birth which begins in us our eternal life with God is a radically new beginning, a new life-view and a new way of life.

338

This new birth man cannot bring about of his own resources, any more than he can accomplish his own physical birth. How then can man achieve this new spiritual life within himself? How can he, unaided, break with his old life, with his old habits of thoughts, and with his past? This is what Nicodemus wanted to know when he interviewed Jesus.

> Nicodemus said to him, "How can a man be born when he is old? Can he enter a second time into his mother's womb and be born?"
>
> *John 3:4*

The Biblical answer to this perplexing question is, that the new birth is effected by God, as seen from the following passage.

> "For I will take you from the nations, and gather you from all the countries, and bring you into your own land. I will sprinkle clean water upon you, and you shall be clean from all your uncleanness, and from all your idols I will cleanse you. A new heart I will give you, and a new spirit I will put within you; and I will take out of your flesh the heart of stone and give you a heart of flesh."
>
> *Ezekiel 36:24-26*

This truth expressed in Ezekiel was restated by the Lord Jesus in His conversation with Nicodemus. Referring to this new birth, He said:

> "Truly, truly, I say to you, unless one is born of water and the Spirit, he cannot enter the kingdom of God."
>
> *John 3:5*

Not only was Nicodemus assured by Messiah Jesus that this new birth — this cleansing of man's heart and the implanting into man of a new nature — is the work of God, he was told that this remarkable change in man will come about through Messiah's death and resurrection.

> And as Moses lifted up the serpent in the wilderness, so must the Son of man be lifted up. That whoever believes in him may have eternal life.
>
> *John 3:14-15*

This thought, communicated to a representative of Pharisaic Judaism at the beginning of His ministry, was reiterated by Messiah Jesus at the end of His earthly ministry, during an interview by some Greek proselytes, these representatives of the Gentile world and forerunners of the Gentile part of the Church of Jesus the Messiah.

> "The hour has come for the Son of man to be glorified.[1] Truly, truly, I say to you, unless a grain of wheat falls into the earth and dies, it remains alone; but if it dies, it bears much fruit . . . And I, when I am lifted up from the earth, will draw all men to myself."
>
> *John 12:23-24, 32*

The apostle John who heard Him speak these words adds the following explanatory remark:

> He said this to show by what death he was to die.
>
> *John 12:33*

All genuine followers of Messiah Jesus who lived at any time in the last 19 centuries since His first advent could testify with the apostle Paul that

> If any one is in the Messiah, he is a new creation; the old has passed away, the new has come.
>
> *2 Corinthians 5:17*

It is through Messiah Jesus that God's redemptive purpose is being accomplished in the human individual who chooses to follow Him; it is through Him that we can have life in eternal fellowship with God.

II. THE REDEMPTION OF SOCIETY

God's redemptive purpose is not limited to the human individual. It embraces the whole of human society. A redeemed society is one which consists of redeemed individuals. To a question as to which of the Mosaic commandments He considers the greatest, Messiah Jesus cited the following:

> You shall love Jehovah your God with all your heart, and with all your soul, and with all your mind. This is the great and

---

1. A reference to His coming death and resurrection.

foremost commandment. And a second is like it, You shall love
your neighbor as yourself. On these two commandments depend the whole Law and the Prophets.

Matthew 22:37-40

The above two commandments, given in the Pentateuch on two
different occasions, were linked together by Messiah Jesus and declared to be of equal rank and to express the essence of God's Will
revealed in the Old Testament Scriptures. There can be no redemption of society without the redemption of the men and women
of whom it is composed. There can be no right relationship to God
on the part of any individual unless it goes together with a right relationship to his fellow men.

If any one says, "I love God," and hates his brother, he is a
liar; for he who does not love his brother whom he has seen,
cannot love God whom he has not seen.

1 John 4:20

In the Parable of the Tares[2] we are told that between Messiah's
two advents the world will grow progressively better in some areas
of life, and progressively worse in other areas; better — in proportion to the influence of the life and works of God's people; worse —
in proportion to the effectiveness of the enemies of God. These two
movements — the good and the evil — will coexist alongside each
other. They will reach a climacting point in their growth at the end
time of history, just preceding the return of Messiah Jesus, who will
cause the evil to be uprooted and destroyed.

III. THE REDEMPTION OF NATURE

By "nature" we mean here man's earthly environmnent. Way
back in Genesis we have the following prophetic statement enun-
ciated in connection with man's original transgression which resulted in his alienation from God.

And to Adam he[3] said, . . . cursed is the ground because
of you . . . Thorns and thistles it shall bring forth to you.

Genesis 3: 17-18

---

2. Matthew 13:24-30.
3. God.

Man's existence is inseparably bound up with the soil, especially the topsoil, on which he lives. Topsoil is the top layer of the soil in which grow trees, grass and crops which supply man with the food and fiber he needs. Human life and animal life, both depend on this topsoil for their existence. Trees on slopes prevent the topsoil from being blown away by winds, or washed away by torrential rains. Grass renders to the plains the same protection against winds. Grass and trees on hillsides and at watersheds allow the melting snows and the rain waters to percolate slowly into the ground and replenish the subterranean water resources.

When trees are removed indiscrimnately, the topsoil of the hillsides is blown away by winds, or carried off by melting snows or rain waters into streams. This phenomenon causes the lowering of subterranean water levels and the raising of river beds resulting in intermittent floods. When grasslands are denuded of their cover, their soil is carried off by winds and we have dust storms.

It is this disturbance of the equilibrium in nature brought about by human greed and shortsightedness which caused famines throughout history, even when the population of the world was small.

As we are approaching the last quarter of the twentieth century the effects of man's reckless abuse of the earth are assuming the character of a world disaster. We are assured by the experts that all, or most, of the known oil reserves in the world will have been used up within thirty years, if not sooner. The earth's known mineral resources are also becoming rapidly depleted. We are killing off much of the wildlife which God created to support human life and to maintain a biological balance. Industries are contaminating the streams, rivers and lakes, and polluting the very air we breathe. Man has been called the earth's greatest plunderer. The most disturbed people in the world today are those scientists whose work brings them face to face with ecological conditions. One of these scientists declared recently that this relentless population explosion coupled with our shrinking food supplies will bring on a crisis such as has never existed since man appeared on earth.[4] "Cursed is the ground because of you," God declared to Adam. No

---

4. Paul R. Ehrlich, in the FOREWORD in BORN TO STARVE, by Joseph D. Tydings (William Morrow and Company, Inc.: New York, 1970), p. VII.

prophetic statement in the Bible has had a more terrible fulfillment than this.

The sense of Biblical revelation is that man is the world's problem as well as his own problem. Nature is cursed because of man and this curse will not be removed until the human heart becomes regenerated. This thought is beautifully set forth in the following passage in Isaiah in connection with Israel's national restoration and spiritual renewal:

> The wilderness and the dry land shall be glad; and the desert shall rejoice, and blossom as the rose. It shall blossom abundantly, and rejoice even with joy and singing: the glory of Lebanon shall be given to it, the majesty of Carmel and Sharon; they shall see the glory of Jehovah, the majesty of our God. Then the eyes of the blind shall be opened and the ears of the deaf unstopped. Then shall the lame man leap like a hart, and the tongue of the dumb sing for joy; for waters shall break forth in the wilderness, and streams in the desert. The burning sand shall become a pool, and the thirsty ground — springs of water; the haunt of jackals shall become a swamp, the grass shall become reeds and rushes . . . And the ransomed of Jehovah shall return, and come to Zion with singing; everlasting joy shall be upon their heads; they shall obtain joy and gladness, and sorrow and sighing shall flee away.
>
> *Isaiah 35: 1-7, 10*

With this Old Testament picture of the rejuvenation of nature in the days of the Messiah the New Testament concurs fully. The apostle Peter speaks of the restoration of all things with the return of Messiah Jesus.[5] The apostle Paul declares that nature groans in her present affliction and looks forward to her deliverance which will take place when mankind's full redemption will have been accomplished when Jesus the Messiah returns to this earth.[6]

---

5. Acts 3: 19-21.
6. Paul's Letter to the Romans 8:19-23.

Hail to the brightness of Zion's glad morning!
Joy to the lands that in darkness have lain!
Hushed be the accents of sorrow and mourning;
Zion in triumph begins her mild reign.

Hail to the brightness of Zion's glad morning,
Long by the prophets of Israel foretold!
Hail to the millions from bondage returning!
Gentiles and Jews the blest vision behold.

Lo, in the desert rich flowers are springing,
Streams ever copious are gliding along;
Loud from the mountain tops echoes are ringing,
Wastes rise in verdure, and mingle in song.

See, from all lands, from the isles of the ocean,
Praise to the Saviour ascending on high;
Fallen the engines of war and commotion,
Shouts of salvation are rending the sky.

Thomas Hastings

352

RABBINIC REFERENCES

The references listed below are those which appear in our text; they constitute a small number of the total body of Rabbinic statements on the subject of the Messiah in the Old Testament.

355